BLOODY BILL LONGLEY

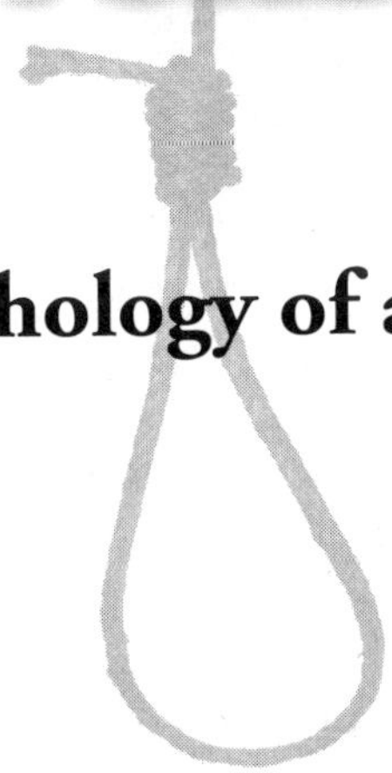

The Mythology of a Gunfighter

Second Revised Edition

Rick Miller

Number 10 in the A. C. Greene Series.

University of North Texas Press
Denton, Texas

Printed in the United States of America.

10 9 8 7 6 5 4 3 2 1

Permissions:
University of North Texas Press
1155 Union Circle #311336
Denton, TX 76203-5017

The paper used in this book meets the minimum requirements of the American National Standard for Permanence of Paper for Printed Library Materials, z39.48.1984. Binding materials have been chosen for durability.

Library of Congress Cataloging-in-Publication Data

Miller, Rick, 1941-
Bloody Bill Longley : the mythology of a gunfighter / Rick Miller ; foreword by David Johnson. -- 2nd rev. ed.
p. cm. -- (No. 10 in the A.C. Greene series)
Includes bibliographical references.
ISBN 978-1-57441-305-2 (hardback : alk. paper) 1. Longley, William Preston, b. 1851. 2. Outlaws--Texas--Biography. 3. Brigands and robbers--Texas--Biography. 4. Langley family. 5. Texas--Biography. I. Title. II. Series: A.C. Greene series ; no. 10.
CT275.L668M55 2011
976.4'063092--dc22
[B]

2010047176

Bloody Bill Longley: The Mythology of a Gunfighter is Number 10 in the A. C. Greene Series.

Contents

Foreword

"When the legend becomes fact, print the legend." So says Maxwell Scott in *The Man Who Shot Liberty Valance*, John Ford's 1962 film based on a short story by Dorothy N. Johnson. It is a classic line in a classic film that, unfortunately, remains all too true in the field of western Americana. The West remains mired in mythology and folklore with defenders adamantly striving to keep it there. The harsh reality is that the West was populated by people, both good and bad.

This is not, of course, to say that there were no bigger-than-life figures. There were men such as Wild Bill Hickok. Hickok was a legend in his time, the topic of newspaper articles and dime novels. Now dead for more than a century, Hickok has been transformed by movies, television, and comic books into a two-gun hero, clean-cut and intrepid. Fortunately, Hickok's main biographer, Joe Rosa, has ably sifted fact from fancy. In Wild Bill's case, the facts are more fascinating than the legend. Hickok, indeed, was of heroic stature, but was also a human being with blemishes.

This is not always the case, however. Less worthy personalities have also assumed a persona far beyond the importance they enjoyed in their lifetimes. The celebrated Wyatt Earp, for example, had a history of involvement with his brothers in prostitution as well as in enforcing the law. It cannot be proven that he ever personally killed a man, even though he was a participant in the noted OK Corral gunfight, and he and his associates were involved in several murders while in Arizona after that gunfight. Yet for all this, folklorists have devoted reams of paper to building the reputation of this perhaps not-so-worthy westerner, whose "glory" was largely due to Stuart N. Lake's fictional biography, *Wyatt Earp: Frontier Marshal,* combined with Hugh O'Brian's portrayal of the fictional Earp on television, not the facts.

In more recent years, historians interested in facts rather than legend have entered the arena of the Wild West to set the record straight. In addition to Joseph Rosa, the preeminent authority on Hickok, there are others, such as the prolific Chuck Parsons, whose works on the Sutton-Taylor War and Texas Ranger Leander McNelly are classics. Paul Spellman and Harold Weiss have captured the realities of legendary Ranger captains John H. Rogers, John A. Brooks, and Bill MacDonald.

Despite this, folklorists still cling to and defend the mythology, seemingly unwilling, or unable, to deal with the realities. So the controversy continues with the Old West. One such individual, Bill Longley, is well known to informed readers of western American history, although he has not achieved the fame or notoriety of such icons as Hickok or Billy the Kid. Unlike Earp, he did not have a modern publicist to transform him from pimp, murderer, occasional lawman, or whatever, into a national hero. Longley has remained a generally dark presence in Texas' frontier history.

William Preston Longley was born October 6, 1851, in Washington County, Texas. The family was well off, but following the Civil War, Longley went bad. He was a contemporary of such men as gunfighters John Wesley Hardin and Ben Thompson, and was well aware of the vicious feuds that rocked Texas during this time, such as the Sutton-Taylor Feud, the Hoo Doo War, and the Horrell-Higgins Feud. Longley took part in none of this epic regional violence, though if his own accounts are to be believed, he brushed elbows with a number of these deadly men, the key word being "if." Longley was a master of spinning a wild tale, with himself as the central focus, and even with several biographies, much of his life remains a mystery today.

To date, there have been three biographies of Longley. His first biographer, Henry Clay Fuller, published *The Adventures of Bill Longley* at the start of the twentieth century. Fuller gathered numerous newspaper clippings, ostensibly of letters written by Longley, and put them into a small book that is now rare. In 1953 Ed Bartholomew, a noted Texas historian, made another effort at a Longley biography, *Wild Bill Longley: A Texas Hard-Case*. Both of these volumes, now long out of print, essentially told Longley's story from his own point of view, giving his own version of the "facts." Unfortunately, neither of these historians had the informational resources available to modern researchers. As a consequence, the story of Bill Longley continued to be passed on as he fancifully told it.

It was not until 1996 that Rick Miller issued the first modern biography of the gunfighter. Miller, a former lawman and currently a county attorney, approached the subject with the critical analysis necessary to determine the truth behind the legend that Longley himself had attempted to foster. *Bloody Bill Longley* proved an instant classic for those interested in the history of this relatively obscure westerner. Miller, author of groundbreaking work on manhunter Jack Duncan and bandit Sam Bass, catapulted the reader into nineteenth-century Texas where justice, or the lack thereof, rode in a man's holster. Tragically, the book was available only in a very limited edition, and Longley's name remained rooted in folklore, with folklorists continuing to spread his tale without any semblance of original research.

We are fortunate to have this revised and expanded biography of Bill Longley available, particularly an edition provided by one of the most tenacious and skilled researchers and historians today. This biography is a veritable feast of little-known history on one of the West's most notorious outlaws.

David Johnson
Zionsville, Indiana

Introduction

The post-Civil War era in Texas spawned a political and social upheaval that generated, in addition to a drastically changed economy for former slaveholders and a fragile new equality of sorts for freed slaves, a few individuals who stepped forward into public notoriety as gunslingers. The most noted was the deadly John Wesley Hardin, followed closely by volatile Ben Thompson of Austin. Legends quickly attached themselves to these singular individuals, legends that survive today and continue to be subject to the humbling scrutiny of nit-picking researchers. Nevertheless, the Texas gunman has continued to be glamorized repeatedly in pulp fiction, movies, and television, and today, more than any other figure, has come to be the most recognized and popular symbol of the "Old West."

Hardin's notoriety erupted from his participation in the violent Sutton-Taylor-Tumlinson feud in South Central Texas that produced an unprecedented number of murders and lynchings. Hardin's involvement in one bloody incident after another, and the subsequent statewide reporting of those events, quickly gave him a reputation, deserved or not, as a "pistoleer" of the first rank. Ultimately, a $4,000 reward was offered for him, an outstanding sum for the time. He was perceived as the most dangerous man in Texas, and not many lawmen were anxious to tangle with him, reward or not. Ben Thompson's gunfighting experiences, though not as well publicized at the time, surely equaled if they did not exceed those of Hardin. And he certainly was in circulation for a greater length of time than Hardin.

Other gunmen came to public attention during the post-war period. John King Fisher was another who attained notoriety, but Hardin and Thompson were at the top of the heap. Both men relished their notoriety, and both had several things in common, primarily a fondness for whiskey, a short fuse, and no lack of nerve when it came to facing an armed adversary. Both were boastful men, especially when drinking, and that certainly helped promote their deadly images. The two men came to epitomize the classic Texas gunfighter.

At the time, the general public was fascinated with men of this ilk, much as we today are attracted to publicized criminal tragedies that occur well outside our daily routines and contrary to our developed values and beliefs. Like it or not, we pay considerable attention to the exploits of serial killers, death cults, and such extraordinary exploits of violence, or "reality" as that term has recently come to be understood, that occasionally dominate the headlines, even though we may, at the same time, consider them aberrations of the human experience. In the late 1860s and during the 1870s, Texans were likewise fascinated by the continuing exploits of the few gunmen who defied the social conventions and strictures of the law imposed after the Civil War. Rumors about these men evolved into legends and folklore about these men, much like those about Jesse James and Billy the Kid, who often took on a Robin Hood mantle as the stories were passed on.

The unsettled post-war era was highlighted by a lack of effective law enforcement as we know it today. The replacement of elected officials by appointed political hacks or incompetents, plus the lack of adequate manpower to carry out local enforcement duties, created a vacuum in which outlaws and gunmen could thrive with impunity. Close friends and relatives, resentful of the new order in the state, gave these men harbor in the local communities in which they operated, and the concomitant lack of community support certainly gave the local marshal or sheriff pause to reflect on his mortality when it was time to do his duty and confront the bad guy. If things truly got out of hand, vigilante groups quickly organized to fill the breach.

The era of the gunman was not long, about ten to fifteen years, from around 1865 to about 1878 or 1880. After that, the outlaws plaguing the Old West could be more accurately described as "common criminals" and bandits, but certainly lacking the fascinating luster ascribed to the "gunfighter," real or imagined. The more notorious early gunmen were mankillers, but there is little evidence that they were horse or cattle thieves or bank robbers. Men such as Hardin, Thompson, and James Butler Hickok were known for their prowess with a firearm and their nerve. They moved in circles and among events that inevitably fomented the kind of violence on which they earned their reputations, regardless of which side of the law they were on, and would not be categorized as "crooks." Thus, they became singular icons of notoriety by virtue of the violence for which they were responsible.

Bill Longley was also a product of these unsettled times, and when he was captured in June 1877, he received his first real public notoriety, *after* he was taken out of circulation by a law enforcement system that had finally achieved some effectiveness and taken hold in the uncertain post-Reconstruction period. Longley's reputation as an equal of the deadly Hardin and Thompson was one of his own creation. He became his own press agent by virtue of a series of letters and interviews that comprised his "autobiography," boasting of killing thirty-two men, and creating for himself the role of a cavalier desperado on the level of a Hardin or Thompson. Many of the episodes he described were greeted with skepticism by the Texas press, but, absent any refuting investigation, these tales over time took on the semblance of fact, and Longley entered the public arena as a worthy peer of the other gunfighters. And despite a last-minute effort to back away from the bloody image he had created when it was time for him to pay the supreme penalty, his name has come down through the years as one of Texas' foremost gunfighters.

However, as will be seen in this book, Longley's self-proclaimed reputation does not survive close scrutiny. Yes, he did kill some men, at least five or six, but the manner in which he dispatched his victims did not approach that level of daring and nerve that is usually ascribed to a Texas gunman. And there are hints of other, darker crimes, such as perhaps the rape and murder of a woman, as well as accusations of robbery and horse theft, which erode his gunfighter aura. But in well over a century, no one has dug into his legend with any degree of dedication to the truth in order to tell the factual story of Bill Longley. Certainly there is fertile ground for the serious researcher to set the record straight. And because Longley has been unjustifiably glamorized, to stand alongside Hardin and Thompson as a legendary peer, the truth or a portion of it has been long in coming.

The problem with digging into Longley's life is the real dearth of documentation in order to either corroborate what he claimed or to prove that he was a liar. Again, until he was caught, very little mention of him could be found in Texas newspapers. When he was caught, he spun a fanciful tale of bloody deeds and wandering that mixed truth and fiction, ranging from Texas to Wyoming Territory and back. Unfortunately, the letters that he wrote to the *Giddings (Texas) News* have not survived, with one or two exceptions. I was unable to find any existing copies of the Giddings newspaper, and it was only through a search of other contemporary Texas newspapers that a few of the letters were located, as reprinted.

The letters written by Longley were supposedly gathered together by Henry C. Fuller in a small booklet printed in Nacogdoches, Texas, sometime in the early 1900s. But Fuller took considerable artistic license in printing these letters, adding Victorian flourishes, although he apparently did not alter the basic facts about which Longley wrote. For example, Fuller's *Adventures of Bill Longley* quoted one letter as follows:

> Sawyer found out by some hook or crook that there was a reward for me, and so he set out to get the reward. He found out that I was probably wanted in Lee County, and he wrote a letter to the sheriff of that county to come and get me and he and the sheriff would share the reward. Sawyer sent the letter to the postoffice by a boy or rather gave it to a boy to take to the office and the boy lost it on the road. I found the letter and read it.

However, the *Nacogdoches News*, on July 20, 1877, reprinted Longley's letter as it had been originally printed in the Giddings newspaper, and the difference is obvious:

> Scrier found out by some means or other that there was a reward for me. He wrote to James Brown and requested him to come and help him capture me, but the boy while taking the letter to the office lost it, and I happened to find it.

Thus, the letters ascribed to Longley that were reproduced by Fuller must be read very carefully for the factual content, but the language is that of Fuller, not Longley. In addition, where there was a chronological gap in Longley's autobiographical narrative, Fuller unfortunately lapsed into third person accounts of rather fanciful and romantic adventures on the part of Longley. These have very little, if any, credibility as primary sources or information helpful to an accounting of the man's life. Alas, this merger of fact and fantasy subsequently became Longley's "life."

The only other source on which chroniclers of Longley's life have relied for details of Longley's life is a lengthy article printed in the *Galveston Daily News* on September 16, 1877, after Longley had been convicted of murder and sentenced to hang. This account, ostensibly related to the reporter by Longley from his jail cell, detailed thirty-one shootings and other adventures claimed by the condemned man. It is very likely that this article was compiled from the series of letters that Longley had written to the *Giddings News* several months earlier, although not with the same amount of detail.

All later accounts of Longley's life can be traced directly to Fuller's book and the Galveston newspaper story in September 1877. Books such as Eugene Cunningham's *Triggernometry* and Ed Bartholomew's *Wild Bill Longley: A Texas Hard-Case* came directly from these accounts without any effort at corroboration (although Bartholomew candidly admitted that his book was written quickly). Even today, so-called historians continue to crank out books about gunmen, including

Longley, relying solely on defective secondary accounts, without any hint of primary sources, perpetuating the distorted myths and legends in the public mind. And in such manner, Longley's self-created legend has attained undeserved respectability simply by virtue of the passage of time and the lack of any real effort to check it out. And it should be pointed out that "Wild Bill" was an appellation coined for Longley in the twentieth century, not one used during his lifetime.

Because of the flimsy, and in most cases nonexistent, contemporary investigation of Longley and the accuracy of his claims, it was necessary to piece together all of the accounts about him and check them out one at a time. Every name he mentioned, every place he claimed to have visited, and every event he recounted had to be individually investigated. Court records, census records, county histories, even secondary sources, all had to be delved into. Here and there some new material turned up, such as some unpublished letters written by Longley and a personal handwritten account by Bill's brother, Jim, of the killing of Wilson Anderson, provided by a descendant, H. Jerry Longley of Farmington, New Mexico.

The result of these research efforts, this book, is essentially a composite of what Longley (and Fuller) claimed occurred, annotated by whatever facts could be established that either backed up that story or refuted it. Unfortunately, much of what was claimed could not be resolved one way or the other, and maybe never will be. But what is revealed is that Bill Longley was not the equal of Hardin and Thompson, a status to which he obviously aspired. There is no doubt that he was a wandering gunman, a loner, and like Hardin and others, was fond of the loose life and boastful talk. But the facts do not back up his self-created image as a nervy gunfighter. It is clear that he was always very careful to gain the advantage or "get the drop" on his prey. But perhaps closer scrutiny of the other gunfighters will likewise diminish their legendary stature and also reveal them as less-than-glamorous figures.

Additional research remains to be done to fully tell Longley's story, new information and sources perhaps yet undiscovered that will likely continue to refute his boastful claims. Longley was fond of adopting alias names as he moved around the country, and it is not improbable that he was arrested or identified under those unknown names. But despite the urge to continue the never-ending search for new information about him, at some point what is known had to be formally documented. A limited first edition of this book was privately published in 1996, but recent events and some new information, such as the discovery and identification of Longley's grave, necessitate a new, revised edition to keep the story current.

I am in great debt to many, many folks, without whom this book would not have been remotely possible. There were just too many places to visit and too many records and sources to check for only one person. Of immeasurable value were the contributions of my peers in Old West history research: Chuck Parsons, Luling, Texas, who kept my mailbox filled with new tidbits, and who accompanied me on a visit to Delta County, Texas, to look into the killing of the Rev. Roland Lay; Gary Fitterer of Kirkland, Washington; Dave Johnson, Zionsville, Indiana, my Old West soul brother, who has kept nagging (and properly so) to get this revision and other books written, as well as writing the foreword to this book; the late Jim Browning of Charleston, South Carolina, who knew the most about the final resting places of Old West figures; and my good friend, archivist Donaly Brice, Lockhart, Texas, who assisted me at the Texas State Library, and who, with his lovely wife, Clare, gave me a place to stay when I visited there. There are many others who were of immense assistance, for which I am truly thankful.

California: Lee Albright, Paradise; Mildred Forester, Paradise; and Dr. Jack C. Longley, Sacramento, who provided an important Longley photograph; John Rudderow, Chico; and Nancy B. Samuelson, Sacramento.

Kansas: Debra F. Graden (Grey Ink, Inc.), Leavenworth; Katy Matthews, Topeka; Charles Strom, White City; Bonnie McClintock, archivist, and Betty Strom, volunteer, Morris County Library, Council Grove; Robert A. Holt, museum administrator, Leavenworth County

Historical Society, Leavenworth; Kathryn H. Nevins, assistant curator, Frontier Army Museum Association, Fort Leavenworth; and the District Clerk, Abilene.

Louisiana: Margie Rambin, Pelican.

Maryland: Ruth Priest Dixon, Mitchellville; and the late Barry A. Crouch, Riverdale.

Nevada: Phillip I. Earl, Reno.

New Mexico: H. Jerry Longley, Farmington; and especially Robert G. McCubbin, Santa Fe, a good friend and foremost collector of gunfighter works and memorabilia, who located the original jail photo of Longley used in this book.

North Dakota: Douglas W. Ellison, Medora.

Ohio: Rutherford B. Hayes Presidential Center Library, Fremont; Robert K. DeArment, Sylvania, whose many fine, well-researched books on the gunfighter west are a mainstay of any respectable library.

Oklahoma: Barbara Longley Bivins, Stillwater.

Pennsylvania: Dr. Louis T. Holz (Second Cavalry Association), Wayne-Strafford.

Texas: Patsy P. Barton (Delta County District Clerk), Cooper; the late Ed Bartholomew, Fort Davis; Katherine Dinsmore Beshears, Mesquite; Kent Biffle, Dallas; Daffy Carpenter, former Bell County District Clerk, Belton; Center for American History, University of Texas, Austin; Lucille Fain, Nacogdoches; Benny Fisher, Paris; Shorty Freeman, Ben Franklin; Vance Hugh Gilbreath, La Vernia; Earl S. Hardin, Jr., San Antonio; Sid Heard, Reagan Wells; Jane Hoerster, Mason; Dr. William T. Jack, Campbell; Jeff Jackson, Lampasas; Darrell Jepson, Angleton; William Johnson, Dallas; Margy Jones, former Lampasas County District Clerk, Lampasas; Vera King, Bandera County and District Clerk, Bandera; Mrs. Elizabeth K. Lambert, San Antonio; Alvis and Pauline Longley, San Saba; Juanita Longley, San Saba; Kenneth Longley, Abilene; Neill B. Longley, Houston; A. T. Mast, Jr., Nacogdoches; Cyndi Mathis, Grayson County District Clerk, Sherman; Lisa May, archivist, Diocese of Galveston-Houston, Houston; Dennis McCown, Austin; Archie P. McDonald, Stephen F.

Austin State University, Nacogdoches; Lind B. McKinney, Nacogdoches; Adeline Melcher, Lee County District Clerk., Giddings; Sue Metcalf, San Angelo; Barbara Meyer, Gillespie County District Clerk, Fredericksburg; Mary L. Meyers, Butt-Holdsworth Library, Kerrville; Scottie Molloy, Uvalde; Linda Cheves Nicklas, East Texas Research Center, Steen Library, Stephen F. Austin State University, Nacogdoches; Pat Norman, Grayson County Clerk, Sherman; Jerry A. Parker, Dallas; Calvin Patrick, Corpus Christi; Berneta Peeples, Belton; Kinga Perzynska, archivist, Catholic Archives of Texas, Austin; Dr. Johnny Spellman, Austin; Mrs. Opal Thomas, Belton; Lydia Steele, Uvalde County District Clerk, Uvalde; Vada Sutton, former Bell County Clerk, Belton; Larry Walker, El Paso; Mrs. Fred C. Willard, Giddings; and the late Woodrow Wilson, Giddings.

Utah: The late Cam and Lee Longley, Brigham City, long-time members of the National Association for Outlaw and Lawman History (NOLA), who were prime movers in this project and always there for encouragement and occasional arm-twisting.

Virginia: Larry G. Shaver, Fincastle.

Washington, D.C.: U.S. Army Center of Military History; Library of Congress; National Archives and Records Service.

Wyoming: Jean Brainard, senior research and oral historian, Parks and Cultural Resources Division, State of Wyoming, Cheyenne; Larry K. Brown, Cheyenne; Buffalo Bill Historical Center, Cody; Rick Ewig, manager, reference services, American Heritage Center, University of Wyoming, Laramie; Todd Guenther, curator, South Pass State Historic Site, South Pass City; and Roberta Olsen, director, Fremont County Library, Lander.

England: Joseph G. Rosa, a renowned expert on Wild Bill Hickok.

In addition to the above, I am indebted to many other elected officials, both district and county clerks, and librarians, throughout Texas, Kansas, and Wyoming, who took time from their very busy duties to help me and let me peruse their records. I am especially indebted to a good friend, Dr. Nora Stafford, former chair of the English Department, University of Mary Hardin-Baylor, Belton, Texas, for scrutinizing the original manuscript in an effort to purge it of split infinitives (whatever those are), comma splices, and idiotic word usage (my phrase).

Finally, the time taken to research and create this book was taken away from my wife, Paula, who has come to recognize that vacant stare and inattention when I am visiting another century. She indulges me this persistent preoccupation, I suspect, because it keeps me from running amok in the streets, and that is a good thing, Thus, her personal sacrifice on my behalf is the noblest of all. Thank you, dear.

Rick Miller
Harker Heights, Texas

Chapter 1

A Good-Hearted Boy

The menacing clouds and threat of rain did not deter the hundreds of people flocking to the small Texas town of Giddings to see Bill Longley die. The newly constructed wooden gallows waited silently some six hundred yards northwest of the railroad depot, where passengers alit by the score from incoming trains.

Although the execution was not scheduled until later in the afternoon of this dark, ominous October day, the main street of Giddings and the surrounding prairie teemed with the growing crowd from an early hour. They came by train, by carriage, by wagon and horseback, and on foot, black and white mingling single-mindedly as they awaited the carrying out of the court's order and the end of the self-proclaimed mankiller's odyssey. Stories circulated about a last-minute escape attempt and there were rumors that Longley had already survived one hanging.

Bill Longley had been confined now for not quite a year and a half, fighting this day as vigorously as he had willingly defied the conventions of his time. When captured, he had boasted of killing thirty-two men, even penning his memoirs in a Giddings newspaper and relishing the sensation he created throughout the state. He adopted for himself a deadly reputation rivaling that of the much vaunted and more publicized John Wesley Hardin. After all, Hardin, when captured, was said to have killed only twenty-seven. Longley had gone to great lengths to portray himself as one of Texas' deadliest gunmen.

But now time had run out for Bill Longley. There was no point to any further boasting. The mass of humanity pouring into tiny Giddings was there to witness his final chapter. The only important thing now was how Longley would make his exit. Would he face his maker with the same reckless spirit that brought him here? Would he keep his nerve and leave mortal Earth in a manner befitting the image of the bold and daring desperado that he sought to portray? Or would he, as some hoped, shrink from his fate in a manner more befitting a coward?

It had been barely a decade since Longley set out on the path that led him most certainly and surely to this day. That path had commenced just a few miles from here. The thousands of milling witnesses camped in Giddings that day exchanged stories and exploits of the doomed man, both true and exaggerated, as they awaited his final procession to the waiting gallows. But there were also folks from that community, from recently formed Lee County, who knew the truth about this man Longley and who could easily separate myth and legend from the truth. They knew Bill Longley well and had their own opinions about the difference between the truth and the legacy he wanted to leave behind. In their minds, justice for Bill Longley would come at the end of a rope.

Campbell Longley was descended from pioneers of the American Revolution. By early in the nineteenth century, his family was located in Tennessee. One of eight children, he was born on September 30, 1816, near the Little Pigeon River in the eastern portion of the state not far from Sevierville. When he was about twelve years old, the Longley family moved to Jackson's Purchase in McMinn County, Tennessee, where his father died a year later. Campbell was the oldest child and became his mother's mainstay in working the family farm.[1]

In 1836 Sam Houston's ragtag army in far-off Texas was in full retreat from the advancing Mexican army led by Santa Anna. The effort by expatriated Americans to live under Mexican rule in this new frontier had not been successful, given their inherent suspicion of the intent and motives of the Mexican government, as well as the paranoid suspicion on the part of the Mexican government as to the ulterior motives and intent of these Yankees on Mexican soil. A clash had become increasingly inevitable, and a state of war had existed, such as it was, since the first shot fired in October 1835 near the small village of Gonzales. A Mexican victory would financially ruin the many impresarios and entrepreneurs who had invested their personal fortunes in bringing settlers to this new Texas land. And a Mexican victory indeed seemed imminent after Santa Anna overran Travis and his men at the Alamo near San Antonio on March 6, 1836. Despite the impatience of the leaders of the newly formed Texas government for some sign of hope, their designated army commander, Sam Houston, continued to fall back with his ill-prepared troops before the oncoming enemy without offering any resistance. There was an ominous feeling that defeat seemed imminent for the Texians once the two armies finally met.

News of the Texas army's poor prospects reached Tennessee, especially distressing one Joe Clay. Clay was an investor in the Robertson Colony, an association of investors initially formed by Sterling and Felix Robertson in Nashville in 1822 to settle colonists in Texas. The Mexican government had granted the association a permit to bring eight hundred families to an area in the Brazos River basin. Sterling Robertson had been attempting to solve some difficulties with Mexico when the Texas Revolution broke out.[2] In order to protect his land investment, Clay was one of a number of entrepreneurs who rallied in response to Houston's call for help by organizing companies of volunteers to reinforce the Texians in the spring of 1836.

Captain Gustavus A. Parker of Georgia formed a unit of some one hundred men and officers from Georgia and Tennessee and was able to lay his hands on a small quantity of arms, ammunition, and horses. Clay greeted the unit when its members assembled in Nashville. The twenty-year-old Campbell Longley, having decided to leave his mother and family behind to seek fortune and adventure in far-flung Texas, was one of the eager new recruits. Clay arranged for temporary lodging for Parker's company and treated the new soldiers, along with other soldiers assembling in Nashville, to a large barbecue as a sendoff. The soldiers departed on a steamer to Louisiana, then on to Texas.[3] As they left, Nashville citizens bolstered the supplies of the departing militiamen with flour, bacon, and coffee.[4]

By the time Parker's unit reached the San Augustine settlement on the Angelina River, however, there was word that Houston and his Texas army were already squaring off against Santa Anna's army at San Jacinto far to the south. They wouldn't be able to get to the battle in time, so Parker was directed to take his company to Coleto in present-day Goliad County where James Fannin and his men had been brutally massacred in the March 27 Goliad Mission surrender. From Coleto, the company joined volunteers in gathering up and burying the bodies of the massacre victims. On April 21 Houston and his men surprised a sleeping Santa Anna and soundly defeated the Mexican force. Santa Anna was captured and, taken before Houston, acknowledged his defeat.

As the new Republic of Texas began to grope for organization, young Campbell Longley remained with Parker's company at Coleto after formally enlisting in the Texas army on June 12, 1836, for a three-month term.[5] On September 12, his term of service completed, Longley was honorably discharged. However, because he owned only a tattered suit of clothes and pair of shoes, he was forced to assign his Texas army discharge to George Green for cash, thus giving up a claim of land under the new Texas republic.[6] Captain Parker went on to settle in Fort Bend County and represent that county in the Texas legislature before his death in 1845.[7]

Campbell intended to return to his family in Tennessee. He had no ties to Texas, the big adventure was over, and he had no reason to stay. But when he and other discharged soldiers set sail from Texas, a shipwreck left them stranded at Matagorda without any money. Unable to return to Tennessee, he went into Austin County, north of

Fort Bend County and south of Washington County, where he decided to settle.[8]

In Austin County, Campbell established himself as a farmer and became involved in local activities. At a camp meeting held in October 1837, the Texas Missionary Society was organized. Robert Alexander, a Methodist missionary, assembled subscribers, including Campbell, to pledge financial support for the new organization.[9] Religion had been and always would be a strong factor in Campbell Longley's life. By 1838 Campbell was on the Austin County tax rolls with $150 in land.[10] More importantly, on July 25, 1838, Campbell Longley married Pennsylvania native Sarah Ann Henry, seventeen years old.[11] Young Miss Henry was an orphan brought to Texas from Cincinnati, Ohio, by Judge and Mrs. Goodnow.[12] Their first child, Mary Catherine, was born on December 20, 1839, to be followed by a second daughter, Martha Jane, on Christmas Day of 1841.[13]

Although the Mexicans were no longer a threat, various tribes of Indians, finding themselves being displaced by the new Texians, were. Regular reports circulated among Texians concerning bloody conflicts between Indian and settler, often involving atrocities committed by both sides. In August 1840, an especially large band of Comanches swooped south in a series of bloody raids. Near Lavaca Bay in what is now Calhoun County, the Indians laid waste the small village of Linnville, then retreated northward with hostages and loot. Alarmed Texians organized a volunteer army under General Felix Huston, Colonel Edward Burleson, Captain Mathew Caldwell, and others, and the army joined with Ben McCulloch's Texas Rangers in pursuit. On August 11, near the present town of Lockhart in Caldwell County, the Texians overtook the fleeing Indians and soundly defeated them in a running battle at Plum Creek.[14] Campbell Longley, his farming routine interrupted, was a part of this expedition, as was noted Indian fighter Big Foot Wallace.[15]

In 1842 Mexico was still smarting from its defeat at the hands of the Texians six years earlier. Sensing that the defense of Texas was now in the hands of a poorly organized and poorly equipped militia, an invasion into the new republic was mounted by General Rafael Vasquez. By March 5, San Antonio had fallen to Vasquez, and once again volunteers flocked to form an army to repel the invader. Campbell Longley was part of an armed contingent marching from Austin County. However, Vasquez subsequently withdrew to Mexico without any attack or pursuit by the Texians. Again, Campbell assigned away his claim for any compensation by the Republic.[16]

Back in Austin County, Sarah Longley gave birth to Frances Caroline on February 15, 1844, followed in 1846, a year after Texas was admitted to the Union as a state, by the Longleys' first son, Alexander. George Washington Longley was born on March 26, 1849.[17] During this period Campbell continued to work his farm and served for six successive years as a justice of the peace. He also assisted in establishing in Austin County the first Church of Christ west of the Brazos River.[18] For the rest of his life, Campbell was a strong supporter and advocate of the minority "Campbellite" viewpoint of the Church of Christ, and this would be the faith into which a young Bill Longley would be baptized.

On October 6, 1851, Campbell and Sarah Longley's sixth child, William Preston, was born in Austin County.[19]

As early as 1839, Campbell Longley owned a headright grant for "one league and one labor" in Washington County, to the north of Austin County.[20] In August of 1851, he was initiated into Hubert Masonic Lodge no. 67 in Chappell Hill, Washington County. He received his third degree in that order on December 14, 1851. He was later a charter member of the J. D. Giddings Lodge no. 280 at the village of Evergreen in Washington County.[21] By early April 1853, Longley, having purchased a farm three miles west of the small village of Evergreen, moved his family to Washington County. Among the property they took with them was a female black slave.[22]

A daughter, Elizabeth, was born on March 23, 1854. Their eighth child, Joseph, was born January 24, 1857, but died on April 3, 1860, of "inflammation of the brain." James Stockton Longley was born on January 21, 1859.[23]

Campbell Longley, the father of Bill Longley, as an elderly man. *Courtesy Pauline Longley, San Saba, Texas.*

When the 1860 census was taken in Evergreen, it reflected the hard work of Campbell and Sarah in building a farm worth $6,000 and personal property worth $4,000. Six children lived with them, including an almost nine-year-old Bill. Their eldest child, Mary Catherine, married Charles M. Tyler on June 29, 1854, and lived with her husband and their two children next to the Longley farm.[24] Also living at the Longley farm was William Carnes, a laborer, who married Martha Jane Longley on August 7, 1860. Frances Caroline married J. T. Lawrence on July 9, 1859.[25]

With the advent of the Civil War, despite the fervent opposition of Sam Houston, Texas elected to enter the Confederacy. Families on farms and homesteads throughout the state saw their young men enlisting and marching off to fight for states' rights. Despite the fact that his father was a staunch Unionist, fifteen-year-old Alexander C. Longley traveled to Houston to be mustered into Captain James S. Lauderdale's company in Nelson's Confederate Regiment of Texas Volunteers on October 25, 1861. Three months later, in January, young Alexander was captured with other members of his regiment at Fort Hindman, Arkansas, and delivered as a prisoner of war to Camp Douglas, Illinois. Paroled in April 1863, young Alexander was hospitalized in Petersburg, Virginia, with "debilitas" for much of the rest of the year. He was subsequently involved in battle near Atlanta, Georgia, in the summer of 1864 and received wounds in his left shoulder and hip. The Longley family Bible asserts that he received a gunshot wound through one of his lungs. Admitted to a hospital at Marietta, Georgia, then to a hospital at Chattanooga, Tennessee, he died on July 31, 1864,[26] the second Longley child to die.

Also marching off to war was J. T. Lawrence, husband of Frances Caroline. A member of the Confederate army, he died on December 9, 1862.[27] His death would have major significance in Bill Longley's criminal career because of his sister's next choice for a husband.

As the war wended its way to ultimate defeat for the rebelling southern states, Campbell remained in Washington County with his family. He was remembered for serving a "special detail in caring for

The Evergreen, Texas, live oak tree today, all that is left of the small village. *Author's photo.*

the war widows and children." In addition, he tanned leather, made and mended shoes, and taught others how to card, spin, warp, and weave cloth.[28]

The name of the small village of Evergreen was descriptive of the variety of trees that abounded in the area. Both Elm Creek and the West Yegua Creek provided clear water and good fishing. The timber from the ample trees in the area allowed for building farms, and the land was quite suitable for corn and cotton. Today the village of Evergreen has totally disappeared, leaving behind only a giant live oak tree, fully five feet in diameter, under which it is said that the local authorities used to administer justice and which gave shade to a blacksmith shop and a number of saloons. The village sat on the Austin-Brenham road and was one-half mile east of the San Antonio-Bastrop-Nacogdoches road.[29] The Longley farm was well located and enjoyed abundant natural resources, requiring only the addition of human toil to make it successful.

Campbell Longley served as a Washington County commissioner from 1857 until the Civil War, although the long trip from Evergreen to Brenham, the county seat, must have grown tedious and frequently took him away from the farm.[30] With the end of the war, young Bill Longley, along with his brothers and sisters who were still at home, continued working on the family farm and attending the local school when they could. Fourteen-year-old Bill was considered "a good-hearted boy, tall, and well-liked by the other boys." The Evergreen children were taught by a medical doctor, G. D. Wilkerson. Two of Bill's younger classmates, Will Grant and Ike W. Sparks, recalled that Bill supervised games, such as "One-Eyed Cat" and "Bull-Pen," for the smaller children and acted as a leader. The school regimen included close study of Webster's "blue-back" spelling book and McGuffey's series of readers.[31]

Less than a month before his execution, Bill reminisced with another schoolmate, Mrs. Bettie Southern, recalling her and her sister, Artimissa, and their pony, Charlie, on which the two girls would ride to school. After school, the boys, smitten with the two sisters, would race to see who could saddle Charlie for their trip home. On one occasion, Bill threw his hat at Charlie, causing the horse to jump and throw Bettie. Bill ran to her and, seeing that she was unhurt, told her that he did it just to have a chance to help her up on the horse.[32] With respect to Bill's formal learning, however, it was said that his education was "by no means of an advanced order; he learned to read and write about as well as farm boys usually do."[33]

The close of the Civil War and the dramatic change it brought to the lives of people living in the former Confederate states led to a period of outlawry and violence in Texas on a scale never before experienced, and the Evergreen community was no exception. A provisional Texas government was declared illegal by the Reconstruction Act, effective March 2, 1867, which created five military occupation districts for the defeated states, Texas being in the Fifth Military District. The state was mandated to write a new constitution guaranteeing

"Negro suffrage," to elect a new government based on the inclusion of black men as voters, and to ratify the Fourteenth Amendment to the United States Constitution prior to being readmitted to the Union.[34]

New fixtures now in the Central Texas area were federal troops and agents of the Freedman's Bureau, their mission to protect the newly freed slaves and the rights engendered them by the end of the war. As might be expected, widespread resentment sprang up throughout the state. The carrying of concealed weapons was a practice universally resorted to by many Texans, but it was an unacceptable notion for the formerly dominant race to now see black men, freely mounted on their steeds, armed with six-shooters, and at will riding over the country instead of attending to those menial duties in which their lives had hitherto been confined. The older and more discreet in every community tolerated in silence this changed order of affairs, but not so with many of the hotheaded youths of the country.[35]

From the perspective of young men and boys such as Bill Longley, and maybe it was true on occasion, some of the liberated young black men were "inflated by their new-given freedom . . . [they] took on airs, were domineering, and were very loose with their talk."[36] Young white men, especially those who did not fight in the war and who were imbued with fanciful, emotional notions of defending "southern honor," chafed under this state of affairs. And the community environment itself often fostered such rebelliousness: "Society was partially disorganized, martial law prevailed, hatreds were engendered, deeds of lawlessness were perpetrated in open daylight, resistance to the military was encouraged, and men who were known to deserve punishment were frequently protected by the good citizens from arrest by those regarded as aliens and enemies."[37] "The violence toward freedmen was due partly to that tendency of rowdyism to attack the weak and unprotected, and partly to resentment at the new insolence and the irrepressible bumptiousness of the freedman himself."[38]

Specifically, the carrying of firearms by ex-slaves was "a proposition that did not readily commend itself to the majority of [whites], who beheld in the armed negro, insolent and swaggering, puffed up with new and indigestible theories of equality, the most intolerable of created beings."[39] But the violence that occurred was not of a political variety; it stemmed from stark racial and rebellious motives, and amounted to very real frontier lawlessness.[40] As Bill Longley himself candidly admitted after he was convicted of murder and sentenced to hang: "My first step was disobedience; next, whiskey drinking; next carrying pistols; next, gambling, and then murder."[41] But even he blamed the path he took on the climate of the times, unconvincingly adopting the Unionist perspective of his father:

> I well remember the heart sickening murders that were committed by the secession party upon as good men as the sun ever shone on, simply because they remained true to the Star Spangled Banner, and the cause of the Union. . . . It was nothing uncommon in those bloody times to see from two to seven men hanging on one liveoak tree, with cards—one pinned on the back of each man with these words written on the cards: "Thus to Traitors." . . . It was the old law of tooth and fang, and [I] made up my mind to live up to that law literally, and to do so I had to fight and kill in self defense when it became necessary.[42]

In this setting, Bill Longley abandoned his school studies and started down the road that led to those waiting gallows and the milling crowd anxious to see him die. But, until he was captured in 1877 and wove the extraordinary tale that caught the fancy of many people across the country, Longley was not widely known in Texas. When his claimed exploits were set out for public examination, it was widely suspected that Bill Longley had highly exaggerated his bloody deeds. But his claim of killing thirty-two men was passed on without much dispute. For generations afterward, the tale as Longley wrote and told it was recounted without clarification or corroboration, and the legend came to be accepted as fact.

As will be shown, Bill Longley was not the bold desperado he sought to portray. Although Longley went to great lengths to camouflage and distort the truth as his sordid path led him to the inevitable gallows, and much of what he claimed could not be countered by documented fact, there was a trail of information that did cast doubt on the outlaw's credibility. But, on the other hand, some of what he claimed *was* true, albeit not as glamorous as he might have recalled.

Chapter 2

These Desperate Scoundrels and Out Laws

The Civil War ended in 1865, and Texas struggled to restore some equilibrium throughout its many communities. Young Bill Longley reportedly dropped out of his schooling and acquired a six-shooter and a horse, like many other young men in those unsettled times. And thus began the confusing mixture of fact and fiction that complicates a straightforward telling of Longley's short criminal career.

Some have written that in 1866, fifteen-year-old Longley jumped a train in order to go to Houston, where he could get his hands on a pistol. This seems a little contrived, given the ready availability of firearms. However, as the story goes, in the teeming streets of Houston, he saw firsthand how "the newly-freed Negroes had taken over the new State Police and created clashes with the white man."

Longley supposedly took up with another young white man, and having nowhere to stay, they decided to bed down in an alley. According to the story, they were confronted by a blue-uniformed black policeman swinging a lead ball on a leather thong, commonly called a mace. The officer demanded to know what they were doing and, instead of searching them, ordered them to undress. Longley's companion suddenly pulled a knife from under his shirt and stabbed the officer to death. Longley grabbed the officer's Texas-manufactured "Dance" revolver and the two boys fled. Longley immediately returned to Evergreen, the proud possessor of his first firearm, or at least so the story goes.[1] Unfortunately, there is no documented basis for this story and it seems a little far-fetched.

Every authoritative source indicates that, indeed, Longley and other young men in the Evergreen area, going out of their way to disrupt community tranquility through assault and robbery under the guise of performing a noble public service, became holy terrors to the local black citizens. Longley later claimed that his lawlessness began in the spring of 1867. He said, "I have always known that I was doing wrong, but I got started when I was just a fool boy, led off by older heads, and taught to believe that it was right to kill sassy negroes, and then to resist the military law."[2] Early researcher T. U. Taylor talked with old-timers who claimed that Bill Longley became an expert with the six-shooter, allegedly able to drill a tree with six balls as he galloped past astride a horse. He reportedly practiced constantly at a small creek near the Longley farm. One witness said that he saw the young man empty two pistols simultaneously into a six-inch spot on the side of a dry goods box.[3] Such tales of exceptional marksmanship are often "recalled" of notorious gunfighters.

Sometime during this period, Longley took up with Alabama-born Johnson McKeown, four or five years older than he, the fifth child of Evergreen farmer James McKeown.[4] James McKeown later became the first sheriff of newly created Lee County in 1874 and pursued Bill Longley the following year. Longley, young McKeown, and others allegedly pledged to disarm all the freedmen they found riding through the countryside, and Longley claimed that they were generally applauded for it.[5]

Stories of general hell-raising by these young men abound. For example, Longley allegedly entered into a horseracing partnership with McKeown, and they rode to various communities to participate in local races. Supposedly in 1867, as Taylor described one incident,

Longley and McKeown were forced to retreat from a certain race when they were "outnumbered" by freedmen. The two boys then went that night to the small village of Lexington, some seven miles north of Evergreen in Burleson County, and rode their horses into the midst of a Negro dance. Longley allegedly fired indiscriminately, killing two men and wounding a number of others before riding off. Supposedly this gave him a reputation as a terrorist among black citizens of the area.[6] However, as with other such tales, there is no corroboration of this incident in contemporary sources.

In another incident, William J. "Will" Grant,[7] a former schoolmate of Longley's, recalled for Taylor many years later how Longley disrupted a traveling circus. Numerous circuses traveled across Texas in those days, moving to a new town every day or so, setting up a single ring and offering a variety of acts. Grant recalled that when a small circus once came to Evergreen, he begged his parents to allow him and his younger sister to go see it. When Longley and a companion demanded admittance to the circus and were refused, they knocked the doorkeeper down and walked into the ring where two clowns were "sassing" each other. Longley reportedly ordered them to "dance," punctuating his command with well-placed pistol shots at their feet. The crowd in attendance stampeded and young Will fled in terror. Only when he arrived at home out of breath did he realize that he had forgotten his sister.[8] As will be seen, there is some evidence that Longley did raid a circus in February 1870, although it was in neighboring Bastrop County.

At some point the confrontational tactics of Longley and his friends were destined only to provoke resistance and end in violence. This is supposedly what led to Longley's first killing, variously described as occurring sometime between 1865 and December 1866, although again the stories stem from hearsay and lack any corroboration.

According to the earliest account, as told to the newspapers by Longley after his capture in 1877, Longley and McKeown attempted to disarm a black man riding through Washington County. The rider refused to surrender his weapon and drew and fired, knocking a pistol from McKeown's hand. The freedman then attempted to ride off, and Longley put a ball into the back of his head, killing him instantly. The body was left where it fell and was not discovered for several days. Although it was suspected that Longley and McKeown were involved, the local authorities did nothing.[9] Another version of Longley's first killing, similar to the first account but a little more "noble," was the story that Longley encountered a "burly Negro" who uttered an unspeakable insult about Longley's father. As Longley leaped to the offense, the black man rode off, casting a shot at the young man. Longley's shot through the fleeing man's head brought him crashing to the ground, dead. According to the tale, Longley rifled the dead man's pockets, freed his horse, then, with a rope around its neck, dragged the body several hundred yards off the road into some woods and buried it in a shallow grave.[10]

If the above-mentioned shooting even occurred, and there was no contemporary account of it other than Longley's, it was before late December of 1868, when a documented killing involving Longley did occur, which may even be the killing first described by Longley as having earlier occurred in 1867. Longley alleged that his first killing occurred three months prior to the documented December 1868 killing and said that his lawlessness did not begin until the spring of 1867. But again, as is so often the case in so many of Longley's stories, there is no record of it.

One author contended that the "first" killing described by Longley attracted no notoriety for Longley and that most folks in the area looked upon it as "merely a transient ebullition of spirit." According to this viewpoint, Longley apparently sought to escape obscurity and, in order to be taken seriously, set out on a deliberate mission to kill black men.[11] The likely truth, however, is that young Longley's rebellious nature, bad habits, and predilection for trouble simply led him to opportunities for mayhem without very much effort on his part, and even without having to kill a man.

In 1868 the new realities of Reconstruction continued to be realized in Washington County, as they were throughout the rest of the state. As one anti-Reconstruction newspaper propagandized:

> There are more negroes in Washington county than in any other county in the State, and more in proportion to the population, as well. The people of Washington have been sorely tried; they have borne with more than Christian fortitude the thousand and one ills heaped upon them. Radical emissaries have been among them, organizing, schooling and drilling the negroes in every sort of mischief. The people for more than a year have steadily confronted threatened riots, bloody and deadly strifes. . . . The people of Washington have tasted the bitter draught of subjugation, carpet-bag and free negro rule, almost to the bottom of the cup. The iron heel of the absolute tyrant has been felt by them in a greater ratio than by any other people of the subjugated State.[12]

In a report dated December 4, 1868, General Joseph Reynolds, commander of the Fifth Military District in Texas, reported to the U.S. Adjutant General in Washington, D.C., that "the murder of Negroes is so common as to render it impossible to keep an accurate account of them."[13]

In mid-December 1868, three of Alfred Evans'[14] former slaves left his farm in Bell County near Salado to visit friends and relatives for Christmas in Austin County. An older black man, known as Ned, was accompanied by two teenaged brothers, Green and Pryor Evans. When the three rode their horses several days later, on December 20, into Evergreen, they were accosted by three young white men who proposed a swap for one of their horses, which was being ridden by Pryor. Pryor told them they were not interested and the three black men rode on. About three or four miles outside of Evergreen, they stopped to eat, and when they resumed their journey, Green Evans swapped horses with his brother. After they had ridden another three or four miles, the same three white men rode suddenly up behind them with pistols cocked and stopped them.

The intruders asked them where they were coming from and ordered them to give up their six-shooters. Green Evans had the only weapon and handed it over. The three black men were searched for other weapons, then ordered to mount up and follow one of the men while the other two trailed them. One of the white men cursed them and said they "intended to learn them manners." After the six had ridden about one hundred yards in the direction of Nails Creek Bottom, a nervous Green Evans asked why they were being taken out into the brush, sensing that they were about to be murdered. When he thought that one of the white men was about to shoot, Green suddenly kicked his horse's sides and made a break for it, hotly pursued by two of the white men. The white man left behind hollered, "Don't Johns, don't Johns!" One of the pursuers fired at the fleeing black man, and the ball exploded in Green Evans' head. In the meantime, Pryor and Ned made a run for it, a shot directed at Pryor barely missing its target. Pryor fled to a house nearby and asked the help of a white man named McDaniel and two freedmen who were with him.

Green's body was soon located, his pockets turned out, a total of $4.30 having been taken from him by the three men. The body was taken back to the house where McDaniel and the two black men were paid to bury it in a temporary grave. Pryor hastily returned to Salado in Bell County, where he told Captain Evans what happened. Evans had purchased the two boys with their mother in Houston when they were quite small and raised them, the family choosing to remain with him after emancipation.

Evans decided to go to Washington County and investigate. He provided double-barreled shotguns to Pryor, Pryor's brother Burrill (or Burl), and their stepfather, Henry Evans, and the four set out for Evergreen. Captain Evans rode through Lexington, having the black men go around town so as not to alert the countryside. South of Lexington, they encountered a rider familiar with the shooting, who said that some local boys were suspected, but the only name he knew was that of a boy named Longley. A description by Pryor of one of the three attackers fit that of the Longley described by the stranger.

At dusk on Friday, Christmas Day, the party neared Evergreen, and Captain Evans had the three black men go to the house where

Green Evans was buried. Evans then went to Evergreen and put up at a local tavern, trying to find out any information without revealing his mission. He was able to confirm that a young man named Longley did indeed fit the description of one of the attackers. On Saturday morning he rode to where the ex-slaves were staying and found that McDaniel had Green's horse. Evans and his three black companions started for Brenham, the Washington County seat, to see about getting a warrant for the Longley brothers, their information leading them to believe that more than one brother was responsible. On the road to Brenham, they stopped at a farm belonging to a man named Burns, where they learned that a "Squire" Maxwell[15] and Deputy Sheriff Nunn had just headed to Evergreen to investigate the shooting. Captain Evans retraced his steps and rode ahead of the black men to catch up with Maxwell and Nunn, but did not find them until he got to town.

Evans told Judge Maxwell that he wanted a warrant for the arrest of the Longley boys, but the official told him that he had no information to act on and that the suspects had to be positively identified first. Pryor Evans was brought into town to see if he could spot any of the attackers, but he did not see anyone resembling any of the three. Then he spotted a young white man walking down the street toward them and pointed him out as one of the men. The white man spotted Pryor, ducked into a nearby store, then came out again and walked quickly away from them. Someone in the crowd said that his name was William Longley, and Maxwell then wrote out a warrant, which was sworn to by Pryor, and Deputy Nunn took the warrant and headed for the nearby Longley farm with a bystander from the crowd.

In the meantime, some unknown person in the crowd slipped a note to Henry Evans to give to Captain Evans. The note stated that Bill Longley, Johnson McKeown, and Jim Gilmore[16] should be arrested for the shooting. Evans gave the note to Maxwell, and the magistrate told Evans that he would insert the names in the warrant. However, Nunn returned to town without any prisoner and said that Longley had taken to the brush and gotten away, along with McKeown and Gilmore. Maxwell suggested that the local authorities had done all they could and advised Evans to go to Brenham for military troops to track them down. It now being dark, Evans realized that any further efforts there would be futile. Three different men warned him that he and the three black men would not be safe from vengeful relatives of the fugitives. The four left in the direction of Brenham to the east, then changed direction and rode north back to Bell County. On December 30, Captain Evans wrote a detailed letter to Texas Governor E. M. Pease describing what happened and asking that a reward be offered for the apprehension of the three men.[17]

In his letter to the governor, Evans observed:

> I found the better portion of the citizens in that vicinity that I conversed with opposed to these murderers, and cut throats, and appeared to be desirous of having them brought to justice, but they are afraid to express there [*sic*] honest sentiments, for fear of being injured in some way by these desperate scoundrels and out laws.[18]

Longley's version of this incident, as reported in a newspaper nine years later, and typically self-serving, was in line with the image that he carved out for himself, claiming that it actually occurred some three months after his alleged first killing:

> Three negroes, two of whom were mulattoes, happened to pass through Evergreen . . . and halted at a bar room to get their drinks. When they returned to their horses one of the mulattoes remarked that Evergreen was the place reported to be dangerous to the well-being of colored people, and added that he would be glad if somebody would undertake to molest him. Young Longley heard him, and at once rallied to his assistance two other young men, and mounting their horses went in pursuit of this party. They overtook them about eight miles from Evergreen, on the Brenham road. No other harm was intended than to disarm the negroes and allow them to go on; but when

> the pursuers came in sight the negroes drew their pistols and spurred their horses into a running speed. They were ordered to halt, but not heeding the command all three of the young men fired, resulting in the instant death of the negro who had requested a difficulty at the bar-room.[19]

While Longley is not identified as firing the fatal shot, and he claimed that all three of them fired simultaneously, he has been generally credited with Green Evans' death.

Whatever the motive for Longley and his young companions to chase down the three black men traveling through Evergreen, and regardless of which story is true, it is clear that the responsible authorities were hesitant to enforce the law, and tolerated such lawlessness. No record exists that any formal charges were ever brought against the three for this incident, and while Captain Evans was sincere in expressing his feeling that the citizens of the area were intimidated and cowed by the hooligans, it is also likely that the young killers were encouraged by the general sentiment opposing the new order wrought by Reconstruction. Throughout Texas, a host of clandestine organizations, such as the Ku Klux Klan, Knights of the Red Hand, Knights of the White Camellia, Pale Faces, White Brotherhood, Constitutional Union Guards, and others, had begun terrorist activities against the freedmen,[20] and the actions of Longley and his companions differed from those of such groups only in the fact that they were not as secretive nor as organized.

Longley's whereabouts after this are clouded. The presence of Captain Evans in Evergreen after the shooting and his insistence that something be done no doubt presented the threat that Longley might be arrested. So it is a fair conclusion that Longley felt compelled to leave the area and his family. No doubt, Campbell and Sarah Longley experienced considerable chagrin at the turn of events and the direction in which their son was heading.

Longley said that he traveled to Karnes County, some three counties southwest of Washington County and southeast of San Antonio.

He stated that he took a job as a cowboy at the ranch of a John Reagan, "one of the largest stock owners in that section."[21]

The next adventure claimed by Longley allegedly occurred in April 1869. DeWitt County is adjacent to Karnes County on the northwest. Longley claimed that he was riding back to Washington County from Karnes County to visit his family and rode through the small village of Yorktown in DeWitt County. According to him, a troop of cavalry soldiers, variously described as from the Fifth or Sixth Ohio Cavalry Regiment, was in the vicinity and spotted him riding along. The soldiers thought that he might be Charley Taylor, a wanted member of the notorious Bill Taylor gang, and they started in pursuit. About a dozen soldiers caught up with him outside of Yorktown and a running gun battle commenced. Longley said that the pursuing cavalrymen sent about forty rounds his way from their Spencer rifles, without any damage, and he returned about five shots, also without effect. A sergeant riding a splendid horse was able to overtake Longley and drew alongside him. According to Longley, he had been about to fire his last pistol shot, but when he extended his pistol back, the hammer of the weapon caught in the lapel of the soldier's overcoat. When Longley attempted to pull the pistol back, the hammer was released, the cap was struck, and a ball plunged into the sergeant, killing him. Longley raced off and the soldiers quit the pursuit.[22]

Again, there is a question as to whether this incident occurred at all. A close review of period newspapers does not reveal any mention of such an episode, and it seems that such a shooting would merit some mention in those turbulent times. There was a Sixth Cavalry in Texas as part of the Union military presence, "used regularly in the interior to assist in upholding the law."[23] The Sixth U.S. Cavalry Regiment first came to Texas in November 1865, establishing its headquarters near Austin at Camp Sanders. In late August 1868, the regiment removed to Fort Richardson near Jacksboro in North Texas,[24] its primary duty that of providing protection from Indians along the cattle trails moving through that vicinity.[25] However, a check of military records for the Fifth Military District provided no mention of such an incident.

It is the sort of exciting tale that a would-be desperado might tell in order to enhance a daring image.

According to a military officer who served with the regiment from 1874 to 1915 and chronicled its history:

> The regiment performed not only the usual frontier service, but, in addition, much of a character not strictly military. The troops were seldom employed together; in fact they were not infrequently scattered all over the State. During the period 1865 to 1871, the duties in Texas were of the most varied and dangerous kind. After the close of the Civil War the country was overrun with desperadoes and outlaws who were even worse than the hostile Comanches and the officers and men were continually called upon to guard the courts of justice, assist revenue officers, aid in executing convicted criminals, supervise elections, pursue outlaws and murderers, and in general to institute lawful proceedings where anarchy reigned. Many soldiers were assassinated for their devotion to law and order, and nothing but incessant vigilance and unflinching courage prevented the guerrilla community from controlling the border counties of that State.[26]

Returning to Washington County, Longley said that he found his father and mother deeply concerned about the direction that his life had taken and that Campbell urged him to leave the state before he was captured. In one account, Longley "promised to amend his life by returning to the principles his parents had endeavored to instill into his mind and heart" and consented to leave for Arkansas.[27] In another account, he is supposed to have learned of a $1,000 reward on his head and then decided to head for Arkansas,[28] but such reward was not offered until March of 1870, almost a year later.

Nevertheless, according to Longley, he headed for Arkansas and the next adventure.

Chapter 3

Murdering, Robbing, and Ravishing

By Longley's scenario, he left Washington County in the spring of 1869 and headed for Arkansas. At some point, as he reached the Texas-Arkansas-Louisiana border area, he said that he fell in with a Tom Johnson, whose family lived in Lafayette County, Arkansas, just east of the Texas state line where Texarkana is located. Johnson was allegedly a "noted horse thief" and a member of the gang of terrorists led by the notorious Cullen Baker. When Longley asked where he might find accommodations that night for himself and his horse, Johnson invited him to his father's farm.[1]

Cullen Montgomery Baker was known as the "Swamp Fox of the Sulphur," leading a band of cutthroats all over northeastern Texas, western Arkansas, and northwestern Louisiana. Repeated raids on blacks, on white supporters of the Union, and on Union troops themselves, dealing death and terror, led Union army troops in the area to focus on his gang, in addition to other marauding groups. Allegedly, Baker's family had been molested in some fashion by blacks, leading Baker to desert the Confederate army in order to seek revenge. Recruiting a band of desperate men, Baker achieved considerable statewide notoriety for his gang's bloody deeds, leading to the continuing manhunt for him.[2]

Longley said that he went with Johnson to the family farm to put up there for the night. Before morning the farmhouse was quietly surrounded by a group of vigilantes who were trying to do something about the violence, beginning with Tom Johnson. According to Longley, he and Johnson were seized, and the crowd suspected that Longley was a criminal colleague of Baker and Johnson. The two prisoners were taken about a mile from the farm where their hands were tied. The mob then placed ropes around their necks and promptly hoisted them from the same tree.

As Longley described it, the knot of the rope caught under his ear and he was well on his way to being strangled when one of the mob, a man named Jones, announced his intention to shoot the dangling scoundrels before someone came along to cut them down. Jones' first shot supposedly hit a money belt containing gold that Longley was wearing. His second shot cut two strands of the rope by which Longley was suspended, and the ball passed through his jaw and broke a tooth. Apparently shots were pumped into Johnson also. The vigilante group promptly left and the rope holding Longley broke, dropping him to the ground. A thirteen-year-old younger brother of Johnson came out from hiding, cut the ropes from Longley's neck and hands, helped revive him, then led him to a spot near the Johnson farm. Tom Johnson was dead when he was cut down, according to Longley.

Longley took about three weeks to recuperate, he said, and he was ready to ride again. Baker and some twelve men came to the farm and wanted to avenge Johnson's death, and Longley was recruited to ride with them.[3]

One author has Longley a willing recruit, Baker spending days in the forest teaching Longley how to handle his pistols.[4] Longley joined the band on raids, and he alleged that, in the course of these activities, the gang captured Jones, the man who had wounded Longley while he was hanging by his neck. The unfortunate prisoner was hoisted by his neck to the very same tree, and Longley claimed that he fired four or five shots into the doomed man.[5]

Longley also claimed that he stayed with Baker and his gang about six months, during which he participated in the killing of seven men with the other desperadoes, but he humbly declined to take any credit for the deaths.[6] It has also been alleged that Longley became a key lieutenant in Baker's gang, often leading a smaller group on raids, then retreating to the safety of some swamp. Finally, Longley decided it was time to return home, and he said that he left Baker's gang for Washington County.

While this makes for a thrilling story, and the hanging episode would lead to a long-standing myth about Longley, there are a number of factual problems that have to be dealt with. First, by Longley's account, he joined up with Baker after the Yorktown incident in April 1869. Cullen Baker was shot to death by his brother-in-law and others on January 6, 1869,[7] and, of course, Longley was definitely in Washington County in late December 1868. Some accounts tried to get around this by backing up the date: Ed Bartholomew has him on a raid with Baker in October 1867; Taylor has him joining the gang early in 1868; Longley's memory placed some of his exploits a year or two earlier than when they actually did happen, perhaps leading researchers to place him with Baker earlier than he could possibly have been there.[8]

Secondly, Longley's name has never been linked with Cullen Baker in any official document or newspaper account, unlike those of other cohorts of Baker. The incident is merely a story told by Longley without any further corroboration and apparently nothing more. When this story was related in 1877, Longley was in jail and busy spinning his own legend in the state newspapers. What better idea than to link himself with someone even more notorious, and, even better, to make that bandit his mentor? But the story cannot be corroborated and does not ring true. In Henry Fuller's *Adventures of Bill Longley*, an edited collection of some of the letters that Longley wrote to the newspapers, he quoted Longley as saying: "There are three years of my life I do not want published, as I do not wish to implicate certain characters who still live in this country. I commenced my wild career in the spring of 1867, and kept it up in Texas for three years."[9] The period in which he allegedly rode with Cullen Baker fell within that three-year space of time, and the incident was not mentioned by Fuller, likely because it never happened.

Longley returned to the Evergreen area, if he ever even left. At this point, it appears that he did indeed fall in with a man who would prove to be a mentor. Longley's sister, Frances Caroline, had married J. T. Lawrence in Washington County in 1859, by whom she bore two children.[10] On September 13, 1866, her first husband having died in the Civil War, Frances Lawrence married John W. Wilson in Washington County.[11] This was not a happy union, as witnessed by an entry in the Longley family Bible after Frances died on January 31, 1868: "after having draged [*sic*] a most miserable existence of 16 months and 17 days with one [of] the most unfeeling fiends in human shape that a good woman ever had to live with—she made a happy exchange."[12] To intimate that one's daughter was better off dead than continuing her union with John Wilson certainly does not detract from an image of a truly bad man.

John W. Wilson, for all of the influence he had on his brother-in-law, Longley, has proven most elusive. "John Wilson" was a common name and a number of John Wilsons can be found in the 1860 Washington, Burleson, and Bastrop County census lists. In 1860 a W. D. Wilson, 30, a farmer from Alabama, was living with J. T. and Frances Lawrence.[13] Plenty of men in Texas named John Wilson were wanted by the law, ranging from Ellis County to Bee and Chambers counties to the south, but there is no information that any of them was Longley's brother-in-law. One of the likeliest possibilities is a John W. Wilson, born about 1842 in Fayette County, Georgia, to farmer Stephen Wilson. Stephen Wilson moved his family to Burleson County in Texas, although son John was not included in the 1870 census of the family.[14] Nevertheless, Wilson and Longley apparently teamed up and began a series of depredations all over South Central Texas, allegedly ranging from horse theft to allegations of rape and murder. Longley referred to Wilson as his "companion and warm personal friend for several years."[15]

Longley asserted that while the two rode together, they killed seven black men, and he took responsibility for four of the killings.[16] That claim is dubious, but there is evidence that they teamed up for purposes of mayhem. Justice of the Peace James E. Brady of Bastrop County, adjacent to Washington County, wrote a letter on February 7, 1870, to Governor E. M. Pease complaining that, on February 2, two white men and a freedman named Cook had gone to the house of another freedman, Paul Brice, ten miles northeast of Bastrop. Brady accused the men of shooting Brice to death and driving off his horses. The judge went on to state that, two days later, when a circus was exhibiting at "Sevorn," twenty-three miles east of Bastrop, four men, "supported by a body of armed men," went inside the circus, drove off a deputy sheriff, and robbed the freedmen present of their money and firearms. Brady said that two of the leaders were named John Wilson and "Long," and one of them boasted that they had shot Paul Brice. Wilson was identified as being from Burleson County and as having murdered a freedman named Record at Bastrop some two years earlier.[17] While Brady was no stranger to trouble himself,[18] he clearly sought the help of the military as violence spilled over into his jurisdiction.

There is no specific account of such a raid on a circus; however, during that same time period a number of circus troupes were performing throughout the area. C. W. Noyes' Crescent City Circus was in La Grange, in Fayette County, on January 28, and at Union Hill, in western Washington County, on February 2.[19] The Orton Brothers Circus, also in the area, experienced a serious disturbance at Union Hill on January 28 between members of the troupe and "some of the young men of the neighborhood," a row that included some shots being fired, but no one was hurt.[20] On February 7, a few rowdies fired their pistols amidst the crowd, wounding two at Noyes' circus performance at Webberville in eastern Travis County.[21] The community that Brady called "Sevorn" is likely the same as Serbin, now located in Lee County about six miles southwest of Giddings and about twenty-five miles east of Bastrop. Perhaps the circus raid described by Judge Brady was the same one witnessed by Longley's schoolmate Will Grant.

On February 11, 1870, Judge Brady took pen in hand once more to complain: "A band of armed men, headed by Jno. Wilson and Wm. Longwell, are murdering, robbing and ravishing colored people in that section of the State, the gang being principally citizens of Burleson county." Brady requested military assistance as soon as possible.[22] No further information could be located that any action was taken immediately by military authorities. Clearly though, Longley and Wilson had cast caution to the winds and were practicing outlawry without any reservation and with the knowledge of the authorities. In early March 1870, a reward was offered for both of them by the military. This was also the first time that there was any mention that Longley might be involved in sexual assaults.

And the record is cumulative that their depredations were more than juvenile pranks designed to terrorize freedmen. In a report dated July 12, 1870, state policeman T. P. Woods made a report to the chief of the newly formed State Police, which replaced the Reconstruction troops that had pulled out of the state the previous April:

> Bill Longley and John Wilson killed a freedwoman near Evergreen in 1870. No warrants issued, no arrests made. ($1,000) one thousand dollars reward was offered for their apprehension by the military but they have not yet been taken. Longley is about 20 years old, about 5'9" high, hair dark, eyes blue, no beard. Complexion little dark. His father now lives in Sal[a]do Bell Co. Wilson is a low heavy set man—will weigh about 170 lbs. Eyes, hair and complexion very light—about 5'6" in height. His family lives 8 miles above Evergreen in Burleson Co. on Austin Road.[23]

The only report located of a murdered black woman in early 1870 was that of a house servant in Fayette County, near Fayetteville, who was found in late February with her throat cut and a knife and a whiskey bottle near the body.[24]

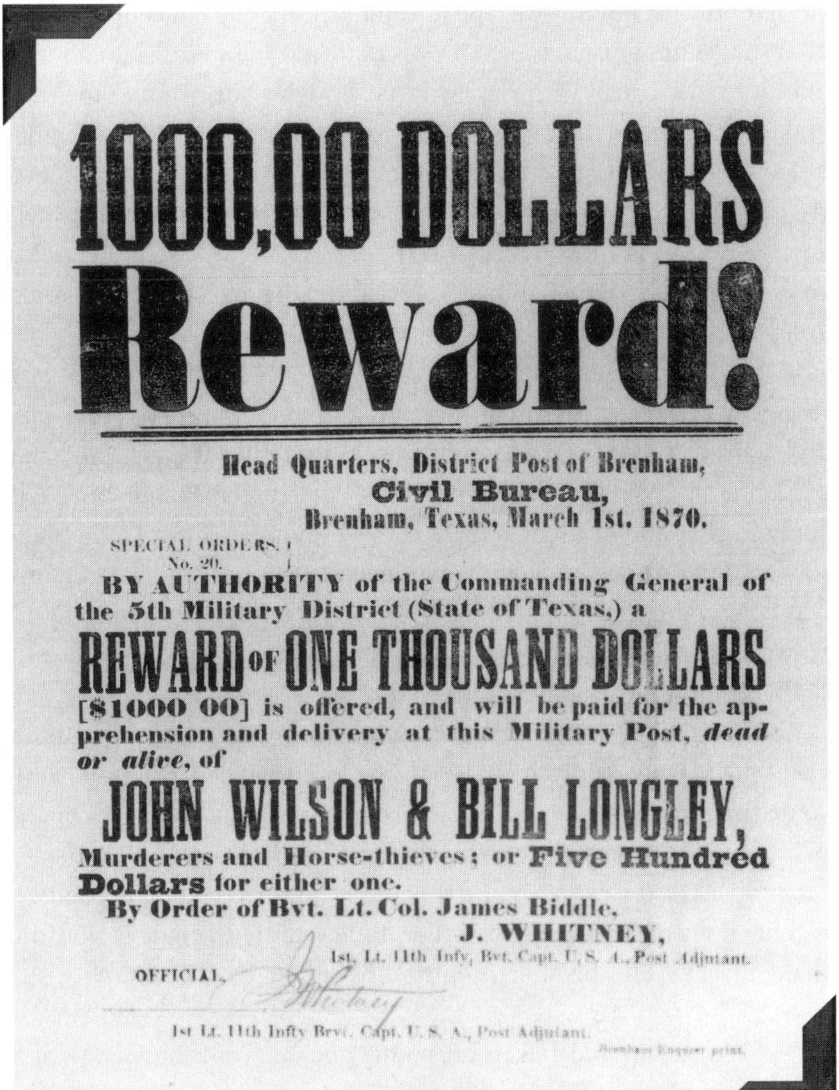

1000,00 DOLLARS Reward!

Head Quarters, District Post of Brenham,
Civil Bureau,
Brenham, Texas, March 1st. 1870.

SPECIAL ORDERS, }
No. 20. }

BY AUTHORITY of the Commanding General of the 5th Military District (State of Texas,) a

REWARD OF ONE THOUSAND DOLLARS

[$1000 00] is offered, and will be paid for the apprehension and delivery at this Military Post, *dead or alive*, of

JOHN WILSON & BILL LONGLEY,

Murderers and Horse-thieves; or Five Hundred Dollars for either one.

By Order of Bvt. Lt. Col. James Biddle,
J. WHITNEY,
1st. Lt. 11th Infy, Bvt. Capt. U.S. A., Post Adjutant.

OFFICIAL,

1st Lt. 11th Infty Brvt. Capt. U. S. A., Post Adjutant.

Brenham Enquirer print.

The March 1, 1870, reward offered by the military for John Wilson and Bill Longley. *Courtesy Dr. Johnny Spellman, Austin, Texas.*

Whether or not this was the murder reported by Policeman Woods later that summer is unknown. It was reported a few years later, during another close brush with the law, that Longley was wanted for rape, and, at the time of his capture in 1877, it was also alleged that he had killed a woman. But beyond this letter, there are no other details as to the crime of which the two were accused. The reward referred to was a $1,000 reward issued on March 1, 1870, by General Joseph Reynolds, commanding the Fifth Military District, for the arrest and delivery of John Wilson and Bill Longley, "murderers and horse thieves."[25]

The reward triggered at least one nibble from an interested lawman. On March 30, Sheriff Joseph Jung of Bastrop County, following Judge Brady's lead, wrote to the governor that Sheriff Charles Wagner of Llano County had advised him that he could arrest Longley and Wilson and that one of them was about seventy miles from Llano about to start on a cattle drive. Jung wanted to confirm how much reward was being offered and where they were to be delivered when caught.[26] However, no details as to any pursuit of Wilson or Longley as a result of this communication have survived.

Available information is skimpy, but John Wilson at some point was killed. One report had the killing occurring in Brazos County some time in the spring of 1870, perhaps in March. In 1875, Longley pointed out Wilson's grave to his younger brother, Jim, somewhere in the prairie northwest of the Bryan community, according to the 1936 recollections of the younger brother. Fuller quoted Longley as writing that he last saw his brother-in-law at Evergreen in early March:

> We sat up and talked all night, not far from the village of Evergreen, on Ridgeway Prairie. There seemed to come to us both as we sprawled on the grass and talked of the past, a feeling that we would never see each other again, and we went back through several years and recounted many a thrilling incident in which we had both taken part, and as a result of which the hand of the law had been raised against us, and we were still hunted men. We talked until the crowing of the chickens in the distant

> barnyards told us it was nearly daylight and then we separated—forever. Wilson went to the house of his father quite a distance away and I slipped into the old home near Evergreen.[27]

However, according to one account from Brazos County in June 1870,

> Two notorious outlaws, John Wilson and Bill Langley [*sic*], for whose capture Gen. Reynolds offered a reward of five hundred dollars each, are still prowling in this vicinity. Of late they seem to be joined by a third party. These, however, are only a branch of an organized band operating from the Trinity to the Colorado, through Madison, Brazos, Burleson and Bastrop counties. Last Thursday, when about half a mile from Evans' ferry in this county, these worthies halted two freedmen and attempted to rob them. Finding they had nothing valuable, they fired upon them and wounded them both—one, at least, fatally. Several citizens of that section are now in pursuit of the desperadoes.[28]

A more authoritative report told of a desperado by the name of John Wilson being shot by a constable in Falls County in 1874 while the lawman was trying to arrest him. Two accomplices, Taylor Young and Jack Lovett, made off with the badly wounded Wilson, and it can be speculated that this was Longley's brother-in-law and that perhaps he did not survive the gunshot wound.[29] Whatever happened to Wilson, Longley was in Wyoming Territory and on his own by June 1870. The above accounts reflect, however, that Longley left behind in Central Texas a reputation as a desperado.

Another episode also allegedly occurred in Evergreen prior to Longley absenting the state—a dramatic meeting between the two self-styled Texas gunmen, Longley and John Wesley Hardin. According to Hardin's egocentric autobiography, he went to Brenham, Washington County, in January 1870 to stay with his uncle, Bob Hardin. While there, he says that his gambling activities earned him the sobriquet of "Young Seven-Up," after a popular card game.[30] It is a fact that Hardin was in eastern Washington County in July 1870, staying with his uncle.[31] Hardin says that because the state police were hot on his trail, he decided to leave his uncle's farm, and he rode to Evergreen in the western part of Washington County, where some races were being held and a number of "hard characters" were congregating, including Longley, Jim Brown, and an associate, Ben Hinds.

According to Hardin, he and Hinds played "seven-up" on a goods box outside in the street of the town, and he won about twenty dollars. Hinds, fifty, a Tennessee native, owned a farm near Evergreen, where he lived with his wife, Mary, and three children.[32] Hinds was a rather volatile man himself, as reflected by an 1877 arrest in Giddings for cutting a man's throat.[33] Hardin said that Hinds was angered over losing and told him that if he were not a boy, he would beat him to death. When Hardin supposedly stood up to the older man and Hinds started for him, Hardin said that he had to draw his pistols and hold off Hinds and about a dozen other men drawn to the dispute. Hardin then claimed that Hinds backed off and apologized, offering his hand. Hardin supposedly refused to shake hands, but did accept the apology. Hinds then told him that Bill Longley would be at the races the next day and invited him to stay over. As Hardin described it,

> Late that evening a dark-looking man came to me and said, "My name is Bill Longley and I believe you are a spy for [McNelly, a state police captain from Washington County]. If you don't watch out, you will be shot all to pieces before you know it."
>
> I said, "You believe a damned lie, and all I ask is that those who are going to do the shooting will get in front of me. All I ask is a fair fight, and if your name is Bill Longley I want you to understand that you can't bulldoze or scare me."
>
> Bill replied, "I see I have made a mistake. Are you here to see the races?"
>
> I told him "not particularly." He invited me to stay over and see the horses. We went and struck a poker game going on

in a crib. We both got into the game. Directly it came my turn to deal. I had three jacks to go on and raised $5. All stayed in, and in the draw Bill drew three cards, while the other two players drew one apiece. I drew two and caught the other jack. Bill filled on aces. One of the other players made a flush, and the other filled on queens. The flush man bet $5, the man with a full went $10 better. I studied a while and said, "You can't run me out on my own deal, so I go $10 better." Bill Longley said, "Well, stranger, you have your foot in it now; I go you $50 better." The man with a flush passed; the man with a queen full says, "Bill, I call a sight."

Bill says, "All right; how much money have you got?"

He counted out $45.

"Well, stranger," said Bill, "It's up to you. What do you do?"

I said, "What are you betting 'wind or money?'"

He said, "Money."

"Put it up," said I.

He went down in his pocket and pulled out four $20 gold pieces and took out a $5 gold piece.

I said, "All right, here is your $50 and I go you $250 better."

He said, "I go you; I call you."

I told him to put up the money. He asked me if his word was not good, and I told him no. He went into his pocket again and pulled out eleven $20 gold pieces and asked me if I would credit him for the balance. I told him no.

"Well," he said, "I call you for $220."

I told him all right. "I reckon you have me beat."

He said, "I reckon so. I have got an ace full."

I said, "Hold on, I have two pair."

He said, "They are not worth a damn."

I said, "I reckon two pair of jacks are good," so the eventful game ended. I was ahead about $300.

Some way or another they all got on to my identity, and they all treated me with a good deal of respect at the races the next day.[34]

Did this episode really occur? Longley never mentioned such a meeting, and it is likely that in his efforts to paint himself as a notorious character, he would have at least described some confrontation with his rival for media attention, maybe even winning the poker hand. It is interesting that Hardin never made mention of any such meeting until 1896, when his autobiography was published, long after Longley had been executed and could not refute the story. Also, the story itself is consistent with the type of tale a boastful man would spin, whether Hardin or Longley. The meeting likely never occurred, as confirmed by a letter that Longley sent to Hardin in February 1878, after both were in custody, in which Hardin quoted Longley as having "never formed my acquaintance."[35] In an interview in the Austin jail, Hardin also told a reporter that he "never knew Longley."[36] However, in another interview while awaiting an execution date, Longley told a Chicago reporter that the two once passed each other on a road in Comanche County, the only contact being a glance between the two. Nonetheless, the tale smacks of braggadocio.[37]

About this time Campbell and Sarah Longley sold their 216-acre Evergreen farm to James Brown of Lampasas for $2,500, the deed being dated April 11, 1870.[38] The Longleys had purchased a number of lots in the small town of Salado in Bell County to the north,[39] and Campbell planned to build a store there.[40] James Brown, the same Jim Brown that Hardin claimed to see at Evergreen, would later play a pivotal role in Bill Longley's life—he would supervise his execution.

Reconstruction ended in Texas on April 16, 1870, when General Reynolds issued a final general order that returned civil authority in the state to the officials elected by the people themselves.[41] This is not to say that the killing stopped, however. One estimate placed the number of murders in Texas between January 1869 and March 20, 1870, at no fewer than 590.[42] An official report by Texas Secretary of State James Newcomb in June 1870, based on less than exact information, asserted that a total of 774 persons had been reported killed during the past two years.[43]

No longer worried about the vigilance of military troops and well aware of the prevailing sentiments of the constituted legal authority, Longley said he felt it was safe to visit his parents in Bell County. After saying farewell to John Wilson, he rode north but "took the measles on the road." It was while he was recuperating at the family home in Salado that he said he heard about the $1,000 reward offered by General Reynolds in early March. Believing that he was too well known to stay there, he decided to leave. His sister Mary Catherine, who married Charles Tyler, had moved with her family from Texas about a year earlier, heading for Salt Lake City and the Mormon faith. They settled temporarily on the Little Arkansas River near Wichita, Kansas, and were planning to go on to Utah soon. Longley decided that Utah was as good a place as any to visit, so he set out that spring of 1870 to catch up with his sister and brother-in-law.

According to Longley, he was still sick and tried to ride quietly out of Salado. However, about a mile outside of the village, he spotted four horsemen galloping after him. He readied his pistols but soon found himself facing four youngsters whom he knew and who thought it would be easy to nab him for the reward. They brashly told Longley to consider himself under arrest, although they were not pointing their pistols at him. Longley said that he brandished his six-shooters and barked: "You bunch of young roosters are in good shape to get a pass to hell, and that mighty quick. You turn around and get out of my sight as quick as you can or I will drill a hole through every damned one of you." That's all of the encouragement it took for the four lads to turn and beat a hasty retreat to Salado.[44]

It may have been that, in the midst of his adventures with John Wilson, Longley never saw an article in the February 15, 1870, issue of *Flake's Daily Bulletin*, published in Galveston, in which the richness of the gold deposits near South Pass City in the Wyoming Territory were touted. In a few short months, though, he would have the opportunity to investigate that claim personally.

Chapter 4

I Kept on Pumping Lead

Longley said that he decided that the most practical way to get to Utah was by joining one of the many cattle drives headed north through the Indian Territory and terminating at the railhead at Abilene, Kansas. According to him, he rode north to near Gainesville, in Cooke County not far from the Red River, and ran upon a large herd. The boss of the herd, a man named Rector, who Longley said came from Bee County in southwest Texas, hired Longley to go along on the drive, offering him pay of a dollar a day. Rector also furnished Longley with an extra horse so that the horse Longley was riding could be turned out with the other extra horses on the drive in order to rest and gain a few pounds. Longley said that he picked out a horse and joined the trail drive as it headed into the Indian Territory.

Fuller quoted a letter from Longley that described his days with the trail drive as tedious, "following a big herd of cattle, seeing that none drop out by the wayside or are stolen and in the days of which I speak Indian thieves as well as white thieves lined the great cattle trails, ready to steal or stampede the cattle and kill the men in charge of them if necessary."[1] Longley said he was assigned to drive the chuck wagon and help the cook in preparing grub for the cowboys. On occasion, he and the mule-driven wagon would get ahead of the herd and have to wait for it to overtake him. As Fuller quoted him, he recalled one stampede:

> One night the herd was rounded up about half a mile from camp, and during the night I was awakened by the shaking of the earth, and a fearful noise. I found that the whole herd was coming down upon our camp in a furious run. I was bunking with another man and as I jumped up and started to run he grabbed me, but I got loose and ran to the opposite side of the chuck wagon. In a moment we were in the midst of a sea of rushing, bellowing, frenzied cattle, but being behind the wagon we were not hurt.[2]

In another incident recalled by Longley, two black soldiers rode up to the cowboys' camp and asked Longley for some food, but he told them he had none. The soldiers were none too courteous, but rode on. Two of the young cowboys with the drive noticed the fine government horses that the soldiers were riding, and suspecting that the soldiers might not have come by the horses honestly, decided to pursue them and take the horses. Longley recounted that when the two overtook the black men, a gunfight ensued and one of the young cowboys was killed. The members of the trail drive dug a grave for the young man with axes and knives, and the drive continued.

On another evening, according to Longley, a severe storm assaulted the drive and, while the chuck wagon had been secured by a chain attached to a long stake pin driven into the ground, everything else was blown away. The cattle stampeded, and the horses got loose and ran with the herd. The storm spent itself by daylight, and the cowboys were able to round up the straggling cattle and resume the drive.[3]

Longley described the trail boss, Rector, as a dangerous fellow, having reportedly killed four or five men.[4] Allegedly, the drive neared a grocery one day, and Rector had the men chip in and buy a ten-gallon keg of whiskey, which was stored in the chuck wagon to last the men until the drive reached Kansas. "Rector himself was a wild, reckless sort of fellow, and there were twelve hands of us besides the cook and Rector, and he would not stand guard at night, but on the contrary would get drunk, run into the herd for pure meaness and cause it to stampede. Then he would curse the hands if they let any of the cattle get away."

About five days after buying the whiskey, Longley said, Rector got into a shooting scrape with one of the trail hands, shooting the man in the shoulder as his own horse was shot out from under him. This incident was supposed to have occurred near Pauls Valley on the Washita River in the Indian Territory, some 100 miles north of Gainesville. This apparently did not slow Rector down, and his drunkenness continued. Longley said that the day after the shooting he remarked to another hand: "Rector had better not run on to me that way, and if he did he would get hot lead poured so close to him that it would not be comfortable." This statement was passed on by a trail hand to Rector.

The drive had stopped for a few days to let the wounded cowboy rest, and Longley said that he expected a row with Rector, so rode his horse out by the herd away from camp. He saw Rector galloping out toward him and anticipated that a fight was brewing. According to Longley,

> He rode right up in front of me until his horse's head was opposite my right leg and stood there a moment looking me in the eye before he said a word.
>
> Then he said "I understand, Goddamn you, that you said I had better not run on to you—is that so?"
>
> "As sure as hell," I answered, "I damn sure did say them very words."
>
> He started to pull his pistol, but I beat him to it, and plugged him squarely in the breast. Before I could shoot him the second time he pulled the trigger of his pistol, but it was only half-cocked

> and he could not pull it down. He kept on trying to pull the trigger and I kept on pumping lead in to him until I had shot him six times, before he died.[5]

When Longley returned to the camp and told the cowboys what had happened, he said that he was advised to turn himself in at Fort Sill as it was certainly a clear case of self-defense. But Longley said that he was concerned that his bloody Texas past would catch up with him and decided to quit the herd and go on by himself. Another young cowboy named Tom Davis decided to join him, and the two packed some provisions, according to Longley, and struck out on the long journey to Wichita, where Longley hoped to find his sister and brother-in-law before they left for Utah.[6]

Again whether or not this episode ever happened cannot be established. No record of a Rector in Bee County can be found. A Mr. Rector from Shreveport brought 18,000 head of cattle through Dallas in May of 1873, three years after the event described by Longley.[7] The only thing that can be established with some degree of certainty is that Longley moved north out of Texas, and a cattle drive was logical as one method of doing that. But there is no record that he killed a man named Rector.

As quoted by Fuller in *Adventures of Bill Longley*, Longley claimed that he and Davis set out on the long journey, "a long, lonely and dangerous ride." We have only Longley's extended description of what happened during that ride, his eloquence likely a result of the added poetic flourishes on Fuller's part:

> We were both very young, not much over 19 years of age. We rode on for about three days and as we saw no Indians, we took the foolish notion that we were perfectly safe and that nobody knew we were in that part of the country. One day late in the evening we crossed the Salt Lake Fork as the stream was called, and presently came upon a large drove of turkeys that trotted along the trail, and were not wild at all. I killed two of them and about

sundown we stopped, built a fire, like two fools, and proceeded to pick and clean the two turkeys after which they were roasted brown, and upon which we made a hearty meal, however, without bread or salt. We had been using considerable caution in our trip up to this time, generally camping at dark, resting a while, then moving off a considerable distance and spending the night. But now, our horses were very tired and we thought as we had seen no Indians that we were safe.

It was a beautiful night. We lay around the fire and smoked our pipes after eating a considerable part of one of the turkeys and watched our horses bite the fine grass which was abundant. The moon was about full, and not a cloud was in sight. My friend Davis was feeling fine and told several funny jokes, as he thought but some how or other I was out of humor. Something kept telling me that we were not safe and that we ought to get up and make tracks and plenty of them, right now.

I had that strange foreboding of evil which seems to come to people sometimes and for which there is no explanation. As we lay there and talked a great horn owl, one of the largest I had ever seen flew silently into view out of the shadows and lit on a dead branch of a scrubby postoak, about forty yards distant. The great bird of the night turned and stared at us, and I noticed as he did so that he formed a wonderful picture. He had perched exactly between two dangling pieces of limbs with dead leaves on them and it gave to him the appearance of a great human head with two horns on it, just like the pictures of the old Norsemen that I had seen in the picture books when I went to school back at old Evergreen. The great bird sat there and stared at us and then uttering a shrill cry as if in warning it disappeared in the adjacent chaparral.

"That was funny, wasn't it?" asked Davis, the first to break the silence.

"Yes," I answered, "and it appears to me that the bird has warned us to get up and be going. That was a peculiar cry it uttered, wasn't it?"

"Yes, but like Poe's Raven, perhaps that 'was its only stock in store,' and it could not say anything else even if it had wanted to indulge in other language."

It was not long until I heard the faraway cry of a wolf and it seemed to me that there was a difference in its tone, to that of the Texas wolf, many of which I had heard at night, on various occasions. The call that I now heard did not sound "wolfish" enough for me and I told Davis so.

"Nonsense," he replied, "that is the genuine call of a real wolf. You are scared and will not admit it."

As we talked the call of another and then another wolf could be heard in different directions. As a matter of fact the calls we heard came from Indians and were signals.

It was about midnight when we got our horses, brought them up close to us, and lay down for a few hours rest. Davis at once dropped off to sleep. But I could not go to sleep to save me. I had a spell of the "big eye," and lay there hour after hour listening to the snoring of Davis and the different calls of the wilderness night. It was certainly a lonely place. It must have been about two o'clock when I saw my horse suddenly turn his head and gaze steadily in the direction of the chaparral, and I knew the animal saw something of an unusual nature. I raised my head slightly and saw an Indian creeping towards my horse, and the animal now began to rear and surge on the rope to break loose. The Indian was very near the rope and as he saw I had discovered him he made a slash at the rope with a big knife which flashed in the bright moonlight. I rose to my knees and let drive at him with my six-shooter. He jumped up, and fired at me, with a pistol I had not seen. I heard the report of another pistol and turning my head quickly saw that Davis was in a fight with several Indians on his side of the camp, his bunch using arrows, which they were pumping into our camp as thick as they could fall. The only Indian that seemed to have a pistol was the one I had first discovered and he kept shooting at me. Every time he shot his pistol he raked at the rope with his

> knife, but missed it. We kept firing at each other until we had fired six times, and then he broke and ran away, without cutting the rope. The other four had continued to advance shooting arrows as they came. . . . So I immediately drew my other six-shooter and ran to the assistance of Davis. I didn't wait an instant but rushed right at the bunch of Indians intending to kill all four if I could get near enough to them, before they hit me with one or more of their arrows. As I started Davis killed one of the Indians and the other three seized him and ran, and left us masters of the situation. We had enough of that kind of business for one night. It was now about two hours until daylight and we quickly saddled our horses and left that place in a hurry. We had two six-shooters each and also plenty of ammunition, and if I do say it, we would have been a bad couple to handle even with odds against us.
>
> Our blankets were shot all to pieces. My blanket had twenty arrows sticking in it, and there were at least a dozen big arrows sticking in the ground around the fire.
>
> Tom was shot through one arm, but not badly. We shook the arrows out of our blankets, got on our horses and rode away, at a lively gait, going about ten miles and stopping just as daylight began to show signs in the east.[8]

This was another melodramatic account spun either by Longley or Fuller that cannot be confirmed by reliable documentation. Essentially the same information was repeated in the account of Longley's life that was published after his trial.[9] Longley said that he and Davis stayed at a second camp a short time and spotted two Indians in the distance leading two horses, the braves likely from the group of five Indians that had attacked them. The two young men moved on and two days later, according to Longley, came upon a large herd of buffalo in a valley. When the buffalo became excited, the two suspected that Indians were in the area, and they concealed themselves in a deep creek with overhanging banks. Longley watched the dust and confusion being created by the running buffalo and thought that it was a hunt. But he said that he then realized that he was actually witnessing a battle between about 150 Osages and 300 Cheyennes, a bloody encounter featuring both rifles and tomahawks. The Osages, badly outnumbered, fled with their enemy in close pursuit. Longley said that he and Davis chose that time to leave the area quickly before the Indians returned to count and claim their dead.[10]

Three days later, according to Longley, he and Davis reached the Arkansas River and a day later the site where his sister and brother-in-law had wintered their cattle, which was about seventy-five miles from Abilene, Kansas. The Tyler family had left for Utah a week earlier. After an hour's rest, the two continued on to try and overtake them.[11]

Longley wrote that on that first evening after leaving the Tyler homesite, he and Davis encountered two men on the road looking for "a pair of fine buggy horses." The men told them that the horses had been stolen in Abilene by two fellows from Texas, and they asked Davis and Longley to join in the search, there being a reward of $100 for each of the horse thieves. Not believing they would ever run into the thieves, Longley and Davis agreed to help and separated from the two men, who were heading back to Abilene by another road. Longley and Davis themselves headed toward Abilene, and about five miles down the road and still about forty miles from Abilene, they came upon a grocery store by the side of the road run by a man named Cook or Cooke. As he went inside to get a drink of whiskey, Longley said that he saw the two thieves leading the stolen stock up to the store. The thieves did not suspect Longley and Davis, since the two were headed toward Abilene, and offered to trade the horses with the two young men. The two thieves introduced themselves as Shelley and Joe McClelland (or McClellan), whom Longley described as "a bad fighting man" and who had supposedly killed a deputy marshal in Abilene. Leaving Davis with their horses, Longley went inside the store to get a drink.

According to another account, storekeeper Cook was acquainted with the Tylers, and Charlie Tyler had given him "a full statement of the young man's [Longley's] reckless life." Their conversation turned to the horses reported stolen in Abilene, just as Shelley and McClelland rode up with the two horses. The two horse thieves then came into the store, had several drinks, and admitted that they had stolen the horses. At some point, according to Longley, he decided to capture the men and take them in for the reward.

Longley said that he took a stiff drink, examined his pistol, then stepped outside the back door.

> I walked unconcernedly around to where the two men were giving Davis the wink, as I walked up, and suddenly covered both men with my pistol. Davis had his gun out and leveled almost as quick as I and the grocery man also came out with a gun in his hand ready for instant use. . . . When I covered the men with my pistols, and yelled for them to throw their hands up and be damn quick about it, McClelland said he would die first and started for his hip pocket. I simply beat him to it, and shot him through the heart. I saw I had killed him and instantly started to shoot Shelley but he threw his hands up and saved himself by a scratch. This is not all of the story. Joe McClelland, quick as a flash had gotten his pistol in his hand, and as he tumbled from his horse it fired and the ball shot Cook, the store keeper, through the body and killed him instantly.[12]

In another account, Cook lived about fifteen minutes, then died. Longley said that he and Davis then took Shelley and the stolen horses back to Abilene. Shelley was turned over to the authorities, and the two men were paid the reward, as well as a sum of money contributed by local citizens.[13] He and Davis lingered in Abilene for a few days, and Longley sold his horse. According to Longley, he and Davis split company, and Longley took a train for the 150-mile trip to Kansas City, then north twenty-some-odd miles to Leavenworth.[14]

Once again, there is no contemporary account of this episode or of the existence of some bad guys known as Shelley and McClelland.

As Bartholomew pointed out in *Wild Bill Longley: A Texas Hard-Case*, the well-known lawman Frank Canton, a deputy United States marshal in Oklahoma, captured two brothers, Bill and John Shelley, in Oklahoma in the mid-1890s after a gunbattle.[15] However, it is unknown whether either of these men was the same Shelley that Longley claimed to have captured.

In Leavenworth, Longley said that he stayed for several days taking in the sights of the town before he went on to Salt Lake City. He became acquainted with several other young men, and they caroused quite a bit. As Fuller quoted him,

> One night I was out in town alone, and got to drinking too much. There were some soldiers there, and they were in the same fix. I was talking about Texas and various things in the Lone Star state. One of the soldiers heard me, and stepping up to me asked me if I was from Texas? He butted into a conversation that did not concern him in the least and his insolent manner and the way he asked the question, told me that I would have to kill him and that right off the reel.
>
> I answered that I was from Texas and wanted to know if he had any particular objections to my having been born in that state.
>
> He replied insolently that if he was from Texas he would be so damned ashamed of it that he would certainly keep it to himself.
>
> I told him that there were many honest people in Texas, however, the population should not be judged by myself.
>
> He answered that there was not an honest man nor a virtuous woman in the entire state.
>
> Before the words were cold on his lips I had sent a bullet through his heart, and as several of his companions made a move as if to interfere I covered them and informed them if they did not want to get a quick pass to hell to keep quiet.[16]

In another account, the soldier supposedly said that all Texans were thieves, and Longley told him his father lived in Texas and was an honest man, cautioning the soldier to "go slow" in his comments about Texas. The remark about the absence of virtuous women in Texas was the final straw for Longley.[17]

Longley said that he escaped from the drinking hall into the darkness, went immediately to his hotel where he retrieved his saddlebags, then took a steam ferry boat across the Missouri River, where he caught a train for the ride north to St. Joseph, Missouri. Thinking he had fled any pursuers, Longley said that at about two o'clock in the morning he arrived in St. Joseph, where he intended to change cars for the trip to Utah. As soon as he stepped off the train, two policemen, who had apparently been alerted by telegraph, laid their hands on the tall, young man and asked him if he was ready to go back to Fort Leavenworth. A third policeman disarmed him, and he was held, Longley said, until a unit of soldiers came to St. Joseph for him. He said that he was returned to Fort Leavenworth where he was kept in close confinement by the army.

Again, there is no record to corroborate Longley's claim as to this killing at Leavenworth. Killings were certainly not uncommon and were duly reported in the local press. For example, Charley Frank, who kept a small store at Fort Leavenworth and was permitted to sell beer to soldiers, attempted to break up a fight between two men on February 28, 1870, and was stabbed to death.[18] And on March 10, a Captain Carpenter of the Seventh Cavalry was shot and wounded in a saloon in town by a disgruntled soldier who had refused to pay for a drink and was ejected by the officer.[19] But there is no mention of an incident similar to that described by Longley.

Longley said that after he had been at Fort Leavenworth for two or three weeks, he overheard some guards discussing his fate: to be court-martialed and shot in a few days. Longley claimed that he boldly offered the sergeant of the guard fifty dollars to let him "run over" the sergeant and get away. Allegedly, Longley had made the soldier a violin out of white pine plank, using a knife that the sergeant had been careful to retrieve every night, and they became good friends. According to Longley, after thinking about the proposal for a few minutes, the sergeant agreed, and Longley was soon on his way again. He said that he was helped after his escape by a number of people in the area who thought he had been correct to kill the soldier. In a letter to his brother, written a year or so later, Longley claimed,

> Jim I am going to tell you the truth now and not waver the thing any further. I shot a man in Kansas and I got captured and there was a strong guard over me and also a ball and chain weighing 24 lbs and I expect I would have bin sent to the penitenchary if it had not bin for a young lady that brought me a file and I got a way. This was near Fort Leavenworth Kansas. I went by a different name there.[20]

If Longley is to be believed, his hair at this time was shoulder length. He said that he cut his hair short, acquired some false whiskers for a disguise, and fled by walking at night, sleeping in the daytime.[21] But as before there is no corroboration of this story, and military records do not reflect any sort of killing occurring. We have only Longley's word that it happened, which he later vigorously recanted.

From Bastrop County in February 1870 until May 1870, there is no record of Longley's whereabouts and activities other than the fanciful accounts given by him after his capture in June 1877, and subsequently edited by Fuller. If he did kill Rector, McClelland, and the soldier at Leavenworth, those killings would have occurred in that roughly three-month period. But beginning in May 1870, Longley's trail can be verified, and his life then took a strange turn.

Chapter 5

We Set Out in Fine Spirit

Whatever happened in Kansas, Longley continued northward, first to Omaha, Nebraska, then on to Cheyenne in Wyoming Territory, where he said that he joined a party of miners preparing for an "exploring expedition" into the Big Horn range of mountains.[1] He was welcomed by the leaders forming the group, including a Captain Kuykendall, and on their instructions obtained necessary supplies and readied to leave immediately.[2]

The record backs up Longley's account at this point. Judge W. L. Kuykendall, late in 1869, had pondered the feasibility of organizing a semi-military group of prospectors to venture into the country above the North Platte River to displace the Sioux Indians there and look for gold. Discussing the idea with others, Kuykendall placed an advertisement in the Cheyenne newspaper for a meeting at McDaniel's Theater. Elected president of the Black Hills and Big Horn Association at the meeting by eager prospectors, Kuykendall began recruiting an expedition, and ultimately, according to him, two thousand men volunteered, each agreeing to bring with him a "repeating gun," one thousand rounds of ammunition, and rations for six months.[3] According to the Territorial Census for 1870, William Kuykendall was a thirty-two-year-old farmer from Missouri, who lived with his wife and three children in the household of lawyer James Whitehead in Cheyenne.[4]

The major obstacle to Kuykendall's expedition was not the Sioux Indians he was arming against, but instead the United States government. After the Civil War emigration west had escalated, and transcontinental trails began to be carved through territories that traditionally had been open Indian hunting grounds. Parallel lines of railroads were being laid as quickly as finances and manpower could allow. The movement west was "tumultuous and irresistible," and the government really had not been concerned about Indians blocking that progress.[5] The Teton Lakota Sioux had reigned over portions of eastern Wyoming, southeastern Montana, and western Dakota and Nebraska for generations. During the Civil War, when the Bozeman Trail was established so that miners could reach the gold fields of western Montana, army troops were sent to protect the prospectors and a number of forts were established along the trail. The Sioux, led by a very capable chieftain, Red Cloud, made war against the invaders, and in 1866 wiped out Captain William Fetterman's command at Fort Phil Kearny on the Bozeman Trail. It was obvious that the army did not have sufficient strength or ability to keep the trail safe.[6]

Given the strategic reality of the situation, a peace movement was started in the East and the government was urged to enter into treaties that would deal effectively with Indian grievances, as well as convince the Plains Indians to move to reservations north of Nebraska and south of Kansas. In July 1867, Congress created a peace commission with very little opposition from the military. In the spring of 1868, at Fort Laramie, Wyoming Territory, Red Cloud and his warriors entered into a treaty with the commissioners that required the United States government to abandon the forts along the Bozeman Trail. In addition, the Powder River country was designated as "unceded Indian territory," and a "Great Sioux Reservation" was created in all of what is now South Dakota, west of the Missouri River. It was expected that the Indians would learn to support themselves through agriculture, despite their history as nomadic hunters.[7] The Indians had a right to hunt outside the reservation in the "unceded territory" only so long as there were sufficient buffalo to justify such hunting. The treaty in effect concentrated the Indians, but the Indians weren't necessarily ready to adapt to a confined life.[8]

Fort D. A. Russell was established at Cheyenne in 1867 to protect the advancing Union Pacific Railroad, and the next year Fort Fred Steele was created near Rawlins where the railroad line crossed the North Platte River. The government also entered into treaties with Shoshone and Bannock Indians to help protect them from their enemies, primarily the Sioux and Cheyennes. As part of those agreements, the army established a military post in the Wind River Valley in 1869, located near present-day Lander on the Popo Agie River. Initially called Camp Augur after the commander of the Department of the Platte, headquartered in Omaha, the name of the post was subsequently changed to Camp Brown. Camp Brown's major missions were to protect the Shoshones on their Wind River Reservation and to guard the miners to the south in the Sweetwater River area and South Pass region[9] on the Continental Divide.

According to Kuykendall, just as the major expedition was preparing to head west into the Black Hills and Sioux country, President Ulysses Grant issued an order prohibiting intrusion into that country by just such expeditions as he was forming. Despite the order, Kuykendall still managed to raise about 130 men, outfitted and divided into two companies commanded by Billy Wise, a thirty-four-year old harness maker from Germany,[10] and a Colonel Farrar. The commander at Fort Russell, Colonel John H. King, ordered the contingent not to move, then, according to Kuykendall, modified the order to allow the men to go no further than the area around South Pass City in the Wind River Range,[11] well south of the Sioux country protected by treaty.

Longley joined the expedition at about this time. When the expedition left Fort Russell on May 20, 1870, he recalled,

> There were one hundred and twenty five men in the crowd, and we had thirty wagons and teams, plenty of provision, plenty of guns and plenty of ammunition. We had picks, shovels, and gold pans. When a short distance out we stopped, made camp, elected our officers, adopted rigid rules and regulations, and then resumed our journey. We were all well mounted on California horses except the teamsters. We traveled slowly so as to keep close to the wagons. . . . We had two pieces of artillery—twelve pound pieces. Our company was composed of middle-aged men and were rough customers. I was the youngest man in the bunch by ten years. We set out in fine spirit and every one expected to become a millionaire in the next few months.[12]

Kuykendall said that the heavily armed company left Fort Russell with a single six-pounder cannon that had been presented to it by Major John Talbot, a thirty-three-year-old Irish saloon keeper in Cheyenne.[13] It is here that Longley's version diverges from that of Kuykendall, whose account is likely the most reliable. Longley alleged that the group reached Whiskey Gap in the Sweetwater Mountains, where they were attacked by some 300 Sioux Indians, led by Spotted Tail. He said that four of the miners were killed, and three were badly wounded, with several Indians killed. After burying their dead, the miners moved on, the Indians watching them closely along their way. At night, he wrote, the miners would circle their wagons with their cattle inside the circle, numerous guards posted to watch for an attack. After one midnight, Indians on horses charged up to within fifty feet of the wagons, he said, and after a fusillade by the guards, retreated into the darkness and sniped at the prospectors throughout the rest of the night. At daylight grapeshot was fired at the Indians from a cannon, and the Indians fled. Longley said that two men were wounded and about twenty Indians were killed.

As the company moved on, Longley said that they followed the California Trail, their path marked with grave after grave of Indian victims.

At one point they saw feathers flying through the air, and Kuykendall told his men that Indians had attacked wagons or a camp somewhere, tearing up feather beds they had found. They came upon the ruins of a ranch that had been attacked, still smoking, and found the bodies of two women and five men: "Their throats had been cut, and their hands and lips had been cut off. The women were about to be confined, when the savages attacked the place, and their entrails were taken out and the babes jerked from the wombs." According to Longley, the company continued its journey, losing one of its men to the Indians when he ventured out alone to hunt for some game. After five more days, Longley said, they came to South Pass City in the Wind River Mountains.[14]

This bloody tale of adventure recounted by Longley must be contrasted with the brief version given by Kuykendall:

> When we reached the Sweetwater River it soon became evident that Indians were congregating and moving parallel with us on both flanks, which they did until we reached Camp Brown, where Lander is now located and where they quit us evidently because they feared to attack owing to the compact marching and presence of the gun.[15]

Most likely, while the threat of Indian attack was ever present, the expedition made it safely to the South Pass area on the Continental Divide, and there were no Indian attacks as Longley claimed.

Digging for gold in the South Pass area began as early as 1842, although mining activity remained sporadic until after the Civil War. Mining resumed in October 1865, and the Lincoln mining district was formed the following month. The rich Carissa mine was discovered in June 1867, and word spread of the major new gold finds in the area, bringing large numbers of speculators eager to find their fortunes. Additional finds were made in 1868 and 1869, and there were an estimated 1,500 claims by 1870. South Pass City was laid out on Willow Creek, north of the Sweetwater River, and it became the county seat of Carbon County in December 1867.

South Pass City, Wyoming Territory, 1870. *By permission of Wyoming State Archives, Department of State Parks and Cultural Resources.*

A second mining community, Atlantic City, was located on Rock Creek about four and a half miles northeast from South Pass City. In addition, three and a half miles northeast of Atlantic City was established the small town of Hamilton City, popularly called Miner's Delight after the major mine in the area. The Wyoming territorial government reorganized in 1869, and South Pass City then was the county seat of Sweetwater County.[16]

Treaty notwithstanding, the Indians did not leave the area alone. In the summer of 1867, on July 22 a party of prospectors was attacked eight miles east of South Pass and three men were killed, the Indians also burning a telegraph at Big Sandy. On July 3, 1868, four miners in the area were killed by Indians, and two more on August 18. In 1869, four more were killed in May and four in September near Camp Brown. John Anderson, a lime hauler, was killed near Miner's Delight, and Charles Latham was killed about one-half mile from Atlantic City while chopping wood.[17]

On March 31, 1870, as Kuykendall was preparing his expedition, Frank Irwin was killed near Atlantic City. On the same date in nearby Smith's Gulch, between Atlantic City and Hamilton City, two miners were killed. One of them, James H. Othic, was found lying on his right side and stripped of all clothing except a shirt. "A pick was driven in his bowels to the eye; three scalp locks had been taken from his head; and his body was pierced with six arrows and one gun-shot wound, also a pistol shot in his head."[18] At St. Mary's Station on the Sweetwater River south of South Pass City also on March 31, the Indians killed three other miners. One of them, a man named McGuire, had suffered five bullet wounds in his neck and face, had eight arrows protruding from him, and had lost three pieces of his scalp. The citizens of South Pass held a town meeting on April 5, 1870, and passed a resolution petitioning the War Department for troops to punish the Indians.[19]

Not waiting for the army, a force of some 275 white men approached 400 to 500 Arapahos camped on the Big Wind River, about thirty miles below present-day Lander. Even though it was suspected that the Sioux were behind the recent depredations, it was determined that the Arapahos did have a large number of stolen horses in their possession. On April 7, 1870, a party of seventy-five men encountered a chief named Black Bear and a small party of Arapahos; a fight broke out, and Black Bear, thirteen warriors, three women, and a child were killed. Eight children were captured and later raised by white families.[20]

By April 3, Wyoming Territorial Governor Campbell had already requested that soldiers be dispatched to the South Pass area, and by May sites were being explored for a suitable post. In the meantime, two companies of the Second Cavalry Regiment were sent to the area, Company D under Captain David S. Gordon and Company B under Lieutenant Charles B. Stambaugh. The soldiers, not aware of the proximity of several angry Arapaho raiding parties, camped in the Big Atlantic Gulch.[21] On May 4, 1870, the Indians hit the area in force, stealing cattle and then retreating. Gordon and Stambaugh led a twenty-five-mile pursuit, killing two Indians and securing the stock. On their return, the soldiers ran into a larger band and another fight ensued. Stambaugh rode too far ahead of his troops and was shot from his saddle. His body was retrieved after the Indians were finally driven off. A sergeant, Alexander Brown of Company D, had much of his jaw shot off.[22]

A permanent subpost of Fort Bridger was established on June 20, 1870, about halfway between Atlantic City and Miner's Delight on Little Beaver Creek. The post was named Camp Stambaugh in honor of the fallen lieutenant and garrisoned with Company B under the command of First Lieutenant James N. Wheelan.[23]

Kuykendall said that as his company of miners neared Miner's Delight, they ran into three men heading toward their claims to the north near Camp Brown, and that he warned them of the Indian danger. They ignored the warning, and he says they were killed that same day.[24] In fact, these three men—Dr. R. S. Barr, a justice of the peace at South Pass City; Harvey Morgan; and Jerome Mason—were killed on either June 23 or 27 (accounts differ, but the June 23 date is more likely) some eight miles south of Camp Brown. The same Arapahos who had killed them had also stolen an estimated 2,000 horses and mules from miners at South Pass City. When the bodies of the three men were found, thousands of moccasin tracks covered the ground. Both Mason and Morgan had been scalped, and the attackers had cut the skin across the back of Morgan's neck, splitting it down the entire length of his back. The Indians had peeled the hide back about three inches on each side and removed sinew, supposedly for bow strings. A wagon hammer was driven through his head, pinioning him to the ground. It could not be removed and Morgan was buried with it.[25]

After they surveyed the death scene, according to Kuykendall, the party proceeded to Camp Brown, continually observed by Indians. Warned that there were at least 1,000 Indians surrounding them, the miners nevertheless left the marked road and blazed their own road, and, defying government orders, moved north into the area reserved by treaty for the Sioux. When they reached the Wood River, south of present-day Pitchfork, Wyoming, they were overtaken by Lieutenant Wheelan and troops and ordered to return south to Camp Stambaugh with them. Ever the lawyer, Kuykendall noted that Wheelan's orders instructed him to take them back if he found them in or moving in the direction of the Big Horn Mountains, so Kuykendall told him that they were moving away from the mountains and were on public domain. After a lengthy conference, according to Kuykendall, he again agreed not to go into the Sioux country, and Wheelan and his troops departed. It was shortly after this that many men deserted the expedition, and it broke up.[26] Kuykendall went on to find some fame as the judge elected by Deadwood miners in 1876 to preside over the trial of Jack McCall for the murder of James Butler "Wild Bill" Hickok, a trial which was subsequently found to be illegal.[27]

Longley's account claimed that Kuykendall's party left South Pass and headed toward Camp Brown, even though the Camp Brown commander had ordered them not to proceed in that direction because of the treaty. Seeking to avoid army troops, the party, according to Longley, moved up the Popo Agie River and then the Wind River to Hot Sulphur Springs near present-day Thermopolis. Longley said that he was taken with the abundance of game in the area, and one day he and a young man named Miller climbed a nearby mountain to view the countryside with a spyglass and maybe do some hunting. They killed a few mountain sheep, butchering and suspending them from trees as they went. That evening the two tired young men descended the mountain, taking up the sheep carcasses as they went, but found two grizzly cubs eating the first one they had suspended. They shot the two bears, killing both, but not before one of them let out a mournful cry of distress. This brought the cubs' mother charging them, and Longley said that he began "pumping lead" at her with his Winchester, breaking one of her front legs, while Miller, who had a shell hung in his rifle, sought safety in a nearby tree. Longley said he emptied his rifle without stopping the rampaging bear, then joined Miller in the tree. The enraged bear shook the tree, trying to dislodge its occupants, Longley said, and they drove her off with several pistol shots into her back. When the bear left, the two men gathered their sheep and quickly made it back to the camp. Several miners retrieved the dead cubs, and with the help of a dog located the mother bear, dead in a pool of water. The bear was skinned and the camp enjoyed a hearty meal.[28]

Longley said the party then proceeded on up the Wind River into the Black Hills country, moving to the Greybull River, again engaging Indians and losing one man killed and having another wounded. He said that the Indians rolled rocks down on them from the top of a steep canyon, and several more men were lost, as well as two wagons. When one of the men was caught sleeping while on guard, Kuykendall tried him and sentenced him to be shot. Longley claimed that he was one of six men selected for the firing squad, only three of whom would have loaded rifles, and the man was shot and buried. He said that when the company reached the Greybull River, probably about the same place as claimed by Kuykendall, "we were overtaken by five companies of United States cavalry, under Captain Gordad [*sic*], and they were a rough bunch, but under the strictest discipline." The party, according to Longley, was ordered to march to Camp Brown and disband, and he said that this is what happened. And what did Longley say he then did?

> The men scattered from Camp Brown, but I stayed there and got a job as teamster for the federal government, and during the time that I was thus employed I had many adventures of a more or less thrilling nature.[29]

Well, not quite. On June 22, 1870, William P. Longley formally enlisted as a soldier in the United States Army for a period of five years and was sworn into Company B of the Second Cavalry Regiment by Lieutenant Wheelan at Camp Stambaugh, between Atlantic City and Miner's Delight. Longley swore that he was twenty years of age, unmarried and without a child, that he had never before been kicked out of military service, and that he knew of no impediment to his serving honestly and faithfully as a soldier for five years. On his enlistment statement, Lieutenant Wheelan noted that the new recruit was of lawful age, had black eyes and black hair, had a fair complexion, and was six feet tall. The assistant army surgeon, James T. Augur, pronounced Longley "free from all bodily defects and mental infirmity, which would, in any way, disqualify him from performing the duties of a soldier."[30]

The accounts by Longley and Kuykendall as to the progression of the expedition from South Pass, with the exception of the ferocious Indian fighting claimed by Longley, are sufficiently similar to conclude they are correct. Since Longley enlisted on June 22, however, the claim by Kuykendall that the expedition encountered Barr, Morgan, and Mason prior to their demise is probably questionable. But now, hundreds of miles from his Texas home, Longley was a soldier at Camp Stambaugh.

Chapter 6

A Man of Low Instinct and Habits

A comparison of Longley's version of his adventures in the Northwest with the official record concerning Camp Stambaugh truly reveals his artful ability to mix fact with fiction in order to project the desperado image he sought. The truth does not do much for that image.

When Longley was captured in 1877, according to the account given by Fuller, he claimed that after the Kuykendall expedition broke up, he was broke and stranded, so he applied to the army quartermaster for a job as a teamster. He said that his job was to drive a six-mule team between Camp Brown and Fort Bridger hauling supplies and equipment. Because of the Indian threat, he said that there were usually four or five wagons in each caravan, guarded by a detachment of cavalrymen. Longley alleged that on September 15 (probably 1870, although no year is given), a caravan was attacked by some 130 Indians between South Pass City and the Green River on a creek that he called the Dry Sandy, which lies to the southeast of South Pass. Longley said that after much shooting and yelling and the loss of one of their men, the Indians were driven off. As will be seen, Longley could not possibly have been present at that fight, if it occurred, even as a soldier.

Longley claimed that he worked as a civilian teamster for about three months, then quit and joined in a partnership with a man named Tom Johnson (by coincidence, the same name as that of the man allegedly hanged with Longley). The two opened a saloon, he said, in Miner's Delight near Camp Stambaugh, each contributing about three hundred dollars to the enterprise. The two made a lot of money, bringing their supplies, he said, from Bryant Station some 100 miles distant on the Union Pacific line. Their saloon maintained two brands of good whiskey, one brand of wine, a barrel or two of alcohol, tobacco, and cigars. According to Longley, there were no women in the country, and their customers to a man were heavily armed.[1]

As the record shows, Longley was a soldier, not a teamster. It would not be until several months before his execution, however, that Longley admitted that he enlisted in the army.[2] A soldier who knew Longley when he enlisted later recalled that Wheelan and his troops took five days of hard marching to overtake Kuykendall's expedition and bring it back to Camp Brown. The soldier, Henry Gross, described Longley as among the most destitute of the party, and "probably not knowing what else to do to satisfy the cravings of his stomach after having disposed of his gun, presented himself for enlistment." Gross insisted that Longley was never employed as a citizen by any quartermaster, nor did he ever keep a saloon in Miner's Delight.[3]

Although Longley enlisted on June 22, Camp Stambaugh itself had been formally organized only on June 20, named after the lieutenant slain the month before. Captain David Gordon, on orders from the Department of the Platte, selected the site for the post, just a little over a mile from Miner's Delight and two-and-one-half miles from Atlantic City. The post was located on a natural plain some one by one-half miles inside a depression formed by a range of the Wind River Mountains. A desolate spot, the alkaline soil was decorated only by wild sage. Pine trees for timber to gather for firewood and with which to

An oil painting of Camp Stambaugh, Wyoming Territory, by an unknown artist. *By permission of Buffalo Bill Historical Center, Cody, Wyoming, gift of Mrs. Gladys H. Ramsey, 28.83.*

construct buildings could be found only in the mountains some twelve miles distant. Springs within a mile or so of the site provided a bountiful supply of good drinking water. The altitude of the post was 7,714 feet.[4] One description said of the hills surrounding the encampment, "Their dark color and very sparse vegetation gives a somber aspect to the entire scenery."[5] There was ample game in the area, ranging from cinnamon and grizzly bear, elk, deer, antelope, gray wolf, and coyote to jackrabbit, porcupine, beaver, gopher, sage hen, and some ducks. The streams teemed with fish.[6]

When Longley joined Wheelan's Company B as a cavalryman, the need to construct buildings for the new post competed with the ongoing, constant scouting that took troops some 400 miles that

Hamilton City, or Miner's Delight, is nothing but a ghost town today. *Author's photo.*

June between the post and the Green River in the Wind River valley.[7] Perhaps it was the desolation or perhaps youthful exuberance for a new adventure withered in the face of military discipline, but, whatever it was, Longley changed his mind about a military career. On July 3, 1870, less than two weeks after he enlisted, Longley deserted, accompanied by John Miller, a five-year veteran of the army who had re-enlisted on March 31 at Omaha Barracks, and who also took with him his army Colt and scabbard. Spurred by a thirty-dollar reward offered for the apprehension of any deserter, troops quickly pursued the pair, capturing them together the next day at Little Sandy Creek, some sixty miles to the west. Longley was supposedly trying to make his way to settlements on the Union Pacific line.[8] The two were placed in confinement at Camp Stambaugh, although no stockade had yet been constructed. Miller may be the same person with whom Longley claimed he shared a tree limb when pursued by the grizzly bear.

A general court-martial for both deserters was ordered to be held on August 15, 1870. General C. C. Augur, commanding the Department of the Platte in Omaha, appointed the same board for both prisoners. First Lieutenant C. H. Shepard of the Ninth Infantry was appointed as Judge Advocate, and the court consisted of the army paymaster, Major R. D. Clark, Captain David Gordon, Captain W. A. Jones of the Engineer Corps, First Lieutenant Wheelan (Longley's company commander), First Lieutenant F. C. Grugan, and Second Lieutenant F. U. Robinson.[9]

Longley was charged only with desertion, but Miller was charged with both desertion and theft of the army pistol. Both prisoners pleaded guilty to the charges without any evidence being presented. Miller, the veteran, told the court-martial panel that the reason he deserted was because he "was not used well in the company" and that he "intended to soldier when he enlisted." After deliberation of the panel, Miller was found guilty of each charge and sentenced to be dismissed from the army, forfeiture of all pay and allowances "except the just dues of the laundress," and confinement in a penitentiary for two years. General Augur later reduced Miller's sentence to one year in the penitentiary at Madison, Iowa. No doubt this sentence had some effect on the waiting Longley.

Longley made no statement to his panel and, after deliberation, they sentenced him to be confined at hard labor for a period of two years, wearing a ball and chain weighing twenty-four pounds, to forfeit all pay and allowances during that period, and to be returned to duty with his company at the end of the two years. General Augur approved the sentence, directing that it be served at Camp Stambaugh.[10] As Longley faced the prospect of imprisonment, Camp Stambaugh became an independent post on August 20. Companies B and D of the Second Cavalry Regiment were assigned there, Gordon commanding D and Wheelan commanding B, and the soldiers began the task of constructing a post before the routinely severe winter overtook them.[11]

On September 25, Lieutenant Wheelan was ordered to transport Miller and another prisoner to the penitentiary at Madison, Iowa,[12] and on the same date Camp Stambaugh was reinforced by Company E, 14th Infantry, under Captain Fred E. Trottin. The next day Captain Gordon moved Company D for transfer to Camp Douglas in Utah Territory. Major J. S. Brisbin of the Second Cavalry assumed command of the post as construction was completed on cavalry stables and a commissary storehouse. Almost immediately, the building of barracks for Company B began, as well as a guardhouse, hospital, and quarters for the infantry company.[13]

Through October and November, the weather cooperated as the soldiers busied themselves with construction of the post, and the Indians presented no problems. Former Major Noyes Baldwin obtained the post tradership and also served as camp postmaster. He built a "commodious and well appearing house," replacing a rough-hewn log sutler's building, in which he stored articles for purchase and maintained a billiard table.[14] Baldwin, forty-one, had formerly commanded Fort Bridger in 1866, but left the army and become a brick mason living in South Pass City with his wife and six children when Camp Stambaugh was created.[15] He reportedly sold guns and food, when available, to neighboring civilians. Alcoholic drinks were sold only by the shot, and soldiers were permitted three drinks a day: one in the morning, one at noon, and one in the evening. Soldiers had to go to one of the nearby mining towns to get drunk.[16]

By November, nearly all buildings were completed. On the fifteenth of November, a party of Arapaho and Cheyenne Indians attacked Chief Washakie and his Shoshone tribe on their reservation some 30 miles from Camp Stambaugh and made off with their horses. Washakie and his braves pursued, killing two Arapahos and scalping one, recapturing part of the herd. Lieutenant Robinson and twenty soldiers from Company B left that morning to scout the country between there and Camp Brown but returned six days later without seeing an Indian.[17] During this same period, the post surgeon reported that there had been few cases of drunkenness and that the men appeared well, although he complained that construction of a permanent hospital was taking back seat to other construction.[18]

The snows came with a vengeance in the first two weeks of December, and the cold hampered continuing construction. On December 6, Longley was released from confinement after fewer than four months and returned to duty with his unit. He forfeited all pay remaining due at the time he deserted, as well as that amount accrued while absent. He was obligated to make good all time lost as well as pay the government for $1.56 in tobacco.[19] Sergeant Gross recalled that Lieutenant Wheelan, a humane and kind officer, "took compassion on him on account of his ignorance of the service, the penalties imposed on soldiers found guilty of desertion, etc., and procured for him a remittal of the unexpired portion of his sentence" from General Augur.[20] On the same day that Longley was ordered released, Private Michael Murphy, of Company E, lost his way in a snowstorm between Atlantic City and the post, and all of his toes had to be amputated because of frostbite.[21] A few days earlier Corporal Patrick Ryan of Company D had gotten into a drunken quarrel at a small ranch between Camp Stambaugh and Atlantic City and was shot to death. All parties to the shooting were discharged because of a lack of evidence.[22]

The only existing record of activities of the soldiers at Camp Stambaugh are the post returns, the muster rolls, and the report of the assistant army surgeon assigned to the post. Sergeant Gross recalled that, upon his release from confinement, Longley was repeatedly used as a member of small parties sent out to hunt beef and game for the post. Longley was recognized as an excellent shot, excelling with either rifle or pistol at weekly company target-practice sessions.[23]

Life as a cavalry soldier was best described by Major Joseph Lambert in his excellent history of the Second Cavalry Regiment:

> On the frontier posts the soldier found his time occupied by many duties. First of all he must be well drilled, then he must learn to be a good marksman. In the smaller posts guard mounting was the only form of ceremony, and was the main event of the day in the soldier's life. Those going on guard spent much time getting ready, as they must clean and polish their

> rifles, brush their clothes, and clean their shoes. In addition to their military duties, the enlisted men often chopped the wood, repaired the buildings, and carried on most of the labor necessary to run the post. In addition to the administrative and fatigue duties, the troops were expected at a moment's notice to be able to perform duties in the field. On the frontier the men were escorting, patrolling, scouting, and occasionally engaging in a campaign or expedition against the Indians. . . .
>
> In campaigns much latitude was allowed the trooper in the amount of equipment he was allowed to carry. He was armed with the carbine, pistol, and saber, and carried about a hundred rounds of rifle and ten rounds of pistol ammunition. There was a lariat and picket pin to tether the animal when he grazed at night. The soldier also carried an overcoat, two blankets, and a shelter tent in cold weather. He had a canteen for water and a haversack for food. He was generally allowed to carry extra articles, such as a frying pan, tin cup, and butcher knife. . . .
>
> On the march the staple articles of food were coffee, bacon, and hard bread. . . . Often when conditions such as the proximity of the enemy permitted, fresh meat was obtained by hunting. . . . On the march there was little protection for the soldiers in inclement weather, either from rain, hail, or snow. While in hostile country, they were not permitted to build fires or to make unnecessary noises. In winter campaign the cold caused great suffering to both men and animals. Often it was necessary for the troopers, after marching all day, to stand on their feet all night, for fear of freezing to death if they lay down. The poor animals stood on the picket lines without covering, and suffered intensely, often uttering during the night melancholy moans.[24]

With the start of 1871, the ravages of the winter did not abate. On January 24, the mercury fell to 35 degrees below zero. The snow on the parade ground was twenty feet deep, and tunnels had to be cut through the snow to reach the guardhouse and the adjutant's office.[25] For those still living in tents, the violent winds at night made life miserable. Construction and improvements continued when the weather would allow. The weather also prevented scouts from looking for Indian parties in the area. The cold weather continued through March, and there was not much activity by the soldiers. It is likely that at about this time Longley wrote a letter to his brother Jim in Bell County, Texas. Dated March 8, but with the year obliterated, he wrote:

> Dear Brother, I seat myself to write you a few lines to let you no that I am wel at present hoping you are the same. I have not any news to tell you only that we are fixing for our summers campaign. You must all write. The letters wil come to the company let it be where it may. It has bin some time since I have got a letter from home and I have not got a letter from Mary for about three months. Jim I am going to tell you the truth now and not waver the thing any further. I shot a man in Kansas and I got captured and there was a strong guard over me and also a ball and chain weighing 24 lbs and I expect I would have bin sent to the penitenchary if it had not bin for a young lady that brought me a file and I got a way. This was near Fort Levenworth Kansas. I went by a diferant name there but I changed back to my right name when I inlisted. There was two dezerters brought back yesterday that I told you about before and I was on guard. I took them to the black smith shop and they was shackled and balls and chains put on them too. They will be sent to Dri Tortougus for two or three years.[26]

This is an interesting letter because, in addition to giving a different version of the killing that he later claimed occurred at Fort Leavenworth, it also describes his own crime of desertion and subsequent punishment. Does the fact of this letter coupled with his account of the Leavenworth killing after he was captured indicate that there *might* be some truth to the story? Absent some corroboration, it can only be presumed that he was again repeating the same boastful account of his "adventures."

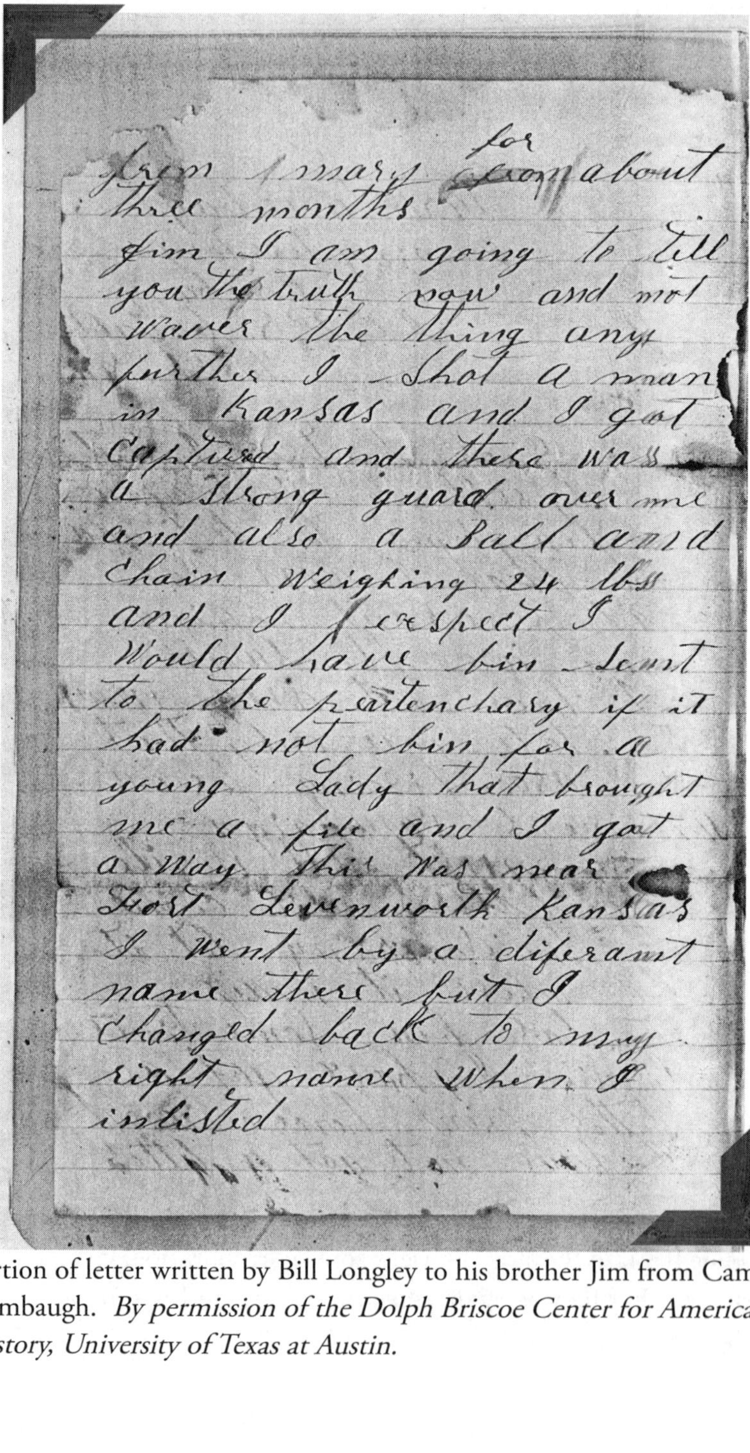

from [illegible] mary for about
three months
Jim I am going to tell
you the truth now and not
waver the thing any
further I shot a man
in Kansas and I got
captured and there was
a strong guard over me
and also a ball and
chain weighing 24 lbs
and I expect I
would have bin sent
to the pertenchary if it
had not bin for a
young Lady that brought
me a file and I got
a way. This was near
Fort Levenworth Kansas
I went by a diferant
name there but I
changed back to my
right name when I
inlisted

Portion of letter written by Bill Longley to his brother Jim from Camp Stambaugh. *By permission of the Dolph Briscoe Center for American History, University of Texas at Austin.*

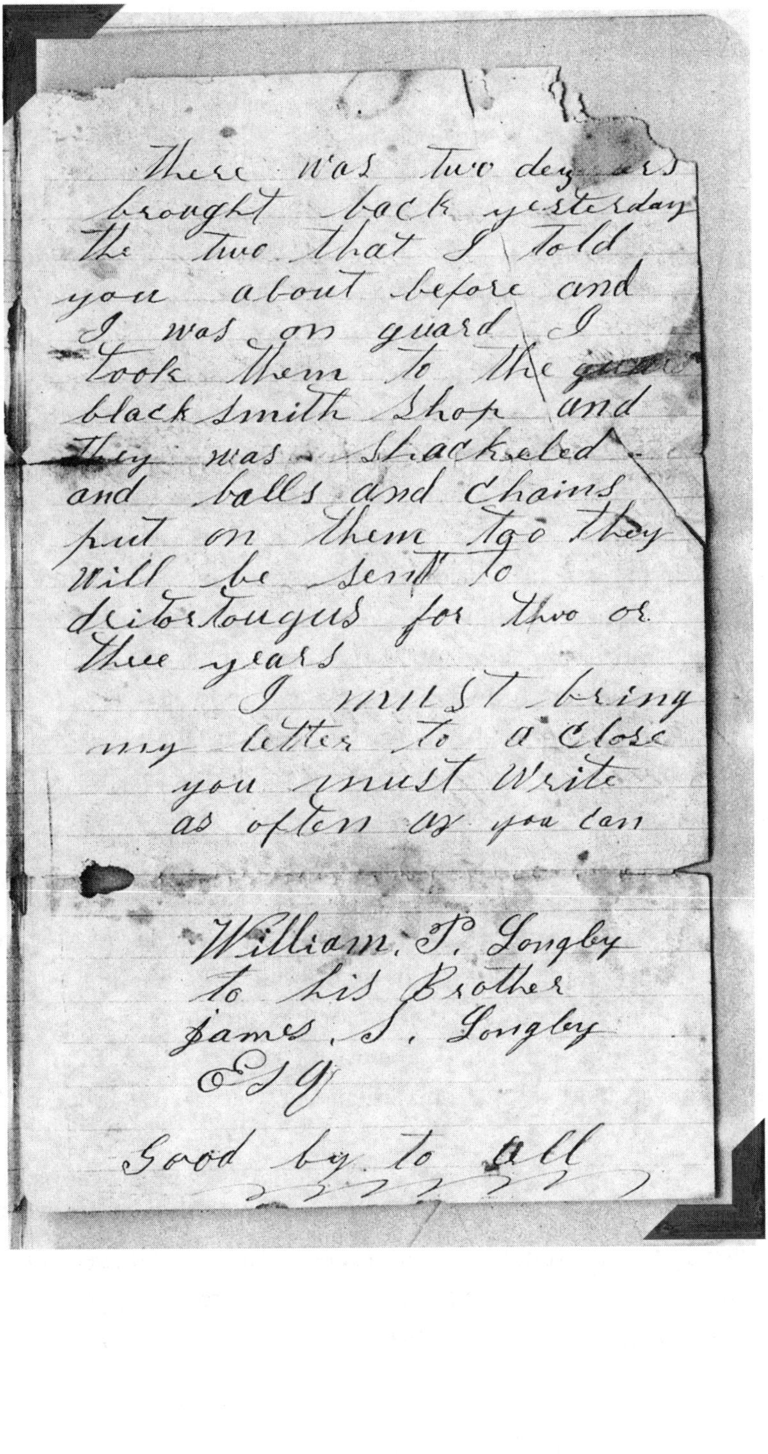
There was two dey[illegible]ers
brought back yesterday
the two that I told
you about before and
I was on guard I
took them to the [illegible]
black smith shop and
they was shackeled
and balls and chains
put on them too they
will be sent to
dritortougus for thwo or
three years
I must bring
my letter to a close
you must write
as often as you can

William. P. Longley
to his Brother
James. S. Longley
ESQ

Good by to all

As spring arrived, renewed concerns about Indians came to the forefront, and scouts were once again ordered. Lieutenant Thomas I. Gregg, a Pennsylvania native like Wheelan, who had been assigned to Camp Stambaugh the previous fall as an assistant quartermaster,[27] took forty-five men out on a five-day scout in the Little Wind River Valley without spotting any Indians. Lieutenant Randolph Norwood, born in Maryland and a Civil War veteran, and who had distinguished himself in several previous engagements with Indians, led a contingent of forty-three men on a seven-day scout in the Hot Springs area.[28] But on April 26, 1871, Longley was temporarily detached, apparently to help with the relocation of Camp Brown.[29] In order to better protect Chief Washakie and the Shoshone and Bannock Indians who were friendly with the United States government, it had been decided to move the post to the south fork of the Little Wind River, and in June work began to dismantle the old post of serviceable lumber and make adobe brick in order to build the new post.[30] A sergeant, a corporal, and fifteen men were sent from Camp Stambaugh to Camp Brown, temporarily deterred by an Indian attack on June 26, which forced a return to Camp Stambaugh.[31] There is a good possibility that Longley might have been one of these men. The detail did not return to Camp Stambaugh until November 14, 1871, as a new winter began to bring its annual onslaught of winds and snow.[32]

Longley was back to the Camp Stambaugh routine again in November: escorts, scouting, and hunting. In the cold weather, reveille was at 6:15 a.m., followed by stable call, then breakfast at 7:20 a.m. After the day's activities, with a forty-five-minute break at noon, retreat was held at sunset and taps was at 10:00 p.m. On Sundays an inspection was held at 9:30 a.m. and a dress parade was scheduled at sunset.[33]

On Christmas Day, 1871, Private William Wilson of Company K, Thirteenth Infantry, left the post to visit Atlantic City while the weather was fair, but on his return a bad storm developed, and he became disoriented and wandered into the mountains where he apparently perished. A search party was unable to find him.[34] The snows became

Shoshone Chief Washakie at South Pass, Wyoming Territory, 1870. *By permission of the American Heritage Center, University of Wyoming.*

Chief Washakie and his Shoshone tribe at South Pass, Wyoming Territory, 1870. *By permission of the American Heritage Center, University of Wyoming*

so bad that a mail carrier had to be rescued from a snow drift, and sleds were unsuccessful in helping soldiers to get to South Pass City.[35] Because supply trains were unable to reach the mining communities in the area, Camp Stambaugh was credited with supplying area miners out of government stores, averting a famine.[36]

At this point the record indicates another event possibly corroborating an adventure claimed by Longley. Longley, of course, did not admit that he was a soldier until just before his execution, but, instead, maintained that he was a teamster, then a saloon keeper in Miner's Delight. Because the snow was so bad, Longley claimed that it was the "rule of claw and tooth and fang," and a man was killed in his saloon almost every day. According to him, one Christmas celebration led to the killing of seven men. He said that he wanted a brief respite from the rowdyism, so in January 1872 Longley and several others decided to take a hunting trip into the mountains for a few days. According to him, they left Camp Brown on horseback, riding toward the Rattlesnake Hills, the snow being five feet deep but firm enough to support them. He said that a snowstorm suddenly caught them about eighteen miles into their trip and the party lost its way. They wandered throughout the night, leading their horses to keep them from freezing. At dawn they sought shelter at a rock outcropping to escape the wind. Unnoticed by the others, one man, George Pierce, wrapped himself in a blanket and went to sleep, but froze to death before the others finally found him.

Wolves began to gather around them, and the cold prevented their rifles from firing. Leaving the carcass of their dead friend to the fury of the wolves, Longley said that the party wandered on into the blizzard, now without any provisions, horses, or mules. They tramped through the snow that night, he said, and on the third night an old Frenchman froze to death when he lay down to sleep behind a snow bank. That corpse was left to a mountain lion. Getting its bearings, the party determined that it was about thirty miles from Camp Brown and headed on frozen feet in that direction. On the afternoon of the fourth day, they ran into a rescue party which took them back to Camp Brown where another man died. According to Longley, their feet were so swollen that their boots had to be cut off. "We all had to lie in bed two months before we could walk a step."[37]

Camp Stambaugh records reflect that in mid-January 1872, a severe snowstorm hit the area. A sergeant and seven privates obtained permission to embark on a hunting expedition. After several days in the mountains, the thermometer dropped to thirty-five degrees below zero and a storm raged. At midnight on January 24th, the party made its way back to Camp Stambaugh and each was frostbitten. Although no deaths were reported, four of the men had to be admitted to the hospital, and it was feared that one faced amputation. The other four were returned to duty. By March, three were returned to duty.[38] Was this the same incident as that described by Longley? The circumstances and timing seem sufficiently similar to warrant a presumption that it was.

As spring came and rumors of Indians once more abounded, very little activity at the post was recorded. In April four of the troopers on a scout were rendered snow-blind for several days as a result of the glare.[39] But army life had apparently again drained the enthusiasm from Bill Longley, and he deserted, this time for good, on June 8, 1872. He owed the government $58.97.[40] There is no further mention of him in military records. His legacy as a soldier was provided by Henry Gross:

> He used to boast of his exploits and adventures in Texas, but none of us believed him, for he did not look by any means like a man of that stamp or caliber. . . . He was considered by the whole company an idle boaster, a notorious liar and a man of low instinct and habits, but tolerated on account of his good nature, gift of "gab" and excellent marksmanship.[41]

But Bill Longley abruptly left his duties as a soldier. His trail would end up back in Texas, littered with more "adventures" that cannot be corroborated. He was still more than six years away from his appointment with the gallows.

Chapter 7

The Worst Indian

As a matter of record, Bill Longley deserted from the army on June 8, 1872, but he does not turn up for the record again until July 1, 1873, in Texas. As before, his version of events in his life during this interim period can be only repeated, not corroborated, and, unfortunately, the sole accounts are lengthy versions of prose colored by Fuller's poetic flourishes.

To begin with, Longley claimed that after his feet recovered from his experience in the snowstorm, he went to Camp Brown. There, according to him, he was hired by the army quartermaster, a man named "Captain Gregory,"[1] and placed in charge of the animal corral. As Longley told it:

> I had been there about one month when I discovered that the quartermaster was tricky, and as he had great confidence in me he told me we could make a lot of money if we could handle the business as he directed. We had several hundred mules inside the corral. He was getting one hundred and fifty dollars per month, and I was getting seventy-five. He would issue full

rations of corn for the mules, and then instruct me to see that the mules were fed only half rations. Corn was two dollars and a half a bushel and we sold what we thus stole from the government to the miners, who did their trading at Camp Brown. We kept up that and several other ways of swindling the government and at the same time were being well paid by the government for our services.

One day one of the mules died and the commanding officer came down and saw it. I had it dragged off and the next night I had it dragged back into the corral and reported another mule dead. I had the same mule dragged off and the next night played the same trick. Then, the next night I took two good mules, went across the mountains to the mining camp and sold them for $250.00 each to some miners who were going to Helena City, Montana. I got back to the post before day and the quartermaster came down to get his share of the money. Then I put my foot into trouble. I thought it was no more harm to cheat him than it was for us both to cheat the government, so I told him that I sold the mules for $350.00 which was $175.00 apiece for us. I gave him $175.00 which left me $325.00. In some way he found out what I had got for the mules, and one day he came to see me about it. He seemed to be very mad and called me a damned rascal. I asked him what did he think he was, and how long did he think he would last if I were to take the fool notion to turn him in to the federal authorities? That had the effect of making him think, and while he seemed to be pacified I could see that he mentally made up his mind to catch me napping and it would be bad for me. I examined my pistols after he left, and made up my mind to be on my guard. In the meantime I picked out a good mule, and got a good saddle and a bridle and rope ready in case I should need them all at once and waited. In a few days I saw him coming toward the corral and I knew the time for action had arrived. I would have to kill him or be killed. I was not going to be killed if I could help it.

> He had killed one man and I knew he was not afraid to tackle me anywhere. As he walked up to the gate I saw that he had his pistol in his hand and I put two bullets through him before he knew what struck him. I then mounted my mule and rode off. I could have put him on one of the mules in the night time and carried him miles away and thrown him in a gulch and the wolves would have eaten him, but I did no such thing. I rode away. There were two companies of soldiers in the camp and I felt sure they would soon be on my track. That is exactly what happened.[2]

Longley said that he struck out across the Wind River Mountains, headed for Salt Lake City some 400 miles away. After several days of hard riding, he shot an antelope for venison to eat and to carry with him, then stopped to rest. He said that he lay down to sleep for a few hours but awoke about midnight to find himself surrounded by about twenty-five soldiers, all with pistols and rifles pointed at him. His hands were tied and, with a rope around his neck, he was made to walk back to Camp Brown, some 110 miles. Longley claimed that the soldiers cursed him and called him a "damn rcbcl," and that his boots had to be cut off the first night, forcing him to walk barefooted. Once back at Camp Brown, according to Fuller's version,

> They made me carry a sand bag that weighed one hundred pounds. A guard walked behind me all the time and when it seemed that I could go no further he would prick me with the bayonet on his gun. I finally felt human endurance could not stand it any longer and then they took me and swung me up by the thumbs, until I fainted. They then let me down, and struck me on the head with their guns. They were a damnable set of cowards. If I could have had my two good pistols for one second I could have whipped the entire cowardly bunch. They made me carry the sand bag, two hours on, and then rest two hours, for six weeks, and tied me up by my thumbs four times and then I made my escape.[3]

He slipped out one night in the middle of a rainstorm, then, according to Longley, "walked ninety miles through the worst Indian country on the plains, without even a pocket knife," existing for four days on only eight crackers that he had brought with him. He said that the soldiers followed him using dogs, recaptured him, and took him back to Camp Brown. Back at the post, he claimed that he was chained down flat on his back for four months. "My hip bones wore through the skin and I fell off until I weighed only ninety pounds. I had on handcuffs, and shackles, straight irons and a chain from my handcuffs to my shackles."[4]

According to Longley, he was court-martialed and "sentenced to be shot on my coffin." But he said that the commander of the Department of the Platte, apparently General Augur, remitted his sentence to thirty years in the penitentiary at Fort Madison, Iowa, the same prison to which his fellow deserter, John Miller, had been sent. However, he said that before he was sent there, one account making it now some nine months after the killing of Gregory, he managed to get hold of a saw and rid himself of his irons. Then he passed on the saw to twenty-two other prisoners in the guardhouse, and they released themselves. The other prisoners helped Longley saw through the bars of the iron cage in which he was kept, then spent three weeks digging under the floor of the log guardhouse, hiding the dirt with their coats. According to Longley, the digging was done with two old, stubby-bladed case knives, and all twenty-three finally made their break on a rainy night.[5]

Once free, Longley said that he parted from his fellow escapees and struck out alone, traveling only at night and following the stage road from South Pass City to Bryant Station. He would hide off the road whenever a stagecoach passed so as not to be seen. At Pacific Springs, he said, he approached a stagecoach driver and offered him $100 to conceal him on his coach and take him to Bryant Station. This was done, and Longley hid in the boot, where the luggage was kept, whenever passengers were taken on at various stops. Approaching Green River, the driver alerted Longley to the presence in town of soldiers, and Longley said that he "took to the chapparal" and made his way up the river.[6]

Again, there is no record to corroborate any of this. Henry Gross, the soldier who served in the area from 1870 to 1875, swore that "no murder was committed by Longley at Camp Brown, nor did he send the post commissary to the happy hunting grounds, neither was he ever employed as a citizen by any quartermaster in those parts."[7] It is interesting to note that Lieutenant Thomas Gregg had been an assistant quartermaster at Camp Stambaugh while Longley was there. This may explain the origin of the name Gregory.[8] And perhaps his account of the guardhouse ordeal reflects some truth as to what happened when he was imprisoned in 1870, albeit a great deal more dramatic in the retelling.

Longley's claim as to his whereabouts after this alleged escape approaches the bizarre. Having left the stagecoach and striking out into the wilderness, he says,

> I was alone and in the Indian country. I was a hunted man, starting at every sound that had any resemblance to the human voice. I was unarmed and didn't have a penny. I was afraid to approach any kind of habitation lest it might be that of enemies, and I did not want to fall into enemies' hands again. I had suffered the agonies of hell at the hands of white men, and this made me wary.[9]

The next day, while on the Green River, Longley said that he heard dogs barking, and upon investigating, came to an Indian village in a beautiful valley. Half starved and no longer caring whether he was killed or not, Longley said that he walked into the village amidst the astonished Indians. He found that they were a band of Snake Indians who were at peace with the white man and who could speak fairly good English. They fed him and he stayed with them a few days, then he moved with them a number of miles to the head of the Wind River. According to Longley, the Snakes, Shoshones, Bannocks, and Utes were friendly with each other at the time, but that peace soon disintegrated into warfare.[10]

Longley said that the chief of the Snake tribe was Washakie. Actually, Chief Washakie was a Shoshone. After an uprising by the Shoshones in 1861–62, a government preoccupied by the Civil War set aside the Rocky Mountain and Great Plains region for them and other tribes in order to have peace in the west. But after the Civil War, and because of intertribal warfare, Washakie sought a more definite, secure reservation for his small tribe. Recognizing Washakie's friendship with the United States, the government, in 1868, allowed him to select an area that included the Popo Agie Valley, and this area was to be shared with the more volatile Bannocks, a subtribe of the Shoshones. But the Sioux continued as an enemy, and raiding parties periodically struck the smaller tribe. Washakie demanded military protection, thus leading to construction of Camp Brown.[11]

The story spun by Longley or Fuller was that the "Snakes" furnished him with a horse and two good pistols, and that he taught the Indians how to ride and shoot!

> It was no time until the most of them could ride by a post or a sapling a few inches through and hit it several times as they passed. I trained them in this way and by and by they had a fighting force that was hard to handle. Then I set in to get even with the United States soldiers who had mistreated me at Camp Brown. Nearly every tribe of Indians on the plains were at war with each other. The Snake Indians made their first big raid in the northern part of Wyoming, and the southern part of Dakota. There were twenty five of us in the raid, me and twenty four Snakes. We came upon a bunch of eight Sioux Indians herding a bunch of horses which they had stolen at Fort Laramie. We surrounded them and a fight started. We killed five and captured eighty head of horses and then started back to our camp on the head of Wind River. We knew that the three Sioux who had gotten away would "carry the news to Mary" and so we traveled day

and night, but on the evening of the third day we were overtaken by about one hundred Sioux, near a range of mountains called the Panther mountains. They came upon us on level ground and a running fight quickly followed, in the course of which we lost all the horses we had taken from the Sioux and also three of our men. . . . The fight lasted until dark when we escaped into the mountains, and we traveled all night.

The next morning we rode into another bunch that were on the way to Red Cloud Agency, about seventy five strong. They charged us in a canyon, and seeing that we could not ride out of the canyon because of the steep walls we dismounted and took to the chapparal. They got every horse we had and left us on foot. We had to walk nearly one hundred miles toward home. We were in desperate straits and fired on some miners about one hundred miles east of Camp Brown, and got sixteen good horses.

Then we concluded not to go home until we had recaptured our losses, and so we turned out of our course, went up on the head of Crow Creek and stole all the horses the Crow Indians had. It was only a small tribe and they did not follow us, perhaps thinking it was a large bunch of Sioux or some other tribe that had taken their horses. Then we pulled out for camp and got back in safety after being out six weeks. We were hailed as heroes, by every Indian in camp, but you can just bet we never told how the bunch of Sioux chased us ten miles, killed three of our men and took all our horses.[12]

Seeking to avenge the loss of warriors, the Sioux retaliated with another raid, Longley said, seizing two Indian women and some seventy-five horses. Three hundred Snake Indians were quickly assembled and gave pursuit, catching up with the party about twenty miles later and killing all but two Sioux. The two prisoners were brought back to the Indian camp and burned alive.

Longley said that Washakie was adamant that his tribe not do anything against the white man, but a number of young Indian braves had heard from Longley how he was treated by the soldiers and "were anxious to have a brush with them." Telling Washakie that they were going to ride to the Sioux reservation "to show them they were not squaws," Longley and the young men headed towards Rollins Springs. Near Whiskey Gap Longley said that they ran into a detachment of the Second Cavalry and a fight broke out. Several soldiers were killed, he claimed, and the Indians took thirty mules and horses. Coming within a mile of Camp Stambaugh, the party found more mules being guarded by three men. These animals were also taken and the party rode on near both Fort Bridger and Fort Douglas. Longley also said that they fired on a wagon train guarded by soldiers, capturing about forty more mules. Heading in the direction of Fort Hall, they came upon a stagecoach and swapped six ponies for the driver's bigger and stronger horses. According to Longley,

> Then we rode rapidly back to our camp and told old Washakee [*sic*] that we had gotten our plunder from the Sioux Indians. We were out nine weeks on this raid and never lost but one man, one killed and two wounded, and we brought in two hundred head of mules and ponies. We were not molested to my surprise and we spent the remainder of the fall in buffalo and deer hunting.[13]

Longley claimed that he spent time hunting with Washakie and his Indians until late autumn of 1872. On one occasion he said that a buffalo killed his horse and almost killed him, and that the last time he hunted with them, a wounded grizzly killed one of the Indians before going down. But Longley said that he told Washakie that he wanted to visit his sister and her family in Salt Lake City and that he would return after that visit. But he said that, in truth,

> I was really getting tired of their wild way of living, and knew that the time would come when one of the raids would end in disaster. It was a wild life, and I tried to imagine that I enjoyed

> it, but as a matter of fact I never did enjoy it. After I had gotten into the tribe, and they had befriended me, I did my best to show my gratitude and the first thing I knew I was riding with them in their marauding and murdering expeditions, and to all appearances was the worst Indian of the entire tribe. They liked me for this, and there was nothing that they would not have done for me, but I knew it was no place for me, outlaw that I was and decided to make my way back to Texas and start life over and in a better way if I could get half a chance.[14]

So Longley said that he bade his Indian friends good-bye and struck out for the Southwest. If he is to be believed, this would have been about October or November 1872.

Longley's next adventure, as described by Fuller in *Adventures of Bill Longley*, is even more questionable, not merely because of its suspiciously melodramatic nature, but also because Fuller told it in the third person. All other letters ascribed to Longley in the book were written in the first person. Perhaps Fuller also discovered a major gap in Longley's story and attempted to fill it in with a little dramatic license.

The story related by Fuller was that Longley rode through desolate country toward a "half-breed Mexican settlement," where Chief Washakie had told him he could rest and be safe. As he slept on his saddle blanket in a small valley, after about a week of riding, a sudden storm awoke him and he walked his horse through a desert that night. In the morning, as he mounted his horse, Longley, according to Fuller, spotted a party of horsemen riding rapidly toward him. Not knowing who or what the men were, Longley, looking for a ravine or some other cover in which he might elude his pursuers, put the quirt to his horse and rode for the mountains nearby. Shots rang out, but he realized that he was out of range, and he counted on his horse to maintain his lead. But an arroyo appeared suddenly before him and Longley was barely able to stop his horse from going over. As in a B western movie, Longley found himself caught in a deadly dilemma as his pursuers raced toward him and their bullets began to fall nearby. As Fuller wrote dramatically,

> Why not end it all by blowing his own brains out and get through with the whole business? He had lived in vain anyway. His life had just about been a miserable failure. He recalled that so far as he remembered he had done such a small amount of good that he could not even recall a single incident. Here he could die, and the vultures and coyotes would gnaw his bones, and his name would disappear from the knowledge of men and be forgotten. But with these thoughts, there came the surge of the love of life. He would not give up until some of his pursuers had also tasted the dust of the desert. He whirled, drew his pistol, and sped back in the direction of the bandits who he now discovered from their broad sombreros or hats were Mexicans, and no doubt bandits or robbers. Surprised at his audacity the Mexicans stopped. Longley rode within one hundred yards of the bandits and then he suddenly wheeled his horse and sped towards the chasm. A frightful cry came from the bandits and on they came. Was the man mad? Urging his horse with all his might Longley flew toward the arroyo, reached it and with a mighty effort as he arose in his stirrups and loosened the bridle reins, the horse without hesitating a second made the frightful leap.[15]

Fuller continued with this purple prose: Longley's horse failed to make the other side and the two of them fell to the jagged rocks below. Longley supposedly struck a projecting branch and was flung under an overhang. When the bandits saw the dead horse, they assumed that his rider was also dead and galloped off.

When the unconscious Longley came around, Fuller said that he found himself on a bed in a small *jacal*, dimly lit by a single candle. A beautiful Mexican girl, Dolores Gomez, brought him a bowl of soup and the two conversed in Spanish. She introduced herself as the daughter of a wealthy Santa Fe herder who spent several weeks each year in the valley. Her father and his friends were off on a hunting trip, but would return in about ten days, giving Longley enough time to recover from his bruises and scratches and resume his journey. After a few days, according to Fuller, Longley was up and around, and he and Dolores took long walks in the twilight. Of course, to make the story complete, they fell in love. Dolores had taken great pains to keep Longley hidden from observation, but as the day drew near when her father's party would be returning, she tearfully told her lover that her father would not hesitate to turn him over to the authorities.

As Fuller related, Longley knew that he had to leave the beautiful señorita, but he promised to return for her and she promised to wait for him. She arranged for her faithful servant, Pedro, to take the fugitive to another pueblo many miles to the southwest, where he would be safe. Dolores told Longley: "Some day you come back—I will be here waiting for you, and may the blessed Virgin protect you. Every night I shall look upon the brightest star towards the south and think of you—the star that rises earliest, and stays up the longest—my star, as it comes above the peak where I first saw you. In one year return—one year, oh, Santa Maria, is it eternity?"[16]

As the faithful Pedro and Longley leave, the two lovers have a "short delicious agony" as they kiss for the last time, and she stands beneath a cottonwood tree waving a final farewell in the moonlight as the two men ride out of sight. Subsequently, Pedro led Longley to a small Mexican village, then left him with directions as to how to get to white settlements.

As stated before, this really seems improbable, and Fuller likely added it as filler for the letters from Longley that he edited. Perhaps he felt that Longley needed some assistance in creating an image as a bold, dashing desperado. Certainly a fling with a beautiful Spanish maiden wouldn't hurt.

Chapter 8

Who in the Hell Are You?

After his 1877 arrest, Longley claimed that "after leaving the Indians, he went to Iowa and 'knocked around' for a month or two, and then revisited the state of Kansas."[1] There was no mention by Longley of the beautiful Dolores Gomez or any injuries received while trying to outdistance pursuing Mexican bandits, as Fuller later wrote. Very likely, Longley leisurely began his way back to Texas without intending much in the way of adventure.

Longley said that he ultimately arrived in Morris County in the east central part of Kansas, stopping at the village of Parkersville (now Parkerville) "to take stock and form his plans for the future."[2] Parkersville, some ten miles northwest of the county seat, Council Grove, was on a branch line of the Missouri, Kansas and Texas Railway that ran from Junction City, north of there, to Parsons in the far southeastern part of the state.[3] The main street of the town paralleled the railroad line, and it was likely that Longley arrived there by train.

Again, Fuller wrote of Longley's next "adventure" in the third person, but Longley also gave a similar account when he was captured. As Fuller related it,

> One day while walking along the only street in the small shack of a town he saw some men playing cards in a saloon and thinking to divert his mind he entered and was soon immersed in the game. One by one the players went broke and dropped out until finally only two remained—Longley and a man by the name of Charlie Stuart. The two men played for several hours, their six shooters on the table by the side of the cards. On entering Parkersville, Longley gave his name as Tom Jones, and let it be known that he was merely on a visit to that section of the country, and was thinking of locating there, provided he found some kind of congenial business that would at the same time bring in satisfactory returns for the money invested.
>
> The game between Longley and Stuart went on several hours and finally, Longley caught Jones [*sic*] cheating. He promptly told him so, Stuart gave the accusation the lie, and reached for his gun, but Longley beat him to it, and Stuart passed to his reward, with an oath on his lips and a hand full of cards that were never played.[4]

In Longley's account after his capture, he claimed that he "left his victim thoroughly dead with a bullet hole in his head and another in his heart."[5] Longley then said that he fled the village as quickly as he could by horseback. Young Stuart was supposed to have come from a wealthy family, and his father, said Longley, offered a $1,500 cash reward for the capture of "Jones," dead or alive. While in hiding, Longley fell in with two men, never identified, who were also "on the dodge." The three men, aware that the reward had been offered, hatched a scheme to lay claim to the money.

According to Fuller, the two acquaintances rode into Parkersville posing as detectives on the trail of some cattle thieves. They formed an acquaintance with Mr. Stuart and confirmed that, indeed, a reward had been offered for Jones, alias Bill Longley. Stuart asked the two "detectives" to do their best to find the murderer of his son, and they instructed him to place the cash in a bank at Council Grove. Accompanied by the two men, Stuart did just that. Furnished a description of Longley, the two men then set off to find Longley and bring him in. In less than a week, as the story goes, they returned to Council Grove with Longley in custody and placed him in the county jail. Stuart was summoned, and he identified Longley as the man he had seen around Parkersville and even as the man he had seen playing cards with his son.

The reward was paid to the two "detectives," and they spent the rest of the day strolling around Council Grove. Toward dusk, they indicated that they intended to be on their way, and they asked the sheriff if they could bid Longley a final farewell. The sheriff took them to the jail and admitted them. Once inside, the two men overpowered the lawman, took his pistol, then locked him in a cell. They released Longley, gave him one-third of the reward, and the three rode out of town.[6] It should be added that, while Fuller related that this escape occurred just after the shooting of young Stuart, Longley's account after his capture had him shooting Stuart, returning to Texas for some period of time, then coming back to the Indian Territory. Allegedly, Longley then fell in with two deputy U.S. marshals and learned of the reward through a newspaper account. These deputies then took him back to Morris County and carried out the escape as Fuller described.[7] Fuller's chronology is more logical, given Longley's subsequent whereabouts, if the incident actually occurred.

Once again, Longley boasted of the killing, but there is no corroboration. The small village of Parkersville does not leap immediately to the mind, so that by itself may be a good indication that Longley was physically present in Morris County. But an examination of local records and historical recollections there produce no record of a Tom Jones or any similar incident. The census for Morris County in both 1860 and 1870 shows only an Alexander C. Stewart, a farmer from Pennsylvania who had three sons, but none named Charles or Charlie.[8] Again, Longley probably mixed fiction with fact, actually gracing the community with his presence, then embellishing it with a bloody deed produced from an active imagination.

And Fuller himself even wondered at several things: why the two men didn't just rob the elder Stuart of the $1,500 while on the way to Council Grove, rather than carrying out the rest of the scheme and sharing with Longley. Or why, once Longley was in jail, did they not simply take their legally obtained reward and ride on alone? Fuller concludes: "The answer is that the old saying that there is honor among thieves was proven in this case."[9]

Longley said that he remained with his two cohorts for several weeks before they separated and then continued his journey back to Texas through the Oklahoma Territory. He said that he was accompanied by a young man named Rodgers, who was a counterfeiter, and the two were apparently passing bogus bills as they went. At Boggy Depot, some fifty miles north of the Red River, they were both arrested, he said, by a U.S. marshal, who started with them for the federal court at Fort Smith. Longley claimed that a $200 bribe ($2,000 in another account) in real money led to their release, the money being the ill-gotten gains they had realized in passing the phony cash. Rodgers then moved on to St. Louis, and Longley continued on to his native state.[10] Of course, there is no record of this.

Once inside Texas, in Grayson County just across the Red River, he said that he caught a ride on a buggy with a Dan Sawyer of Fayette County. In fact, Daniel A. Sawyer was a farmer from Fayette County, near La Grange, not too far south of Evergreen, who later moved to Smithville in Bastrop County.[11] The two rode south to Bell County, where, at Shaw's Crossing on the Lampasas River, Longley said he left his traveling companion and struck out on foot for his parents' farm nearby. He later stated that he could have robbed Sawyer, but charitably added that Sawyer was "a first class gentleman and need never fear any harm at his hands."[12] Campbell and Sarah Longley had moved their family from Salado to the Wilkinson Valley in southern Bell County, south of the Lampasas River, between Keys Valley and the Union Grove community.[13]

An unaltered photograph of a young Bill Longley taken at an unknown date. *Courtesy of Dr. Jack C. Longley, Sacramento, California, and the late Colonel Cam and Lee Longley, Brigham City, Utah.*

An altered copy of the previous photograph, allegedly done at the behest of Longley's mother. *Courtesy of Pauline Longley, San Saba, Texas.*

Fuller did not include any information on Longley, in either first or third person, from the time of the alleged killing of Stuart until November of 1875, and the only account for that period must be taken from the newspaper account given after Longley was captured. As related by Longley in his 1877 interview,

> He remained at home doing farm work for his father for three months, but his stay was by no means satisfactory. Rumors of coming trouble on account of old scores were being constantly brought to his ears, and finally, while engaged at work one day in the field, a young man came to him and said that a mob from Lee County [Washington County; Lee was not formed until 1874] were coming up to effect his capture, in order to secure the $1,000 reward offered for him by the military authorities while they were in power in the state. At this time Longley had hoped that his troubles were drawing to an end; he was anxious to settle down, and had gone so far toward a reformation of his character as to forswear the ownership of a six-shooter. When the tidings of the Lee County movement reached him he went into the bushes and remained there until he could send into Belton [the Bell County seat] and purchase a couple of "Colt's Improved." So soon as he got his six-shooters belted around him and was mounted upon a splendid animal his father gave him, he felt that he was ready once more for anything that might turn up.[14]

Longley said that he then rode northwest to Comanche County and went to work herding cattle for Willis Johnson.[15] Johnson would be remembered as an early pioneer of the Brown and Comanche counties area, who began as a cowboy and ultimately bought his own land and became wealthy. He apparently walked the line, befriending many outlaws and often going their bond when they got in trouble and even hiring their lawyers. He was ultimately mixed up in a kidnapping situation when a sixteen-year-old girl, not against her will, was taken from her parents and married off to a much older man. The upset parents

The gate to the cemetery, all that is left today of Williams Ranch, Mills County, Texas. *Author's photo.*

charged Johnson with abduction, but before it could come to trial, he was ambushed in Mills County and killed. Supposedly, his death led to a major feud that resulted in many deaths.[16]

After Longley worked with Johnson for about two months, he had occasion to ride over to a visit at Williams Rancho, then in Brown County and now in Mills County. Pioneer John Williams had come to

Brown County from North Carolina, establishing a ranch in 1855 on Browns Creek just a few miles northwest of where the village of Goldthwaite would be laid out thirty years later. A settlement grew up around Williams' ranch, and since Williams Rancho was on the Austin to San Angelo road, it was a stopping point for many travelers. Gradually, the ranch became a trading post for the area, and a school and several stores were established, as well as a mill. One mercantile establishment was run by the Ware family, from where Texas Ranger Dick Ware would go on to fame in the 1878 shootout with the Sam Bass gang. One source asserted that just after the ranch was established, a man named Chancellor abandoned a large number of Negro slaves there.[17]

Over the years, Williams Rancho acquired a significant reputation for rowdyism and became a magnet for tough characters. Little wonder that Longley found his way to this place. Among the residents of Williams Rancho were W. J. "Bud" Forsythe and his brother, Robert. They came to Ellis County with their parents in 1851, then the two brothers settled near John Williams' ranch in 1866, where they operated a store before getting involved in cattle ranching. At one point, they employed Willis Johnson. Robert lived with Bud and Bud's wife, Caroline, and their two children, and until his death in 1871, John Williams also lived with them.[18]

According to Longley's account, a black man who had once been a state policeman under Governor E. J. Davis rode into the settlement. At the Forsythe place, he ordered Caroline Forsythe to prepare him a dinner and to feed his horse. Another account described the black man as one of the former slaves left behind by Mr. Chancellor. The black man supposedly went to a store where Longley happened to be. As the man walked in, he spotted Longley and reached over and pushed Longley's hat back, asking insolently, "And who in the hell are you?" Longley replied by bringing his pistol up and shooting the man twice. Oddly, the riddled man remained upright and, even though Longley had already started to leave the store, he said he saw the man standing, so he turned and fired at him again, striking him two more times. The man still did not fall, but, as Longley raised his pistol to fire again, the man then stumbled and went to the floor. Lying at Longley's feet, the man begged Longley not to shoot him any more so that he could pray before he died. Longley said that he told the wounded man that the devil had come for him and that there was no time to spare. Longley's next shot hit the man at the hairline of the forehead and he died instantly. Longley then returned to Johnson's ranch, "fixed up his affairs," and according to him, left for Coleman County with two others, Joe Mitchell and a man named Martin.[19]

In 1877, a major feud centering around alleged cattle theft erupted at Williams Rancho, and the Frontier Battalion, or the Texas Rangers, was called on to protect the residents there. Bud Forsythe was then arrested for both cattle theft and arson growing out of that conflict.[20]

And a question about the authenticity of this account by Longley is again raised. Local records do not reflect any such killing. However, in a letter dated February 28, 1873, State Police Sergeant J. M. Redmon wrote Texas Adjutant General F. L. Britton that he had sent Rangers Haffe, Roy, and Evans to investigate a death in Brown County:

> I started Pvt. Haffe on the 20th inst. with two men Roy and Evans out west to investigate the murder of George W. Hughes & Robt. T. Payne, also the murder of Price, a colored man who was most brutally murdered for his money in Brown Co. at Baker's Ranch on or near the 2nd day of Feb. 1873 by Bill Longley, John Jones, Joseph J. Alberts, __ Hammond & two other men names not known. Mr. Haffe taken [*sic*] a full statement of a colored man who was an eye witness to the affair, which affidavit accompanies this letter.
>
> Longley & his gang is 15 miles above Camp Colorado on Hordes Creek at some ranch where they can stay most of their time . . .[21]

This letter fixes the approximate date that Longley was in Brown County, and refers to the killing of another black man, similar to the killing of Brice in Bastrop County complained of by Judge Brady in

February 1870. Was this the same black man that Longley described as having a problem falling down after being shot?

Hordes Creek runs west from its juncture with Jim Ned Creek in Coleman County, into where the present town of Coleman is located. The ranch above Camp Colorado referred to by Redmon was probably that of Sam S. Gholson. Longley said that he, Mitchell, and Martin went to Gholson's ranch. Gholson was born in the early Robertson's Colony in Texas on November 13, 1840, and as a young man came to Mills County, where he served with his brother, Benjamin, as a Ranger in Captain John Williams' company from October 1858 to March 1859. He was remembered as a buffalo hunter and a tough Indian fighter, once being hit in the thigh with an arrow and pulling it out himself. Later, he was a cowboy for John Chisum.[22] Another well-known Texas Ranger, Jim Gillett, recalled the first time that he saw Gholson in Coleman County in 1873 while Gillett was driving a remuda of horses:

> I saw a man approaching me from the rear. As he came up I thought he was the finest specimen of a frontiersman I had ever seen. He was probably six feet tall, with dark hair and beard. He was heavily armed, wearing two six-shooters and carrying a Winchester in front of him, and was riding a splendid horse with a wonderful California saddle.[23]

Longley said that when they reached Gholson's ranch, they told the rancher about the killing of the black man at Williams Rancho. Gholson told him, he said, to go on west to Joe Franks' ranch. Gholson and Franks had served as Rangers together, and Franks had lived with Gholson and his family as recently as 1870. Gholson promised to alert Longley if anyone came looking for the three.[24] Gholson went on to become a prominent citizen of Coleman County, serving as its first treasurer, and building a significant ranch house, later moving to Lubbock County, then to New Mexico, where he died in 1926.[25]

Rather than heading west, however, Longley and his companions, when they got word that a party of men was in pursuit, headed south, stopping to camp near the Santa Anna Mountains some ten miles south of Gholson's ranch. According to Fuller,

> While they were camped near St. Anna Mountain they were overtaken by five men, who were ordered to halt, but instead of obeying they drew their guns and got ready to fight. Longley fired, bringing one of them to the ground. Martin also fired, killing a horse. Their own horses stampeded, but were followed and finally recaptured. Longley does not know to this day who these men were.[26]

Apparently, if this shooting incident did occur, and there is no record of it, the parties determined that a draw had been achieved, and the pursuers withdrew.

Longley said that he parted company with Mitchell and Martin and returned to his parents' farm in Bell County. He rested there for four or five days, then mounted up and rode off again, "looking for a secure place in which to locate."[27] Apparently he didn't get away from Bell County soon enough, as A. M. Guthrie, William Smith, Dave Cave, George Pate, Joe Gauntt, and George Washington all saw Longley carrying a pistol on July 1, 1873, and the offense was reported to

The Santa Anna Mountains where Longley claimed that he had a gunfight. *Author's photo.*

the sheriff, although an indictment was not brought until September 25, 1873. Longley was never arrested for the charge.[28] Amanda M. Guthrie, along with her husband, Shadrack, owned and operated a general store in Salado.[29] H. D. Cave was an Arkansas-born farmer in Bell County,[30] and Smith was a farmer from Alabama.[31]

Longley left Bell County in July 1873, headed south and toward another episode in his life, this one on the record.

Chapter 9

Desperate-Looking Character

Although Fuller did not mention it in his account, Longley claimed that after he left Bell County, he went southwest to Mason County, where he moved about under the alias of "William Henry." He said that he attended a horse race at old Fort Mason, which had been abandoned by the army in 1869, and met James J. Finney, the sheriff of Mason County.[1] A former blacksmith,[2] Finney was first appointed county sheriff in October 1869 under the military government of Reconstruction, then elected in his own right in November 1872.[3]

Longley said that Finney suspected his true identity because of descriptions that the lawman had received, but the two talked, drank, and gambled for four or five days. Longley claimed that he was suspicious of the sheriff. By mere chance, according to Longley, when Finney was ready to spring his trap, Longley happened to ride up to Fredericksburg in Gillespie County. He had not been there but a few hours when Finney and another man arrived in town, talked with Longley, and invited him to a saloon to take a drink. In the saloon, Longley said, he carefully avoided getting between the two men and kept the bar counter between them, frustrating their intent to surprise and overwhelm him. He said that he accepted their invitation to meet there again later that night to play cards, but that he instead mounted up and rode southwest some twenty miles to Kerrville in Kerr County.[4]

Claiming that he was on the way to El Paso, Longley said that as he went through Kerr County, "Frank Eastwood, the celebrated desperado of that county, had just been killed, and the whole county was in arms." He alleged that he was met by a group of vigilantes, but that he cursed them and rode on. He said that he stopped at a house near the Edwards County line, ate supper, then rode on about a mile before bedding down for the night. As he awoke the next morning, he said he was surrounded by eighty-seven men, including Finney, and after posturing with his pistols, vowing never to be taken by a mob, he said he surrendered when Finney told him he had papers authorizing his arrest and that he intended to take him in for the $1,000 reward. According to Longley, he was taken to Kerrville.[5]

It was true that Longley was arrested by Finney and others on July 16, 1873, but he left some details out of his account. Frank Eastwood was indeed the celebrated desperado that Longley described. Eastwood and James Johnson were two of a number of men from Kerr County who fought for the Union army in the Civil War with the First Regiment, Texas Cavalry Volunteers.[6] After the war Eastwood quickly established himself as a premier horse and cattle thief. He was indicted in 1867 in Williamson County to the north for theft of a mare[7] and found not guilty by a jury of theft of a steer in Kerr County in 1870.[8] Another Kerr County jury found him guilty on June 3, 1870, of theft of forty cattle hides and sentenced him to six hours in jail.[9] In October 1870 he and Johnson were again indicted in Kerr County on four charges, ranging from shooting and killing a steer to illegally branding and driving cattle, all alleged to have occurred in August.[10] Eastwood lived with Johnson and his family in Kerr County in 1870.[11] In November 1870, Eastwood, Johnson, and Young Stockman were also indicted in Gillespie County on nine counts of cattle theft, each pleading guilty to one count and paying a $15 fine and costs in July

1871.[12] Eastwood was indicted again in Gillespie County in November 1871 for another cow theft.[13]

But the killing of Frank Eastwood in July 1873 was only part of the story, and there is every indication that Bill Longley rode inadvertently into an aroused countryside. The various newspaper accounts, when pieced together, reflect a bizarre tale. Late in 1872 and early in 1873, Eastwood staked out an area in a remote spot north of Kerrville, near a creek referred to as Buffalo Branch, which led into the south fork of the Guadalupe River. The branch was surrounded on both sides by high cliffs and dotted with caves. Intent on pursuing his cattle-and horse-thieving career, Eastwood began to recruit gunmen to help him. "Some of the most noted outlaws in Texas" were attracted, notably from Bell, Coryell, and Williamson counties, and they in turn notified others to follow them.[14] Almost immediately the outlaw gang began raiding neighboring settlers and ranchers for miles around and taking their stock. The number of men flocking to join Eastwood numbered as many as twenty or more, and the gang included John Jamison (also known as Pinkney, from Williamson County), George DeGraffenreid, James Ratliff, Tom Odum, and a young boy from Bell County, William Baker. In order to try to avoid detection, Eastwood and his gang sometimes actually made their raids dressed as Indians, complete with bows, arrows, and war paint. When not in use, the Indian garb and implements were stored in one of the caves along Buffalo Branch.

Near the canyon frequented by the outlaw gang was the homestead of a farmer named Madison (or Mattison), who frequently observed their comings and goings with large numbers of stock. The suspicions of other settlers in the area were already high. Desiring Madison's place, gang members at first attempted to buy him out, then threatened him if he didn't leave the property by June 5, 1873. Madison steadfastly refused to leave and, on Thursday, June 5, Eastwood and Jamison came into the field where Madison was working and shot him to death. They then dragged his body into some bushes. The plan, now that Madison's place was in their possession, was to run off several other settlers so that the gang could drive stolen stock without being observed.[15] They ran off a German farmer named Hubner and threatened another named Wachter by raising an issue about a lawsuit over a pistol.[16]

On Sunday, June 8, blistered and decomposed by the hot Texas sun, Madison's body was found. The next day an inquest over the body was held. Nine or ten men from the area were sworn to testify, likely including some of the gang, and they all "cleared themselves," but alleged that young William Baker had been seen arguing with Madison and had not been seen since Thursday. Although Baker was an obvious suspect, there were suspicions that the gang of rustlers raiding throughout the area was behind the killing.[17] On the following Friday it was reported that a young man had been seen riding Madison's horse, well known for a lame front hoof. On about the twentieth or twenty-first of June, a group of men on the north fork of the Guadalupe River stopped a young man riding a horse belonging to Tom Brazill, but ascertaining that he had swapped for the horse, they let him ride on. Then one of the men wondered aloud if the young man could be Baker. The next day the boy was captured and returned, and he was identified as Baker. He was also identified as the boy seen riding Madison's horse.[18] When Madison's horse was located in Mason County, where Baker had sold it, it was also learned that Baker had boasted of Madison's killing to the buyers of the horse.[19]

Kerr County Sheriff John M. Tedford quickly convinced young Baker to talk, the prisoner no doubt intimidated by the very real threat of mobs and lynching, and he agreed to testify as a state's witness against Eastwood and his gang. Tedford was first elected sheriff in 1869 and re-elected the following December. He suffered a crippled arm as the result of both an Indian arrow wound and an inexperienced army surgeon.[20] Baker fully briefed the lawman as to how the gang operated, including the wearing of Indian garb, and even showed them the caves used by the outlaws.

Even though the sheriff was thoroughly investigating the murder of Madison and trying to apprehend the gang members, it was obvious that he lacked the resources to do the job. A citizen vigilante group organized secretly and, vowing to rid the county of these desperadoes, set out to find the outlaws.

On Tuesday, June 24, 1873, Tom Odum and Eastwood were ambushed by hidden vigilantes while riding, and Odum was severely wounded in the head. Eastwood, suffering a flesh wound in his thigh as well as a ball going through one hand, fled his pursuers on foot, his horse also being shot from under him.[21] Eastwood boldly made his way toward Kerrville for medical help and was promptly arrested for Madison's murder. As he was placed in jail, the bandit leader boasted that forty men stood by, ready to rescue him, and that he would have vengeance. On the same afternoon, Jamison and DeGraffenreid were also ambushed, and Jamison was killed. DeGraffenreid fled with his and Jamison's horses, leaving his hat beside Jamison's body.

In the early hours of Sunday, June 29, a band of some forty or fifty men surrounded the house of Deputy Sheriff Pruett, threatening his life if he didn't turn over the keys to the county jail. The keys were promptly surrendered and the mob took Eastwood out of the jail. The next morning he was found about six miles from town with seven bullet holes in him.[22] An inquest was held for Jamison's death that same afternoon. Sheriff Tedford then rounded up about twenty-five men and proceeded to James Ratliff's place. Surrounding the building, Tedford tried to gain the surrender of eight or ten armed men holed up inside with women and children. A compromise of sorts was worked out without shots being fired, and Tedford left some dozen men to guard the house. The barricaded men agreed to surrender the next morning provided the sheriff had no writs or warrants for them from other counties. The next morning Ratliff was arrested and jailed, but, because he could not be connected to the Madison murder, he was released. However, Tedford rearrested him on a Blanco County warrant.[23]

Bands of vigilantes now scoured the area for remnants of the gang. George DeGraffenreid, a half-brother to Ratliff, turned himself over to Sheriff Tedford on July 1 and was jailed with Ratliff. While the vigilantes rode through the countryside, another party of men from Mason County, a posse of several deputies led by Sheriff Finney, came to Kerr County coincidentally looking for some of the same outlaws.[24]

The Kerr County jail had been guarded daily by a group of "minute men" led by a Captain Watson, as well as Rangers under Captain Henry Schwethelm. For whatever reason, this guard was removed on Saturday, July 5, and the men went home. The next evening, a mob confronted Sheriff Tedford, and Ratliff and DeGraffenreid were taken from the jail to share Eastwood's fate. Two days later, on July 8, their bodies were found on Town Creek, about one-and-a-half miles from Kerrville, hanging from the limbs of a live oak tree. An inquest determined that the badly decomposed bodies came to their deaths by hanging at the hands of unknown parties.[25] This was the state of affairs when Bill Longley rode into Kerr County.

What was left of Eastwood's band had disintegrated and was running for cover, and this included their families and followers as well. On the evening of July 16, just such a party was seen. As a San Antonio newspaper reported,

> A party of *emigrants* passed through our little burgh [Kerrville], bound up the river. The teams were driven by women, and the men were mounted and well armed, wearing the alert look so becoming to fighting men in an Indian country, seeming ready for a shot or a chase in either direction. Their gait was quickened going through town and the party camped just above, on the creek, and were interviewed by some neighbors in passing, but the meeting was brief. On the following day the Sheriff of Marion [Mason] county appeared in pursuit and the next morning the party was arrested about dawn, by Capt. Watson's minute men. The comment was that, "the mountain fellows had a lively way of recovering emigrants."[26]

Another account of this arrest said,

> Last Friday [Wednesday] a party of suspicious looking characters (four men and two women) passed through Kerrville traveling in the direction of the "Headquarters." A few hours after, the Sheriff of Mason county accompanied by several deputies arrived at this place. He had been following them for some time. With the information gathered at this place and with the assistance of the Sheriff of Kerr county and the parties who had been successful in arresting other members of the gang, proceeded to a place about 13 miles above this, where they found them encamped for the night. After surrounding them they rested until nearly day-break, when they were quietly informed that they were prisoners. They evidently had not heard of the trouble that their "pals" had met with and were proceeding as they supposed safely and with[out] suspicion to their den.[27]

Finney and his posse arrested three of the men—Bill Longley and two brothers, Jeff and Bill Ake—and the remaining man and two women were released. Finney took his prisoners back to Kerrville. Why was Longley in the area? Had it been his intention to join Eastwood's gang, or was he merely passing through, in the wrong place at the wrong time? Clearly, if he was in Bell County on July 1, he could not have been a participant with the gang. But other "toughs" had been recruited from Bell and surrounding counties; perhaps Longley was one of them.

On July 17, while in Kerrville, Finney took Longley before Kerr County District Clerk A. McFarland and had him stand by while he took the deposition of two men regarding Longley's crimes. A. J. Murray swore that he knew Longley personally and affirmed that he knew that Longley was charged "with a murder committed in Burleson County near the Brazos River at or near Evans' or Moseley's Ferry in or about the year 1862 or 1863." He also swore that Longley was charged with a murder near Evergreen in Washington County where "one or more negroes were killed," as well as a horse theft from one "Thomas Evans" around the time of the Burleson County murder.

Obviously Murray was aware of the killing of Green Evans in 1868, but the other crimes are unknown. There was no A. J. Murray in the 1870 Kerr County census, but there was an Andrew Murray in Burleson County in 1870, a twenty-one-year-old farmer from Virginia,[28] and an A. J. Murray, a forty-five-year-old farmhand from South Carolina, in Fayette County in 1870.[29]

The second affiant, Thomas J. Carson, swore "that he knows the said W. P. Longley for no character. That he the said Carson is familiar with the charges alleged against the said Longley at Evergreen from owner only."[30] A Tom J. Carson, a farmer born in Texas in 1833 and a Confederate veteran, can be found in both the 1880 and the reconstructed 1890 Kerr County census.[31] Carson had just married Mary F. Faulkner in Kerr County some eight months before the affidavit was given.[32] While several Thomas Carsons can be found in the 1870 census for Burleson and Washington counties, they are not the same as the Carson in Kerr County. How Carson knew Longley is unknown.

Longley and the Ake brothers were placed in the county jail at Kerrville while Finney ate dinner and refreshed himself. As one correspondent from Kerrville wrote to a San Antonio newspaper on July 21,

> The citizens of Washington and Burleson counties remember William. As a "trimmer of the census" he had but few equals in Texas, and it *did* seem that "no law could touch" him. William had a few hours rest in our jail, for safe(?)keeping, where he consoled young Baker with the assurance that friends were at hand who would effect his release, giving Baker full instructions as to his conduct of himself till his clearance. . . .
>
> This Longley is charged with a triple murder in Burleson county, near some ferry, another murder in Washington Co. and a rape in that vicinity—the murder of his victim and the rope being at home. He boasts of having been in the hands of the police eleven times. Oh, no! "no law can teche him!"[33]

Another correspondent to a San Antonio newspaper described Longley as a desperate-looking character:

> It is said that he has already been indicted for no less than two murders and that he is supposed to be guilty of several more. He appeared, when arrested, to know "where all of them men came from" that arrested him, for, said he, "we didn't see nary house all day yesterday but Kerrville."[34]

Longley's fellow prisoners, Jeff and Bill Ake, were just as notorious as he was. A review of Williamson County district court records reflects arrests and indictments of various members of the Ake family going back to 1858. William or Bill Ake's first arrest was in 1865 for assault with intent to murder, and in subsequent years he appeared before the court for other assault offenses. Prior to his arrest by Finney, Bill Ake's last appearance in a Williamson County court involved a $10 fine in July 1872.[35] Illustrative of his violent nature was his effort in May 1869 to gun down the Williamson County sheriff in Georgetown as the lawman drew water from a public well. Ake's shotgun failed to fire and the sheriff was spared.[36] In the spring of 1877, there was an outstanding $375 reward for Bill Ake's capture.[37]

Jeff Ake was no less a scoundrel than his brother. The Ake family helped settle Williamson County, their father, John, building the first log house in Georgetown, the county seat, and operating a hotel there for many years.[38] Jeff's numerous brushes with the law began in 1868 with an indictment for disturbing the peace (for which a jury found him not guilty), but he quickly graduated to assault offenses, not to mention numerous charges of cattle theft. Not long after his arrest with Longley, in February 1874, Governor Coke offered a $750 reward for both him and his brother, Bill, because of their Williamson County indictments, which totaled twenty. The following November, Jeff was arrested in Cass County for horse theft by Hunt County lawmen. One of the men he was arrested with, a man named Glass, killed one of the arresting deputies, Robert Hagood. Jeff Ake was held in

Hunt County for some time until he was spirited off to Williamson County to stand trial for his crimes there.[39] After an escape and recapture in Arkansas with his brother Bill, Jeff Ake later went to prison in 1878 for multiple horse thefts.[40] He was subsequently pardoned, but arrested again in Austin in January 1882 for being involved in a whorehouse shooting.[41]

As an old man, Jeff Ake reminisced about his life, without, of course, mentioning his criminal life and time in the penitentiary. Basically giving a rambling oral history, Ake claimed to have known all of the old outlaws, even alleging that he sold cattle to Cole Younger and Jesse James posing as the "Rector brothers." As to Longley, he described him as a "noted killer, but he always killed on the square; a fair fighter." "Bill was the gamest man I ever knowed; and quiet, pleasant, polite and self-confident. He told me once he never killed a man he was sorry for, and that he believed in an eye for an eye and a tooth for a tooth. A right-down game man."[42]

Finney took his prisoners on to the jail at Fredericksburg during the evening of July 17.[43] The next day, he released the Ake brothers, apparently because there was no pending warrant against them that he could find.[44] Longley said that, while at Fredericksburg, a mob threatened to lynch him,[45] but there is no contemporary account of such an incident. Longley was probably correct, however, when he quoted Finney as stating an interest in the $1,000 reward on Longley's head. Finney arrived in Austin with his prisoner on July 20, 1873, and checked in at the Raymond House.[46] But there is no official record of what happened. Longley said that Finney was told by Texas Governor E. J. Davis that no reward would be paid. He said that a cousin of his, William Patterson of Austin, gave Finney $563 in gold and Longley was released. "A fresh horse and two new six-shooters were secured, and Longley was ready for the road again."[47] Again, this is Longley's account and there is no corroboration, but the facts circumstantially support him. The census for Austin, in Travis County, for 1870 and 1880 shows a William or W. T. Patterson from Tennessee who had no family.[48]

Longley's account has him leaving Austin and returning to Bell County to spend a few days with his parents at their farm, then heading north to the Indian Territory again.[49] In the account of Longley's life that he gave and which was published in the September 16, 1877, *Galveston Daily News*, he claimed that while in the Indian Territory, he fell in with two deputy marshals and went with them to Morris County, Kansas, where they then tricked Mr. Stuart out of the $1,500 reward. Fuller's account, described earlier in chapter 8, which had Longley in Morris County after leaving Wyoming seems like the correct chronology. Then, Longley claimed, he returned to Texas and ended up in more trouble at Frio City in Frio County, southwest of San Antonio. Fuller did not include this account and it also cannot be corroborated:

> Longley had traded horses with [a] Mexican, and in a short time the owner of the animal held by Longley came forward and claimed his property. Longley went to the Mexican who had traded his horse off, and having money and declining to rectify the swindle he had effected upon him, Longley brought the services of his six-shooter into recquisition [*sic*], and after shooting him four times the Mexican was pronounced to be dead.[50]

Longley said that he then left Frio County and went to Madison County, falling in with a local desperado by the name of Bill McKiver. He later told his brother that he went to work for a Dr. McKiver there, apparently Bill McKiver's father. According to the 1877 newspaper account, Longley said that he fell in love with McKiver's sister, Laura, and invited her to go with him in a buggy to hunt for huckleberries. He made a pass at her, trying for a kiss, and the frightened girl jumped from the buggy and started for home on foot. Longley said that he was unarmed and was afraid that when Bill McKiver heard about his brashness, McKiver would "go for him." Longley said that he drove alongside the walking girl, pleading with her to get back in the buggy. The girl finally did get in, and he said that when he declared his love for her, she relented and let him kiss her. Longley claimed that McKiver did indeed hear of the incident and challenged him to a duel, but friends interfered, he said, and Longley left the area.[51]

A review of the Madison County census for 1870 and 1880 does turn up a McIver family. Dr. Joseph McIver was a North Carolinian who maintained a household near Madisonville with his wife, Alice, and nine children, including a daughter, Laura, age fourteen in 1873, but no son William is shown in that or any other household. The McIver family, building a large log home, settled west of present-day Normangee and engaged in farming and cattle raising.[52] A clue as to the existence of a Bill McIver, desperado, if there was a Bill McIver, may be in the following account from Bryan, Texas, in 1870:

> HORRIBLE MURDER—Yesterday, our city was the scene of one of the most unprovoked and cruel murders ever perpetrated in a civilized community. One McIver, of Leon county, with his father had been in the city for some days, and both had been drinking to excess, the younger being especially noisy and boisterous. Yesterday he was especially abusive and violent, causing great commotion on the streets. Police officer A.G. Hearn, one of the bravest and most faithful officers the city ever had, approached him, and, in a kindly manner, attempted to persuade McIver to keep order. Hereupon, McIver drew a knife and approached Hearn, with the evident intention of cutting him; Hearn, acting on the defensive, struck at McIver with his club, the blow being dodged by the latter, who then plunged his knife into Hearn's abdomen, inflicting a terrible and mortal wound. Hearn knocked McIver down, planted his knee on his breast, and took from him his knife and pistol, remarking in a tone of almost unparalleled magnanimity, "I could kill you if I wished—but I won't. I am a dead man."
>
> Mr. Hearn lived but a short time after he had lain down on the bed. His last words were: "Tell the boys I died, discharging my duty, like a man."[53]

The McIver in the above-mentioned account was apparently captured and placed in a military prison but escaped sometime in March 1870.[54] In March 1876, Governor Richard Coke offered a $300 reward for McIver's arrest for the killing of Green Hearne.[55] A William McIver was charged in Brazos County with two unknown offenses, one of which was dismissed in February 1877, and one that was continued after a jury failed to reach a verdict in September 1876.[56] William McIver also had a criminal charge against him dismissed in Madison County in November 1877.[57] Dr. McIver, who may have been the father referred to, was apparently himself a violent man, as witnessed by an 1869 incident in Grimes County in which a "Dr. McKeever" killed a Monihan during a fight resulting from a long-lasting feud.[58] And in an 1876 account in Madisonville, "two old men named Dr. M'Iver and Mosely" engaged in a drunken "rough and tumble fight in which Mosely received such a kicking and stamping that he handed in checks and gave up the ghost."[59] Joseph McIver was indicted for murder in Madison County in December 1876, but the charge was dismissed in July 1879 because of a defective indictment.[60] A "J. R. McIver" was indicted at the same time and this charge was also dismissed.[61] This "J. R. McIver" was likely John R. McIver, who had been found not guilty of carrying a pistol by a Madison County jury in 1874.[62] Joseph McIver was again indicted for murder in Madison County in July 1879 but acquitted by a jury in 1882,[63] and J. R. McIver, also indicted at the same time for murder, was acquitted in December 1879.[64]

Dr. Joe McIver and his family would ultimately be buried in the Hopewell Cemetery in Leon County.[65]

As a final confirmation that Longley at least knew Dr. McIver, he told his brother Jim in 1875 that he had once worked for Dr. McIver and had fallen in love with his daughter, Laura.[66] If Longley's story was true, and Laura was fourteen years old, it is no wonder that Bill McIver wanted to kill him for trying to seduce his sister.

Chapter 10

Shot Him Dead

Between July 1873 and Christmas 1874, there is no real record of Longley's whereabouts. We only have his story that, after being released in Austin, he killed a man in Frio County and then worked for Dr. McIver in Madison County. The 1877 account of his adventures found in the *Galveston Daily News* had him leaving Madison County, which is in East Texas northeast of Bryan, visiting his parents again briefly in Bell County, then riding on to old Fort Ewell on the Nueces River in LaSalle County, at the junction of the San Antonio and Laredo roads. The fort had been established in 1852, but abandoned in October 1854 when army troops there were transferred to Fort McIntosh on the Rio Grande above Laredo.[1] Fort Ewell and Dog Town, forty miles northeast on the Frio River, became two principal stage stands between San Antonio and the Rio Grande. Fort Ewell was not much of a town, being principally occupied by Mexicans and a storekeeper known as Peg Leg Stuart.[2]

Longley said that he was at Fort Ewell only a short time when he got into a fight with "a noted gambler named Dave Clark." He said that he shot Clark "a couple of times" but did not kill him.[3]

After this, according to Longley, he rode northeast back to Madison County where he again visited Laura McIver, presumably without interference from her desperado brother. He said that he then went on to the Sabine River, separating Texas from Louisiana. Near Logansport, in DeSoto Parish, Louisiana, he said that a Negro had insulted an "old gentleman" in that neighborhood who was a friend of Longley's, and Longley "killed him for accommodation."[4] There is some evidence that Longley's excursion to East Texas and this killing may have actually occurred, but in 1877, not 1873–1874 (see chapter 15).

Moving southwest, into Angelina County, about fourteen miles from tiny Homer, which is just southeast of Lufkin, he said that he came upon a white man and a black man fighting. Their two wagons had collided, resulting in a broken wheel on the black man's wagon. Longley said that the infuriated black man "concluded to thrash the white man for his carelessness," but Longley, "feeling in a good humor and to stop the difficulty," shot the black man once, breaking his neck.[5] Once again, there is no corroboration of this incident.

Continuing to move westward, Longley said that he rode into Lovelady, in Houston County south of Crockett, near the Trinity County border, where he "cracked a negro on the head with a six-shooter."[6] Being broke, he said that he put up his horse in a raffle there, then bought two chances himself and "cast the first throw." While other men were trying their chances, Longley, with cash in hand, slipped outside and rode off on his horse.[7]

Longley returned to his parents' farm in Bell County, and every account seems to confirm that this was around Christmas of 1874. Fortunately, Longley's brother, Jim, sometime in 1936, penciled an account of what subsequently occurred, and that account is somewhat corroborated by accounts written by Bill Longley himself. The following series of events is pieced together from those writings.

Young brother Jim was set to turn sixteen on January 21, 1875, some four weeks off. He idolized his older brother and certainly was glad to see him ride up to the farmhouse. According to Jim, Bill told their parents that he was going to get married and wanted Jim to go with him, although who and when was not clarified by Jim in his account. Perhaps he still had Laura McIver on his mind. Campbell and Sarah consented and allowed Jim to go with him, although, given Bill's lifestyle up to that point, there must have been some nagging concern for Jim's welfare. Nevertheless, Jim said that the two rode off about 8 p.m. Christmas night in a misting rain, headed south.[8] Bill later wrote that they left on New Year's Day.[9] Bill also claimed that, while he was at his parents' farm, they heard about the death of his cousin, Little Cale Longley, as the result of an accident with a horse near Evergreen,[10] but that was not Jim's recollection nor the account given by the *Galveston Daily News* in September 1877.

There may have been another reason that Bill didn't want to hang around in Bell County. At about one thirty in the morning some seven months earlier, on Tuesday, May 26, 1874, a large mob of masked men rode into the county seat, Belton, from the east. The sheriff was sixty miles north in Waco retrieving a prisoner confined there. The masked men rode to the Bell County jail on the banks of the Leon River and were confronted by Deputy Sheriff S. E. Wilkerson and some guards. The deputy, faced with a determined force, relented and was allowed to take his wife and child from their living quarters on the second floor. With the deputy and his men under guard, the mob used axes, hatchets, and crowbars to break into the downstairs. Once inside, they found nine prisoners in an iron cage. They were, for the most part, horse and cattle thieves, although one was being held for murdering his wife in adjacent Coryell County. The mob opened fire and within minutes all nine men were dead, their blood running freely across the jail floor. None in the mob was ever identified, and it was conveniently claimed that they were all from outside the county. The reason for the lynching? It was supposed that friends of the prisoners would try to rescue them.[11] It was quite apparent that the good citizens of Bell County were not of any mind to tolerate the presence of lawbreakers, perhaps including the notorious Bill Longley.

The two Longley brothers rode through the rain southward about twelve miles, staying the first night with a William Clark. The next day, it still misting rain, they rode on to Florence in Williamson County, where Bill had his horse shoed by a "John Yoarbro." Actually, this was William "Billy" Yarbrough, a twenty-six-year-old native of Mississippi, who had moved to Florence in the late 1860s with his aunt and uncle.[12] Leaving Florence to visit a friend, "Uncle Billie" Mullen, the two brothers rode along Salado Creek leading out of Florence and soon realized that they did not know in which direction to go. They stopped when they ran across some playing children and asked the way. Jim recalled that one young girl, about thirteen, stood out because of her blue eyes and wavy brown hair, and that this girl, Elvira Draper, would one day be his wife.[13]

After riding on some two-and-a-half miles, at the point of a low mountain, they arrived at the Mullen farm. They stayed for several hours and ate dinner while they were there. William S. Mullen, an Indiana native born about 1838 or 1839, was the son of a Mexican War and Confederate army veteran, and had run for Williamson County sheriff in the 1860s.[14] And Mullen himself was really no stranger to the courthouse at the county seat in Georgetown, given his numerous arrests between 1861 and 1873 for gaming, one of which was with another old friend of Bill Longley, Ben Hinds.[15] In April 1870, Mullen was indicted for murder, but a jury found him not guilty in November of that same year.[16] Clearly, Mullen was the type of individual that Longley would be attracted to as a friend.

After finishing their dinner, the brothers rode on to Pond Springs, just north of the Travis County line on Brushy Creek near present-day Cedar Park. They spent the night there with "Uncle Jimmie" Standifer, about sixty-six. Formerly called Live Oak Prairie, a pond had been formed there by an underground spring, thus the change in name. The Rutledge family had operated a store there on the stage road between Lampasas and Austin.[17] James Standifer, a Tennessee native, had fought with Houston at San Jacinto in 1836, and after settling at Pond Springs, served on the first Williamson County grand jury in 1848 under a live oak tree in the new county seat of Georgetown. One of his daughters married a Williamson County sheriff, Jack Champion.[18]

Standifer told the brothers that he had been forced to kill a man in Mississippi in self-defense, and though acquitted, was forced to come to Texas before more trouble occurred. A son-in-law, Tom Holiday (or Holaday), operated a store nearby.[19]

Continuing their journey in the cold and misting rain, Jim and Bill Longley rode on to the double-log house in Travis County of a Mr. Liston. The 1870 Travis County census includes Henry Liston, a Georgia-born farmer, who lived with his wife and five grown children.[20] Jim recalled that farmer Liston had a great number of cattle, horses, geese, and other fowl. The Longleys enjoyed their visit there, especially a lively conversation with two of Liston's sons, and they got a good night's sleep in a "big fat feather bed."[21]

Moving on the next morning toward Bastrop County, they stopped for a sumptuous meal at the immaculately clean log home of a black woman, for which Bill paid her a dollar. The two finally arrived in Bastrop County, and after riding through the town of Bastrop and crossing the Colorado River on a ferry, they took the road leading to Lockhart to the southwest. The misting rain having grown even heavier, they looked for a place to spend the night and came upon the one-room log cabin of a poor man and his wife. The man gave up some of his meager supply of corn to feed their horses, and the two brothers were given a meal of corn pone, bacon, and coffee. Bill was afraid that the man would attempt to steal their horses, so the two alternated staying awake that night, but without event. They slept on mattresses filled with corn shucks, and an occasional cob would poke them in the ribs, leading Jim to dig one out with his pocket knife. The next morning they paid the couple two dollars and rode on.

Coming to the Austin-Lockhart road, they stopped for dinner at the home of an Englishman named Hamaks. While dinner was being prepared, Jim saw mist on the window and, in large letters, wrote JS LONGLEY with a finger. Bill spotted him and wiped it off quickly with a handkerchief, at the same time forcefully mashing Jim with a knee pressed into him as he sat. Bill warned him not to reveal his true name, instructing him that they would identify themselves as Jim and

Bill Patterson. Jim later wrote, "I never knew one day what our name would be the next."[22]

As they ate dinner with the family, Bill inquired about any work that might be available to them. Hamaks suggested they try Bill Baker on the Red Rock road, about half way between Lockhart and Bastrop. Bill asked Hamaks where Baker was from and was told Missouri. Bill told him that his and Jim's name was also Baker, and since they were from Missouri too, they might be related to Bill Baker. Apparently they had not yet introduced themselves to their hosts by the name of Patterson.

The Baker house and farm was a nice one, and Bill and Jim "Baker" were hired for general farm work. Jim was paid $15 per month, but Bill was raised to $20 because he was a good worker. William Baker was about forty-eight years old and lived with his wife, Elvira, who was believed descended from Texas hero Stephen F. Austin.[23] Jim's chores included gathering stove wood in the evening and milking fifteen cows both morning and night. One frequent guest who used to stay with the Bakers was William "Buck" Walton, a prominent Austin attorney who would a decade later write a biography of Texas gunman Ben Thompson. Bill Longley was leery of Walton and cautioned Jim not to let his guard down when the lawyer was around. One night after Jim had gone to bed, Bill engaged Walton in conversation, asking if he was "not a bit afraid to go through the Evergreen country of Bill Longley." Walton said he was not and that he carried a good pistol and shotgun, which would be more than enough to finish Longley off quickly. They went on to discuss Longley's "daring deeds" into the night. Before they left the Bakers, Jim and Bill revealed their true identities to the family and told them of the joke they had played on Walton. Jim said that the Bakers "got a thrill out of it."[24] Bill Baker continued to be a good friend to the Longley brothers.

According to Jim, they left the employ of the Bakers toward the end of February 1875 and headed back to the old Evergreen community.[25] However, two other accounts conflict as to when they left. In the 1877 *Galveston Daily News*, it was indicated that Bill learned that a cousin of his had been killed near Evergreen, and that this was the reason they left.[26] However, in a letter written on September 12, 1877, after his arrest, Bill wrote that while they were at the Baker farm, he heard that he had been indicted for shooting at some black men, so they left on March 28, 1875.[27] No such indictment has been located. Regardless, the two brothers headed for Evergreen, now located in newly formed Lee County, which had been carved from Washington, Burleson, Bastrop, and Fayette counties.

Jim and Bill rode northeast through Bastrop and decided to separate at what Jim called Hogey Prairie. Bill reached the Lee County farm of his uncle, Caleb Longley, about fifteen minutes before Jim rode up. According to accounts by both brothers, accounts that would be hotly disputed by their uncle, Bill was standing with his horse while Caleb pointed at the nearby grave of his son, Caleb, Jr., claiming that he had been murdered by Wilson Anderson. Bill recalled that "Uncle Cale" met him at the gate, crying like a child and putting his arms around Bill's neck, telling him, "Bill, there lays poor little Cale, and the man that murdered him still lives here in one mile of me."[28]

Caleb B. "Cale" Longley, brother of Bill's father, Campbell, came to Texas about the same time as his brother, settling in the Evergreen area. His third son, Caleb, or "Little Cale," had been born about the same time as his cousin, Bill Longley, in 1851. During the Civil War, Caleb, Sr., had fought with Dick Dowling at the Battle of Sabine Pass.[29]

According to both Longley brothers, Caleb urged Bill not to leave there until he had avenged his cousin's death by killing Anderson. When Bill asked why some of Caleb's other boys, O. P. and Charles being the oldest, didn't kill Anderson themselves, Caleb had various excuses. But to add fuel to Bill's fire, Caleb told him that Anderson had also accused Bill of stealing his horse and had threatened to kill Bill. Jim heard Bill agree to kill his cousin's alleged killer.[30]

As early as 1860, Henry and Caroline Anderson, who married in Washington County in 1849, had farmed in the household next to Caleb and his family. The sixth of eight Anderson children and their second son, Wilson grew up with both Little Cale and with Bill Longley. Caroline Anderson's father, Archibald Willingham, moved from Washington County in 1850 to Bell County, where he settled at Salado.[31] In 1853 when an older child, Henry, died, a saddened Caroline sent her father locks of hair from both Henry and Wilson, describing eleven-month-old Wilson as "the finest boy in the country."[32] Wilson Anderson now lived in the Loebau community, just a few miles northwest of Evergreen.[33] Even though he was a farmer, Anderson was also known to go armed, having pleaded guilty to carrying a pistol the previous summer.[34]

As Bill recalled the entreaties of his uncle the day they arrived,

> The boys then concealed our horses, and uncle Cale talked all day about the matter, and nothing would do him but that I should kill Anderson next day. You all know there is no one but can be influenced by some one else, and he touched my sympathy by his talk in various ways. Some time that day J. M. Brown came there to get a load of corn, and I wanted to talk with Mr. Brown to see what the general opinion was in regard to the suspicion for Anderson, but uncle Cale would not consent for me to do so, because he said Jim Brown would try to arrest me, and I thought if that be the case I would not show myself, for I did not want to hurt Brown nor get hurt, for I never had anything against him.[35]

How did Little Cale die? No contemporary account has been located. However, Miley L. Wooley, the son of Virgil Wooley, a contemporary in Lee County, later recalled that several months prior to the Longley brothers' arriving at their uncle's farm, Anderson and Little Cale had spent the day at Giddings, some eight miles south of Evergreen, and both had been drinking rather freely. The two rode out of Giddings late in the afternoon, and Little Cale's horse became unmanageable and ran off with him. The horse ran under the low-hanging limb of a live oak tree and young Longley was knocked off, dead with a crushed skull. The Longley family did not accept that explanation and, instead, contended that Anderson dispatched him with a club.[36] There is no indication that Anderson was ever charged with a crime in this incident.

The Jim Brown referred to by Bill Longley was the same Jim Brown that he and Ben Hinds had allegedly gambled with in Evergreen just a few years earlier. Born in Alabama in 1839, James Madison Brown came to Texas with his family in 1850. He served in the State Rangers in 1858 and 1859, and fought Indians in 1861. By 1870 he was a resident of Washington County near Evergreen, farming with his wife and children, but rubbing shoulders with the likes of Ben Hinds, Bill Longley, and John Wesley Hardin. In addition he was a passionate horse racer and took horses to various races around the state. He served as a state policeman as well as with McNelly's Texas Rangers, and this may have been why Longley feared arrest when Brown came to his uncle's farm.[37] In April 1870, Brown purchased the Longley homestead near Evergreen for $2,500.[38]

Jim Longley grew alarmed about the impending violence and tried to head it off. As he described it,

> I was only sixteen then, but I thought I knew best and soon as I got a chance to see Bill by his self, I talked and reasoned with him. I told him that our uncle had several boys living there in the same neighborhood and if they wanted Anderson killed let them do it their selves, that he Bill had plenty against his self, and that he could beat any thing that there was against him, and reform and settle down and make a good citizen, and he promised me he would take my advice.
>
> But we stayed there three days, and every time I caught them by their selves, Cail [*sic*] would be talking and crying. I never so worried and uneasy [*sic*]. But I would talk to Bill again and he would promise to take my advice. Once I came in the room where they were loading the shot gun. They put five layers of buck shot in each barrel and Old Cale, as I called him, put one

> extry shot in this Grade 31 shot, and as he put it in he said I hope it will go through his dam brain.[39]

Bill recalled that his uncle gave him "twenty-six buckshot" to load in his shotgun and told him, "Bill, don't leave no life in him," also warning his nephew that Anderson would be armed with a Smith & Wesson pistol and ready for trouble.[40] It was also later alleged that on March 30, an old schoolmate of Bill ran into him, and Bill, heavily armed, was riding a mule. Longley was supposed to have demanded of the person whether he recognized him, and the schoolmate was "wise enough to deny the recognition."[41]

When Bill later wrote his account of this episode and after his execution in October 1878, Old Cale vehemently defended himself, denying that he greeted his nephews with open arms or that he implored Bill to kill Anderson. He later asserted,

> Bill Longley came to my house March 30, 1875, in company with his brother Jim, and stayed all night. I was sick in my bed when he came. Never met him at the gate; never put my arms around his neck, as his wicked fancy would picture, and did not tell him of the threats that Anderson had made. I told him the evidence against Anderson at the examining court. Bill wished to know the reason why we had not killed him. I replied that we did not want him killed. "Yes," said Bill, "you are all too much like brother George–to [*sic*] big cowards." He then cursed Anderson, and said he would burst his skull if he saw him, and that he owed him a killing for accusing him of stealing his horse. I had but little talk with him, but told him for my sake not to trouble Anderson nor any one else, but to leave as he came, for it would bring us into trouble. He then said, "Uncle Cale, I won't on your account." Some time during the day he asked if we had any buckshot, and was told that there was none on the place, which was true. He then drew the wads off the loads in his gun (which he said he had taken from a negro), took the buckshot out, fired the

powder off and reloaded with same shot. He said he didn't want to travel with a gun unless it was fresh loaded. It is needless to trace his letter through, for all his charges are false, as can be proven. The last words I told him were, to go out of the country peaceable for our sake, and he said he would."[42]

The uncle went on to put some distance between him and his nephews:

> Suffice it to say, that Bill Longley, when he came to my house, was always a terror to us, knowing what a character he had. . . . Why he entertains such enmity toward me is because we didn't spend our living on him and go to killing and breaking jail for him, besides sending him word by his father to keep away from me. I say let the law handle his sort to the letter, for he was a notorious horse thief, a wholesale murderer, a highway robber, a woman slayer, a woman abductor and seducer, according to his own contention and public knowledge.[43]

Given the consistency between the account given by Bill and, many years later, by his brother, Jim, as to what occurred, Caleb's protestations ring rather hollow and likely not true.

In the early afternoon of March 31, 1875, Bill and Jim rode away from Caleb Longley's farm, but Bill did not tell Jim where they were headed, and the obedient younger brother followed. Jim did not know where Anderson lived, although he knew it was nearby. After a few miles, Bill told Jim to stay in some timber while he went to see a man. Suspecting that Bill was going to find Wilson Anderson, Jim hurried after him. He rode up in time to see Anderson plowing in a field and Bill telling Anderson that he was going to die for killing Little Cale. Jim described what he saw:

> Anderson started to raise his right hand to his left shoulder as Bill fired. This charge struck him in the breast and as he was

> half fallen, Bill fired again. This charge struck him from his knees to his head, one coming out at the top of his head. There was a man cutting sprouts near by, and he ran across those four foot cotton beds that Anderson was putting up. Bill pulled a pistol and started to shoot him, but I put my left arm over his and held on to his arm. This fellow would look back and as he did he would fall. [I thought] that he never would get away, but he made it.[44]

In 1878 another account of Anderson's death stated that when Anderson saw Longley standing by the fence with a double-barreled shotgun, he called out not to shoot him. But Longley fired one barrel at him and Anderson began to run. The charge from the second barrel then killed him instantly.[45] An even more melodramatic version has Longley hitting Anderson with the first shot, and Anderson exclaiming, "Oh, God, What did you shoot me for?" Longley's response was simply, "Just for luck."[46]

The death of Wilson Anderson was soon laid at the feet of the Longley brothers. The initial newspaper reports stated that Anderson was killed by two unknown men who shot him twice with shotguns and that Anderson had been tried about a year earlier and acquitted for the murder of a man named "Langley."[47]

A more thorough account also said that two men were responsible:

> The *News* has been informed by two responsible and reliable gentlemen who were in Giddings yesterday, that on Wednesday last [March 31], some four miles from Giddings, two men rode up to where a man named Wilson Anderson was plowing in a field, and shot him down, completely riddling him with buckshot. They fired twice, the second shot taking fatal effect. A man in the same field at a distance witnessed the shooting. The sheriff and a number of citizens started in pursuit of the murderers, but returned without effecting their capture, having failed to come up with them.[48]

Longley, who would never admit Jim's presence in order to protect him, simply said, "I found him where I expected, rode up to the end of his row, shot him dead and rode off; I met brother Jim in the branch and rode off."[49] Bill and Jim quickly rode north to Burleson County, where it was said that they told an aunt and uncle (Caleb Longley?) that they had killed Anderson.[50] Bill also was said to have told an acquaintance named Wash Harris that he had dispatched Anderson.[51]

On May 10, 1875, the Lee County grand jury handed down an indictment for murder against both Bill and Jim, alleging that Wilson Anderson died from a wound fired by Bill that was six inches deep and one inch wide, and that Jim Longley had stood by encouraging him with words and by using threatening gestures.[52] Texas Governor Richard Coke promptly offered a $175 reward for the arrest and delivery of each of the brothers.[53] By this time, Jim and Bill had put a great deal of distance between them and Lee County.

Chapter 11

Bill Was Still Fighting

The Lee County sheriff mounting the search for the Longley brothers was James McKeown, the father of Bill's early criminal companion, Johnson. Sheriff McKeown was elected as Lee County's first sheriff on June 2, 1874.[1] But the posse led by James McKeown never came close to the fleeing brothers, who headed north after leaving Burleson County.

Jim later recalled[2] that they initially steered clear of settlements where they might be recognized. Camping out in the open each night, Jim hunted and killed swamp rabbits to eat with the bacon and bread they had brought with them. They approached the Brazos River, heading toward Bryan, and encountered a black man with three yokes of steers that he was taking to Caldwell. The two outlaws, apparently feeling their oats, made the man "dance," riding on after rewarding him with a half-quart of whiskey. One can only suspect what happened to the other half-quart.

Riding into Bryan, Bill stopped at a saloon to get more whiskey. When he came out, he saw some half dozen young men talking and laughing and looking their way. Bill decided to go back in for another quart, telling Jim that if they were laughing when he came back out, he would make them dance. Bill came back out again, mounted, and rode over to where one of the fellows was still laughing. A shotgun aimed at the young man very quickly led him to "cut the pigeon wing," while the other men evaporated into a nearby store. Feeling sorry for the dancing man, Jim rode between them and urged Bill to leave town with him, and the two rode out.

Bill was apparently under the influence. As they left town, Bill spotted a man hoeing a field while chickens picked around him for worms. Bill unlimbered a pistol and began firing at the chickens. The man threw himself to the ground, the bullets throwing dirt on his back. Bill dismounted and went to the man's fence, supposedly to get a better shot, and Jim threatened to get the sheriff and have him jailed. Bill then agreed to ride on with him, much to the relief of the man hugging the ground.

A few miles outside of Bryan, they spotted horsemen pursuing them. Bill elected to stay and fight them, but Jim argued in favor of making a run for it to nearby timber. The group turned out to be a party of black men, the leader riding a spirited iron-gray horse. Bill again talked about someone dancing, and the leader rode off quickly. Bill fired off a shotgun blast, but Jim knocked the gun down before it could do any damage except to the ground. Jim said that a short, fat black woman, weighing some 350 pounds, was with the party and cheerfully volunteered to dance. She hiked up her long skirt and broke into a jig that put Bill "in a fine humor," and the boys rode on. Just northwest of Bryan, Bill showed his brother the grave of his former companion and brother-in-law, John Wilson.

Jim and his drunken brother came upon an old log house, and they rode off the road and stopped to let their horses graze. Jim left Bill to build a cooking fire, and walked to the house where he bought two dozen eggs and two dozen biscuits. The lady of the house loaned him a frying pan and some spoons. Back at their camp, Bill was getting drunker. He put the bacon in the pan to fry, then promptly broke twelve eggs into the pan, but they were only half-cooked when he ate them. As he started to break the remaining eggs, a disgusted Jim picked up Bill's two whiskey bottles and threw them both up and shot them before Bill could stagger over and rescue them. Jim made do that evening with bread and bacon, and vowed not to let Bill get near a town or saloon anymore.

The next morning, the two crossed the flooded Navasota River into Madison County and passed the school where Laura McIver, Bill's young love, was on the playground. She ultimately married Leroy Thomas in Madison County in 1884.[3] The brothers shared a meal with Dr. McIver's son-in-law, Jim Gardner, and Mrs. Gardner baked them bread and gave them some bacon. That evening, they continued their journey, working their way north. The next evening, two families camping in a large tent let the two riders sleep inside, feeding them both supper and breakfast. Bill gave them some beef, and they again rode on in a cold rain. Before noon, Jim said that they came to the ranch of a bachelor named Zolner, some ten or fifteen miles east of Rockwall, where they ate dinner and Bill traded the ranchman a shotgun for a Colt Army pistol. The countryside was soaked from the continuing rains as Jim and Bill rode north into Collin County, then veered and headed for Sherman and Denison, just south of the Red River.

They continued north, periodically trading for food. Crossing the Red River on a ferry north of Denison, they encountered three men eating lunch. Jim described the scene from memory some sixty years later:

> Bill told me who they was. They was Missourians and high powered bad men. They knew Bill and told him that they was hanging out at Caddo and waiting for the payroll for the soldiers at Fort Sill, and wanted us to help. They planned that the four would go in the express office and get the money and throw it out to me, and we would scatter out and meet at a designated spot and divide the spoils. But that little play house was broken up when fifteen U.S. soldiers came in a week before the money arrived. They decided that five of those soldiers was our equal. There was

> one in particular, they called him Billie, and always have [suspected] that he was Bill McDonald, an old Texas Ranger. Two men held him up between town and their camp one night and he killed both of them. There never was a man so bad. But there was another just a little better. I was the proudest boy you ever saw when those soldiers made camp at Caddo. I thought of my dear good mother that had loved and taught me right and for me to turn out to be an outlaw and break her heart, and how she would grieve and die broken-hearted. I thought it all over and told Bill that I would not go in to anything crooked or unlawful.[4]

Bill agreed to take him back to Bell County and sold their horses and saddles to raise some cash. With the help of some gambling, he was able to increase their assets to about $500. Perhaps itching for new adventure, he broached Jim with a proposal that they go to the Black Hills and join Custer in fighting the Indians, but Jim turned that proposition down. They took a train to Denison, across the state line in Texas, then walked through the nearby town of Sherman to tiny Van Alstyne, above the Grayson County line. Named after the surveyor who laid the town out, Van Alstyne's first business in 1873 was Oscar Riddle's saloon. Subsequently, four more saloons opened their doors, and two wholesale liquor houses prospered.[5]

The Longleys slept on the ground near a railroad section house, and a railroad foreman saw their weapons and warned them that the Grayson County sheriff lived at Van Alstyne and would take the guns from them. James W. Vaden was elected sheriff in December 1873.[6] Bill informed the railroad man that the sheriff couldn't take their firearms, and the two walked on into Van Alstyne where Bill began drinking and gambling in a saloon. Jim took ten dollars from him and put it in his watch pocket, then sat down in a chair in a back room and fell asleep. After a few hours, Jim said, he was rudely awakened,

> And what woke me was Sheriff Riggels [*sic*][7] in my pocket. I had a .22 caliber gun that I used to kill rabbits. My first thought

was robbers, so I came up hitting that sheriff in the face fast as I could. He was about my height and about 45 years old. He kept backing gun in hand. Finally he said I'll just whip the dam little devil and was trying to put his gun up and give me a fair fight, but I kept pouring it in his face like Joe Louis does in these days.

I heard a voice behind me say you are not going to hit the kid and when the fight was over and that was soon as I found it was the sheriff, there was a tall man about fifty years old with his back to me keeping Riggels' deputies from hitting me in the back. Things quieted down then and the sheriff and all of us had come up in the front of the saloon. I felt around in my pocket and found the end of a Colts 44 barrel that we had sawed off. It had the long brass sight so I grasp it so it would look like a derringer and poked it in the sheriff's face. He bent down and taken hold of his gun, but he was stooping over til he could not make the draw, when a deputy poked me in the side with a six-gun and I threw the thing on the floor and as it rolled across the floor there was an awful roar went up from the whole crowd, officers and all. Even the sheriff was so relieved that he laughed heartily. The real fight was to come for when Bill saw a deputy coming with the handcuffs (I had never saw a pair and did not know what they was), and when the deputy got close enough Bill floored him with his fist or rather grounded him as we was out in the street then. There was eight trying to put handcuffs on him by this time but every time one got in kicking distance Bill would kick him and hit him at the same time, and he never failed to lay him out. I saw an opening and ran. It was about five miles to a creek bottom so I lit out, but two big long-legged deputies chased me some three hundred yards, and when I saw I could not make the creek, I fell down on my back. They came up all tuckered out and taken me by the legs and said we will drag you back. I looked at them and said there is nothing but a gun case, and we will beat that and if you move me an inch I will kill you both when I get out, and they decided to carry me back. I just limbered myself and tried to weigh two hundred but they carried me back to the battle ground and Bill was still fighting the whole bunch. One big deputy that had one of Bill's guns ran up behind Bill and stuck the gun in his right boot and said I can put them on him. I just pulled the gun out of his boot and said hands off. At just then there was four or five guns stuck in my back and ribs, so I threw the gun on the ground cocked and every body tried to put their feet in their pocket at once.

But they finally got the cuffs on one hand, and then it came my time. There was so many holding Bill [that they] could hardly get me close enough to get my arm in. I just walked up nice and no one holding me and as I made as if I would put my hand in, I quickly ran this time all around the saloon stores and street. The crowd hurrahed for the kid and I would do my best running and dodging and then I ran up and told the sheriff I was ready to be yoked up.

The crowd all dispursed [*sic*] and the sheriff taken us over to the depot and he went inside and left a little fellow to guard Bill and I with one of Bill's guns. This fellow was standing on the depot platform on the edge next to the track. Bill and I was sitting on a bench with our back to the wall. We whispered that my right hand was loose, so we sprang and I made a grab for the gun. I just touched it with tips of my fingers, the fellow fell on the track and it knocked him out. I tried to pull Bill off the platform. I seen he was knocked out, but Bill pulled me on in the depot office and the sheriff covered us with his gun. So sure enough the section foreman knew his sheriff.[8]

The sheriff wasted no time tossing the two rowdies into the local jail. The jail was quite dark, almost too dim to see the other men in the cell with them. A Sherman lawyer, handsome, blond-haired J. W. Finley, visited them at the jail. Born in Tennessee in 1847, Finley became a lawyer in Georgia in October of 1873, moving to Texas the following month.[9] Finley told them that he would handle their case for ten dollars, and Jim gave him the money he had stashed in his watch pocket. The two were subsequently released. When they went to the county jail to retrieve their guns, and while the jailer was getting them, they saw the sheriff and Finley coming toward them in a hurry. Bill suspected that they might know about the Anderson murder and whispered to Jim that he would take care of the sheriff and that Jim should take care of the jailer. But Finley alerted them that the sheriff intended to arrest them for a second offense growing out of the row at Van Alstyne, and the lawyer said that he would sue the county for $5,000. The two brothers were taken before a judge where Finley advised of the pending lawsuit, and the judge ordered them released. Unhappily, although they were free to go, they had each picked up body lice while in jail.

Jim was concerned about their safety in the area and suggested to Bill that they sell their guns for a dollar apiece and get out of there. Bill asked about work, and the sheriff said that if he could lay brick, there was a building being constructed on the far side of town. Unarmed, the two walked in that direction through a creek bottom. When they heard horses running several hundred yards behind them, Jim and Bill ran toward a house being built, jerked some boards loose, and crawled under it. They saw five officers ride up, including one who Jim identified as W. A. Knox, a one-legged deputy. Apparently, Jim's recollection was confused, as W. A. Knox was the name of the Lee County district clerk who would play a major role in Bill Longley's capture, and who had but one leg.[10]

The Longleys were convinced that the lawmen were looking for them and managed to run to some nearby timber for cover without being noticed. On foot they hastily made their way west, and four days later found themselves at a farm in the Trinity River bottom some twelve miles east of Dallas. They went to work at the farm for about two weeks, but discovered that they would not be paid until the cotton was gathered. They decided to move on unannounced, but waited until the people at the farm left for church on Sunday, leaving them behind. The first order of business was to boil and wash all of their clothing with lye soap and salt in order to rid themselves of the lice; then they left and headed for Hutchins in southern Dallas County.

They arrived at Hutchins in the late afternoon. Hutchins, located on the Houston and Texas Central Railway, would gain fame in three years as the site of a train robbery by Sam Bass and his gang. Inquiring for farm work, the brothers were directed by a merchant to contact a man named Holiday. When Bill took their last fifty cents to get them something to eat, then returned with a pint of whiskey, a considerable portion of which had already been consumed, Jim was enraged and smashed it on the plank sidewalk, threatening to beat his brother to death. They made their way to Holiday's place, where Bill got a job. Jim went to work for a Mr. Schoolfield about a mile away. After about a month Bill went to work for J. B. Miller, who rented to Schoolfield. The Longleys were going by the name of Bill and Jim Jackson. Bill also managed to fall in love with one of Miller's daughters.

While they were there, a revival was held on White Rock Creek, a branch of which ran west of Hutchins. The evangelist was General Richard M. Gano, whose father had reportedly baptized George Washington, and who himself had been an outstanding Texas cavalry officer for the South during the Civil War. In addition to dealing in real estate and raising livestock after the war, he devoted much of his time to religion and took pride in the thousands of people that he had baptized.[11] One of those was Bill Longley, who, at least for now, professed religion, at least temporarily, and was immersed in the creek. Alice Schoolfield, daughter of Jim's employer, was escorted to the revival by Jim, and she sang at the gathering. One can't help but believe that Longley was merely trying to impress his female companion.

Jim quit working for Schoolfield and went to work for about a month for "Cas" Floyd. Toward the end of July 1875, Jim grew homesick for his family and the seven months since he had left with Bill seemed like a century. He and Bill said good-bye and set out again for Bell County. The first night they stopped at a camp meeting of black worshippers south of Lancaster, still in Dallas County, and were offered all they could eat for fifty cents. They rode on, but didn't have very good luck in finding anyone with food to share. After they crossed the Navasota River, they found themselves in a thick bottom and, leading their horses, had to cut their way through the thick brush with their pocket knives. They came upon a small two-room cabin, and the woman there could provide them with only a low grade of flour. The three shared a meal of biscuits, butter, and fresh buttermilk, and Bill paid her with a silver dollar.

On the next day they finally arrived at the Longley farm, and Jim was happy to be home. Campbell told them both that they had been indicted for Wilson Anderson's murder, and Jim said that he surrendered himself at once.[12]

At this point it seems appropriate to put to rest at least one incorrect statement concerning Bill Longley. In his pioneering work on Wyatt Earp, historian Ed Bartholomew asserted that, in July 1875 "Wild Bill" Longley killed a cowboy at Kingman, Kansas, just west of Wichita.[13] This grew out of a newspaper article in the *Wichita Beacon* reporting an incident in Kingman on July 8, when a Bill *Langley* killed a John Riley. Both had been cowboys on a trail drive for W. B. Grimes of Texas, who maintained a sizeable ranch in Matagorda County.[14] Clearly, Bill Longley was in Texas and could not have been the same fellow. Also, it sounds like a killing he would have relished for his autobiography, but he never mentioned such an incident.

By August 10, Jim had surrendered to Bell County Sheriff Robert Halley. With several deputies as guards, the sheriff took the young man to Lee County. Jim readily admitted that his brother had killed Wilson Anderson, but denied that he was involved. "He seemed anything but a murderer in appearance, young and very fair looking."[15] Within a week, Jim was released on a $5000 bond, and, on August 24, 1875, the governor offered a $250 reward for Bill Longley.[16] But Bill Longley had disappeared, not to resurface until November.

Chapter 12

I Will Not Be Captured

Bill Longley's whereabouts after he left Bell County are unknown, but the best evidence indicates that he returned to his old haunts in what was now Lee County, around Evergreen. Not aware that his brother was in custody and hearing numerous rumors in the neighborhood about his own well-being, Longley wrote a remarkable letter to Jim Brown, likely in September or October of 1875, although it could have been later:

> Devils Pass
> Hell's Half Acre
> Septober the 41st 7777
>
> Kind friend. This lieves me stil floating through the gentle breeses of misrie and feel just as happy as a big sun flour that boes and bends in the breeses. Well Jim I understand that I have threaten your life and if I done it it must have bin when I was a-sleeping. For I know nothing about it myself. I killed the only one in that country that I had any thing against at that time. now

Jim Brow[n] if I ever kill any man in that country it will be eather for killing some of my kinfolks or els it wil be in resisting being captured for if the court knowes its self I will not be captured in that country alive tho I wil come there just when I pleas. I wrode by your house the first Monday night in August 1875. I stoped near the old yard fence and stood for an hour and my mind run back over my whole life and I thought of my childhood and the hapy hours that I had passed in the old cabin home.

Oh what dreadful thoughts pierced my hearts intermost core for a little while but I cursed my weekminded soul and treated myself to a drink of good old brandy and wrode on with a bold heart. It hurt me very bad when I heard that Johnson McKeown had bin hunting me with the intention of betraying me and geting me in to a snair to be killed for I loved him like a brother. Oh the hapy hours that I have passed with Johnson but now they are oer.

Two nights before I passed your house I was at home and my own Dear Father told me never to put my foot in his house again. and Brother Jim quit me and said I was too bad for him and my kinfolks is all so D____D cowardly. they don't want me to come about them so I stil alone tread the living land destitute of friends but G____d the world and every son of a bitch that don't like me for I am a wolf and it is my night to howl. I expect to get killed sometime but you may bet your sweet life that I will keep the flys off of the son of a bitch that does it while he is at it.

Jim I have got nothing against you and do not blame you for hunting me if you thought I had threatened you but now—if you will all let me alone I wil not bother none of you nor your property. I understand that some fellow in that country intends to get in with me and help me do mischief a while and then kill or capture me but you can tell the son of a bitch that I play a lone hand or I would like very much to fall in with him. Tell old Anderson he will find me some where between the Rio grand

> and the Rockey mountains and if he ever hires any one to kill uncle Cale—he might find me some where near his yard fence some dark night. You all know that Wils Anderson did kill little Cale and why in the hell does outsiders want to take a hand in it, for why not just say it is dog eat dog and all of you go on about your business and let the biggest dog eat the most dog if he can and I will bet old Bill wil get his shir of dog. Brother Jim did not have any thing to do with Killing Wils Anderson—he did not know that I was going to do it until it was done and if they arrest him and you wil use your influence in giting him out I wil be your Busome Friend and wil do anything for you that I can. I will be back through there in two weeks and I wil come and see you—so no more at present. I remain ever your true friend until further orders—do not doubt me Jim for I am true.
>
> W. P. Longley
>
> [Give my kindest regards to Mr. Cole for I never hear of him doing anything against me.][1]

From this letter, it can be deduced that Longley's past was catching up with him. His failure to be a God-fearing, law-abiding son had led to his parents' abandonment of him. Once in his old haunts, he now feared that he was open prey for reward-hunters, including those who were formerly his close companions. He did not dare take anyone into his confidence or establish any friendships for fear of betrayal and death. The letter starts off gaily, but quickly turns morbid and fatalistic, revealing rather starkly the dark mood of Bill Longley, now realistically aware of the direction in which his life was headed. There is a hint of realization that, in a few short years, times had changed, and there was no longer any tolerance for those who once so freely defied authority with youthful exuberance.

And indeed there was no more patience for Longley and those like him. As the *Giddings Tribune* editorialized concerning continuing outlawry and violence in the area:

> Where is this thing to stop? How is it to be stopped? There is but one way to stop it, and that is to make these ruffians who are so ready at homicide, feel that punishment for their crimes will come surely and swiftly. We must have some hanging. . . . A little more hemp applied in the punishment of murderers and outlaws would no doubt have a more salutory [*sic*] effect upon society, and especially upon the vain and bloodthirsty aspirations of some of the young men of the present day. . . . Do away with the penitentiary for cold-blooded and premeditated murder and substitute the ROPE in its stead, and law and order will again prevail throughout the land.[2]

With this menacing atmosphere in place, Longley retreated from Lee County, perhaps as early as August 1875 and moved north to the Waco area in McLennan County above Bell County. Using the alias Jim W. Patterson, he took a job at the farm and cotton gin of John W. Sedberry, which was located about eight miles above Waco on the northeast side of the Brazos River, about two miles below the Chalk Bluff community and just west of present-day Lacy Lakeview.[3] The Sedberry family came to McLennan County from Tennessee in the early 1850s,[4] and John Sedberry was one of several men who formed a Confederate militia unit in the county at the outbreak of the war.[5]

It did not take much time for Longley's predilection for trouble to affect events around him. He became close friends with a young man named Robert Rushing. It was later alleged that on August 10, 1875, Longley and Rushing robbed James T. Duke of a pocketbook containing $25.[6] The 1870 McLennan County census shows Missouri-born Duke, thirty, and thirteen-year-old Edward Duke living with the household of East Waco teamster Joseph Perry and his wife.[7] Unfortunately, there are no contemporary accounts nor descriptive court papers to reveal what happened, and no indictment was brought until after Longley left the area. "Jim Patterson" continued to work at Sedberry's gin.

As November arrived, Longley allegedly took a shot at one Seth Robinson on the tenth of that month, and was later indicted for attempting to kill Robinson.[8] A few nights later, on November 13, after several days of rain, a frosty chill was in the air.[9] "Captain" Sedberry proposed a fox hunt and a number of men, including "Jim Patterson," set out late in the evening for a nearby area known as White Rock. Supplied with ample amounts of whiskey, the group soon abandoned its fox hunt and began racing their horses. By midnight (another account puts it at about 7 p.m.), as the whiskey took greater effect, several arguments broke out, followed by fights. According to Longley,

> There was a young man along by the name of George Thomas, who was considered the worst fighting man in the country. Thomas and myself had a few words, and the first thing I knew he snapped his pistol at the back of my head. I turned and leveled my pistol at him, but before I fired a friend of mine by the name of Bob Rushen [*sic*] caught his pistol, and then I would not shoot him. He then proposed a fist-fight. I handed my pistol to Capt. Sadbury [*sic*] and fought him [for a while until we quit and] neither of us was satisfied, and then I proposed to fight him next day, "ten steps with pistols," and he agreed to it. They then gave him his pistol and he started toward a grocery. He had not gone far before he came back and told me that he would not meet me at any certain place, but that we would settle it the first time we met. It was some time before Capt. Sadbury would give me my pistol, and I promised him that I would not follow him, but as soon as I got my pistol I started off after him. I came up with him at a store. He had awakened the store-keeper and was sitting on his horse at the door. I rode up to him and told him that I was ready now to settle that difficulty, and he said "alright." He had his pistol out, and as he turned round I shot him through the heart. His pistol fired as he fell. I fired three more shots in quick succession, each taking effect in his breast and bowels.[10]

According to the *Waco Daily Examiner*, after the fistfight between the two men, Thomas left the party and rode to the store of a man named Miller, but was followed by Longley, Rushing, and R.B. Dickens. After Thomas was shot, Longley returned to Sedberry's party and told them that he had killed the man. Miller came out of his store to examine Thomas' body and found three bullet holes, including one in the breast and one in the hip.[11] Longley's indictment subsequently alleged that Thomas was killed by a pistol shot in the back near his spine.[12] The 1870 McLennan County census shows a George Thomas, fifteen, from Louisiana, living in the household of the Reverend Thomas Lockett and attending school.[13]

Longley, apparently stealing a gelding belonging to a Daniel Lyons, fled the area.[14] In the aftermath of this murder, the true identity of "Jim Patterson" was determined, and Rushing and Dickens were arrested, although it was not initially believed that they were responsible for Thomas' death.[15] On November 18, 1875, the McLennan County grand jury indicted Longley for Thomas' murder, as well as the assault earlier on Seth Robinson. Among the listed witnesses to the murder were Rushing, Sedberry, and Dickens. Other witnesses were T. R. Gray, a man named Smith, Frank Rust, who was a thirty-one-year-old farmer from Germany, as well as W. A. Miller, a twenty-two-year old from Mississippi who boarded with Rust.[16] Another witness, Charles M. Dabney, from Tennessee, twenty-four, lived with his mother and sister on John Sedberry's farm.[17] Longley was again indicted on November 20, along with Bob Rushing, for the Duke robbery, and Longley was also indicted for the theft of Lyons' horse. Rushing was tried for the Duke robbery in 1876, but a jury found him not guilty.[18] In January 1880, Governor O. M. Roberts offered a $250 reward for Rushing's arrest for the Thomas murder. At the same time, Rushing was sought by the state of Arkansas for extradition to that state for some unknown offense.[19]

Longley said that after the shooting he immediately struck out for Bell County, for his father's farm, where he got a fresh horse.[20] Another account had Longley killing Thomas with one shot, then riding to

Sedberry's farm where he packed his clothes, told Mrs. Sedberry who he really was and what happened, then left McLennan County with another young man.[21] After leaving Bell County, Longley continued traveling southwest.

According to Longley, he stopped for a night at a Mexican ranch on the Medina River about eighteen miles west of San Antonio. There were four Mexican cowboys there, and during the night he heard one of them get up and go outside. After a few minutes Longley arose and went outside to check on his horse, only to find it missing. He waited for the Mexican to return and, about two hours before dawn, saw him return. Longley said that he slipped back into bed again, then later in the morning confronted him and demanded to know where the horse was located. When the Mexican refused to tell him, Longley said that he shot the man through the head and warned one of the others that he would die also if he did not retrieve his horse. Longley put his saddle on one of their ponies and rode with the Mexican to where his horse was located about seven miles away. Longley claimed that he then saddled his horse, shot the Mexican dead, then rode back to get the other two, but they were gone. As might be expected, there is no corroboration of this incident.[22] Longley turned his horse toward Uvalde County and a deadly rendezvous with Lou Shroyer.

William L. Shroyer's origins are obscure, although it is known that he was born at Northumberland, Pennsylvania, sometime around 1845 or 1846. During the Civil War he was a private in the 149th Pennsylvania Infantry Regiment, serving as a "substitute" in a three-year enlistment. He mustered out at Elmira, New York, on June 24, 1865.[23] When Shroyer came to Texas is unknown, but there is mention of a "Lew Soyer" in charge of a herd of cattle belonging to a J. D. Hoy, and the Comanche Indians taking the herd away from him in 1867 in what is now Val Verde County.[24] By 1870, he was raising stock in Lampasas County, although for some unknown reason he was listed in the census as William Sawyers.[25] This would be part of a general confusion as to his name, as he would be variously identified as Lon Sawyer or Sawyers, Shriers, and Scriers. He even signed his name as "Shroyier."

William "Lou" Shroyer. *Courtesy of Mrs. Opal Thomas, Belton, Texas.*

Shroyer, known as Lou, married Mary C. Slaughter, the daughter of Philip and Melvina Slaughter, who had founded the community of Slaughterville near present-day Kempner in Lampasas County.[26]

Shroyer's first child, William, Jr., was born in March 1871.[27] But the new father was not an easy person to get along with. Lou was remembered in Lampasas County for an episode on Christmas Day in 1871 when, waving a pistol, he rode his horse into a local saloon.[28] And the wildness reflected by that episode continued to bring him to the attention of Lampasas County authorities. In January 1872, likely for the saloon incident, Shroyer was charged with disturbance of the peace. He was found not guilty on January 12.[29] In May 1872 he was charged with theft of a horse, but he was also acquitted of that charge on January 16, 1873.[30]

On July 10, 1873, while Shroyer, Thomas Briscoe, and a black youngster, Lewis, were working Shroyer's cattle, a neighbor, William Owens, and his son, Russell, climbed over the rail fence separating their properties in order to retrieve a dog that had run onto Shroyer's land. Shroyer ran over to them with a drawn pistol and told Owens to get off his land. When Owens attempted to climb back over the fence, Shroyer struck at him with a piece of railing. Owens complained to the sheriff, and Shroyer was indicted on September 9, 1873, for aggravated assault.[31] However, just prior to that indictment, it was alleged that on September 1, Shroyer stole a pistol belonging to the State of Texas and in the possession of George Haynie.[32] Because of lawlessness in Lampasas County, Haynie had been selected in August 1872 to command a company of "minute men," which he did until February 1873,[33] and Shroyer was subsequently found guilty and fined fifty dollars.[34] On September 10, 1873, he pleaded guilty to an unnamed misdemeanor offense and was fined five dollars.[35] Shroyer went on trial in January 1874 for the Owens assault in Judge Ezekiel B. Turner's court and a jury found him guilty. Shroyer's attorneys appealed, and the appeal was granted in February by the Texas Supreme Court.[36]

Apparently Shroyer decided to take his family out of Lampasas County, an area smarting from violence on the part of the bloody Horrell brothers, who would be involved a few years later in a violent showdown with rancher Pink Higgins and his men. In fact, Shroyer was sued in June 1873 by Sarah Horrell for $100 claimed due on the sale of a wagon and team.[37] A second son, Stephen, was born in September 1872.[38] By late summer and early fall of 1875, the Shroyers settled first in the Frio Canyon and then in the Dry Frio Canyon in Uvalde County. The area was rugged and still occasionally beset by Indian raids, one such raid occurring in early August 1875, when four horses were stolen from a Mr. Thigpen. Thigpen, a man named Fulgham, and a third man went in pursuit, overtaking the Indian party and engaging the marauders in a gunfight. Two or three Indians were killed, and one horse was recovered, with only the unnamed man being wounded.[39]

As excursionists to the Dry Frio Canyon in August 1875 described it:

> This is a narrow valley, lying along the river of that name, some 20 or 25 miles in length and from one to three miles in width. The river sinks near the center of the valley, to rise again somewhere to the south. . . . The dry, rocky bed of the stream winds and twists about, and across the valley. . . . The lower part of this valley is one dense cedar brake.[40]

The Fulgham who helped pursue the Indians was likely William Eldridge Fulgham, who settled in the Dry Frio Canyon earlier in 1875 and filed for a land patent claiming 160 acres located on the west prong of the Frio River in the canyon, about twenty-one miles northwest of the town of Uvalde.[41] On September 29, 1875, Fulgham signed a deed transferring his interest in the 160 acres to William Shroyer for the sum of $235.[42] At the time Shroyer and his family were apparently living on the adjacent survey claimed by L. P. Heard, who had been visiting with his son in the canyon when the Indian raid took place in August. Sometime between October 1, 1875, and January 1, 1876, William Fulgham disappeared, and it was presumed that he had been killed, the rumor being that Shroyer had killed him. Fulgham's wife then abandoned the claim, but Shroyer and his family never moved onto that land.[43]

Lou Shroyer was not well thought of by his neighbors in the Dry Frio Canyon and stories about him made local conversation lively:

> Lew Sawyer [*sic*] just before coming to this community stopped at the ranch of an old bachelor (whose name has been forgotten) and stayed all night and was well treated. The next morning this old bachelor took him out and showed him some fine horses of which he was proud. The man was killed, the horses gone (which were never heard of again), and Sawyer was missing from the neighborhood.[44]
>
> Lew Sawyer was a man of mystery. . . . He was considered a desperate and dangerous man, a wonderful shot, with plenty of nerve and as quick as lightning; is supposed to have killed several men; was always on the watch, carried a six-shooter and winchester rifle and was ready for business in the fraction of a second. Sawyer was a petty thief; he attended the dances, but never went in the houses nor mixed with the people who were there. He always herded around alone, and when the time came for the dances to break, Sawyer was always found missing and so were a rifle, a six-shooter, a hat, a saddle, quirt or some other thing. A great many of these articles were stolen by Sawyer, but were never found. After he was killed, his wife told that he had hidden them in a cave somewhere nearby in the canyon where they still remain.[45]

Many years later, Canyon old-timers added several stories to Shroyer's legend. G. W. "Fuzzy" Van Pelt recalled that Shroyer first settled in the main Frio Canyon and "never mixed with anyone," and that when he came into the little settlement there on business, "he had little to say, but no one missed the fact that he wore his gun all the time." Van Pelt said that Shroyer once came to a blacksmith shop where the men in the neighborhood generally gathered to talk. A man named Skinner asked to see Shroyer's pistol. Without a word, Shroyer handed his pistol over, but then pulled a knife and pressed it against the hapless Skinner, telling him to take a good look at the pistol but that he should never ask anyone to hand over their weapon and leave themselves unprotected. Van Pelt said that Shroyer's peculiar behavior led folks to believe that he was on the dodge from the law.[46]

On another occasion, according to Van Pelt, the Uvalde County sheriff George Johnson once came to arrest Shroyer, accompanied by a deputy, George Hammer. Actually, Van Pelt was incorrect about the sheriff; it had to have been Pat Dolan, who served as sheriff from November 1872 until February 15, 1876, and was later also a noted Texas Ranger commander. Johnson did not become sheriff until after Dolan.[47] The two lawmen were invited inside, only to be met by Shroyer with a pistol pointed at them. He bade them to share dinner with his family, at gunpoint, then he let them leave, saying, "Goodbye, gentlemen. Come back and see me sometime." The lawmen reportedly did not return.[48]

Reminiscent of the theft story, Van Pelt also described a dance at the house of Bill Shores in the main Frio Canyon, where all of the men were required to "park their guns." Shroyer was supposed to have stealthily swiped most of the pistols, as well as a hat belonging to Van Pelt's brother, without anyone seeing him. He was suspected of the theft, but no one accused him because of his sinister reputation as an outlaw. Later, after Shroyer and his family moved to the Dry Frio Canyon, someone looking through Shroyer's old place found the stolen pistols under the floor.[49] As a matter of record, "L. Shroyer" was sued by the estate of J. P. Gibson on September 29, 1875, for failing to pay for stock that had been delivered to him.[50]

Bill Longley rode into Uvalde County, and, using the alias of Jim Webb, stayed at the home of Captain Theophilos Watkins in the Main Frio Canyon. Many would remember "Webb" as a "gentlemanly man, well liked, polite and [who] had the respect of the whole community."[51] Watkins, born in Kentucky in 1819, first came to Texas with his brother in 1845 and settled in the Sabinal Canyon. He went to California in 1848 as part of the gold rush, but returned to Texas. In 1860, he was the captain of a home guard at Fort Inge, Texas. Watkins was a partner in building an irrigation ditch bringing in water from the Frio River.[52] Longley said that he intended to find work in the area and stayed with Watkins for about two weeks. He became acquainted with Shroyer, whom he remembered as "Bill Scriers," recalling that "he had the name of being a very bad man, and every one in that country dreaded him."[53] Longley said that he was aware that the county sheriff had several warrants for Scriers. According to Longley, "I formed his acquaintance in a short time, and he seemed to want to get very intimate with me."[54]

When Shroyer moved over on the Dry Frio, near present-day Reagan Wells, Longley stayed with him about two weeks. Longley said that Shroyer was more than candid with him, telling "Webb" that he had killed the man who had sold him his ranch on the Dry Frio, who would be William Fulgham, although Longley recalled him as Elk Fulsom. Shroyer told him that a "quarter breed Indian" by the name of Jack Bolt helped him kill Fulgham. A Jack Bolt can be found in the 1860 Leon County census, and, in Mason County, a number of criminal cases were filed on James, Frank, and thirty-year-old Jacob "Jack" Bolt in 1883. One of Jack Bolt's brothers was legally hanged in Lincoln County, New Mexico, in 1886.[55]

Longley asserted that Shroyer somehow found out who he was and that there was a reward for him. Shroyer did carry a personal leather notebook to record stock brands and wrote "J. Web" on one page.[56] Shroyer supposedly wrote a letter to Jim Brown, asking him to come to Uvalde County and help arrest Longley, but Longley said that a boy carrying the letter to a post office lost it, and Longley happened to find it.[57]

Deciding to take action of his own, Longley said that he went before a justice of the peace in Uvalde, the county seat, and was deputized to arrest Shroyer. Longley said that he now learned that Scriers' name was "Lou Sawyer." Recruiting and deputizing a young man named William Hayes to go with him, Longley returned to the Dry Frio Canyon "determined to either take him, kill him or get killed."[58]

Longley and Hayes arrived at Shroyer's place on January 10, 1876, according to Longley. They told Shroyer that they had killed a "very nice beef" at a clearing about a mile from his place known as

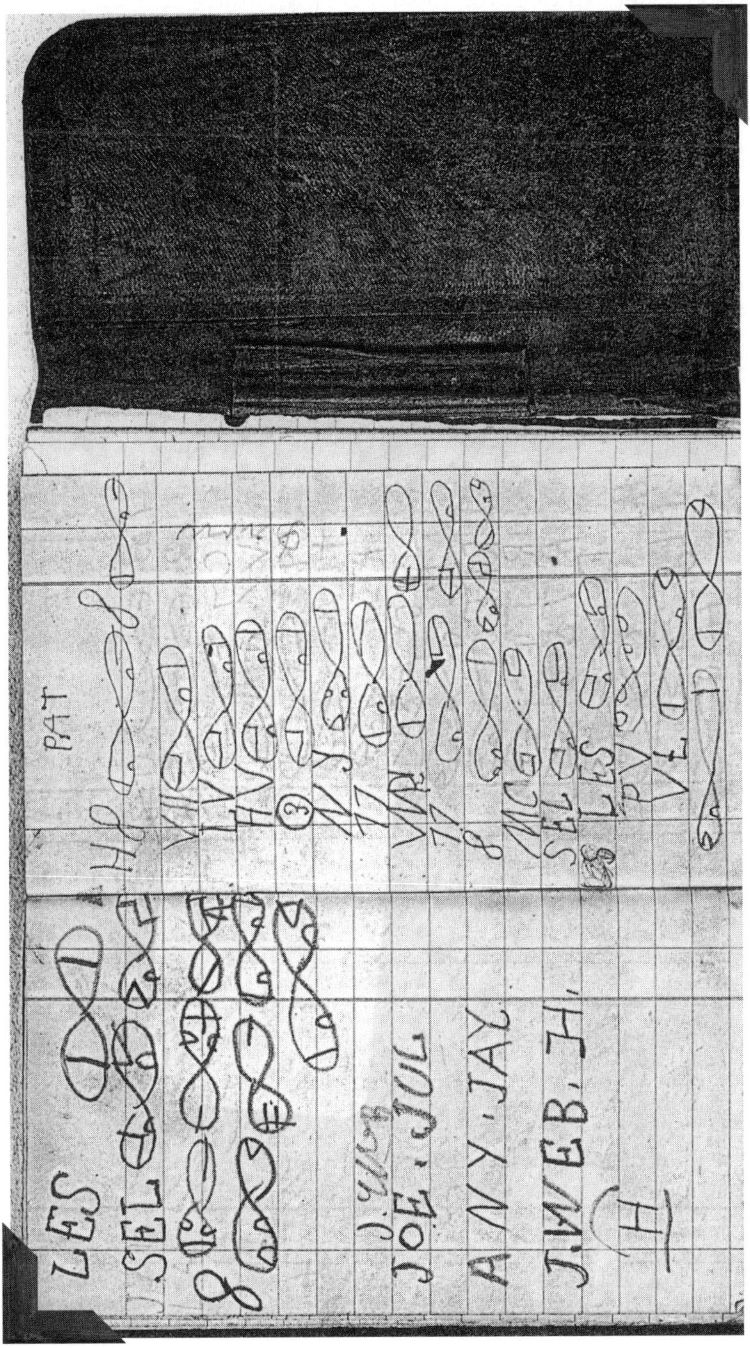

Two pages from Lou Shroyer's personal notebook. Longley used the alias "Jim Webb" when he met Shroyer. *Courtesy of Mrs. Opal Thomas, Belton, Texas.*

"Thompson's Flat" and wanted to share it with him. According to Van Pelt, Hayes was passed off as a horse thief who was in cahoots with Longley to bring in a bunch of horses in several weeks.[59] Shroyer asked the two to go with him and help him skin the cow, as he intended to bring the meat back home for his family and his pack of about twenty dogs. As Longley described it in another one of his letters to a newspaper, without embellishment by Fuller,

> He told a hired man to hitch up his wagon and come on, and Sawyer, Hayes and myself started on horseback. We had rode about a half mile from his house, and the three of us were riding along abreast, when I checked my horse, leveled my pistol on him, and told him that I would just take him to Uvalde, when he remarked that he would see me in hell first. As he drew his pistol he put spurs to his horse and yelled as loud as he could. I fired the first shot which took effect under his right shoulder. Sawyer fired the next, but missed. Hayes' horse was a very spirited one, and as shooting commenced he turned off into a cedar brake, and was of no use to me. We was riding through a cedar-brake, and there was a little glade in front of us about two hundred yards long. He ran right down the glade and I followed him closely, shooting at each other all the time. By the time we had reached the end of the glade we had emptied our pistols. I put four balls out of six in his back, one in the hind-tree of his saddle, and one in his horse which disabled him. He jumped off his horse, drew his carbine, fired at me and killed my horse. He was about ten steps from me, and it was about twenty steps to a very dense cedar brake. I drew another pistol (it was a cap and ball pistol) but the caps were wet and not a barrel would fire. Sawyer ran into the brush, while I turned and ran to the wagon. While going to the wagon I met Hayes coming. I told him to hurry on and take his trail from where he left his horse, as the blood was running down his back in streams. I then ran to the wagon and took a cow-boy rifle from the fellow that was driving, but he had

only three cartridges. I cut one of the horses out of the wagon and jumped on him. I rode across the cedar brake in order to cut him off from his house. I had not gone far before I rode right in among his dogs, and I knew he was not far off. While I was there looking for him he fired at me with his carbine, and came very near hitting me in the head. I dismounted, dropped to my knees, and fired at him, shooting his gunstock off at the small end. I then fired the other two cartridges I had at him and killed two of his dogs. The dogs were running all around him, and they ran in the way. I then drew my pistol which I had reloaded and commenced firing at him. I got behind a tree, as he continued firing at me, and I at him. I fired eight more shots at him with my pistol, and he fired six times at me. He then called to me and said he wanted to talk to me. I stopped firing and told him that I would hear anything he wished to say. He told me to come to him. I told him if he would throw his pistol away from him I would come to him, and he said he would do it. He was then laying on his side, and was not able to crawl. I then walked up to him with my pistol in my hand. When I got within a few feet of him he presented his pistol and said: "Oh G__ damn you, I've got you now!" and fired at my head, but missed me. I fired just as he did, (so near the same time that you could not have distinguished but one report) striking him just over the left eye and killing him instantly. My friend Hayes was coming up about that time, about forty yards off, and the ball struck him, passing through his thigh into his saddle. Sawyer had a pistol in his bosom that I did not know of, and when he threw his pistol away from him I thought that was the only one he had. I went to him and straightened him out. His gun-stock was shot in t[w]o, and broken into two pieces. One ball had struck the guard of his pistol and mashed it upon his finger. Sawyer had become so sick from the loss of blood that he could not walk, and stopped. He had pulled off his coat and belt, and laid out his cartridges in separate piles and never intended to surrender. I must say he was the bravest man I ever met.[60]

Longley said that the only damage inflicted by Shroyer's fourteen shots was on Longley's horse and the wound in Hayes' thigh. Of the eighteen shots fired by Longley, he said that thirteen were effective, killing Shroyer, his horse, and four dogs.[61] One account recalled by old-timers was that Longley took Shroyer's gloves and returned to Shroyer's house. He supposedly asked Mary Shroyer if Lou had returned home, and when she replied that he had not, Longley supposedly threw the gloves in the yard and said, "Here are his gloves; he never will return."[62]

Other accounts passed down by word of mouth in the area didn't make the killing of Lou Shroyer as daring as Longley painted it. One pioneer recalled that Longley and his companion waited until Shroyer was engrossed in dressing out the beef, then sneaked up behind him and shot him in the back.[63] In another version, Shroyer's dogs gave away his hiding place and a dialogue broke out as described by Longley. However, rather than walk up to Shroyer, Longley slipped up behind a tree and "shot out his brains." The man on the wagon found Shroyer's body and hauled it home. A coffin was fashioned from a water trough and Mary Shroyer buried her husband in the yard. According to this account, when she left the area about a year later, she exhumed the body and took it off to some unknown place.[64]

Fuzzy Van Pelt said that Longley and Hayes came to his father's house where they laughed about Shroyer's killing. The Van Pelts were not impressed that "Webb" was a very brave man.[65] No one in the area ever suspected Webb's true identity until they read Longley's account in newspapers in 1877 after he was captured.[66] For years afterward, the skeletons of a horse and several dogs could be seen in the cedar brake where Shroyer died.[67] By sheer coincidence, on the same day that Longley killed Shroyer, Texas Governor O. M. Roberts signed a land patent to L. P. Heard for the land adjacent to that of William Fulgham, which had been sold to Shroyer. Descendants today believe that the Heard family bought Shroyer's land from his widow for $50,[68] but Texas Land Office records show that the 160 acres bought by Shroyer were transferred by Mary Shroyer to Charles B. Jones.

Mary Shroyer McMasters and her sons. The son directly behind her is by James McMasters; the other three are Lou Shroyer's sons. *Courtesy of Mrs. Opal Thomas, Belton, Texas.*

In 1880, Jones filed an affidavit claiming that the document of transfer had been lost and that, since Mrs. Shroyer had left the country for some unknown place, and because he had lived on the property since February 1876, he was entitled to a deed to the land. Interestingly, Jones' affidavit swears that "some time in January 1876 Shroyers was killed by a special constable in attempting to arrest him."[69] Obviously, this lends a great deal of credence to the story told by Longley. In addition, the obvious relish with which Longley recited the details of this episode goes a long way in confirming that it indeed happened.

Longley later wrote his brother Jim from jail that he had fond memories of the Frio Canyon:

> Well that is good country and a good neighborhood. I know John Lakey [Leakey], but old George Lakey is my old friend and his son Tom Lakey, and the Pattersons. I killed Lon Sawyers [*sic*] 20 miles on the other side of the canyon on Dry Frio River. I went by the name of Jim Webb out there. Old George Lakey used to have the prettiest girl you ever saw. Her name was Fannie. I don't know whether she is married or not. I had a sweet heart in the canyon—her name was Miss Nannie Ringer—every body in that country was my friends. The morning I left there Tom Lakey drove 45 head of saddle horses in the pen and told me to take choice. He made me a present of the best horse he had. Mine got shot in the fight with Sawyers. If you go out there, don't have much to say about Sawyers. I expect his wife lives there. I don't know. [70]

Longley said that after Shroyer was killed, he went to John Leakey's place. Leakey was a Tennessee native who came to Texas in 1847, settling in Uvalde County in 1853. He was said to have built the first house in Frio Canyon, had fought Indians, and was a partner with Captain Watkins in building the irrigation ditch from the Frio River. Sometime during this period, he was involved in a difficulty of some sort and had to kill a man. In 1870, he was living on the Sabinal River as a grist miller and running a sawmill, later moving to Bandera County where he farmed.[71] The county seat of Real County, Leakey, was named for him. Getting the horse from Tom Leakey, Longley rode to Uvalde, where he returned the warrant and reported that Shroyer was dead.[72]

Mary Shroyer, pregnant with a third son, returned to Lampasas County with her two sons, William and Stephen, likely returning to her parents at Slaughterville. In July 1876, she gave birth to Louis, who would always be known as "A." Shroyer.[73] In November of that year, she applied to be named guardian of her children's estate.[74] On January 17, 1878, she married James O. McMaster, and a son, James, but called Mackey, was born to them in November.[75] But on July 16, 1878, while still pregnant, she was once again widowed when her husband of seven months was mysteriously shotgunned to death as he slept outdoors by a haystack, a brother-in-law sleeping only forty feet away.[76] She would never marry again and died in Lampasas County in 1926.[77]

Oblivious to all of this, Longley moved on.

Chapter 13

The Last of "Pea Time"

The murder case against Jim Longley, arrested in August 1875, was severed from that of his brother. His lawyer asked for a change of venue, likely because of hard feelings in Lee County about the murder of Wilson Anderson, and the court agreeably transferred venue of the case to the district court in Fayette County at La Grange. Jim was released on a high $5,000 bond, his father, Uncle Cale, and H. C. Jones acting as sureties.[1]

Still on the move, Bill said that he left Uvalde County about January 20, 1876, ten days after Shroyer was killed. Riding with three unidentified men, he rode east. Approaching Castroville, in Medina County west of San Antonio, the three men revealed that one of them had a brother in the jail there for killing a Mexican. Concluding that Longley was "a pretty solid sort of fellow, one who would do to tie to," they asked him if he would help them get him out. Longley said that they offered him $250 and that he reluctantly agreed, provided that he was in charge of the operation.

According to Longley, the three men stayed outside of Castroville, instructed by Longley to come into town in an hour and meet him at a certain "beer joint," which was about a hundred yards from the county jail. Longley rode into town and went into the place to have a few drinks. He had been there about thirty minutes, he said, when the Medina County sheriff came in. Valentin Vollmer, a native of Bavaria, had been a farmer until he was elected sheriff in December 1869. An election for the office was to be held in a few weeks on February 15, 1876. He was also the tax collector.[2] Longley invited the sheriff to join him and have a drink, which he did. While they sat at a table and talked, Longley's three companions rode into town, hitched their horses, and came into the beer joint.

Vollmer looked at Longley's clothes and surmised that he was from the Rio Grande region. Longley said that he told the officer that he was a special officer from Uvalde County and on the trail of an outlaw named Jack Bolt. According to Longley, he had returned to Uvalde, after killing Shroyer, to return the warrant and Sheriff Dolan had given him some additional warrants, including papers on Bolt, King Fisher, and John Wesley Hardin. He said that Vollmer reached over and took the papers out of Longley's breast pocket and noticed that one of the warrants was for a man who fit the description of a man he had in jail, the same man that Longley and his companions wanted to release. Longley asked the sheriff, he said, if it wouldn't be too much trouble to let him take a look at the prisoner out of curiosity. The sheriff agreed and they started for the jail.

They stepped outside into the dark, and Longley said that he unhitched his horse and led him as he and Vollmer walked to the jail, discussing where he could stable his horse for the night. At the jail they were greeted by the jailer, who gave the keys to the sheriff. Once inside the jail, Longley supposedly whipped out his pistol and ordered Vollmer to unbuckle his gun belt, which he did. Longley's three companions then entered the jail. The alarmed Vollmer asked the meaning of this, and Longley said that he told him it was just a little joke and that he would not be harmed as long as he remained quiet and followed instructions. Longley agreed not to turn out the other prisoners, and he had the sheriff change places in the cell with the man they wanted. The released prisoner strapped on the sheriff's pistol and rode off behind one of his three friends. The five men rode together until about midnight, then stopped in a thicket to rest for a few hours, having a good laugh. Longley said that he then rode on alone.[3] There is no corroboration of this incident in Medina County records. On February 15, perhaps because the escape did actually occur, Ferdinand Niggles was elected Medina County sheriff.[4]

Longley said that he rode on east, and near Lockhart in Caldwell County, encountered a rider toting a large pistol. The man, apparently a lawman, asked Longley for his authority to carry a pistol, and Longley said that he showed the man the warrants he was carrying. This appeared to satisfy the man, and Longley then asked him for his authority to carry a pistol. Since the man could provide no papers, Longley said that he took the man's pistol and rode on to the northeast through Bastrop County.[5] The only account of such an incident is Longley's.

The next day late in the evening, according to Longley, he rode into Lee County. Some six miles west of Evergreen, on Bluff Creek, Longley said that he stopped and took supper with a man named Meldas, an old German farmer whom he had known several years before. The 1880 Lee County census lists Andrew Meldas, a farmer from Saxony, who had a wife and eight children.[6] An Andreas Meldas, born in 1825, sailed to the United States from Germany on the *Ben Nevis*, settling on Bluff Creek and acquiring title to his land by virtue of the Texas Homestead Act.[7]

Meldas did not remember Longley, but, according to Longley, proceeded to have a lot to say about the notorious Bill Longley, claiming that if he were to see Longley, he would "know his hide in a tanyard." Longley said that he pretended to be from Williamson County and that he maliciously ordered three hundred bushels of corn from the farmer before continuing his journey.[8] And it was likely that Longley did not stick around in Lee County, because the local citizens were still upset about lawlessness. In the early morning hours of February 29, 1876, some forty armed men seized the county jail in Giddings and removed three prisoners. One of the prisoners, Pet Shaw, was taken about two hundred yards from the jail and riddled with bullets, his clothing catching fire from the close proximity of the weapons shooting into him. The other two, the brothers Jim Tom Irvin and Tom Irvin, were taken to the corner of a field a half mile from town belonging to a man named Carlyle and hanged about ten feet apart. The younger Irvin was about seventeen years old.[9]

In May a jury panel of thirty-six men was called in Fayette County for the trial of Jim Longley for the murder of Wilson Anderson.[10] Young Jim was represented by R. M. Russell, an attorney from Austin who used to practice in La Grange, and by E. W. Fay of Belton in Bell County, no doubt hired by Campbell Longley. Fay had gained some notoriety in Travis County by suing an Austin newspaper for libel on behalf of a local horse thief.[11] Robert Russell had been a clerk at the Texas General Land Office in Austin,[12] and Fay, who lived on Cross Street in Belton with his wife, Emma, practiced with Belton attorney A. M. Monteith.[13]

On May 26, 1876, Jim's trial commenced, and "the testimony and argument took up nearly the whole day, when finally the whole matter of law and testimony was submitted to the jury. After a few moments' consultation, they returned a verdict of 'not guilty.'"[14] Some sixty years later, Jim recalled that the trial came "clear without a witness before the finest looking jury and judge that ever sit on the bench." He described the aftermath of the trial:

> I must say that I never did get so many hugs and kisses, advice and tears from those elder mothers as I did there and a few pretty brunets about my age. Thos good womans prayers must have went up for me and help to save me. They all told me to go back to my little sweet mother and be good, and I promised I would, and I kept my promise. Four fifths of the spectators was women and young girls. I went back to my sweet mother and worked on the farm and helped my mother with her work with all my spare time, as she never had a girl at home.[15]

As a side note, lawyer Fay returned to his practice at Belton in Bell County, but was caught in a real-estate swindle and subsequently imprisoned.[16]

Bill Longley said that he did not remain in Lee County very long, but went to Arkansas where he visited with friends. He then returned to Texas, finding himself in tiny Delta County, just across the Sulphur River from Lamar County, from which the small county had been partially established in 1870. He said that he stayed at the house of Thomas P. Jack, a fifty-six-year-old farmer from Tennessee, who lived in the Ben Franklin community with his wife, Sarah, and their seven children.[17] Longley, with the help of Fuller's editing, said that he did not expect what happened next:

> I only intended to stay with him a day or so, and take a little rest, but fate willed it otherwise. It was there that I met the first girl I ever loved, and never on earth will I forget the feeling of my heart the moment I laid my eyes on her, and I will never be ashamed to acknowledge that I did love her with all my heart.
>
> It was on the 12th day of February 1876 that I met her. I introduced myself as William Black, of Missouri, and had lived in Texas about three years. We sat up late that night and I related many of my adventures, all of which the beautiful girl listened to with great interest. The family was composed of the old man Jack, his wife and two grown daughters—Jennie and Louvenia, the last named being the younger, and it was her with whom I fell madly in love.
>
> Louvenia was sweet sixteen, and of a religious family, but very lively. I was finally shown to a room to which I retired, but not a wink of sleep came to my eyes that night. I never felt such feelings on earth as now seemed to take possession of me. I lay and thought of all my past life, and never before did I realize my condition.
>
> That desperate revengeful disposition left me, and I thought I would give all the wealth of the world, if I had it to give, if I was

> only a plain, civil and pious young man. I did not know what to do. I thought I would get up an excuse so I could stop and rest for a day or two, and perhaps in that time I could make up my mind what I should do.[18]

An examination of the 1870 census for Thomas Jack's family shows that he had a daughter named Virginia, who was twenty-two in 1876. She had two younger sisters, Julia L. Jack and Rachel L. Jack, who were nineteen and fifteen respectively in 1876.[19] Fifteen-year-old Rachel Lavinia Jack, born on July 20, 1860, was one of eight children born to Thomas P. Jack and Sarah K. Pearce Jack, who married in Rhea County, Tennessee, in April 1844, and came to Texas prior to 1857.[20]

Longley said that he arose before daylight, took a small nail from the Jacks' mantelpiece, then went out to the stable and drove it into "the frog of one of my horse's feet." He then returned to bed. After breakfast, pretending to resume his journey, Longley found that his horse was too lame to travel, and Mr. Jack invited him to stay for a few more days, which, of course, the outlaw was willing to do. He said that he wrote a note to "Miss Louvenia," which she answered that day. When he had a chance to talk to her, he told her that he would like to stay in the community if he could get some work. She referred him to a preacher who lived about a mile away and who had been trying to find a sharecropper to bring in his crop and share half of what the renter made. Longley said that he leaped at the chance, seeing it as the best way to stay near his new love.[21]

Longley went to work for, and moved onto the farm of, William Roland Lay, a preacher and farmer born in October 1843, who lived with his wife and children, which included at least two sons, Willy, six, and Bobby, four.[22] Lay's origins are shrouded and little information on him can be found. Longley said that he received a rude awakening from his idyll when he discovered that he had a competitor for Miss Louvenia's affections, a young man named Foster. Likely this was Mark L. Foster, who turned seventeen on March 12, 1876, seven years younger than Longley.[23] Young Foster lived with his father, also named Mark, a Confederate veteran and farmer from South Carolina.[24] To make matters worse, according to Longley, Foster and Miss Louvenia had once been engaged to be married, but Jack and his wife were bitterly opposed to the union, and young Foster was a cousin to the Reverend Lay. Longley said that a sister of Mrs. Lay, who herself was a Foster, was determined to make trouble between him and the Jack girl, as well as with the entire Foster family. Longley had initially grown to like the Reverend Lay, but said that the man was now trying to add fuel to the flames, all the time professing great friendship for "Mr. Black."[25]

Despite this turn of events, Longley continued to work the farm of the Reverend Lay, starting a fairly good crop and keeping his eyes and ears open. An anger at the actions of the Lay and Foster families began to grow, but he said that he vowed to keep his temper and not be the first to start any trouble. Longley felt, however, that because he did and said nothing, the Fosters assumed he was afraid. To counter that, he found an opportunity one day to confront and curse a group of Fosters, telling them he stood ready to face them at anytime. He said that the Fosters then began carrying guns.

Even though Parson Lay and his wife treated him quite coldly, Longley said that he continued to work the fields, ignoring their every insult, such as leaving only table scraps for him when he came in for dinner. Longley said nothing, later claiming that "I did not intend to kill any of them if I could help it."[26] Finally, Thomas Jack ordered young Foster not to come around his house for any reason, although Longley said that he remained welcome.

About May 15, 1876, Longley said that as he once more prepared to toil in the fields, he found a note tied to his plow handles:

> Bill Black—Do you know the danger that is all around you? If you don't know it, then this is to tell you that if you do not get out of this country at once, your d__d hide will not hold shucks. Don't lose any time. Go at once.[27]

Longley was infuriated. Suspecting that whoever placed the note on the plow was probably watching him from somewhere in the brush, he said that he stood there and laughed out loud for a few minutes, then wrapped the note around a rock, tossed it in the air, and blew it into a thousand pieces with his six-shooter. Then he hitched his horse to the plow and resumed his work as if nothing had happened.

A day or so later, when he was visiting the love of his life, Longley's ego got the best of him and he told Miss Louvenia that his real name was not Black, but that she would find out his true identity in due time. They laughed together about the note on the plow; she had already heard about it. She suggested that he keep quiet about it and that the conflict would likely die once it was clear that he was not leaving. But Longley said that he found another note on the yard gate on May 18 (Longley said it was a Saturday, but it was a Thursday). He kept the note in his pocket. The next day being a Sunday, according to Longley, he was returning from White Rock Church when he found another note tied to the limb of a tree which contained many threats if he didn't leave. Longley said that the image of the sweet face of his love calmed his fury. He said that he examined the note closely and found that it was written on a part of a piece of paper that Parson Lay had borrowed from him the previous day, and which had been torn from a sheet of paper on which the lovelorn outlaw had written a poem. The two pieces fit exactly, he claimed. His anger now focused on Lay, Longley said that he packed his clothes, readied his two pistols, and prepared to fight.[28]

The next day when Longley confronted the preacher, Lay denied knowing anything about the notes, and Longley said that he cursed him. Longley suspected that Lay intended not to pay him for bringing in a crop and threatened to kill Lay if he didn't pay him for his work. He said that Lay paid him what he was owed on the spot. Longley then left and went north into Lamar County, where he went to work for a man named Lane for $15 per month, and his horse died while at Lane's.

Although Lay and Longley supposedly had an agreement to leave each other alone, the other Fosters remained upset, according to

Longley. The following Sunday, Longley went over to the White Rock church, then afterwards rode to the Jack place with Miss Louvenia. The two sat and talked on the gallery of the house. The barking of a dog in the yard alerted them to the presence of Mark Foster and others riding by, and young Foster shot the dog when it ran out to bark at them. Longley, wearing both of his pistols, said that he jumped into the saddle and chased down Foster. Catching the quarry, Longley said that he whipped him with his quirt, took his pistol away from him and hit him on the head several times with it, then broke Foster's pistol against a tree and let him go.

When Lay heard about the incident, according to Longley, he went to the county seat, Cooper, and swore out a complaint against Longley.[29] Actually complaints were made against "William Black" for false imprisonment, likely for detaining and assaulting Mark Foster, and against Thomas Jack for making threats.[30] Longley said that he was arrested at Lane's place on June 6, taken to Cooper before a justice of the peace who set a bond of $2,000, then placed in the Delta County jail.[31]

The sheriff of Delta County was James G. Hamilton, fifty-five, from Tennessee, who had been elected in November 1872.[32] His deputy was Nathaniel Corbet, sixty-three, a New York native, who had lived in the Ben Franklin community next to Thomas Jack, but moved to Hopkins County, then back to Delta County to live with his son, Henry.[33] Longley described the county jail as "a small dirty, plank affair, not fit for a rat, much less a human being."[34] When the Texas legislature created Delta County in 1870, Hamilton was given responsibility for building the jail for a cost of $700. It was an oak cabin, about fourteen feet square, with a ceiling about eight feet high. There were small barred windows on the north and south walls, and entrance was gained through a heavy oak door. There were supposed to be iron cages inside and an iron pipe to come up through the floor "for the convenience of the prisoners."[35] On May 29, 1876, Sheriff Hamilton and Deputy Corbet were ordered by the Commissioners Court to have the jail repaired "so as to keep securely prisoners confined now or may hereafter [be] confined therein."[36]

Longley said that he suffered the indignity of the filthy jail for six days. In the early morning hours of Tuesday, June 13, he burnt a hole through the bottom of the jail door and made his escape. A horse was tied up some two hundred yards from the jail, and Longley said that he took the horse and made tracks northwest to the Ben Franklin community:

> It was eight miles to the residence of Mr. Jack and day was breaking as I rode up to the front gate. In the distant field I heard the familiar cry of the whippoorwill, which once heard is never forgotten. Old man Jack had just gotten up and come out on the front gallery where he was sitting and putting on his shoes. I bade him good morning, went into the house, got his double barrel shotgun, went out, [and] mounted my horse. As I did I heard a scream at the house and I knew that Miss Louvenia, bless her dear heart, had just been told of my act of taking the gun. She had heard of my recent trouble and knew well enough now that worse trouble was close at hand.
>
> It was about eight miles to where the parson lived. I hitched my horse out of sight of the house, and walked up where I could see the house from the adjacent timber.
>
> The parson was in the cowpen milking. He had just come out to the pen and I noticed that his gun leaned against one of the gate posts of the cowpen. Evidently he was anticipating trouble. Presently he stooped over and went to milking one of the cows, and as he did so I walked into the cowpen and stood between him and the gun. He looked up and saw me and turned as white as a sheet. He seemed to know that his time had come and that he would get no mercy at my hands.
>
> When he saw me, I told him it was the last of "pea time" with him, and if he had anything to say he had better be at it. He said he hated to die and leave his wife and family. Then I asked him why he did not let me alone when I was at peace with him and all his kinfolks. To this he gave no answer and I dropped my gun to

> a level with his body and fired. The gun was heavily loaded with turkey shot. He fell backwards and I left him. I heard later that he died at one o'clock the same day.
>
> I then went on to the home of Mr. Lane, in Lamar County, where I had been at work, told him what I had done, got an extra pistol that I had left there, went to Red River Crossing and set out up through the Indian nation.[37]

It was subsequently reported that "Black" had been confined in jail for not being able to post an $800 bond for threatening to kill the Reverend Lay. After being shot, Lay identified his killer before dying that evening.[38] Basically, the version of the Lay killing as detailed by Longley was the same as that passed down in the Lay family.[39]

Revoking all prior bounties, Texas Governor Richard Coke announced a reward of $500 for "William Black alias William Longley." The outlaw was described as twenty-six–twenty-seven years old, spare build, six feet tall and slender, black hair and eyes, and a dark complexion.[40] In Delta County, "William Black" was indicted for murder, and the false imprisonment charge was dropped. Surprisingly, Nathaniel Corbet was also indicted for permitting Longley to escape, as was Constable William Kennedy, twenty-one.[41] On August 19, the Delta County commissioners approved payment of $32.93 for repair of the jail.[42]

Longley fled Delta County, avoiding his pursuers, and said he headed for the Indian Territory.

The grave marker of the Reverend William Roland Lay, Simmons Cemetery, Ben Franklin, Delta County, Texas. *Author's photo.*

Chapter 14

Plenty of Ammunition

After killing the Reverend Lay, Bill Longley left Delta County, but there is only his fanciful account of where he was for the next year, as provided in Fuller's heavily edited *Adventures of Bill Longley*.

According to Longley, on June 13, 1876, he rode north from Delta County and camped near the Red River as it grew dark. He hid off the main road, ate a cold meal that he had gotten at Mr. Lane's place, then slept on his saddle blanket. The next morning he took a ferry across the river and said that the ferryman told him of several parties who had crossed the night before into the Indian Territory looking for a man who had killed a preacher. Longley said that the ferryman looked at him with suspicion as Longley asked him questions, but Longley said that he learned that most members of the posse believed that the fugitive was still in Texas and that they planned to set up on roads leading into the Indian Territory and waylay Longley when he headed north.

Leaving the ferry, Longley said that he took to the river bottom, leaving the road, and headed northwest until he came to the Blue River, which would likely have been the Boggy River, and followed it, finally riding west and passing to the south of the town of Caddo, in present-day Bryan County, Oklahoma.

He said that he rode steadily northwest for nine days, eating an occasional rabbit that he shot and broiled. With distance between him and Delta County, Longley said that he felt more secure. Late in the evening of the ninth day, he encountered an Indian who could speak English, and they struck up a conversation. The Indian told him that he was in the Creek Nation, and, eyeing Longley's horse, proposed a horse swap, if Longley would throw in the double-barrel shotgun that he used to kill Lay and which was now empty after shooting rabbits along the way. Longley said that he still had his two pistols and agreed to the swap.[1] Longley put his saddle on the Indian's pony and they separated. According to him,

> My troubles were about to start. I had not gone but a few miles before I heard the gallop of a horse and on looking back I saw the Indian coming full tilt. He rode right up to me and said: "You d____ lying white man, your horse no good, me want my horse back, or me kill you." I refused to swap back. We got into a quarrel, and then he said he had killed three d____ white men and I would be the fourth and with this he sprang from his horse and made for me with a big knife in his hand. Then the fun started. I put one ball through his body and another through his head before he sprawled on the ground—too dead to kick. Under his blanket I found two Colt's improved cartridge pistols, and feeling that a dead Indian had no use for them I left the shotgun and horse with him, remounted and continued my journey.[2]

Longley said that he just then noticed three Indian women standing in the yard of a nearby cabin who had witnessed the shooting. The women began to scream loudly. He said that he rode quickly away, but as he topped a small hill, he found that he was at the edge of a large Indian village and that the cries of the women had excited the village. The three women trotted toward him, still screaming. Trying to keep his wits in the face of being outnumbered should the Indians pursue him, Longley said that he left the road and headed for some mountains about ten miles distant. Looking back, he saw a party of about twenty Indians a mile behind him in pursuit, so he checked his horse's gait to preserve some of the animal's strength in case the Indians got closer. He said that he reached the hills at dark, still with a comfortable lead over his pursuers, and once more turned to the northwest. Riding all night with one eye on the North Star and riding all the next day, he finally stopped the next night to rest himself and his horse.

Longley said he rode on in the morning, although his horse was quite stiff. Looking back, he saw dust, which could have meant cattle or Indians, and stopped to see what it was. The dust turned out to be the Indians still on his trail, and he said that they also had a bloodhound with them.

Longley rode on, he said, and soon came to a small cabin belonging to an Indian, but saw no one there, although a hobbled pony was grazing nearby. Longley saddled the Indian pony just as the bloodhound ran up and began baying at him. Longley said that he shot the dog, then mounted and rode off, and an Indian woman in the cabin began crying shrilly.

Riding hard, Longley said that he did not stop until late that evening when he came upon a herd of antelope, shot one, and was soon enjoying a broiled steak, his first meal in three days. After that, he prepared some venison, then rode on that same evening, and in only a mile or so, came upon what he later learned was a Seminole Indian village. Riding down into some timber at a nearby creek, Longley planned to steal a fresh horse that night. As he unsaddled his horse, he said that an Indian mounted on a splendid paint steed rode by a short distance away, but the distance was still too great to try to get the animal, so the Indian rode unawares into the village. Longley said that he slept until about midnight, saddled his horse, then rode down within a few hundred yards of the cabins in the village. Taking a bridle, he slipped up on foot into the sleeping village and spotted the paint horse tied to a gallery post and eating corn off a blanket spread on the gallery floor, two Indians sleeping nearby. With a cocked pistol in one hand, Longley said that he sneaked up to the horse, cut its rope, then silently led it away back to where his own horse was. He changed saddles, turned his old horse loose, and rode off.

Longley said that he traveled all night and all the next day, and in the late afternoon came to the Arkansas River, which runs across present-day northeast Oklahoma. This was country that he had been in before, he said, and gave him an opportunity to contemplate what had brought him to this point.[3]

> It was a lovely scene that spread out like a map before me. I crossed my legs as I sat on my horse, and became lost in thought. My whole life seemed to pass in review before me, and as usual I was a hunted man. Why was Fate thus cruel to me? Was I the arbiter of my own destiny? Why was it that I persisted in choosing for myself this hard and unsatisfactory life—this constant race from my kind, like some wild and hunted animal?[4]

These musings past, probably contributed by Fuller, Longley said that he figured that he was about forty miles west of Fort Wichita in the Indian Territories and nation. Enjoying a lovely vista across the river, including a valley covered with grazing buffalo, he rode down, killed a buffalo calf, and roasted a side of ribs. As he rested, smoking a pipe, he said that in his mind he could still hear Miss Louvenia's piercing scream when he left her house to kill Lay, "and it went to my heart like the thrust of a dagger."[5]

Suddenly his rest was disturbed, he said, by the appearance of thirteen Indians riding hell-bent for him, still on his trail. Longley leaped into the saddle and was off, leaving behind his hat and saddlebags, the Indians yelling and firing rifles at him. They rode within one hundred yards of him, and Longley said that he leaned low in his saddle, firing back at them. One of his shots killed an Indian's horse, which slowed them somewhat, and he dashed for the river about four miles away. Although his horse was fresh and he could easily outdistance them,

Longley said that his "blood was up and I wanted to show this bunch of red devils that they had better remained at home and let the man from Texas alone."[6]

He said that he fired four more shots without doing any damage, but one of the Indians was leading the others and coming uncomfortably close with his shots, so Longley made a special effort to nail him, and the Indian spilled from his saddle. The nearby buffalo, alarmed by the shooting and yelling, stampeded and ran in the same direction as the running gun battle, dust billowing and the ground shaking. Another Indian took the lead, cursing Longley in English and punctuating his epithets with gunfire. Longley drew another pistol and fired at him, but missed. Longley said that as the Indian rode within twenty feet of him, Longley's horse stepped in a prairie dog hole and fell to its knees. As the horse stood up again, the Indian rode up to him, but the Indian's pistol was empty, so he struck Longley on the head with it as his horse flew by. Longley said that he put a bullet into the back of the Indian's head, but this didn't cause the other Indians to check their pursuit.

The leader of the party exchanged horses with another Indian, who had the strongest horse, one that could most likely catch up with the fleeing white man on the paint.[7] As Longley described it,

> Then after me the leader came like a tornado. He ran right up on me. When he fired he would say, "Wake up, you ____ scoundrel, wake up." I started in to shooting at him and my first shot got him in the right shoulder, for I could see the blood running down his breast. The first shot he fired cut one of my bridle reins, the second passed through my hair, and the third hit me in the right side and broke one of my ribs. This shot knocked the breath out of me and I turned as blind as a bat, momentarily, but quickly recovered. My pistol fell from my hand, and I came near falling from my horse, and then he shot my horse and killed him dead, although I am sure he did not intend to kill the horse as that was what they were after, but intended to kill me first.

> My horse fell a fearfully hard fall, and in doing so fell on my right leg. The Indian ran by me and fired at my head while I was struggling to extricate myself. He did not know that I still had a pistol. He ran by me a few steps, then turned and came back, ready as he thought to show his companions what a brave fellow he was. As he came on I suddenly reached up, seized his bridle reins and shot him through the head. I sprang on the dead Indian's horse and with the shouting demons all around me still shooting at me I sped for the river which now seemed to be near.[8]

Longley said that he reached the river bottom, but could not ride his horse into the thick brush. He then cut the horse's throat and headed on foot through the undergrowth for the river. He said that he was bleeding badly and found a hiding place to stop and check his wound. Pulling off his clothes, he said that "the ball had glanced off when it struck the rib and the end of the broken rib was sticking out of the bullet hole."[9] He said that he tore up his "drawers" to bind his wound with, then tied his clothes on his head, buckled on his pistols, and began to swim the high river. When he got his legs entangled in some vines, he lost his clothes and had to struggle to keep from drowning. Reaching the other side naked with nothing but his pistols, he struck out again through the undergrowth, now aware of pesky mosquitoes plaguing him. Growing sick and vomiting every few minutes, he sat by a tree to rest as the sun went down. He said that he fainted, then later awoke in the darkness, dizzy and his head spinning. He tried to walk in the darkness, then sat down and gathered a bed of leaves in which to lie down and maybe die.

He dozed fitfully, suffering from a terrible thirst, and said that he dreamed of old Evergreen and the bubbling creeks that he had enjoyed as a boy. He mused once more about a life gone wrong as he contemplated what he felt was a "most terrible fate." But then he heard the call of a man not very far away, answered by another man, and he said that he realized that his pursuers were still hunting him, feeling their way carefully through the dark woods. Longley remained still and the voices disappeared. As Longley recalled, "I had made up my mind to sell out at a dear price if they found me, and I would have killed several perhaps and been killed by the others as the entire pack would have come to the scene of the noise made by the firing of a pistol."[10]

At daylight he found a stout limb to support him and started walking very slowly up the river bottom, looking for a house or a path or road that could lead him to help for his wound. He said that, at about two o'clock in the afternoon, he came upon a well-worn path and heard chickens nearby. Following the path, he came to a clear spring and thirstily gulped down some water, then bathed his wound. Figuring that someone would come to the spring, he said that he concealed himself, intent on killing any man who came, stealing his clothes, and moving on.

As sundown approached, he said that he saw a young Indian girl, about seventeen, and called to her. Frightened at first, she spoke good English, and after Longley explained his situation and wound to her, she told him that she was already aware of him as Indians hunting him had stopped by her father's house, and in fact several were still there at that moment resting from the hunt. She introduced herself, Longley said, as Mary, a "pleasant looking girl," who was the half-breed daughter of a Cherokee. Mary told the naked, wounded man that her father was going to help bury the dead Indians that Longley had left behind, as well as to look for him. She agreed to help him.[11] According to Longley,

> I told her that my life was in her hands and that she could have me killed or she could save me if she would.
>
> She cried and told me that she would die before she would tell anybody about me, and that she would do everything she could for me, and she hoped that I would not doubt her.[12]

Mary returned to her house with water from the spring, and a still-suspicious Longley said that he rolled some rocks together as a sort of barricade in case she revealed his presence. But she returned, he said, and brought him fried chicken and hot coffee, as well as some clothes. He removed himself to another hiding place further from the spring, and he talked with the Indian maiden about their lives. Longley said that he stayed there about nine days, and, before moving on, the fair Mary gave him some moccasins, four dollars, and some provisions that would last for a week. The Indians had finally given up looking for him. He said that he knew that Mary wanted to go with him, but he knew that she would be an encumbrance, but one which he would have given his life to protect had she gone with him. "I sure hated to tell her goodbye, but it had to be done and so one night I pressed her to my heart, left her standing by the spring and walked away, following directions which she had carefully laid out for me."[13]

About ten miles from the spring, he found a railroad, which he said he followed until he came to a nearby "Fort Barker." He apparently did not stay there long, as he said that he caught a freight train on the Missouri, Kansas and Texas Railway for Fort Gibson. That military post had been established as early as 1824 near the confluence of the Neosho or Grand River with the Arkansas River, between present-day Muskogee and Tahlequah, Oklahoma, and was an active army post at the time Longley said he was there.[14] Recalling that he had a friend who lived in Sebastian County, Arkansas, Longley said that he checked a map and took some six days to walk ninety miles to near Greenwood, southeast of Fort Smith. He said that his rib, though still sore, was healing nicely. Longley said that he stayed with his friend from July to October 1876, then, outfitted again with a "good horse, plenty of ammunition and new clothes," he set out for Evergreen in Texas.[15]

According to Longley, he apparently left Arkansas, rode across the Indian Territory, then crossed the Red River north of Denison. He described his visit:

> I came down through Denison, and as I had not had any whiskey in some time, I decided to stop and get a drink or two, something I should not have done by any means. I took too much

> and got drunk. I got loud and boisterous and the first thing I knew several officers were detailed to arrest me and place me in jail. I knew this would never do, and so I made it to my horse just in time to keep from being arrested, and as it was they chased me out of town, shooting at me several times as I went. I did not fire back, for fear I might kill one of them, and so they thought they were running an ordinary drunk out of their town.[16]

This account is reminiscent of the story told by brother Jim as to their wild visit to Van Alstyne in 1875, and it may, indeed, be Bill's version of the same episode, since he never wrote about the adventures he shared with his brother.

Longley said that he took the road to Bonham in Fannin County with the idea of returning to Delta County and visiting Miss Louvenia. About eight miles from Denison, he said that he encountered "Deputy Sheriff Bryant" bringing two prisoners, "Jim and Dick Saunders," to Denison. The two prisoners were tied on their horses, and the horses were tied together at the neck with the rope tied to Bryant's saddle horn. Longley said that he knew the brothers and winked at them. A conversation was struck with the deputy, and Longley said that he offered the lawman a drink from a bottle he had in his saddlebags. As the deputy took a long swallow, Longley said that he covered him with a pistol, ordered him to unbuckle his pistol and toss it down, along with the two pistols belonging to his prisoners, and not to make any suspicious move.

According to Longley, Bryant was determined to argue with him, and Jim Saunders warned the deputy that the stranger with the pistol was none other than Bill Longley and that he had better do as he was told or Longley would kill him. Bryant complied and Longley said that he had the now-chastened lawman ride off a little while he had him covered. Longley cut the rope binding his friends, handed them their pistols; then all four took another drink before Longley and the brothers rode off. Longley said that three wagons had driven up and watched the incident, and several men at a nearby house had also watched, but no one attempted to intervene. While no contemporary account or record that this incident occurred, or the identity of a Deputy Bryant, could be located, there is some evidence that it did happen. In June 1878, when it was reported that a Richard Sanders was being taken to the penitentiary by the Fayette County sheriff, he was identified as a "chum and bosom friend" of Bill Longley, and that "upon one occasion, and during the height of Longley's career, that enterprising brigand took Sanders away from the sheriff of Grayson County, in Blossom Prairie, Fannin County (actually Lamar County), and managed to get his friend for the time being safely out of the clutches of the law."[17] Another account in 1877 recalled that Jim and Dick Saunders "were released from a deputy sheriff" by Bill Longley.[18]

Actually Jim and Dick Sanders (not Saunders) were friends of Longley. As early as 1860, Alabama-born nine-year-old Dick and five-year-old Jim lived with their parents and six other siblings on a farm near Union Hill in what was then Washington County.[19] Another brother, Jack, was killed in March 1876 near Victoria when a Fayette County posse, pursuing him for horse theft, met resistance and returned fire.[20] Richard Sanders, Jr., was indicted in 1874 for theft of a gelding in Washington County, and Dick Sanders was indicted in Grayson County in October 1877 for theft of a mare. A Richard Sanders was also wanted in Lee County for rape and robbery.[21]

As the sun went down, the trio overtook two black men who were returning to a farm after selling some cotton. The air being chilly, the three men took leather gloves away from the black men and filled a quart bottle from whiskey that the unfortunate men had in their wagon; then the three rode on toward Bonham. After riding all night, they pulled up at Thomas Jack's house at Ben Franklin in Delta County about midnight and carried on a lively conversation until nearly dawn.

Longley said that Miss Louvenia told him that Sheriff Hamilton had searched for him at the Jack place after Lay was killed and seized a photograph of Longley that the outlaw had given her. Supposedly, this photograph was reproduced on wanted posters and sent throughout the area, the authorities having discovered his true identity. No such poster has been discovered. At daylight he bid her goodbye once more, and the three rode on to the south.[22] To avoid suspicion, Longley said that he tied Dick Sanders' hands to the horn of his saddle and his feet beneath the horse, somehow also acquiring a warrant for a "Bill Taylor," in the event that they were stopped by a lawman.

In this manner, according to Longley, the three rode south, finally reaching Milam County, where they stopped with a George Sanders and ate supper. George Sanders was an older brother and may have been the G. W. Sanders who was indicted in San Augustine County in 1874 for selling mortgaged property.[23] The three rode out that night and the next morning were overtaken by a Milam County deputy, Matt Shelton, who wanted to see their authority.[24] James "Matt" Shelton, born in 1814 in Tennessee, had farmed in Milam County with his wife, Martha, since the 1850's, raising 13 children.[25] According to Longley,

> I told him I was an officer—a deputy sheriff of Bell County, and was hunting a man who had stolen a horse. We had turned "Bill Taylor" loose, thinking we were safe at this distance in Texas. I asked Shelton if he was an officer and he said he was. He then asked me if I was going to Milano, a station on the railroad, not far from Rockdale. I told him I was. He said he would go with us, but I knew he would ask me for my papers when we got there, so I thought I would just take his pistol and quit the road. I did so and we left him standing in the road, a-foot as we took his horse which we told him we would turn loose, a mile down the road and we did so. The pistol I took from him was a nickel plated Smith and Wesson.[26]

This episode did occur, and was confirmed almost a year later when Shelton rode to Giddings to take Dick Sanders into custody and return him to Milam County.[27] In a November 1876 newspaper account, Shelton was returning to Milano from Cameron when he came upon three men armed with shotguns and pistols. As he passed them, they asked him about some horse thieves they said they were tracking. They then got the drop on him and ordered him off his horse. He was compelled to turn over twenty dollars and his six-shooter. The three men left with his horse, leaving it about a mile off. Several posses scoured the countryside, including the Brazos Ford, where they had been spotted late in the evening, but to no avail. Not suspecting that it was Longley, the authorities assumed that the men belonged to a local gang.[28]

Longley said that, after disarming Shelton, they rode into Lee County and spent a few days in the vicinity of Evergreen. Jim Sanders left them, and Longley and Dick Sanders rode north to the Longley farm, from where Dick rode on back to Denison to his wife. Longley said that he rested a few days, apparently welcome once more back in his parents' home, then prepared to ride to East Texas.[29] But Longley's presence in his old stomping grounds in Lee County didn't go unnoticed, as one Giddings newspaper reported:

> We have been creditably informed that Bill Longley and crowd, the notorious gang of outlaws, was seen in this county during the present week, they having stopped some three hours at a certain farmer's house (we learned the farmer's name, but have forgotten it). Look out, boys, "they are coming one hundred strong."[30]

Longley was headed for East Texas late in 1876, but he was now better known to lawmen around the state, and a keen lookout was being maintained. On March 10, 1877, Texas Adjutant General William Steele, who supervised the Frontier Battalion, instructed Sergeant Joseph S. Leverett at Blanco, Texas: "You will proceed to Kerr County and if Sanders & Longley can not be captured, proceed by the most direct route to Lampasas."[31] Ranger Captain John Sparks of Company C responded on March 20 that his men were unable to find the two.[32] Indeed, Longley was at the other end of the state and ready to leave it again.

Chapter 15

We Want Him

Bill Longley likely visited his parents in Bell County in the late fall and perhaps early winter of 1876, during which time Dick Sanders may have left him and returned home. It is also possible that in March 1877 Longley and Sanders might have been in Kerr County. From March 10 to March 20, a detachment of Texas Rangers from Company C, responding to some source of information, was sent into the county to look for them.[1] The Rangers returned empty-handed. No doubt concerned that the authorities would get wind of his whereabouts in his old haunts, Longley said that he went to East Texas, and he ultimately made his way into Nacogdoches County, across the Angelina River. An educated guess would place this trip in the spring of 1877.

For whatever reason, Longley decided that he would detour around the town of Nacogdoches, rather than ride through it. Fuller, who himself was a resident of Nacogdoches, and speaking again in third person, said that the outlaw had "heard something" about Nacogdoches Sheriff Milt Mast and his deputy, Bill Burrows, and did not want to get into "fresh trouble."[2] About four or five miles west of the town, Longley stopped at the farm of George Washington Clevenger, Jr., a twenty-six-year-old who lived with his wife, Missouri Caroline, and two daughters, Ida and Nora.[3] Clevenger had a brother who may have been living with him at the time, Joseph Phlemester Clevenger, who was shy of his twentieth birthday, and whom Fuller described as a "good-sized boy."[4]

Joe Clevenger remembered the tall visitor as "a talkative fellow, lively, a good story teller and [he] did not look in the least like a bad man."[5] The next morning Longley prepared to leave the Clevenger farm, bantering with George about a horse swap, which was made. According to Joe, the horse that his brother acquired from Longley was a swift one and won races in the neighborhood under the name "Bill Longley." Longley asked how to get to the road to Logansport, Louisiana, after going around Nacogdoches, and George had Joe guide him around the town.[6]

Once beyond Nacogdoches, Fuller said that Longley rode into Shelby County and stayed a few days with a man named "Welch" in the Buena Vista community, locally called "Bucksnort," just east of the present-day town of Timpson. The 1870 Shelby County census lists a William Welch, a farmer from Kentucky, who is likely the same as the William Welsh listed in the 1880 census, who worked at a sawmill.[7] In 1870 there was also an older William P. Welch in Shelby County, a farmer living near the younger Welch and likely related.[8]

Fuller said that Longley was an "expert violinist" and made a fiddle for his host out of white pine using a pocketknife. This violin reportedly remained in the possession of the family for many years.[9] Longley left the Welch place and rode east across the Sabine River into Logansport, Louisiana, where he rested for several hours.

After Longley was captured and convicted and the *Galveston Daily News* printed his "adventures" in September 1877, it was alleged that Longley had killed a black man near Logansport after he had visited the McIver family in Madison County in 1873–1874 (see chapter 10). There is some evidence that this event may have occurred, but logic would seem to indicate that it more likely happened in 1877, rather than three or four years earlier, and Longley got his timeline wrong, if it indeed happened. The editor of the *Mansfield Enterprise* in DeSoto Parish, Louisiana, who was editor of the *DeSoto Democrat* at the time of Longley's capture, told T. U. Taylor the following story:

> He [Longley] claims to have killed a negro near Logansport in this parish, and the story is probably correct as an incident similar to the one he described did occur as follows: A gentleman living near Mansfield left his horse hitched to a rack on our streets, and someone rode it off. He learned that a negro living near Logansport had ridden his horse away and he went down to recover his horse, and returned saying that a Texan had shot and killed the darkey. The story was accepted with a grin, the people thinking that the gentleman had killed the negro himself. However, Longley says he did it, and at this late date the truthfulness of our citizen's story is substantiated.[10]

According to Fuller, Longley left Logansport and headed for Shreveport through the village of Keatchie (pronounced *Kee-chy*). Keatchie was the home of a female college and had been a noted slave center prior to the Civil War.[11] Along the road, he encountered a man named Adams. It is likely that Adams was sixty-year-old T. R. Adams, a farmer in DeSoto Parish.[12] Adams' son-in-law, W. T. Gamble, operated a farm six miles northwest of Keatchie and needed some farmhands. Gamble asked his father-in-law, who was headed to Shreveport to pick up some supplies, to see if he could also pick up several farmhands for him. When Adams ran into Longley, he let him ride on his wagon, and Longley told him that his name was William T. Jackson, that he had worked out west at a cattle ranch, but that he had tired of that life and was coming east to find a good job on a farm. "Jackson" said that he had traveled quite a lot but was looking for a place where he could buy a home and settle down. Adams invited his new young friend to come home with him, and agreed to take him to Gamble's place to see about a job.[13]

W. T. Gamble was almost thirty years old when he met "Bill Jackson." Longley went to work for him the next day, the agreement being the same as that which Longley had with the Reverend Lay: Gamble would furnish the land, team, and supplies, "Jackson" would work the crop, and the two would split the proceeds.[14]

As "Bill Jackson" began his labors on the Gamble farm, he became acquainted with June Courtney, who had recently been elected constable in the area. Courtney, thirty-eight, was born in Alabama, and his wife, Cornelia, a Louisiana native, was a teacher. Together they were raising three children.[15] Courtney was described as being an "enthusiastic criminal officer" and as having made several important arrests. Courtney and his friends were ardent fox hunters, and soon "Bill Jackson" became an associate. Courtney struck up a friendship with the newcomer and even had "Jackson" assist him in making arrests, noticing that "Jackson" took great delight in doing so.[16]

As was the practice among law enforcement agencies, circulars regarding wanted criminals were distributed throughout all parts of the country. Constable Courtney also received circulars and apparently received one giving a description and offering a reward for the noted Texas mankiller, Bill Longley. The description closely fit that of "Bill Jackson," the young man working Mr. Gamble's farm. Perhaps the circular also had Longley's photograph on it. Courtney began to pay closer attention to "Jackson" during their activities together and finally concluded that "Jackson" had to be the wanted Longley. He contacted the sheriff of Nacogdoches County, Milton Mast, who had sent him the circular, about his suspicions.[17] Fuller said that Courtney was urged to contact Mast by W. B. Peyton, a twenty-four-year-old friend, the son of a prominent Keatchie merchant.[18]

Milton Mast was born in Nacogdoches County in 1834 to Jacob and Rebecca Mast, formerly of North Carolina, who settled in Texas in 1826, establishing a farm of 1,800-acres. Milton Mast did not receive much early schooling but learned how to manage a farm. In 1854 Mast engaged in an occasional expedition against marauding Indians and for a year was a member of a Ranger company led by Captain John

S. Walker, being involved in several skirmishes. In August 1861, after Texas entered the Confederacy, he enlisted in Company K, Eleventh Texas Volunteer Infantry Regiment, under Colonel and future Governor O. M. Roberts, and was named captain of the company. One account said that he refused promotion to stay "with his boys." He fought in battles at Pleasant Hill, Mansfield, and at Saline, Arkansas, where he sustained a serious wound to his hand and fractured a forearm. After a short furlough home to recuperate, he rejoined his regiment at Minden, Louisiana, where he stayed until the end of the war.

In October 1861, Mast married his cousin, Nancy A. "Nannie" Mast, and they ultimately had nine children, seven of whom were living when Longley was in the area. After the war, Mast returned to Nacogdoches County and farmed until his election as sheriff on December 2, 1873.[19]

Assisting Mast as his deputy was William Muckleroy "Bill" Burrows. Born in Tennessee in 1835, he was a resident of Nacogdoches County by 1848 and married Lydia E. Coats in 1856. During the Civil War he served with Company D, Seventeenth Texas Cavalry. In February 1868 he was indicted in Nacogdoches County for assault with intent to murder, but the case never came to trial. By 1877, he was living with his third wife and two children by his first marriage. He had two more children by his third wife.[20]

Upon hearing from Courtney about his suspicions, Sheriff Mast, on April 24, 1877, wrote a letter to the Lee County District Clerk, W. A. Knox, asking for more information concerning Longley, and specifically for any information as to rewards offered. On May 18, Knox sent his response:

> Dear Sir: Your esteemed favor of April 24th was received yesterday. Allow me to thank you for your interest in the arrest of criminals. Longley is today the worst man in Texas—He has committed many murders in this vicinity— even murdered a woman. He is about 6 feet high, weighs 150—tolerably spare built, black hair, eyes and whiskers, slightly stooped in shoulders. I am told

by those who know him that he can be recognized in a crowd of 100 men by the keenness and blackness of his eyes. There are several large rewards offered for him by citizens, one from this county for $250. He has many assumed names. You will have to take the advantage of him—he will fight and is a good shot. Please keep me posted—we want him. Our sheriff followed him once to the La. line. Thanking you and tendering you all official courtesy that I may be able,

I am very Resp'ct'lly yours,
W. A. Knox[21]

After receiving the response, Mast and Courtney consulted with each other to come up with a plan for Longley's capture. On May 28, District Clerk Knox caused a capias warrant to be issued to any sheriff or constable in Texas to arrest "William Longley, alias Bill Black, alias Chadwick" and deliver him to Lee County, and this was received by Mast on June 2, likely by telegraph.[22] Courtney had observed the fugitive, and informed Mast that "Jackson" always carried his six-shooter, sometimes hanging it on his mule as he plowed. But he also noticed that sometimes, when hoeing, Longley left his pistol in the house.

Mast and Courtney determined to try to capture Longley, and just after the first of June 1877, Mast and Deputy Bill Burrows rode to Keatchie and met with Courtney. On June 6, prior to going to Gamble's farm, the constable told them that Longley was hoeing cotton with Walter Burgess, nineteen,[23] and that Mr. Gamble was not home at that time. They would have to take a chance that he was not armed. Taking a circuitous route, the two Texas lawmen positioned themselves on the gallery of Gamble's house while Courtney went to the field to ask Longley to help him arrest a "bad negro," telling him that he had two other men to help them. As Courtney and Longley approached Gamble's house and Longley spotted Mast and Burrows, he stopped and asked Courtney who they were. When Courtney responded that they were part of their posse, Longley was reassured and opened the front gate. At that point Mast and Burrows drew down on the fugitive, and Courtney shoved a six-shooter against his back. And the Texas badman was not armed.

Longley was enraged and cursed Courtney for his trick, telling the lawmen that if he had had his pistol, he could have killed them all. They quickly handcuffed him, placed him in a wagon, and headed for Texas, some fourteen miles away.[24]

There are other accounts of the arrest. One account had him renting land from the DeSoto Parish sheriff, living with the sheriff, and even falling in love with and becoming engaged to the sheriff's daughter, who told her father when the fugitive foolishly told her who he really was.[25] But Parish Sheriff W.P. Sample played no part in the capture, and he never had any children.[26] In another account, when Longley realized that he had been taken prisoner, he was supposed to have gracefully surrendered, telling his captors, "Gentlemen, I know what you want; you are after William Lungley [*sic*]; I am the man," and inviting them to attend his execution.[27] And in even another account, Longley was supposed to have made various excuses to go inside the house, but Mast would not permit it, and Bill said, "I would have played you a lively tune if you had."[28]

Mast and Burrows did not waste time with extradition proceedings; their prisoner was too dangerous and elusive. They hustled their prisoner across the state line by wagon to Henderson, Texas, in Rusk County, some sixty miles west of Keatchie. They spent the night there, and Mast told a reporter for the *Henderson Times* that different counties had offered a total of $1,050 for the man, and he quoted Longley as having claimed that he had killed thirty-two men.[29] They took the I&GN train to Palestine, then transferred to the Houston & Texas Central to Houston, from where the prisoner was taken to Giddings in Lee County and placed in the county jail on June 9, apparently greeted by a large crowd.[30] Sometime prior to turning their prisoner over, Mast and Burrows posed for a photograph with their tall, lanky, manacled prisoner standing between them, pistols held at the ready by their sides.

In June, 1877, a manacled Bill Longley is flanked by Nacogdoches County Deputy Sheriff Bill Burrows (left) and Sheriff Milton Mast (right). *By permission of the East Texas Research Center, R .W. Steen Library, Stephen F. Austin State University, Nacogdoches, Texas.*

Mast returned the warrant to District Clerk Knox, claiming a fee of $1.00 for arresting Longley, $5.00 for mileage going to make the arrest, $25.00 for mileage conveying the prisoner, and $37.50 for railroad expenses, a total of $68.50.[31]

Having been successful with Longley's capture, Courtney didn't rest on his laurels. The following month he became suspicious of a man named Collins and learned he was wanted for an October 1876 murder in Tarrant County, Texas. Courtney arrested the fugitive and returned him to Texas for a $400 reward.[32]

But now it began. With Longley at last in a cell, his boast of killing thirty-two men was carried statewide. Now came the stories of the killing of Rector, of McClelland, of Quartermaster Gregory, and of all the others. The *Brenham Banner* contended that the claim was "probably doubtful" and accused Longley of committing depredations with various local gangs.[33] In Waco, a dubious writer stated: "We are not inclined to believe this number really as great as stated by Longley, who seems to glory in and boast of his bloody deeds, but there can be no doubt that a great many men have received their death from this brutal fiend, who seems imbued with no other feeling than a desire to murder."[34] Longley now began writing a series of letters, beginning on June 11, to the *Giddings Tribune*, detailing his claimed exploits. Some of these accounts were picked up and printed by a few newspapers around the state.

But Longley was careful to distinguish between his exploits and those of any common criminal. As one newspaper summarized his claims:

> Bill seems to be in good spirits and tells of all the men he has killed, how they groaned, and what they said, etc., with as much pleasure as an old hunter would of the luck he'd had in killing a fine lot of game. He said, as we have heard from different parties, that he has killed thirty-two white men, to say nothing of negroes and mexicans. He does not seem to care as to being charged with having killed different parties, but don't like the

> idea of being called a horse thief, and says he never stole a horse in his life; that he would occasionally kill a fellow and take his money, but he wouldn't steal a horse.[35]

The *Giddings Tribune* of June 22 printed a two-column letter by Longley, claiming that while he may be a murderer, he had never ridden with local horse and cattle thieves and that "no man can say he ever stole anything in this country," nor kept company with local thieves. Longley also claimed that unknown persons had forged his name to various threatening letters that had turned up in the area.[36]

Longley was now in the custody of Sheriff James Madison Brown, the same Jim Brown with whom he had been friends and who had bought his parents' homestead at Evergreen. Brown was elected sheriff of Lee County on February 15, 1876,[37] and on April 29, 1876, was shot off his horse by a shotgun blast directed at him by two concealed men near his farm.[38] In a different episode, Brown shot to death Giddings City Marshal Hugh McKeown on May 4, 1877, the result of a long-standing feud, and was out of jail on bond at the time of Longley's capture.[39] McKeown, incidentally, was a brother of Johnson McKeown, Longley's boyhood cohort in the Green Evans killing.[40]

Longley quickly took over operation of the jail, at least as far as the inmates were concerned. In between composing his memoirs for the *Giddings Tribune*, he presided over an official greeting for Jeff Arnold. Arnold, a black man, was arrested for the murder of Henry Chapin, a white man, at Lexington, north of Evergreen. Another account said that Arnold killed his nephew.[41] When Arnold was placed in the Lee County jail, he was "tried" by the other prisoners before "Judge" Longley, found guilty, and sentenced to death. As a rope was fashioned, the terrified black man was given time to pray, then hanged in the jail. However, the rope was tied so as to slip, and the condemned man tumbled to the floor amidst laughter. Then the man's clothes were taken from him to be burnt

Lee County, Texas, Sheriff James Madison Brown. *Courtesy of Chuck Parsons, Luling, Texas.*

so that smoke would drive out the mosquitoes plaguing the jail. Longley promised Jeff that the next man placed in jail would be stripped and the clothes given to Jeff. There is also some indication that Arnold may have been administered twenty-five lashes as an "initiation."[42]

A rusting iron cage in Lexington, Texas, is purported to be the one in which Bill Longley was held in Giddings. *Author's photo.*

On June 21, as soon as he returned to Nacogdoches, Mast wrote W. A. Knox with an inquiry as to payment of fees and rewards. Knox responded:

> Dear Sir: Yours of the 21st received. I attached the account to the capias and Sheriff Brown will give it his personal attention when he makes out his fee. Did you not get the reward from this county? If not let me know and the reason why. The $500 received I suppose was from Delta county. You should correspond with Capt. Gadberry [*sic*], of McLennan county. Bill says there was a large reward offered for him by the citizens of that county. Bill is lively; talks freely; thinks you and your deputy are good men; has taken quite (?) a liking to me. He is well ironed and well guarded; he will fight for a continuance. He is a regular correspondent for the Giddings Tribune. . . . Bill wants me to

intercede with the governor in his behalf if he is sentenced; says he will catch every thief in Texas, but I prefer to have him hung; he deserves it, and should he get out he might take [illegible] fit to you, let me know. Our entire community are indebted to you, and all will join to assist you.

Very truly, your friend
W. A. Knox

P.S. Bill says if he should get out, that the man who reported on him will "smell h_ll," all send regards to you and deputy W. H. Burrows. W. A. K.[43]

Early in July a reporter for the *Galveston Daily News* visited Longley and gave his impressions of that meeting:

Your reporter visited the noted desperado, Bill Longley, in the Giddings jail. The jail is a good one of the iron cage kind, is kept clean and tidy by the sheriff, who watches William like a hawk. Longley is a tall, well made young man of 20 years of age, black hair and eyes, of very pleasing address, has not a repulsive feature in his face. His eyes are sharp but not savage. He has no hesitation in speech, but laughs and talks freely with all. The listener would not, if ignorant of his history, dream that he was talking with perhaps the most desperate and bravest man in the west.

He has not traveled about like Wesley Hardin and King Fisher with a crowd of murdering followers, but has usually operated on his own individual hook and responsibility, asserting his rights to liberty and freedom under Magna Charta through the prowess of his own right arm. He divides honors with none. His weapons are pistols, which he uses with perfection only to be attained after years of practice. Yet he is not

> so particularly wedded to them as to not upon occasion resort to the shot-gun. He acknowledged the efficiency of the latter weapon when he practiced successfully with it upon the person of a preacher who had offended him, but Colt's repeaters have been his favorites.[44]

The reporter noted Longley had already sawed his iron manacles off once and came near escaping, but the jailer let interested spectators come in to view him, though they were not allowed to stay for very long.

No doubt the security of his prisoner was uppermost in Sheriff Brown's mind. The area in and around Lee County was experiencing widespread violence in the form of vigilante lawlessness. On June 27 in Bastrop County, near the town of McDade, a group of fifteen masked men took four young men out of a community dance and hanged them to one limb for alleged horse theft.[45] This led a correspondent in Giddings for the *Galveston Daily News* to discuss the widespread stock theft occurring in the county without any arrests and the fact that local citizens had been engaged in "pursuing extraordinary means." It was estimated that about fourteen persons had been hung or shot in the last several years by vigilantes in Lee County. The temper of the citizenry was one of exasperation, and there was even a threat that if Longley obtained a continuance in his court case, he would be removed forcibly from the jail and lynched.

> The people of the county have been sorely tried by the depredations of thieves and murderers, and if anywhere lynch law is justifiable it has been here, and if any case I have ever heard of could be singled out as one of greater enormity of turpitude than Longley's, it does not occur to me now, and it may be that in the absence of proof in the particular case he is now charged with in this county he may escape punishment and lynch law be provoked. But until the court fails the mob should desist.[46]

As the exploits of Bill Longley continued to be played out in the Texas press, there was some concern about the effect that such boastful approach to murder would have on young boys. As the *Brenham Banner* editorialized,

> No good purpose can be subserved by the publication of these adventures or more properly speaking yarns. As already stated they are read with avidity by the young and are calculated to exert a baneful influence. If published in book form the circulation would be immense and the harm done would be in proportion. Although Longley always puts himself in the position of being the aggrieved party, there is much genuine cowardice displayed in many of his shooting scrapes. To use a familiar expression he has always managed to place himself in a position to have "the drop."[47]

The *Dallas Daily Herald* echoed those comments: "We have never seen a loud-talking, blustering, abusive bully yet, who was not at heart an arrant coward, and who would not quail before the immediate prospect of death. Bill may 'die game' when the time comes, but we doubt it."[48]

McLennan County authorities issued a capias warrant for "J. W. Longley's" arrest and return to Waco to stand trial for the assault on Seth Robinson, but Jim Brown returned the warrant, noting on it: "I have confined in jail one W. P. Longley charged with murder in Lee County."[49] McLennan County would have to wait its turn, if it ever got one.

Chapter 16

The Most Successful Outlaw

While he sat in the Lee County jail awaiting trial, Longley continued his letter writing. Ink, pen, and paper were provided by Sheriff Brown, and he was allowed to write to anyone he wished, provided that Brown saw the letters. He wrote his father, Campbell, telling him not to employ any counsel for him, that the state would be bound to appoint one for him because it was a death penalty case. According to Brown, Longley wrote his father that he only wanted a lawyer to postpone his case for six months, and that if he could not escape in that time, he deserved to be hanged.[1]

Longley's murder trial was initially set for August 24, 1877, and Samuel R. Kenada was his attorney, perhaps appointed by the court because this was a capital case that could result in the death penalty upon conviction, although Longley later claimed that he was hired for fifty dollars. Kenada, born in Alabama around 1839, came to Texas and settled in the Evergreen community where he was both a merchant and a farmer.[2] He and his family moved to Burton, about halfway between Giddings and Brenham, where he studied for the law. In March 1876, he underwent a thorough examination in the law by prominent attorneys Seth Shepard, C. R. Breedlove, Dan McIntyre, and J. T. Swearingen, and was admitted to the practice of law.[3] Kenada advertised that he could represent clients in district, county, and justice courts, and that he gave "prompt attention to the collection of claims."[4] However, Longley could not have taken much assurance from the fact that he had an inexperienced lawyer who was likely handling his first capital murder case.

One of Kenada's first subpoenas was for William Hayes in Uvalde County to come and testify on Longley's behalf.[5] Hayes had been Longley's deputy at Uvalde when Lou Shroyer was killed. The writ of attachment was filed with District Clerk Knox on June 25 and returned on June 30 when the Uvalde County sheriff, George S. Johnson, could not locate Hayes. Sheriff Johnson wrote: "There is no man in this County by the name of William Hays that I can find or ever heard of[.] [W]hen the man Sawyers or <u>Shrier</u> was killed in Frio <u>Canon</u> there was a man went by the name of Hays with the party that killed him. I have never heard of him since and satisfied he is not in this part of the County."[6]

By the end of July, Longley completed his "memoirs" for the *Giddings Tribune*, but he had yet to resign himself to being tried, convicted, and executed. Late in July, a man named Lott was caught throwing a file through the jail window.[7] Sheriff Brown promptly served notice through the *Giddings Tribune* that "hereafter no one will be allowed to visit Bill Longley in the jail." Brown assured the community that Longley would be "heavily and securely ironed, and guards will be perpetually on watch."[8] He admonished that "if the good people of the county do their duty in rendering him necessary assistance, there will be no danger of Longley being released."[9]

Newspapers around the state freely expressed their opinions about Bill Longley and his attempts at exploiting his own career in crime. The *Galveston Daily News* said "There is no accounting for taste even in the most serious affairs" and suggested that in addition to Longley's being hanged, "It may save the county future expense if a few of his confederates would attempt a rescue and are shot in the meantime."[10] From Dallas, "Bill Longley promises to rival Scott, Bulwer, Trollope or any other of the prolific novel-wrights who have ever played a vivid fancy at the stomach."[11] And the *Bonham News* seconded the idea that Longley's letters were "dangerous literature, and ought not to be placed before the youth of Texas," urging the *Giddings Tribune* to "Give more home news and less of Longley, and your paper will be a better one than it is."[12]

In Delta County the District Court ordered Sheriff Hamilton to retrieve Longley from Lee County to stand trial for the murder of William Lay,[13] but Lee County had first claim on the outlaw. The East Texas area citizens would have rejoiced "to see him and hear his account more definitely of the murder of the preacher . . . that he speaks so complacently about in one of his published letters."[14] Longley was not the only prominent badman in custody either. The notorious King Fisher was in custody in Castroville, and the local newspaper there carried Fisher's complaint that the citizens did not provide prisoners in jail with fruit, current newspapers, and magazines "as well regulated communities do." The newspaper dryly responded that "The letter is unique in its way, and about as original as those of Bill Longley."[15]

On August 23, 1877, in Pensacola, Florida, John Wesley Hardin, the most wanted gunman in Texas, was finally brought to bay by Texas Ranger Lieutenant John Armstrong and Ranger Jack Duncan, formerly a Dallas policeman, with the help of the local sheriff, William Hutchinson, and others.[16] Hardin, returned to Texas and placed in the Austin jail, had been far more celebrated in Texas newspapers than Longley, and the two were to become rivals in disdain for the exploits of the other. Reportedly, Hardin was credited with killing but twenty-seven men; perhaps this explains why Longley claimed thirty-two.

In the meantime, an old friend, Dick Sanders, was arrested and returned in August to the Giddings jail. He and Longley immediately got into some sort of argument and, "after a war of words they had a war of fists." Longley came out the winner.[17]

A trial date in Longley's case was reset for Monday, September 3, 1877, and Jim Brown was ordered to secure a special venire panel of thirty-six men from which a jury could be selected.[18]

District Judge Ezekiel B. Turner. *Archives Division, Texas State Library, Austin.*

The district judge presiding over the trial was Ezekiel B. Turner, the same judge who presided over the trial of Lou Shroyer in Lampasas County a few years earlier. A native of Putney, Vermont, born in 1825, Judge Turner studied law in Michigan with his brother and in 1848 became a lawyer in that state, where he was also a justice of the peace and a prosecutor. In 1853 he moved his family to Williamson County, Texas, and practiced law until the outbreak of the Civil War. Being from a Union background, he opposed secession and took no part in the war, an unpopular stance. However, after the war, in 1866, as a Republican he was appointed the U.S. attorney for the Western District of Texas, but he resigned in order to serve as attorney general in the provisional Texas government. In 1871 he was appointed the Thirty-second Judicial District judge in Lampasas and in 1876, running as an independent, was elected judge of the Sixteenth Judicial District of the large Travis County district. Turner had not been everyone's choice, at least in Washington County, where he was criticized for running away from Texas during the war, and for making a speech at Georgetown after the war in which he was supposed to have said that "Jeff Davis, and every man who had carried a musket in the war should be taken out and hung to the nearest post oak."[19]

In anticipation of the security problems surrounding Longley's trial, Jim Brown swore in additional deputies on August 27.[20] Virgil P. Wooley, a longtime Evergreen farmer, was born in Alabama around 1837 but settled in Texas by the start of the Civil War. At one time Bill Longley had worked for Wooley on his farm.[21] One of Wooley's seven children, Miley, asserted many years later that Longley saved his father's life once "by warning off at a circus the brother of a man intent on killing Virgil because he had booted his brother out of the courthouse during a factional dispute."[22] Another deputy, William J. McClellan, was the son of a Lee County pioneer and was born about 1858.[23] The other deputies were R. E. Harris, a thirty-three-year-old Evergreen farmer from Mississippi, who later became the Lee County Surveyor;[24] O. Bixby; S. Atchison; forty-nine-year-old William M. Davidson;[25] and twenty-eight-year-old William M. Brown from Missouri, a single farmer born April 13, 1849, who maintained a farm for his mother and six other relatives.[26] William Brown would succeed Jim Brown as sheriff of Lee County in 1884.[27]

Prosecuting Longley for the state was Seth Shepard, assisted by his law partners, C. C. Garrett and N. A. Rector.[28] Shepard was one of the attorneys who had approved defense attorney Kenada's admission to the Texas bar almost a year-and-a-half earlier. Born in Brenham in Washington County on April 23, 1847, Shepard was the son of

Prosecutor Seth Shepard. *By permission of the Dolph Briscoe Center for American History, University of Texas at Austin.*

lawyer and former Texas senator Chauncey Shepard. His uncle, James Shepard, had been a member of the Texas legislature prior to the war, and served as a judge prior to the military occupation. As a seventeen-year-old, Shepard enlisted in Company F, Fifth Texas Mounted Battalion, in the Confederate army, but was never in a major skirmish and was discharged as a private in June 1865. In 1868, he received a law degree from what is now Washington and Lee University, then set up his law practice in Washington County at Brenham. Although he would be defeated in a race for the Texas Senate by a black candidate, Matt Gaines, who was later prosecuted for bigamy, Shepard did ultimately serve as a state senator. He lost three successive primary races as a Democrat for U.S. Congress and was defeated in a close race for Congress in 1880.[29]

Shepard was an excellent choice to carry the state's case against Longley. When Shepard died in 1917, his career after 1881 as a lawyer in Galveston and Dallas, his 1893 appointment as an associate justice of the Court of Appeals for the District of Columbia, and finally his lectures for the Georgetown University School of Law, were recalled in a eulogy by Charles F. Greenwood. But Greenwood especially remembered Shepard for his personal talents as a lawyer:

> He was magnificent and pleasing in person and impressed every one with his scholarly bearing and absolute sincerity. As an advocate before juries he was eloquent and convincing. His jury speeches were models of eloquence and argument combined. With an almost inexhaustible fund of historical information, coupled with a lively imagination, he was well-nigh invincible before a jury. . . . [He was] young, handsome, educated, brilliant and eloquent, and was in literal truth the idol of Washington County.[30]

C. C. Garrett, also a Washington County native, was born in 1846. Admitted to practice law at Brenham in 1871, he was the current city attorney for Brenham, in addition to his partnership with Shepard.[31] N. A. Rector had moved his law practice from Austin in March 1876 to Giddings where he was in a partnership with the Brenham-based Shepard and Garrett law firm.[32]

The players were in place for the trial. Certainly Kenada must have felt somewhat intimidated by the legal talent opposing him. And his client's big mouth was also likely very little consolation.

On Monday, September 3, only twenty-three of the thirty-six men summoned for jury duty could be located.[33] Because Lee County's first courthouse was not yet completed, a group of rooms on the second floor of A. B. Farrell's house had been rented for a temporary courthouse.[34] Farrell, born in England about 1852,[35] was a farrier and advertised himself as a "wholesale and retail dealer in all kinds of hardware, stoves, furniture, tinware, wood and willow-ware, iron, steel, wagon and buggy material, lamps and lamp fixtures, and a general assortment of agricultural implements."[36]

Kenada's first strategy, likely at Longley's urging, was to secure a continuance in the case to buy more time. He filed a motion on the first morning of the trial asking Judge Turner to continue the case until a witness, the elusive William Hayes of Uvalde County, could be located and attached as a witness for the defendant, Longley.[37] Judge Turner denied the motion when Kenada was unable to state relevant facts that would be proven by the absent witness.[38] Longley was formally arraigned by having the indictment read to him, and he pleaded not guilty. Both sides announced ready for trial, and the process of jury selection began. While it had been thought that it would take several days to pick twelve jurors, the task was completed the same day.[39]

Longley's shackles were removed in the courtroom, which was densely packed with spectators. Brown had in place "a numerous guard of resolute men, who are well-armed with shot-guns and six-shooters," and it was noted that Longley "exhibits or affects exuberant spirits."[40] After consultation with Judge Turner, Brown had fifteen men posted inside the courtroom for Longley's protection, to prevent a lynching if Longley obtained the continuance that he sought.[41]

R.W. Brooks, one of the jurors, was one of two R. W. Brookses, each listed in the 1880 Census for Lee County and each of them farmers with families.[42] Daniel M. Cameron, fifty, came to Texas from Milledgeville, Georgia, about 1850 and was a stockman and farmer, raising a large family.[43] A. Gaines was also selected. Another juror, Ira F. Golden, was born in South Carolina.[44] William T. Griffith, an

Alabama-born farmer who was raised at Evergreen, was thirty-one and had a large family.[45]

Juror Abram A. Harrison, born in Tennessee in 1833, was a farmer with another large family. During the Civil War, he had been a Second Sergeant in the Evergreen Mounted Guards, formed in Washington County in July 1861.[46] Z. Madison was selected as a juror, as was Richard Puckett, a fifty-nine-year-old farmer from Georgia. In 1873 in Burleson County, from which part of Lee County had been formed in 1874, a Richard Puckett and a "Bud" Puckett had been charged with several offenses, including murder and theft of a gelding, but it is unknown if either was the same as the man who sat on Longley's jury.[47] John Stubar (or Shibar) was another juror selected.

Fred S. Wade was born in Canada about 1837 or 1838 and came to Texas where he was a schoolteacher, then raised horses and cattle, and by 1877 had five children. His farm was about nine miles from McDade. Only a year before he had achieved some small notoriety by catching a swamp rabbit with "seven horns on its head," some of them three inches in length.[48] Finally, juror Robert M. Whitfield was a twenty seven-year-old farmer from North Carolina.[49]

Longley and Kenada were entitled by law to twenty peremptory strikes of the prospective jury panel, requiring no reason to be given to the court, but they exercised only twelve challenges. The state was entitled by law to only ten such strikes in a capital case. Jim Brown later said that Longley and his lawyer were personally acquainted with every member of the jury.[50] Once the jury was impaneled and sworn in, Judge Turner recessed the trial until eight thirty Tuesday morning.[51] Ironically, in Burton, in adjacent Washington County, Kenada's home, famed Texas Ranger Leander McNelly died on the same day as the trial.[52]

In a 1937 book, the author alleged that Longley made a desperate escape attempt on Tuesday morning:

> On the second day of his trial they came out of the jail, the prisoner and a dozen heavily armed deputies, led by Sheriff Jim

> Brown. The guards were laughing and joking over something, Longley joining them, as they marched down the street.
>
> Hundreds of men stood around. A few jeers and threats were hurled at him, but he shuffled on, his chains stirring the dust, and his head down. But all the while his sharp, dark eyes were darting this way and that. He was watching for that one chance to make a break.
>
> Suddenly he felt he saw it, and his big arms went up and the chains came down upon the head of an unfortunate guard. The man dropped to the road, and Longley swung himself free, sweeping right and left with his linked arms, using the chains as a whip. In another second the street was a milling mob of flying fists and legs. This was as Longley had expected. He was hoping his chance of escape would come during the confusion he planned to stir up by striking down the guard.
>
> But Sheriff Brown was not to be caught napping; his voice boomed above the uproar, and he ordered his men to pin Longley to the ground. Commanding them to keep their heads and fire no shots, he refused to draw his own pistol. This cool, wise action probably saved the lives of many in that jam. A single shot would have been the signal for many more. The scuffle was brief. Longley saw that his opportunity had gone, and he gave up. No use to get himself beaten up for nothing. But he was scratched and bruised, and his shirt was torn off. They had to return him to the jail for patching before he could be presented to the court.[53]

Whether or not this episode actually occurred cannot be corroborated as there were no contemporary accounts about this incident. On the face of it, such an escape attempt does not seem likely for a chained man amidst a heavily armed guard and hundreds of angry onlookers.

Kenada apparently had also summoned Joseph Hemphill of Bastrop County to testify on Longley's behalf. He was likely related to "Uncle Billie" Hemphill, an acquaintance of Longley's, and with whom brother Jim would live after the trial. Unfortunately, before he could consult with Longley and his lawyer, Joseph Hemphill was arrested in Giddings on a warrant for murder in Bastrop County. In late August, four or five shots had been fired from ambush by two men at a Jack McDonald and a young man named Holligan, who subsequently died of his wounds. Bastrop County Sheriff William E. Jenkins took custody of Hemphill for this murder on Wednesday, September 5, and returned him to Bastrop County without the opportunity to testify for Longley.[54] A Joseph R. Hemphill was married in Bastrop County in October 1866,[55] and a Joseph Hemphill was before the Bastrop County district court for an unknown charge in December 1873,[56] but whether this was the same person is unknown, as is the reason Longley wanted him to testify. A Joseph Hemphill of Bastrop County was shot to death in an ambush in December 1878.[57]

Amazingly, the capital murder trial took only that one day, Tuesday, September 4. Seth Shepard did not call many witnesses. Fuller wrote that the main witness was Wash Harris, who testified that Longley had personally told him that he had killed Wilson Anderson.[58] Longley later claimed that Harris, whom he accused of being a cattle thief from Caldwell County and a relative of Wilson Anderson (which he was not), had lied.[59] Wilson Anderson's wife told the jury that she saw Bill and Jim Longley ride off after the shooting, and that one of them was wearing a white hat (which Bill later denied).[60] Longley's aunt and uncle from Burleson County (Caleb and Ardelia Longley?) were "unwilling witnesses," but had to testify under oath that on the day of the killing, Longley told them that he had killed Anderson.[61] Three men summoned by the state, who were with Wash Harris when the alleged statement was made by Longley, testified basically that they did not recall Longley's saying expressly that he killed Anderson, but that his conversation left that impression on their minds.[62]

Shepard also called Sheriff Jim Brown to the stand to testify as to the letter he had received from Longley. Brown identified Longley's handwriting on the letter, in which he admitted that he had killed Anderson (see chapter 12).[63] Longley later claimed that he had three witnesses to present, but, in addition to Hemphill's being arrested and not appearing, one was "impeached without cause," and he decided not to call the third friend, who he said was afraid that he would be mobbed if he testified. Longley also claimed that the letter sent to the sheriff was forged, like ten or twelve other letters that he said had been signed with his name.[64] Kenada apparently rested without presenting any defense witnesses.

After both sides rested, a charge to the jury was prepared prior to final argument of the lawyers. The law given to the jury by Judge Turner for the offense of murder stated, "Every person with a sound memory and discretion who shall unlawfully kill any reasonable creature in being within this state, with malice aforethought, either express or implied, shall be deemed guilty of murder."[65] The jury was instructed, in accordance with the Texas Penal Code, to determine that, if they found Longley guilty of murder, to distinguish whether it was in the first or second degree, i.e., whether or not the murder was committed with malice. Murder in the first degree carried the death penalty, while the punishment for second degree murder was imprisonment from five years to life.[66] The jury was further instructed:

> If in this case you find from the evidence that this defendant did in cool blood kill Wilson Anderson because he had hatred, ill will, or malice toward him and the killing was done to carry out a previously formed design to take the life of Anderson and the design to kill was formed at a time when the defendant was self-possessed, his mind capable of cool reflection and cool deliberation and that the killing was done because he was mad at, or had hatred toward the deceased, then you would be justified in returning a verdict of murder in the first degree.[67]

Under Texas law at the time, both sides were allowed no less than two arguments to the jury after the charge was prepared, but the state was entitled to argue last, primarily because the law placed on the prosecutor the burden of proof in the case.[68] There is no doubt that Seth Shepard brought to bear all of the eloquence at his command to convince the twelve men in the jury box that he had, indeed, met that burden. There was even evidence in Longley's own words from his letter to Jim Brown admitting that he killed Anderson: "You all know that Wils Anderson did kill little Cale. . . . Brother Jim did not have any thing to do with Killing Wils Anderson—he did not know that I was going to do it until it was done."[69] Other than whatever cross-examination had been made by Kenada, Longley presented no witnesses, and likely on the advice of counsel, he did not testify himself for fear that Shepard would tear him apart on the stand based on his writings in the *Giddings Tribune*, which would certainly further paint him in the jury's mind as a calculating killer.

Longley later said that Kenada made a very short concluding argument to the jury, asking that they find there was no malice and at least spare Longley's life. But Longley was certainly impressed by Shepard's presentation: "Then Seth Shepard got up and gave me a blast, and bemeaned [*sic*] me to the lowest pitch, and said that I had committed many dastardly and cowardly murders, and he thought that I certainly ought to die."[70] Longley also complained that Kenada abandoned him after making his brief presentation to the jury, but not before the lawyer whispered to his client they would hang him "in spite of hell," and if not by law, then they would kill him before he got back to the jail.[71] So much for Longley's defense.

After arguments, at about three thirty in the afternoon, the jury retired into another room to discuss the evidence and reach a verdict. No doubt, a nervous Longley, watched closely by Brown's deputies, felt some desperation at his fate being in the hands of others. An hour and a half later, the jury sent word that it had reached a verdict, and the courtroom filled to hear the decision. Fred Wade had been elected foreman and handed the written verdict over to the court clerk, likely W. A. Knox, who read aloud: "We the jury find William Longley the defendant guilty of murder in the first degree."[72] It was death for Bill Longley.

Judge Turner accepted the jury's verdict, then remanded Longley to jail to await sentencing.[73] One newspaper reported that Longley received his verdict with a laugh, adding that Longley still had not given up the idea of escaping his fate.[74] Yet another observed,

> No change was noticed in the countenance or actions of the prisoner upon this announcement. A cold smile played around his lips, and he nodded to some of the jurors as they passed out from the box. He was heavily ironed and remanded to jail.[75]

Longley waited another week in jail. On Tuesday, September 11, he returned before Judge Turner for the pronouncement of his death sentence. As Longley's parents no doubt read in the *Belton Journal*,

> Bill Longley to-day received his sentence of death by hanging. Judge Turner evinced deep emotion. Longley, with a serious air, unusual to him, but without the slightest agitation, responded that while the sentence might be just, prejudice had much to do with the verdict of the jury, and as he did not wish to be hanged by their say-so, he applied for appeal. If the Appellate Court affirms the sentence, he would not murmur at his doom.
>
> This secures him at least seven months longer. His hope is to effect escape. Interrogated in prison as to his expectation, he has uniformly replied, "None at all, except to make escape. I have got out of worse places than this."[76]

Judge Turner noted that Longley had not filed a motion for a new trial or in arrest of the judgment, and therefore approved the jury's verdict. He sentenced Longley to be "hanged by the neck until he was dead."[77] It was reported that Longley was caught off guard by the emotion evinced by the judge, and on being returned to his cell remarked, "I feel for the judge."[78]

The next day a self-pitying, unrepentant Longley wrote an open letter to the citizens of Lee County through the pages of the *Giddings*

Tribune, which was picked up by other newspapers throughout the state, including the *Belton Journal* in Bell County:

> Well, the blow is over, the die is cast; and I am condemned to die without the sympathy of a single one that I know of. You are all eager, and hope to see me brought upon the scaffold. Then I hope your vengeance will be fully glutted and that you all will be satisfied when you see my soul hurled into eternity. Then, gentlemen, for God's sake, I hope your prejudice will cease when I pay this dreadful debt which is exacted of me by the law. I am willing to pay this debt for the good of the rising generation, and I hope now that the law will triumph over all lawless characters, for of course you know that the world would run back into barbarism if the laws of the land were not enforced. Certainly life is sweet; yet I can not expect to escape the penalty of the law. For though I escape, either by pardon or by breaking jail, it would be encouraging to all boys that are now growing up who are disposed to be lawless. I have two dear brothers who are now in their boyhood, and are disposed to be wilder than I was, and hope this will be a warning to them, for I would freely die rather than see them live the life that I have lived; yet I believe I have been the most successful outlaw that ever lived in Texas, as far back as I can remember. But look at me now, after all the victories I have gained over my enemies, during the past ten or twelve years; where I now sit bound up in irons, awaiting the doom that I know is certain. Yet I am thankful to Almighty God that I have this opportunity to repent of my sins and fit my soul for the blind step that it will soon take off into the realms of an unknown future, and also to advise the rising generation, and tell them [of the] evils and dangers of a reckless life. There are many who may not take my advice, but if I can be the means of saving only one soul from eternal ruin, it will pay me for all the writing I have done since I have been in jail; for that is what I have been writing of my life for. Not for any good that it could do me, nor to boast

> of my exploits, but only to show the rising generation the great danger and folly and final end of such a life.
>
> A man now only destroys his happiness in this world by leading such a life, but he runs a great risk of being cut down in sin without one moment's time for reflection. Yet I am one of the fortunate ones that have been blessed with a little time, and I think I should devote every minute of that time now in doing good, after having thrown away so much precious time that I could have put to much more profitable use than I have. But now it is too late for me, but it is not too late for all young boys who may read this, and who are now blessed in being in possession of a happy home, and have the daily advice of Christian parents, as I once had, but never availed myself of the opportunity. And now, boys, remember the road Bill Longley has traveled in disobeying his parents, and when you go to do wrong remember that a very small wrong leads to a still greater one, and so on, until finally nothing will seem wrong to you if you follow the wrong road. My first step was disobedience; next, whiskey drinking; next, carrying pistols; next, gambling, and then murder, and I suppose the next step will be the gallows. I hope my father and mother will never be blamed for what I have done, for they tried to raise me right.[79]

Obviously, Longley still held out hope that he would escape before his head was inserted into a noose, but this statement was also quite self-serving. He had to have realized that the boasts of his adventures had been ill-received throughout the state, so he sought to redeem himself by characterizing them as object lessons for the youth of the state not to follow his path. Also, his own words had come back to haunt him during his trial; might not the same device be used to paint a positive picture for the appellate court which would finally decide whether or not the jury's verdict would be carried out? If he appeared appropriately repentant, his life might be spared.

But Longley went on to discuss the killing of Wilson Anderson from his perspective. He blamed his Uncle Cale Longley for lying that

Wilson Anderson had said things about Bill and continuing to urge his nephew to kill Anderson.

> Now, some will blame me for telling all this on Cale Longley, but I think it is right for me to do it, for he was [the] cause of it all, and God holds him accountable for the murder of Wilson Anderson, although I was not justifiable in killing him. I have got to hang for it, but his blood rests on none other than uncle Cale Longley, and he knows he is guilty. I would not have made a clean breast of it, but he has treated me very bad. When I was first put in jail he was in town one day, and he would not come down to see me. I sent him word to send me a mattress to lay on, as I had nothing to lay on but the iron floor. He said I did not need anything. Not one of the Longley name has ever come near me, or paid one dollar toward getting me counsel. Even my own dear father has never noticed me or come near me while in prison. I don't ask any of them to come now, but they are the cause of me being right where I am—but I don't ask any of their sympathy. I can die like a man, and the people will believe what I have told [in] this letter, for it is true—every word of it, as certain as there is a God in Heaven! I have always been put up as a target between the Longleys and the world, and have done the jobs for them they were too cowardly to do, and thus the thanks I get for it. No more at present. I will write more before I am executed, and I expect more than a few will like to hear from WILLIAM. P. LONGLEY[80]

This appeal for sympathy was not very effective throughout the state's press, as evidenced by this comment in the *San Antonio Daily Express*:

> There seems to be a gentle regret expressed by the papers of this State that Bill Longley, the convicted murderer, cannot be hanged at once, without enduring the vexacious delay of an

> appeal to the Supreme Court, to say nothing of the danger of the escape of the prisoner in the meantime, or the danger of absence or death of important witnesses in case of a new trial. What a wail would go up [on] account of his premature death, should Bill Longley die before he can be hanged.[81]

Another newspaper, justifying why it refused to print Longley's letters, declared that Longley was "a fraud of the fourteenth water" and that "he is a liar and braggert by birth, education and instinct; . . . his numerous letters are written for the sole purpose of 'blowing,' and especially to influence public opinion in his favor."[82]

Chapter 17

I Have Killed A Many Man

After Longley was sentenced on Tuesday, September 11, 1877, Jim Brown discussed with Judge Turner his concerns about the security of the Lee County jail while Longley was awaiting the outcome of his appeal. Turner agreed that it was "not a safe jail for the confinement" of Longley, and ordered that he be conveyed to the Travis County jail in Austin "for safekeeping during his appeal."[1] Turner initially ordered Longley sent to Galveston, but crossed it out in favor of Austin.

Apparently there was no room for Longley in Austin where John Wesley Hardin was currently being detained. Brown sent a telegram that evening to Sheriff Christian Jordan in Galveston: "I want to imprison Bill Longley with you. Answer instanter. Can you take him?"[2] Jordan promptly responded that the county commissioners of Galveston County had prohibited him from receiving prisoners from other counties until the county jail could "be placed in a more secure condition." On the 13th, Brown again telegraphed him: "By request of many citizens I telegraph you again to take Wm. Longley for safekeeping. He is convicted of murder and is threatened by mob."[3]

The Galveston County jail where Longley was kept. *Courtesy of Chuck Parsons, Luling, Texas.*

Apparently the message appealed to Jordan's sense of responsibility as a lawman, and he realized his duty to render assistance in order to uphold the law and prevent violence. He replied to Brown that if Longley was delivered to him for safekeeping, he would not refuse to receive him.[4] That evening Sheriff Jordan and several deputies stood by at the Galveston depot expecting the notorious prisoner, but he did not arrive.[5] That same evening in Giddings, Dick Sanders was turned over to Deputy Sheriff Robinson of Milam County, who confirmed that Sanders and Longley had disarmed Deputy Matt Shelton several years before.[6]

The next day, on Friday, September 14, as the *Giddings Tribune* planned to publish Longley's letters in the form of a book, Brown left

Giddings with Longley and four other prisoners who were sentenced to the penitentiary at Huntsville.[7] At noon, hundreds crowded the Galveston depot to get a view of the noted mankiller when he arrived. But he was not aboard the noon train, and the disappointed crowd returned to homes and businesses. However, a crowd of boys, including newsboys, bootblacks, and those whose parents didn't know they were there, continued to congregate around the station. A *Galveston News* reporter left the station with Galveston Chief of Police Owens and a Sergeant Finn, followed closely by deputies Billy Owens and Prowse and Captain Grey Nichols of a special force. When the bevy of some two hundred boys saw the delegation of huddled lawmen walking away, the cry of "by jiminy, there he goes" rang out, and they rushed to get a glimpse of Bill Longley, followed by a large number of men. The reporter would later shake his head over the many comments made by the crowd as to what a "bad looking" fellow that Longley was.[8]

That evening, Longley arrived in Galveston on the 11:10 train. "He was as heavily ironed as could be, and looked like anything else but a desperado as he appeared amid the scenes of his arrival."[9] Longley arrived in this coastal city just in time for a major hurricane that did some damage to Galveston over the next several days.

On Saturday, a *Galveston News* reporter called on Longley in his cell at the county jail to hear from his lips "the many scenes through which he has passed and the many hairbreadth escapes he has experienced in his remarkable life."[10] On Sunday, September 16, the *News* printed three full columns of his exploits. This relating of the killings, which totaled only thirty-one, not the thirty-two claimed by Longley, would provide the primary source for the facts of Longley's criminal career, along with the heavily edited letters by Longley that Fuller included in his book *Adventures of Bill Longley*, printed in the early 1900s. The reporter quoted Longley that if he had to hang, he would do so like a man.[11] Now the *Galveston News* came under the same criticism that the *Giddings Tribune* had received for showing interest in Longley:

> Whatever fate overtakes sweet William in the future, the *News* and the Giddings *Tribune* have provided for the immortality of his name. William is peculiarly fortunate in his biographers. Boswellian indeed. Ah! William, you little knew to what lofty heights you were about to ascend, when the shrieks of your murdered victims first saluted your ears. So the world goes.[12]

Galveston Sheriff Christian Jordan was elected to his position in February 1876.[13] Born about 1824 in Germany, he married his first wife, who died December 21, 1864, then promptly married his second wife, Ann Maria, on February 4, 1865. He was a grocer in Galveston until his election and would die in 1885.[14] At the time that Longley was incarcerated in the Galveston County jail, the outlaw shared confinement with eight other men charged with murder, three from other counties also being held for safekeeping. One of these was W. L. Grissom, who had been convicted in Houston for killing a doctor and who was transferred to Galveston in July.[15]

At the end of September, the *Giddings Tribune* announced that it was temporarily suspending its publishing for a few weeks in order to change its format. In the meantime, *The Life and Adventures of W. P. Longley* was being printed and soon would be available at fifty cents a copy.[16] The editor, J. W. Bell, provided copies for sale in Austin.[17] No copy of this publication seems to have survived.

Safely ensconced in jail, Longley resumed his varied and active correspondence. On October 5, 1877, the day before Longley's twenty-sixth birthday, he wrote his captor, Milt Mast:

> I suppose you heard about my trial. I am under sentence of death. They gave it to me at Giddings, you bet, they did. They swore bushels of lies on me; and I did not have a friend nor a witness. My own father and brothers never came near me. I have not seen one of my kinfolks since I was captured, and was not allowed to write letters to them or receive any, and I am now

flat broke, as most men are in jail, and I am compelled to make this call on you, not that I consider you under any obligations to me at all, but as a friend I would ask you and Bill to send me $15 or $20. I am out of tobacco, and, as the county does not furnish coffee, if I had money I could get it made for me, and if you will, I shall appreciate it as a very great kindness from you. I understand that you failed to get but one reward for me. You remember you said you would give me a few dollars, but I hope you will not think that I consider you under any obligations, or that you ought to pay me any of it, for I know that you hardly made expenses, and if you should be so kind as to send me a few dollars, I should regard it as a kindness in you, and not a duty. You know I told you when you left me that I had no hard feelings toward you and Bill for capturing me, and would always be a friend to you, though you may not believe me, but you ought to know enough about me to know that I am neither treacherous nor cowardly, and it would be no use to tell you this, no how. But you know I told everybody publicly that you and Bill Burrows deserved great credit for the capture of me, and you do, too. And I must say that I never was treated better by any one than I was by you and Bill. Tell old Bill I would like to help him crack a big bottle of whiskey once more. I will be here until next March, and if you or Bill have any business in Galveston, I want you to come and see me at my office, and you will be apt to find me in my office, for I am so busy that I seldom walk out in town. Sheriff Jordan will be apt to know where I am at most any time, for he and I are very intimate. He takes a great interest in my welfare. I have been thinking of immigrating to parts unknown, but the sheriff insists on my staying here. I had collected some transportation material in the shape of a few old case-knives, files, etc., but the sheriff conceived the idea that I wanted to abscond, and made application for my tools the other day on very short notice, and succeeded in getting a very good supply out of my office; and, owing to such luck, I guess I shall have to spend the winter in the city. But the sheriff and all his guards are good, jovial fellows. They never get angry at me, but they are wide-awake and full of fleas. Well, I must stop my foolishness. You and Bill must write to me sure, tell me what you heard in Delta county.

W. P. Longley[18]

To this letter, which was published, one newspaper would scoff at his desire to "walk out in town" by observing that he "will get out and off to a strange land, materially aided by a scaffold and a twisted piece of hemp."[19]

On October 11, obviously concerned about his appeal, Longley wrote a long letter to "an eminent criminal lawyer in Richmond, Texas," inquiring as to his availability to handle the appeal and answering questions that the lawyer had previously asked about the conduct of the trial. Longley complained about the lack of experience of Sam Kenada, alleging that he employed him at a fee of $50 only because Campbell Longley had been threatened with death if he assisted his son in any way. He said that he was not allowed to receive or forward any letters, nor allowed to talk to his attorney privately, and that Kenada did not return to the jail after one of Brown's deputies insulted the lawyer. He said that he did not see his lawyer again until they were in the courtroom at the time of trial.

Longley also complained of being chained hand and foot when he was taken to court, the chains to be removed by a blacksmith while in court at the order of the judge. He said that the twenty armed men inside the courtroom kept their weapons pointed at him throughout the trial: "I believe if I had raised up on my feet, they would have shot me into doll rags." To bolster his image, Longley observed that when a guard got too close to him, the guard would become so afraid his teeth would chatter.

Of course, Longley was not happy with the defense presented by Kenada, saying that the lawyer had failed to get a change of venue for the trial, and had made a short argument to the jury and then walked out. Longley pleaded ignorance as to the procedures required for a new trial and no motion for one was filed. To the attorney's question as to whether or not a "Statement of Facts," i.e., a transcript of the testimony, was written out by the attorneys, he said that Kenada had written nothing down, nor had he taken any "Bill of Exceptions" to the rulings of Judge Turner.

Longley told the lawyer that one "Dutch man" on the jury had been whipped some twenty-five years earlier by his father and others for stealing hogs, and that he was convinced that all of the jurors had been part of a mob that had come to the Giddings jail about a month earlier and demanded the keys. According to Longley, the jailer told the mob that they could have Longley if he was not convicted. He complained about the man that summoned the jury, and said he did not know if the jury separated during the trial. Texas law prohibited a capital murder jury from separating once the trial began.

> And I don't know of any misconduct of the jury, only they were very unconcerned while Kenada was speaking, and would laugh very heartily at him. Sometimes some of them were reading papers, and others were engaged in conversation with some of the guards in a low tone. One of them looked at me and gritted his teeth at me while Shepard was speaking.[20]

Longley was also put out with the public joy with which his conviction was received, and told of one man who came to the jail and teased him, even pointing a pistol at him through the bars threatening to blow his brains out while he was chained to the wall. He said that after the trial he wrote a letter to Judge Turner relating his bitterness at how his trial had been conducted and that he was told that the judge cried when he read it.

In requesting the Richmond lawyer to handle his appeal, a bitter Longley took the jury to task:

> If I must hang I intend to hang like a man, but there is one thing I do know, and that is certain, and that is, every one of them fellows has got to die some day as well as me, and I am going to try [to] meet my God in peace, and I hope the good Lord will forgive them too, for if I don't get a new trial that jury has murdered me, in colder blood than ever I did a man, and I have never harmed one of them in no way in my life, and the great God of Heaven knows I have not. If they had given me a fair trial it would not have been so bad, but I had no showing on earth they had just as well went and killed me in jail.[21]

The lawyer forwarded Longley's letter to the *Galveston Daily News*, which printed it on Sunday, October 21, observing that if Longley's complaints were valid, there should be "serious reflection," his guilt notwithstanding, that the law was not "faithfully, fairly, and impartially administered."[22] Infuriated, Sheriff Jim Brown quickly responded in a letter to the *News* written on October 24 and printed two days later.

> Your issue of Sunday contained a letter from W. P. Longley which, although its statements do great injustice to the court and people of this county, as well as to me personally, I should not have considered worthy of an answer were it not that you in some editorial remarks on the subject seem to imply that there might be some foundation for Longley's statement in fact. Where Longley is known no denial of any charge he might choose to make would be necessary, if the charge rested on his unsupported testimony, but the wide publicity given his statement by the *News* seems to render some answer necessary, lest the sympathies of some good, but ill-informed person should be extended—not to the officers of the law, engaged in a necessary but unpleasant duty, but to the hardened desperado now about to expiate in some slight measure his terrible array of crimes.[23]

Brown denied that Kenada had been insulted by a jailer and discussed the presence of armed deputies in the courtroom for Longley's security, stating that no guns were pointed at the defendant. "He was treated by me with all due consideration, not only in the court room, but in the jail." The sheriff defended the jury as being "composed of the very best men in the country," and argued that Longley and his lawyer had been satisfied with the jury, foregoing eight peremptory strikes that remained available to them. He said that the members of the jury would have been as likely to be a part of a mob as the editor of the *News*. According to Brown, the jurors did not converse with guards, and his trial "was in every respect fair and impartial." The evidence, said Brown, contrary to Longley's assertions, was so conclusive as to leave the jury no choice, especially because Longley had repeatedly admitted the killing of Anderson.

To Longley's assertion that Campbell Longley was prevented from assisting his son, Brown stated that the old man feared his son, "as did every one in the community." Then Brown quoted a letter that Longley had written him on October 20: "I have wrote a long letter which will come out to-morrow in the Galveston *News* about the way I was tried. You need not tax it to yourself at all. I done it to try to *change* public opinion a little, though it is nothing against you. Not at all."[24]

In closing, Brown expressed regret that the name of the Richmond lawyer was not published, wondering "if he be the same eminent lawyer of Richmond who paid Longley (according to Longley's statement) $250 to kill a Negro for him."[25] From this letter, the *News* concluded that Brown's comments were "for the most part in excellent temper and taste, and in point of force is so masterly that, we doubt not it will strike impartial readers as conclusive against all the material allegations of Longley."[26]

The furor subsided, and Longley continued to languish in his Galveston cell. On October 14 he wrote his brother Jim describing his routine. He had a cell to himself, but remained shackled at all times. A man named McCaleb had communicated with him and was supposedly at work on a 600-page book about Longley that he intended to send to a New York publisher. Longley promised Jim that he would avoid telling any tales that might get his younger brother indicted, but said, “Jim, I think I will put in our fight on the Brazos River where I got the buckshot shot through my hat and coat, If I put [it] in I put it in as being unknown parties not any sheriffs posse. You know how it is yourself. Be careful what you write in regard to such things for all my letters are opened before they get to me.”[27] He continued:

> I wish I could talk to you a little while. Jim, I am just as lively as ever. Jim, I never have passed the time with no one on earth as happy as I did with you. I all ways did injoy your company better than any of the family even when you was a little child. I never have saw the time when you and me could not rais a little fuss. We all ways had fun where ever we was. Do you remember our fish fry we had up on the Lampasas River one day and you was rideing behind me and you held out your hands to show me how long that big fish was you caught and I spurred Creole and made her jump from under you. Ha, ha, what a scaley fish a frog is. Well, Jim, I think it is a good idea for you to not live at Paps [Campbell Longley] for some cowardly s____ might waylay you on my account. I dont want you to take up anything that has or will be done to me unless they mob me some time and then you must be careful and take your time for it. Every body knows you are the only one that would every [*sic*] try to avenge my blood and they would like to get away with you too. Now you just let them go ahead with there [*sic*] rat killing and if I am hung don’t say a word about it for you know I have killed a many man myself and you can’t expect me to run allways and Jim you must believe what I say. Death is no punishment to me. I don’t dread it one bit as shure as you live I don’t and I would rather die a thousand deaths than to hear of some cowardly son of a bitch killing you while I was in jail for if I was fast loos I would wade through hell to kill the one or ones that would kill you but I hope you will be all right.[28]

Longley told his brother about a photograph that had been taken of him in the jail, and promised that when Campbell came to see him, he would send some back by him:

> Tell Ma and Pap that it is all stuff for them to be taking in about me. It is the most foolish thing in the world for them to do so; it is so strange to me that sensable [*sic*] people will grieve about any thing. Why in the name of God will you grieve about things on this earth that God intends to be. Do you not know that we all must die. Oh why will you not take the right view of things and rather rejoice to leave this troublesom [*sic*] world.[29]

Milt Mast responded to Longley's October fifth letter and sent him some money. On October 29, Longley used a letter to Captain Mast not only to thank him, but also to project himself as an equal of the notorious John Wesley Hardin, who had recently received a twenty-five-year penitentiary sentence for the shooting death of Brown County Deputy Sheriff Charles Webb in the town of Comanche a few years earlier:

> You know what I told you about John Wesley Hardin, and myself and all such cases. When the right one jumps a fellow they always take him out of the wet. I told you that John Wesley Hardin would get picked up some time for all he and his friends, has told it everywhere that he would never be captured alive. There never was a man so fast but what he found a man just a little faster than he was. But, then Captain, you know that you and Bill Burrows got the dead drop on me, and so did Lieutenant Armstrong get it on John Wesley Hardin. But drop or no drop, John Wesley Hardin and myself now inhale the gentle breezes that flow through prison windows. Did you see the interview that was given out by John Wesley Hardin when he was first brought to Austin? He said in that interview that he had never had anything to do with Bill Longley, nor any other such characters, and that he never had anything to do with anybody except gentlemen

William Preston Longley in a photograph taken while in jail at Galveston, Texas, in October 1877, while awaiting a decision on his appeal from a murder conviction. *Courtesy of Robert G. McCubbin, Santa Fe, New Mexico.*

of honor. Now as a matter of information I would like to know where these gentlemen of honor friends of his are now? They certainly are not in jail where the Honorable John Wesley is himself. I wonder if it is King Fisher, Brown Bowen [Hardin's brother-in-law], Bill Taylor [friend of Hardin jailed for killing Gabriel Slaughter], [George] Gladden[,] Ringe [John Ringo], Scott Cooley, [Fayette] Grissom and two or three dozen more whom I might name. I wonder if John Wesley Hardin thinks it honorable to take two or three dozen men, of the same stripe that I have just named, ride to Cuero and shoot to death the man named Rube Brown, the town marshal, simply because Brown had arrested one of the pals of Hardin and collected a reward of $500? Also when Hardin and Jim Taylor and Dickson killed poor Charley Webb in Comanche, for absolutely nothing? Webb was one of the best and bravest officers Texas ever had. The only excuse Hardin and his bunch had for killing Webb was that Webb had arrested one of their gang, a fellow named Jim Buck Waldrop, of Brown county for cattle theft, and who had been run out of the Llano country for the same offense. It is probable also that Charlie Webb had made the remark somewhere that he was not afraid of Hardin which was the truth. Hardin was afraid of Webb, and when he killed him he took every cowardly advantage that it was possible to take. It seems that it was death by their law—the law of Hardin and his gang—for a man just simply to say that he was not afraid of Wesley Hardin, and poor Charlie Webb could not help saying that, for he was a man, that never was known to tell a lie, and so one day when somebody asked him if he would tackle Wesley Hardin, he said he would certainly do so if he had the necessary papers that called for his arrest. Then again Brown Bowen, another pal of Wes Hardin killed a man in Gonzales county by slipping up and shooting him while asleep. Wes Hardin says the people of Texas need not be afraid to turn him loose. I am like him about that they need not be afraid to turn me loose either, for you may just bet your sweet life that I would get

> fast and far away from Texas, for we never know how dangerous it is until we get picked up and locked in jail for keeps. Now I do not mean to say that Wes Hardin is not brave, but the woods in Texas are full of brave men, and I suspect Hardin remembers at least one—and that is old man Reagan, who captured him near Palestine several years ago. I heard that when Hardin got back to his crowd in the brush, he said: "Boys don't ever let old man Reagan get after you, for he is h____ I tell you."
>
> Well I do not propose to boast of being brave at all, but I have had no help in my meanness, when it came to killing a man. I have done such things on my own account and always alone, and I am not trying to justify myself in the least, but I do think that as far as Wes Hardin is concerned in the matter of honor, that neither Hardin nor myself are overburdened. I have always known that I was doing wrong, but I got started when I was just a fool boy, led off by older heads, and taught to believe that it was right to kill sassy negroes, and then to resist the military law. So the first thing I knew there was a reward of $1,000 offered for me by the military authorities of Texas. But the Yankees never laid their hands on me and when martial law was over in Texas I thought I could stand a trial, but my father told me that it would bankrupt him to get me out of the trouble I was in bad so I kept out of the way, because I did not know what else to do, and then the civil officers were trying to catch me all the time for the reward that was offered and so it went on until finally I was caught, and brought to this place. They all get caught soon or later. It has not been for gain that I have lived the life that I have lived. It is due to the situation the country was in during the year that followed the Civil War.[30]

Longley's bitterness was compounded by the differences in punishment received by Hardin and him: "Don't you think it is a one-sided thing to kill me for my sins and only give Hardin 25 years in prison?"[31] No doubt, Longley was disgusted not only that he would continue to be obscured in the shadow of the celebrated John Wesley Hardin, but also that Hardin would live to dance on Longley's grave as the premier outlaw of Texas. In the meantime, an unnamed Texas Ranger from Cuero who had visited Hardin in his cell in Austin observed: "I found him to be a great talker, though not near so boastful as the outlaw Longley."[32]

As Longley continued to wait for the result of his appeal, he likely read the *Galveston Daily News* about events with which he was familiar. In November, an article from Lee County mentioned that a Dr. A.J. Gilder purchased Jim Brown's "fine stock farm . . . near Evergreen," which was the old Longley homestead.[33] Also, Lee County authorities calculated that Longley had so far cost the taxpayers about $800.[34]

By November 1877, Jim Longley was settled in Bastrop County, staying with W. A. "Uncle Billie" Hemphill, a thirty-five-year-old farmer in the Red Rock area a few miles northeast of the Bastrop-Caldwell County line, where he lived with his wife and six children, including a set of twins. Hemphill had been a private in Co. D, Third Battalion, of the Mounted Reserves in Bastrop County at the end of the Civil War. Jim assured his parents that he was working hard, that he was seeing a girl just to "pass time," as he had little money, and asking them to pass on any news they heard from Bill.[35]

In January 1878, Lee County Sheriff Jim Brown left to bring back Dick Sanders who had escaped from Milam County and had been captured in Mississippi.[36]

As was its custom, the Galveston County grand jury on January 22, 1878, reported to the court that it had inspected the county jail. The jail was reported "in as good condition as the nature of the building will admit." The group recommended that the basement floor be raised some eight to ten inches to head off periodic flooding, and that the jailyard likewise be raised to provide runoff for water after rains. "We further recommend for sanitary reasons that the prisoners receive twice each week dessicated [*sic*] vegetables, vinegar, etc."[37]

About this same time Jim Longley became involved in a plot to break his brother out of jail when the convicted murderer was returned to Giddings after his appeal was decided. Jim wrote his parents that he was still working for Billie Hemphill for $14 a month, then,

> Read this to your self, Pap. Well, I have got the trigers [*sic*] spinning. I met with a [illegible] fellow. His name is Henry [illegible]. He is a cousin to the Tailor boys. He says he will go with me to release Bill and that he will meet me here with five others of the Tailor [Taylor] party. T[w]o of them will be Tailors. Tha[t] will be when Bill comes to Giddings. Bill got a chance and told me how to do. He says make the attack in day light about 2 o'clock in the eavening. I will have 7 besid[e]s my self. Bill Baker will go to[o]. Now tell me what you think about that under taking. There will not be any g[u]ards in day light. Only Brown and Deputy. Bill says Brown is all right. So no more.[38]

Somehow, Bill had apparently gotten a secret communication to his brother in Bastrop County. Bill Baker was a fifty-two-year-old farmer in Bastrop County, likely the same Bill Baker that Bill and Jim Longley had worked for in 1875 prior to the killing of Wilson Anderson.[39] And it is just as likely that Campbell Longley communicated with his young son, sternly admonishing him to steer clear of such foolish and dangerous schemes. Such an escape effort was never attempted, but, nevertheless, Bill Longley was not yet resigned to being hanged.

The court of appeals in Galveston, on February 4, 1878, sustained a motion by Assistant Attorney General George McCormick to require the trial court of Judge Turner in Lee County to forward to the appellate court a complete record of the Longley case. District Clerk W. A. Knox traveled to Galveston from Giddings to make sure that the high court got whatever it wanted.[40] McCormick, a Virginia native, born on October 12, 1848, came to Texas with his family in 1858, settling in Colorado County. During the Civil War he was wounded at the battle of Harrisburg, near Holly Springs, Mississippi, and, while a Union prisoner, had a leg amputated. Returning to Texas after the war, he studied for the law and was admitted to the bar. Removed from the position of

Assistant Texas Attorney General George McCormick. *Archives Division, Texas State Library, Austin.*

district clerk in Colorado County by the military after the war because he could not take the "ironclad" oath, he went on to represent Colorado and Lavaca counties in the Texas Constitutional Convention of 1875. In 1876, he was appointed an assistant attorney general by Governor Richard Coke. In 1878 he would be elected Texas attorney general, and from 1884 to 1892 would serve as a district judge of the Twenty-fifth District. His death would come in 1905.[41] It was McCormick's task to prepare the legal brief on behalf of the state in Longley's case and urge the court of appeals to affirm his death sentence.

Longley's attorney on his appeal was Jacob H. Catlin, a sixty-seven-year-old lawyer and farmer from Bellville in Austin County.[42] On March 6, 1878, Longley's case was placed before the court of appeals in Galveston in the form of legal briefs prepared by the two attorneys.[43] This was a most inopportune time for Longley to attempt an escape. As a Galveston newspaper reported,

> Mr. Henry Miller, the jailer, reports that a short time ago W. P. Longley, confined in the jail of this county under sentence of death by the District Court of Lee county, succeeded in getting two bottles into his cell, which he had filled with water, and with which he intended to make some ugly bruises about Mr. Miller's head. The end of the effort was in Longley getting himself unbottled by force to be even more closely watched by his keepers in the future.[44]

The court of appeals rendered its decision on Wednesday, March 13, 1878. The opinion was written by Judge John Preston White. Like McCormick, he was a Virginia native, born in 1832. White graduated from Emory and Henry College in 1850, studied law at the University of Virginia, and began the practice of law in 1853. After an early visit to Texas, he returned with his family in 1855 and settled at Seguin. During the Civil War, he commanded Company E, Sixth Texas Infantry. White served as mayor of Seguin and county attorney of Guadalupe County, then was appointed a District Judge in 1874. In 1876, he was elected to the Galveston court of appeals. White would go on to be presiding judge of the court until 1892, after which he was the reporter for the court of criminal appeals and the author of important Texas legal case books.[45]

The problem faced by Catlin, in trying to shape an effective argument on behalf of Longley that he was not properly and fairly con-

Judge John P. White, Galveston Court of Appeals. *Archives Division, Texas State Library, Austin.*

victed, was that an insufficient record was forwarded from the trial court to the court of appeals. As Judge White noted: "We are placed in the embarrassing situation of having to pass upon his appeal without the transcript of the record disclosing a single bill of exceptions, or a statement of the facts adduced upon the trial."[46] Catlin argued that a defendant had a statutory right in Texas to have a certified statement of facts included as part of the trial record, and that for the high court to affirm Longley's conviction without having access to such record would be a violation of due process. However, the court noted that the law left it up to the parties to cause a statement of facts in the case to be written up, and that the judge was not required to do so on his own initiative. Judge White pondered the problem:

> As to who is to blame for the failure to have a statement of the facts made out in the present case, it would be perhaps unprofitable for us to inquire. In a case involving the life of a defendant, and especially after a verdict of conviction imposing the death penalty, and notice of appeal given, it would hardly be presumed that the condemned criminal would quietly suffer the punishment without having first availed himself of every remedy afforded by the law. And yet he himself alone may be to blame; or his attorneys, conversant with the law and the facts, may have been willing to assume the responsibility, honestly believing that a statement of facts could and would admit of but one conclusion—the undisputed establishment of his guilt. The better practice would be, in all such cases, to make out and certify the facts, let the consequences be what they might.[47]

Without any testimony or evidence to consider, the court of appeals could only examine the basic trial documents, i.e., the indictment and jury charge, and determine if they were sufficient legally to support the jury verdict and the court's sentence. The court quickly found that both were adequate, finding that the charge was "a clear, able, full, and complete exposition of the law, so far as it is possible for us to determine in the absence of a statement of facts."[48]

In the preface to its opinion, the court of appeals expressed regret that the record failed to disclose the facts of the case, "which probably concludes the career of one of the most noted malefactors of the state, whose imputed exploits have contributed largely to the most sanguinary chapters of her annals."[49] Having found all documents that had been submitted to be in proper order, and obviously well aware of all of his boasts, the court affirmed Longley's death sentence.[50]

"The news of Bill Longley's sentence being confirmed is received with great satisfaction," crowed the *Galveston Daily News*.[51] Because Judge Turner's court was adjourned at Giddings while he held court elsewhere in his district, Longley continued to be held in the jail at Galveston. He wrote his brother Jim on March 14 chiding him for some difficulty that Jim had with unknown persons, when he had to "take to the brush." Longley warned him about Virgil Wooley, his former employer and one of Jim Brown's deputies, referring to him as the "damdest s...b in the whole county . . . a treacherous scoundrel," and not to be trusted.[52] The mandate of the court of appeals was filed with the district court in Lee County by W. A. Knox on March 30.[53]

Time was running out for Bill Longley.

Chapter 18

Same Old Rattling Bill

Longley now languished in the well-guarded Galveston County jail until Judge Turner returned to Giddings in August to open the term of the district court. Although constrained by an iron bar connecting his ankles and affixed to chains,[1] he kept himself occupied with a prolific frenzy of interviews, as well as writing letters when he could obtain writing materials and postage. Much of what he was reported as saying and wrote during this period gives insight into Longley's mindset as he sought to both justify himself and rationalize his self-created reputation, at the same time beginning to reconcile himself to his pending fate. But throughout his writings can be detected a continuing glimmer of hope that he might yet avoid the hangman.

In one interview with a Chicago reporter, Longley boasted of yet another killing that he had not previously mentioned. This involved an alleged duel with a man named Grady in Mexico, supposedly in revenge for the killing of a friend of Longley in Texas. Longley also claimed that he was at this time invited, but declined, to participate with Mexican bandits on a raid into Texas.[2] As with his other claims, this one also appears to be another idle boast. Although it is possible, there was never any evidence that Longley went to Mexico.

On March 25, he mailed an extensive letter to the *Illustrated Police News* complaining about the description written of him in a previous issue as a "cold-blooded, wilful murderer," claiming he always acted in self-defense. In this article, Longley sought to rewrite the sordid events in his life, vigorously denying the killings he had so fervently boasted about only months before, insisting that the stories were the product of a vivid imagination on the part of the Giddings editor and the *Galveston Daily News*. "I had no showing for my life and I have so many enemies, that it is no use for me to say anything." He proclaimed: "All those reports about my killing a soldier in Gonzales county, and the cattle drover, Rector, and the Osage Indians and then the soldier at Leavenworth, Kansas, and the quarter-master, in Wyoming, is all a conglomerated, damned lie."[3]

In early April 1878, he wrote his captor, Milt Mast, his language an attempt at eloquence, expressing some sense of remorse, but nevertheless still self-pitying. His "unknown future" had become a source of increasing concern, and he sought to rationalize the extent of his crimes:

> I take my pen in hand to let you know that I still float through the greater [illegible] of misery, destined to that inevitable doom that awaits me sooner or later, but "Let the wide world wag as it will, I am still the same old rattling Bill."
>
> Well, Captain, about eleven years ago I launched my boat upon that mighty river that leads to destruction, and without the least idea where it would land me. Of course you are aware that when once one gets under good headway going down this mighty channel it is very hard to check up. I have found that this great river has but one landing place, from its head to its mouth. The name of that place is Reformation-town, and after one passes Reformation-town there is no stopping place between him and

eternity, no, none; but O, how few there are who get off at this landing!

The reason of it is, the country looks beautiful on either side, and still more promising ahead, and on we go, until finally we begin to strike our boats against the terrible boulders and snags. Then it is we begin to see our companions wrecked and lost on either side of us; then it is that we see whither we are going. But, alas! too late, for we are then beyond the help of human hands. Then we cast a look or a thought back to our happy home, and Mother!

Well, Captain, this is my condition, and I have lost my oars, so that now I can do nothing but fold my arms and sit back and "let-er [illegible]," but, at last, I am trying to concentrate my thoughts upon the great mystery of my unknown future, but, Oh, what strange thoughts pass through my mind! I sometimes ask myself these questions: Is this world or this life only a dream? Is there nothing beyond the grave? Will all, then, be a universal blank, without a single prize? Oh, certainly not! Most undoubtedly there is a future, but is it a future of happiness, or will it be an eternal punishment?

No ministers ever came near me, and I have never read the Bible a great deal, for I have spent my life, from a fifteen year old boy, in the wildest parts of the country and in company with the most [illegible] men on earth, but withal, there has always been a spark of Christianity in my heart, and it has kept me from committing many evil deeds which I would have committed had I been void of that feeling. I have done enough, however, to ruin me, at least in this world, but I hope not in the world to come.

Now, Captain, I believe I could die a Christian if people would quit tantalizing me. It does seem that everybody glories in making me feel as miserable as possible, especially the newspapers of the country. I don't think I deserve to be abused as much, for I have never killed a man for money. It is true I have killed several men, but I always thought at the time that I had a good cause for doing so.

William Preston Longley[4]

About this same time, on April 12, Longley wrote a letter to Rudolph Thatcher, an inmate in the state penitentiary at Huntsville. Thatcher was charged with stealing pistols and clothing from three persons at Hilderbrandt's factory in Galveston, and was arrested in Louisiana and returned to the Galveston jail in November 1877.[5] On November 30, he was found guilty of burglary and sentenced to two years in prison,[6] and likely transported to Huntsville by Sheriff Jordan on December 5.[7] Again Longley sought to make an eloquent plea of redemption, but an element of self-pity shines through:

> I will drop you a few lines this morning to let you know I am yet on time's side of eternity, but I expect soon to pass to that bourne from whence no traveler ever returns. But you may first bet your sweet life I am the boy that is able to stand the racket. You must not take me for an idle boaster or a braggart when I boast that I am able to stand the racket. For it is by the help of our blessed Lord Jesus Christ that I stand the storms of this life. I do not, neither can I, fear mortal man. But I do both fear and love God, and I must say from my heart that if it be God's will that I must end my days here on the scaffold, I will meet it with pleasure.
>
> My friends are all the time saying to me, "Bill, old boy, die like a man—die game," and so forth. Well, I am going to die game, but not a braggart. Suppose some people think I will walk out and dance a jig, like Loss Kimble did. But that is not my style. I don't want to pass my last moments cursing the world and everybody in it, just to leave a name behind me of being game. God knows whether a man is game or not, and I don't care what the world thinks. The Lord Jesus has been with me through

many a dangerous place, and he will be with me to the end. Now, Thatcher, you know my disposition; if you did not, I would not write the way I do, for I know you will believe what I say. Now you must not imagine I am putting on the old Pharisee's face. O, no, not a bit of it. I am as gay and lively as I ever was in my life. I can't be any other way but lively.

My father wrote to me he was going to do everything in the world toward getting my sentence commuted to life-time imprisonment. But he can't do anything, because everybody is my enemy, and I have no friends. So you see I have no hope of that, and then for my own part I would as lief to be hanged as go to the penitentiary for life. But on the account of my poor old mother and father I would be willing to go there, instead of hanging. You know we have all got to die sometime, so why not at once, rather than hammer out a few miserable years in prison and then die? For I suppose life-time prisoners are not allowed any privileges whatever.

Well, Thatcher, old boy, it's ruff both ways sure. It is six of one and half dozen of the other. You must not think hard of me for not writing sooner, for I have had no stamps, nor money to buy any, and it looks like an impossibility for me to get one of my pictures, but I will get one before I leave here.

Write when you can, and I will do the same. I remain, as ever, your friend,

William Preston Longley[8]

But Bill Longley was far from giving up the ghost and waiting to die on the gallows. He was one of four convicted murderers under the death penalty in the Galveston jail, there being thirty-six other prisoners also held. On the same evening that he wrote the letter to Thatcher, he was caught by a jailer with a saw trying to escape his cell. One bar of his cell door was "cut in two," and his shackles were partially severed. The sheriff told the newspaper that the saw had been acquired from W. L. Grissom, a murderer convicted of the killing of a doctor in Houston who, like Longley, had been held for safekeeping in the Galveston jail since July 1877 and who likely had brought the saw with him from Houston.[9] Afterwards Longley wrote to a newspaper that he would never "give away" the man who furnished him the saw, remarking that the jailer appeared "to want a saw a darned sight worse than he did," and that he unhesitatingly gave it to him.[10]

Longley's letters to Mast and Thatcher were subsequently printed in newspapers, and the *Austin Daily Democratic Statesman* sarcastically commented on his eloquence:

> Such is the Christian sweetness and tenderness and simple trustfulness of Bill Longley's character and taste and gentle affections illustrated in his unique letters, that it would be a great pity to hang him. We don't see how Governor Hubbard, with all the overflowing buttermilk that forever bubbles up in his swelling bosom, can refrain from pardoning this splendid Christian gentleman Bill Longley.[11]

On May 14, 1878, Longley again wrote his brother Jim, who had written him about riding down to the Frio Canyon area where Longley had killed Lou Shroyer. Longley recounted his experiences there. He advised Jim not to change his name there unless he did something wrong and warned him that Texas Ranger Captain Lee Hall and his men "were all over that country." He told Jim to look up the Saunders brothers, one of whom, Charley, was the "best boy I ever saw."[12] Charley Saunders was a twenty-five-year-old Ranger who lived with his brother, farmer D. H. Saunders, in Bandera County.[13] Jim and Bill were corresponding weekly. Bill wrote a little of his life in a jail cell, revealing that he could be crude at times when he didn't like someone, such as his jailer:

> Well, Jim, I don't know one thing to write this time. I sent you three papers last Tuesday. I get a letter from you every

Tuesday regular, and I generally answer it as soon as I read it. I got a letter from the editor of the Police News last week. He told me he would send me tobacco pipes, cigars, books, papers, pens, pencils, postage stamps or anything in the world I wanted to make me comfortable, and I have wrote to him to send them along, and next time I write I think I will send you the paper with my picture in it. I got a good letter yesterday from a preacher in Lampasas Springs that I never saw nor heard of before. I get lots of letters from different parts of the world and from persons that I have never saw. I got one from a young lady the day I left Giddings. She said she had heard so much of me she wanted to correspond with me. I wrote to her but I came down here and I never heard no more of her. She lived at Spring Hill, Navarro County, Texas. Well, I guess I had better stop. I don't know what to write. My yellow girl brought me a bottle of kimbal yesterday. Jim, she is a pretty trick. She wants to come in my cell, but the sheriff won't let her for fear she might bring me a saw. Henry Miller, the jailer, comes to the jail of mornings and laughs at me and tells me he crammed my girl last night. He says he crammed her for that dollar that she bought the kimbal with, and I expect he did. But she says he is a liar, but I rather think that she is the liar. Miller fucks every woman in the city in twelve months, and a good many of the men. I guess he wount see this letter as it goes out. So no more at present. I remain your affectionate brother forever more.

William Preston Longley[14]

Longley's "preacher from Lampasas Springs" was Dr. Thomas Denny of Lampasas, who had seen one of Longley's letters to Mast published in a newspaper. Dr. Denny was licensed as an Episcopal lay reader in 1873 for St. Mary's Episcopal Church in Lampasas.[15]

Longley was also trying to establish some correspondence with Campbell and Sarah Longley, but unlike the light tone he took with his brother, he was intent on assuring his parents that whatever happened, it would be all right. They were apparently not answering his letters, but he continued to write them, as he did again on May 17, 1878. After mention of a letter to Mast being published ("They all say it was a splendid letter"), he discussed the latest news of his case:

> Well, I heard some little news last night after I went to bed. One of the night guards came and called me and told me that he had just bin talking with a man from Giddings up at the city market. [Letter torn] man he talked too was in the jury that tried me. And he said that the jurimen and states attorney and the judge was getting up a petition to the govner to have my sentence commited to life time imprisonment. I understand that the jurymen now says that they had to find me guilty of murder in the first degree to keep me from being killed in the court house. Now if all this be true, the govner will commute the sentence, but the question is whether it is true or not, but I know this guard heard what he said he heard. Well, here is how I stand. If they do anything its all right, and if they don't, all right, with me, because they can do nothing unless it be the will of God. Therefore I am perfectly easy on the matter. Now here is one thing shure. If it is Gods will that I must hang, you may just rest asshured that I will hang, and if not, why then I will not be hung. Now that is so as certain as I live. Mortal man has nothing to do with me only as God sees fit to use them in the case. And I can neather blame them nor give them credit for nothing they do. But give the credit to God, the only rightous one, and I hope you will look at it as I do for I am certain that I am right. Well, I have nothing more worthe to write. I believe Lizzie has quit writeing to me, but I gues Ney stopped her, but that is all right. Now Pap if you and Ma and Cammie and Jim was all to go back on me, it would not set me back any, for my mind is beyond this miserable world, and my trust is in one that never betrays none who trust in him. Of course I love you

> all but God should be loved more than all els, am I not right, I think I am.[16]

Longley added a note to his little brother, Alexander Campbell Longley, or Cammie. His younger brother had been born to Campbell and Sarah Longley on October 27, 1867, when they lived at Evergreen, when Sarah was forty-six years old.[17] As a postscript, he noted the fate of another notorious Texan:

> Brown Bowen will be hung today at Gonzales. His sentence was affirmed the same day that mine was. He is a brother in law to John Wesley Hardin. It is but a few hours until he will be hurled into eternity from whence no traveler ever returns. May God have mercy on his soul.[18]

On the same date that Longley started this letter, May 16, another accused murderer held in the Galveston jail, the notorious Bill Taylor, was taken into custody for return to Calhoun County and trial for the murder of Gabriel Slaughter in Indianola in March 1874. The killing was an outgrowth of the bloody Sutton-Taylor feud that had propelled John Wesley Hardin to prominence, and Taylor's previous conviction had just been reversed by the Texas Court of Appeals.[19] Longley had claimed that he was pursued at Yorktown by soldiers after being mistaken for a member of Taylor's gang.[20]

Longley's correspondence with Mast, still complaining about his trial, continued on May 22:

> I received your kind letter and was glad to hear from you, and, as I still languish on time's side of eternity, I will scratch you a few lines to-day. Well, Captain, I am in the best of health, and I expect I am in better spirits than you or any one think I am, notwithstanding my would-be dreadful doom, that is if I was inclined to make it dreadful. I am not going to die until my time comes.

Them fellows in Lee County are so fraid they will not get to see me hung that they have been writing letters down here to the sheriff begging him not to let me receive any letters from my poor old father and mother, for fear the letters might be saturated with poison. That looks mighty hard, that they would try to cut me off entirely, and not even allow me to get a letter from home, after telling my poor old gray-headed father that they would kill him if he came to see me or assisted me in getting a lawyer.

Then they wrote a long letter and had it published in the Galveston News, saying in it that my father was glad that I was condemned, and that that was the reason he never came near me or assisted me in getting a lawyer. Colonel Belo, the editor of the Galveston News, will publish anything in the world against me that any one writes, but he will not publish my side of the story. He published one letter for me, but as soon as he found I had no friends he would listen to nothing I would say no more. The Galveston News always pounces on the bottom dog.

Now, Captain, it does seem to me that them fellows in Lee County ought to be satisfied with taking my life without tormenting me what few days I have got to live. If I had done anything in my life worthy of being treated the way that they have treated me, I would not say one word about it, and then, if they had give me only a dog's showing when they tried me, I would die without a word.

But it hurts me to have to die at the hands of a mob under the pretense of hanging one by law. It is not death that I dread at all, but it is the thoughts of having to die without a trial, and then, afterwards, they will say that I had a fair and impartial trial. They say that I have killed men without giving them a trial. So I have, too, but I done it alone; I never had 200 or 300 men to help me, and then I thought law was framed for the purpose of giving every one a fair showing. But in my case they have only used law in the shape of a kangaroo court—just to satisfy their vengeance. I know I have done wrong, but, then, we all do wrong; we are all mortal beings and liable to sin; none are saints; but all must stand before God as sinners. There is no difference.

Well, Captain, it is getting dark, and I must come to a close. But you know you told me in your last letter that there were some people in your county that sympathized with me, and that they would sign a petition to the Governor to get my sentence commuted to lifetime in prison. Of course that would be preferable to death, but, sir, it would be no use, for there is so many against me and then it is about election time, too. So, I don't think it worth while. But, Captain, I am truly thankful and under many obligations to the good people of your county, who would be willing to show me that much mercy, and you must tell them that I thank them and will never forget them while I live, though that is not long.

They have set the 4th day of October for their execution. Captain, you must write to me; this may be the last letter that I will write to you, but I guess we will all meet at the hatter's shop when Gabriel blows his horn. So, no more; write soon. I am, your friend,

W. P. Longley

P.S. Now, Captain, they are talking so much about poison. I will tell you this: that if nothing will save me from the gallows but poison, you may bet your life that I will hang, sure; for you bet I will never be the murderer of Bill Longley—no, never.[21]

Fuller, in *Adventures of Bill Longley*, quoted an undated letter written by Longley about this time, which was similar in wording to the letter he wrote the *Illustrated Police News*, published on April 20, 1878, in which he sought to give a testament justifying his life and again denying the deeds he had boasted about when captured:

I have noticed in various newspapers published in different parts of the United States, sketches of my life and adventures which do me great injustice, and which have greatly tended to arouse public opinion throughout Texas against me. But I do not insinuate regarding any of the aforesaid papers, for I firmly believe that they have been misinformed by men who have sworn that I shall swing by the neck from the gibbet.

I do not intend to attempt to justify myself in everything, but I am justified in some things that I have done, and there is one thing that I do deny, and that is the charge that I am a cold-blooded murderer as the newspaper correspondents persistently represent. I have always acted in self defense and have not been dodging the law for the past ten years. It was the high toned murderous mobs that I have always feared for in western and middle Texas, it is a well known fact that mob law has been the rule and not the exception since the country was first settled.

There has been two parties in central Texas and what is known as west Texas since 1861, which was the year I believe that the great Civil War started, or rather the year when it go [*sic*] in full swing.

I was a small boy then, but I well remember the heart sickening murders that were committed by the secession party upon as good men as the sun ever shone on, simply because they remained true to the Star Spangled Banner, and the cause of the Union. If all the bloody deeds that were done in Texas during the war could be written down on paper, without exaggeration, it would chill and freeze the blood of every human being, and would shame and shock the civilized world. It was nothing uncommon in those bloody times to see from two to seven men hanging on one liveoak tree, with cards—one pinned on the back of each man with these words written on the cards: "Thus to Traitors."

The meaning of that was that they had simply voted for the Union. I have known mobs to go to houses and pull the very best men out of their beds, while on their knees praying to God, while their wives and helpless children begged the leaders to have mercy and spare the lives of their husbands and fathers. But mercy was unknown and the poor men were ruthlessly butchered and murdered in the presence of their heart stricken wives and innocent children. My father voted a Union ticket and came very near being murdered on the spot. All that saved him, was that he was one of the oldest settlers in Texas, had served in the Mexican War between the United States and Mexico, and was with Sam Houston at the battle of San Jacinto. He still lives in Bell county, Texas and is very old. Several threats were made against his life. He was shamefully abused and his property stolen from him.

I will now explain why the "mobocracy" got incensed against me. Soon after the war the sons of these murdered men grew to manhood, and of course wanted revenge for their murders [*sic*] relatives. I sympathized with them and befriended them on numerous occasions. Because I did so the people became embittered against me, and I was waylaid and shot at, and the boys whom I had helped were getting killed on every side. What could I do but keep out of the way. It was the old law of tooth and fang, and made up my mind to live up to that law literally, and to do so I had to fight and kill in self defense when it became necessary. I knew perfectly well what my fate would be were I to fall into the hands of my enemies. They all knew that I had never stolen anything. I staid at my fathers house and there is not a man on earth who can say that he ever traced a stolen horse to me.

The report of my killing negroes for pastime just to see them kick, is an ungodly falsehood. It was the villainous Ku Klux bunch that did all the killings among the negroes, and laid it on me in order to get the United States troops turned against me, and they succeeded in doing it, causing General Griffin to offer a reward of $1,000 for me dead or alive. Now they had me where they wanted me. I had no protection and my father advised me to leave the state. I left and went to Wyoming territory and enlisted in Company B, second United States Cavalry. After serving two years I ske-daddled from the company and came back to Texas.

All I want in the world is simple justice for there is no possible way on earth for me to do any other way, than the way I have done. If I had surrendered myself or been captured at any time, previous to the time that I was captured, I would certainly have been shot or hung without a trial. However, I might as well have been strung up by a mob, as hung at last by a jury that was picked and stocked to condemn me. My trial was a mere mockery of justice. Perjured testimony was taken against me. My witnesses were driven from the country. I had no lawyer to defend me. My father received threatening letters that if he took any stock in securing counsel to defend me he would certainly be assassinated and my father and mother were not even allowed to see me while I was confined in the Giddings jail. It is over three years since I have seen them, and it is nearly a year since I was captured.

I was tried for killing Wilson Anderson in Lee county. I have been charged with killing my uncle Cale Longley, in Lee county, but that is untrue. It was the killing of Cale Longley's son, my nephew [*sic*], by Wilson Anderson, that caused me to kill Anderson. It has been stated that he was unarmed when I killed him, but that report was circulated in order to influence people against me. Anderson was well armed and was on the look out for me, when I came upon him and he had a fair chance. There was not a tree nor anything near us, and it was about one o'clock in the broad day light, in an open field when I rode up to him. He made the first break at me, and in self defense I killed him, and I consider myself perfectly justified in doing so.

I have been condemned to death on the blood-thirsty and perjured testimony of a sworn gang of cutthroats and murderers, and God knows that I had no showing for my life. I am not afraid to stand before His judgment seat for then I know that I will be dealt with fairly and impartially. I feel hurt that I should have been so misrepresented by the press throughout the country charging me with murders in Texas, thereby naming me the king of Texas man killers.

I am satisfied that people would form a different opinion of me if they were acquainted with all the circumstances connected with each case, in which I was forced to take life in my own defense, but I solemnly re-iterate that I never killed 32 men as has been reported throughout the country. I understand that I am to be hanged by the neck until dead, sometime next October, although the governor has not as yet set the day. I am in good health and in good spirits—as good as a man can be under the circumstances. I am well aware of my present precarious condition. I have no hopes of commutation, because I have no friends to intercede for executive clemency. But I want the world to know that I am cheerful, for I do not see any use of a man pining away, or fretting himself to death before his time comes, and if I must die on the scaffold, you can bet your bottom dollar that Bill Longley will die as becomes a brave man.[22]

Longley continued to write to his parents, although it is not known if they had yet tried to communicate with him. On June 1, 1878, he wrote:

Dear Father and Mother and brother Cammie—

As I have nothing to do I will write you a few lines this beautiful Saturday eavning. And I can say that I am in the very best of health and spirits hopeing that they may find you in like happiness. Well, the old wheels of time are still rolling on. Every day brings me a little nearer to that mighty abyss from whence my soul will be wafted far into the relms of the great unknown future, where pain and death are fealt or feared no more. Oh strange but happy thought it is, and is a thought that was never rightly weighed in my mind until lately. Great God how foolish I have bin to live the life that I have, but I have don [*sic*] it shure, and I can do nothing now only depend on the merits of Jesus Christ in the future. But he is able and willing to blot out my sins and make me as pure as any that live. He says he will, and I believe his blessed word, and if it be his will that I should drink this cup, of which I do most rightly deserve, I will drink it with pleasure. Well, I suppose you know now about how I feel and I wish you could all feel as I do. I got a long letter yesterday from a Christian lady in Mobile, Alabama. She saw a letter of mine published in a Mobile paper and she said she thought she would write to me and console me in my lonely cell. It was a purely religious letter and it suited me exactly, and I answered it and [letter torn] her eight pages. I receive a great many religious letters from people who I never heard of. I am saveing all of them. I will send them all home some time. This lady saw the same one that the person at Lampasas saw which caused him to write to me. I told you about his letter. Dr. Denny was his name. That letter of mine was published all over the United States. Not only that one but several others. I have received another letter from an unknown lady in Navarro County, Texas, and a minister of Dallas wrote to me and another one wrote to Rev. [illegible] Bird, rector of Trinity Church here and he come to see me twice and is going to come regular. He gave me a prayer book and tracts hymn books and so fourth and I get religious newspapers from all parts of the world. Well it is getting late in the eavning and I must close. I sent you a Police News three days ago with a letter in it. Tell me if you got it. While I write this line I hear the band playing a beautiful piece. The band wagon is going along by the jail. I hear the band every night. So I will close. I want to send this off this eavning. Write soon. Cammie be a good boy.

W. P. Longley[23]

A strange occurrence on the evening of Friday, May 30, injected Longley's death watch with a touch of mystery. A man entered the office of the clerk of the Court of Appeals in Galveston. He identified himself with the name of Wilson, telling the clerk that he was a messenger from the governor and that he wanted a copy of the judgment in Longley's case with the court's official seal attached. "Wilson" was asked to come back the next day, and the clerk worked until three in the morning to prepare it. But rather than wait for the messenger, the clerk decided to express it on to Austin. When "Wilson" returned and was told what happened, he was upset and left. The clerk had suspected that something was not quite right, which was confirmed when the governor's office sent word asking why the judgment had been sent.[24]

Longley was now one of twenty-nine prisoners in the Galveston County jail, including six women. Said the *Galveston Daily News*: "First-class jail soup and a liberal supply of good bread and meat, make this resort a desirable one to a good many of the inmates, who prefer prison fare to none at all."[25] On June 15, Longley wrote a letter to his brother Jim, telling him that he was out of clothes. He asked Jim if he and Campbell could send him $25 by the first of August for the purchase of a new suit to take to Giddings when he was returned there for his execution. "You know there will be many eyes on me and I hate to go out looking ragged." On the other side of the letter, Longley directed a message to his younger brother, Cammie, and enclosed a photograph of Mast and a lock of his own hair:

> Cammie wouldent you feel funny if you was to see me come rideing up some day. Who knoweth what a day may bring fourth. Well Cammie that may never be. But if you will live a Christian as long as you live, you are certain to meet me in the beautiful land that is farer than day. Remember what I say. Hurry and learn to write so you can write to me. I would rather see you now than any one on earth. But I dont suppose you remember much about me, as I have never bin with you much.[26]

The Rev. Louis Claude Marie Chambodut. *By permission of Catholic Archives of Texas, Austin.*

It was during July that Longley was baptized into the Catholic Church. His spiritual advisor was the Reverend Father Louis Claude Marie Chambodut, born at St. Just-en-Chevalet, Loire, France, on March 25, 1821, to a well-to-do farmer. Attending seminary in Lyons, he became a deacon of the church in 1845 and decided to emigrate to

Texas. He went to Nacogdoches in 1846, then moved to Galveston in 1851.[27] A priest of St. Mary's Cathedral in Galveston, the cigar-smoking Reverend Chambodut had previously attended to another convicted murderer, a black woman who was hanged in 1857 in Galveston for killing her mistress with a flatiron then throwing her body in a well.[28] Longley's baptism was sponsored by the Reverend Chambodut and Mary Viola Slocovich.[29]

During July, a number of events occurred that peripherally touched Longley's life. He likely read in the July 21 issue of the *Galveston Daily News* that a James O. McMasters was shot to death in Lampasas County without realizing that McMasters was the second husband of the widow of Lou Shroyer.[30] On July 19, Sam Bass and his gang were shot to pieces in Round Rock, north of Austin, displacing Longley from the newspapers temporarily. For many weeks, the pursuit of Bass and his men all over North Texas had entertained the state. George McCormick, who had argued for the state on Longley's appeal, became a Democratic candidate for Texas attorney general.[31] More important, petitions were being circulated in Nacogdoches to commute Longley's death sentence to life imprisonment. Among the reasons given for the petitions being signed "by numerous citizens of the very best class" were opposition to capital punishment, sympathy for Longley, and "confidence in his honor and honesty of purpose."[32] In a letter home on July 31, Longley's spirits seemed somewhat upbeat:

> As I have made a rais of a stamp, I will write a few lines. I would write oftener, but I have exhausted every sours of borrowing stamps. I have borrowed out the whole jail. Jailors and all. I owe stamps to everybody. Well I am in good health and the very best of spirits. My time is getting short, but it cannot shorten faster than I want it to. Everyday seams like a week. If it is God's will that I must be hung, I would rejoyce if it was tomorrow. I am in better spirits now than ever was in my life, and I hope you are all in good spirits. I have bin baptized some time, and will in a

couple of days pertake of the sacrament here in jail. The preast has just leaft my cell. He has bin talking to me all morning. Well I have no news to tell you. I am sorry you could not make arrangements with some merchant to get me some clothes, but I guess you would have done so if you could. I am almost barefooted, and I have no coat at all. But I hope I will soon be where I will have no use for this worlds goods. I care not for my body nor what is on it. So my soul is safe that is all I want. Sometimes I am all most afraid that I will not be hung. I am tired of this world. Well, I want to write some to Jim. So I will close. I will be here about 20 days yet. So you can write one more letter to me here. I will write when I get to Giddings. I remain your affectionate son until death.

In the same letter he wrote his brother Jim:

I hope you are in good spirits and health. I see in the news that the citizens of Nacogdoches county has got up a petition to commute my sentence to the penitentiary. Over three thousand men & women have signed it, and it will be sent all over the state. Captain Milt Mast is the one that is doing it. I suppose you have saw it in the Galveston News. It was in the Daily News. Well Jim I expect you will get a very religious letter from a lady in Mobile, Alabama, and her little daughter Viola, 13 years old. Now if you do you must be very careful what you say when you write to her. They are not no love letter writers at all. They have written a great many letters to me. They are the ones that got me to join the Catholic church. They commenced writing to me on account of a letter of mine that was published. You know the one I wrote to Mast about floating down the river of destruction from my youth. I sent it to you in the Police News. I will send you a paper next Saturday with a long piece in that I wrote in a paper called the Thunderbolt. Well, Jim, if God is running the petition it will work and if not, then you know it will not amount to anything.

So I won't bother myself about it, for I allways say in all things, O God, Thy will be done, not mine. So no more at present. Write soon. Your brother,

Bill Longley[33]

The likelihood that Governor Hubbard would heed any petitions was not a great one. In an address the governor made at Corsicana on July 10, he described the standard he would require in considering leniency for any criminal, and it was clear that Longley's appeal would not reach a sympathetic ear:

> In the matter of pardons, while I respect the courts and the applications for clemency, I have made it my rule to hold up the juries and courts. I must feel a wrong has been done and find some mitigating circumstances that will justify my imposition to act otherwise.[34]

At dawn on Sunday, August 4, W. L. Grissom and Dave Drake, both convicted murderers, escaped from the Galveston County Jail with the help of a saw left them by another prisoner. Grissom cut away his leg shackles and, with Drake, who was not wearing any irons, broke out of their plank-lined second floor cell and through a window with a rope made out of blankets. Sheriff Jordan's security precautions were found lacking. Normally there were three guards on the night watch at the old jail, one in the office and the other two patrolling the jail. Routinely at 5 a.m. the cells were entered to remove human waste from the prisoners. After 6 a.m. there was only one guard. By 11:45 p.m. Sheriff Jordan and a posse, after receiving a tip, had recaptured the two escapees.[35]

Immediately, the Galveston County commissioners authorized the sheriff to hire two additional jail guards until a new jail could be constructed.[36] The old jail holding Longley was appropriately described by one newspaper:

> The county jail is just now a menagerie, which only needs the inspired invention of a Barnum to place it first among the menageries of the world. There are upwards of fifty men and women convicted or accused of every grade of crime, and possessing all the conceivable eccentricities to which human flesh is heir. No half hour passes without a fight, and the religious and national anthems blend harmoniously with the blasphemous swell which comes from the lips of others. [J]ailers Miller and Schmidt have their hands full.[37]

But Longley was soon to leave his noisy home of the past eleven months.

Chapter 19

Hanging is My Favorite Way of Dying

As Bill Longley faced his transfer to Giddings and coming one step closer to the gallows, his father was apparently not faring very well. Bell County Judge Erastus Walker submitted a petition to the state government on behalf of Campbell Longley requesting a petition for financial assistance stemming from his service in the Texas army in 1836. Walker described the sixty-two-year-old Campbell as "too old to labour for a support, that he has several in family to provide for and has no one to assist him to make a support for himself and family—that his health is not good—that he is poor and needy, in fact in indigent circumstances and that he was in said condition on the 1st of July, 1876."[1] In May, 1874, Campbell had filed a pension claim, which was approved for $250.[2]

Whether or not Bill Longley was aware of this is unknown. His uncle Alexander Preston Longley, known as "Pres," sent a letter in August on behalf of his condemned nephew to President Rutherford Hayes, blaming "politics" and asking for a presidential pardon.[3] "W. P. Longley is very young, and, I think, has a good heart, and might, in case you reprieve him, under other skies do some thing to make amends for any misdeeds he has done."[4] Campbell Longley's brother, Pres Longley, had long ago migrated with another brother, William Tennessee Longley, to Butte Creek Canyon in California in search of gold, but was largely unsuccessful and certainly never wealthy as would later be rumored. In addition to being noted for a fondness for drink and festive occasions, he gained local prominence in Butte County as a poet and, it was claimed, personally met President Hayes in Chico, California, in 1881.[5] The letter was forwarded to the Department of Justice, which sent it on to the United States attorney in Houston. That official being out of town, his wife forwarded it to Texas Governor Hubbard. No record exists of any response to this plea.[6]

On Saturday, August 24, 1878, a day after Judge Turner convened the district court in Lee County, Sheriff Jim Brown and several deputies retrieved a heavily ironed Longley from the Galveston jail for his last train ride to Giddings. "He was in good spirits when he left, was laughing and talking with the crowd at the depot, and seemed to be in a better humor for a feast than a hanging."[7] His hope for any last-minute reprieve was growing slimmer, although it was rumored that only three men in Nacogdoches County had refused to sign the petition to commute his sentence.[8]

Another bizarre episode occurred at this time. On August 30, 1878, Amos Ben Hadley and Diomed Powell were hanged at Longview, Texas, for the December 1877 murder of a Gregg County grocer. Prior to their execution, Hadley was interviewed, at which time he made a rambling statement to the "people of Texas" claiming that he was with Brown Bowen and John Wesley Hardin just prior to a murder for which Bowen was executed, but asserting that Hardin was responsible. Then he went on:

> Those murders that people are putting on Bill Longley God is putting on mob law. He is not guilty of the third of them. I was with him the day before he killed Anderson. He had a good right to kill him, for Anderson made the first attempt.[9]

Longley denied any knowledge of Hadley and his claims.[10]

Returned to jail in Giddings and placed in an iron cage on the first floor, Longley appeared before Judge Turner on Friday, September 6. He appeared "haggard and pale" from his long confinement.[11] The mandate of the court of appeals affirming Longley's conviction had been returned, and it was now Judge Turner's duty to set a date for the execution. On this same date Longley's jailer, Sheriff Jim Brown, defended by Seth Shepard, Longley's prosecutor, was found not guilty of murdering Hugh McKeown.[12]

Reading from a prepared statement, and appropriately contrite, Longley stood before Judge Turner:

> Judge Turner, your honor, I stand before you, sir, condemned to die for the murder of Wilson Anderson. I have been tried and convicted of murder, by an honorable jury, I suppose, as far as I know of them they are.
>
> Still I cannot help but think that there was prejudice against me. But I thank God that I have had time to reflect calmly on the matter. I now feel quite different to what I did one year ago, when your Honor, sir, pronounced the sentence of the law, when I appealed to a higher court, by which the sentence of death was affirmed. And by the grace of God I am ready to abide by the decision of the jury. I have said a great deal since, during my confinement at Galveston, in regard to my trial, all of which I do not take back, but I said more than I should have said, but I hope that all who are interested will consider the dreadful state of mind under which I labored. Place yourself for a moment in my place and probably you will not blame me too much.
>
> It is true I killed Anderson, that you all know, for I have never denied it, but had I not believed so strongly that he killed my cousin, Cale Longley, I would not have killed him, but still even suppose that Anderson did kill Cale Longley, that did not justify me in killing him, in the eyes of the law here on earth, neither in the sight of God, for God never made me an avenger of blood. I am sorry I killed Anderson, and also of many other things that I

have done, but what is done cannot be recalled. There is no hope for me in this life, but God is more merciful than man, and he will forgive when man won't. People generally condemn the acts of others, when at the same time, if they were placed in similar circumstances, they might do the same thing, which they condemn in others.

I know I did wrong in killing Anderson, but I didn't see it in that light when I killed him, for really I thought it was just and right, for me to take his life, in retaliation for his killing Cale Longley, but now I think the majority of the people think it very doubtful whether Anderson killed Cale or not, and he may not have done it, yet I believe he did; whether or not he did, availeth me nothing now, but I would like to be thoroughly convinced before I die, one way or the other. I wish to make this request, that is I would be glad to have the jury that held the inquest over the body of Cale Longley, to come to the jail and let me ask them a few questions if they please, I ask them as a special favor, I do not know who they are, but some one here may know them. In conclusion, may I say to your Honor, sir, that you have ever done your whole duty and nothing else in my case. I know you have not the least prejudice against me, you even exhibited sympathy for me, and I hope I said nothing to wound your feelings.

I thank you, sir, for giving me the privilege to say what I have.[13]

Eloquently and sadly, Turner then addressed the accused man standing before him, and carried out his grim duty in what was described as a "feeling manner":

Mr. Longley, the time has arrived at which I am called to perform the last act which is devolved upon me in the case of the State versus yourself, viz: To pronounce the final sentence. It is a duty that I approach with reluctance and regret. It is painful enough to consign a fellow being to the confines of the penitentiary for life, or for a limited period, but when called upon to take a part, as an instrument in the hands of the law, to consign a fellow mortal to the grave, by passing sentence of death, which sends one across the dark waters, from beyond which no voice has ever yet returned, you may well imagine how great the solicitude must be to the sensitive mind to feel and know that the part taken has been controlled and governed by the rules laid down in the law for guidance. And I assure you that I am heartily glad that, so far as my conduct in the trial of your case is concerned, it has all passed in review before the court of last resort, and that I am assured that, in so far as the action of the court in this case is concerned, it has been in strict conformity to law. The bill of indictment in this case was returned into this court on the 10th day of May, 1875. In the bill you are charged with the willful and deliberate murder of one Wilson Anderson, in this county, in the month of March of that year. After a trial which ended on the 15th [*sic*] of September, 1877, the jury who tried the case returned a verdict of guilty of murder in the first degree. To that finding by the jury the law attaches the death penalty. In addition to the testimony, which was pointed and conclusive, you have, over your own signature, published to the world, as well as openly declared here this morning, the fact that the verdict was the very truth; and, under the law, your life must pay the forfeit. Without law, society could not exist; civilization would be impossible. By it our rights are assured, and life, liberty and property protected. It is the ligament that binds the universe, that controls the movements of the planets and prevents utter chaos and destruction. It binds communities together, regulates the conduct of nations toward each other and binds poor, weak and crying humanity to God himself. What may have been your early training, I know not, nor is it in my place to inquire—to what temptations you may have been subjected no mortal may know. It is not possible for human institutions to take these things into consideration when laying down rules to govern the conduct of men towards each other. But, if in the great hereafter, as we hope to believe there is an all wise and all beneficent law giver and will be taken into the account, and that strict justice will be meted out to all the erring sons and daughters of men. Let me, in all kindness and sincerity, urge you to turn your thoughts inward and upward, and to prepare yourself for the terrible ordeal which awaits you, and to secure, if possible, forgiveness and remission. If you can accomplish this, and feel and know for a certainty that this has been in your behalf accomplished, you can then say with the poet:

'Tis a dreadful thing to die,
But the dark vale once trod,
Heaven lifts its everlasting portals high,
And wings the immortal soul away to God.

Life is short at best, and, so far as time is concerned, it is but a difference of a few short years, or, perhaps, months and considered merely as a matter of time, no great importance can be attached to the few short years of our sojourn here. Punishments are inflicted with no feelings of animosity. The State much prefers to protect rather than destroy, but, in its wisdom, it demands that when a person deliberately takes the life of a citizen, the party so offending shall pay the forfeit with his own life, in order to prevent a repetition of the offense, and, more especially, to deter others from offending in a like manner. It is, therefore, the final sentence of this court that you be detained by the Sheriff of this county in close confinement in the county jail of Lee county until the 11th day of October next, 1878, and that on that day, between 11 o'clock a.m., and the going down of the sun on that day, you be, by the Sheriff of Lee county, hung by the neck until you shall be dead-dead-dead. And may God have mercy on your soul.[14]

Judge Turner then signed Longley's death warrant, which directed Sheriff Brown to carry out the sentence of the court on Friday, October 11.

Longley returned to his cell to await the trip to the gallows thirty-five days later. Once again, he resumed letter writing, mentally preparing himself for his execution. To an old schoolmate, Mrs. Bettie Southern, he wrote on September 19:

> Yes, Bettie, I am happy to say to you that I am ready to die, and I look forward to the day of my execution as being the end of all trouble. It is the gate, dark as it may seem, to endless happiness, and oh, too true it is, that I have been a wild and reckless boy since our old school days. That you well know yourself, but as you say, Bettie, God is more merciful than man, and is willing to save all who come to Him with a penitent and contrite heart, and though I may be chief of sinners, I have no right to doubt God's mercy if I ask it from my heart and if I will freely forgive my enemies, both of which I have done, and am daily trying to do.[15]

After reminiscing about school days, Longley went on:

> I am lively yet, and expect to be as long as I live. It is no use to be sad, and then I cannot be sad when I know that I am soon to be released from all trouble, for I well know that I will be better off. Hanging is my favorite way of dying, if I have to die. I would rather die that way than any other way on earth, that is except a natural death; and I would be glad if everybody would forgive me before I die, but I will forgive all my enemies whether they do me or not.[16]

As the time grew closer, Longley likely realized there was little hope, but he still looked for good news. On September 26 he wrote his heartbroken parents:

Dear Father & Mother,

This leaves me well and in good spirits. I received yours and Jim's letter of the 19th of Sept. this morning and was glad to hear that you was all well, but sorry to know that you are takeing things so hard. Of course, I know you cannot help but feel bad, but then if you will look at things right, you will not take it so hard, is it not better for me as it is than for me to have went on as I was going and got killed some time without time to think of the future? Well, I have nothing of interest to write. I got another letter from Uncle Preston. I will send it to you in this letter. I sent you his other letter, and it seemes that you never got it as you did not say nothing about it. I would like to know if you got it and also if you get this one. You ought to write to him shure. I have wrote to him several times. It was Uncle Preston that wrote to President Hays and he wrote to Gov. Hubbard too. I have a petition written out and Jim Brown will send it to Judge E. B. Turner tomorrow and if he signes it I am going to try how many of the juriman will sign it, if any. A lawyer by name of Lott wrote out the petition for me. Well, I have nothing worth writing. You must write soon. I will write yet again. Cammie, dear little brother, keep in good spirits, and be a good boy. I am all right. I would not give my chance for no ones. I mean my chance for a happy eternity. You must all do the best you can. We will all meet again in the sweet by and by. Your affectionate son until death.

W. P. Longley

To C. Longley and S. A. Longley. Give my love to all inquireing friends.[17]

The next day, in a letter to brother Jim, Longley seemed more focused on dying than on living:

> I was glad to hear you talk as you did in your last letter. That is right to be a man. Dont give way to old Nick. The Devil will lead you in to temptations and ruin you and then laugh at you for being a fool. God is our only friend. Why not love him and him [*sic*] with all our might. It is the Devil that puts men up to seek revenge. Now just quit drinking whiskey and swearing for the sake of God who loves you, and be peacible with all on earth, and beare no malice in your heart against no man. If you dont do this you shall never be happy in eternity. You have a much better chance now than I had when your age to do right. Well Jim I don't expect to die like a braggart at all. I hope to die as becomes a Christian. God will be with me and the blessed Virgin Mary will be a mother to me in the last trying hours, for she is the comfortress of the comfortless and mother of mercy. Jesus Christ himself has said so, and has appointed her the mother of all dejected sinners. Jim, I sent you and Cammie a letter with several little sacred pictures and some prayers in it. Did you get it? Write soon and keep in good spirits. I am in the best kind of hopes. I care nothing for this world. If God will be with me through death and strengthen me, I would rather die than not, and I know he will help me. So good by until next time.[18]

In the weeks before the scheduled execution, Sheriff Jim Brown's primary concern was the security of his prisoner until the court order could be carried out. According to T. U. Taylor, because of some apprehension that cohorts of Longley might attempt to rescue him, Governor Hubbard sent Ranger James E. Lucy from Austin to Giddings to make an investigation.[19] Born in Maryland in 1854, Lucy served in Captain Lee Hall's Special Ranger Force for about six weeks in 1877, then served with Captain Dan Roberts' Frontier Battalion Company D.[20] According to Taylor, Lucy spent about one week in Giddings, then returned to Austin and reported to the governor that there was no probability of an attempt being made to save Longley.[21]

In response to a letter from Campbell and Sarah Longley to Hubbard, asking that the death sentence for their son be commuted to life imprisonment, the governor responded that he would not be doing his duty to "disturb the decision of the courts," and invoked "the mercy of God for your unfortunate son."[22] All that there was left to do was to count the days and hours and wait. One man stated that Longley's father had visited his son in jail (although that never happened), and that Longley played a violin, one of his melancholy tunes being a ditty called "Gentle Annie."[23] The word from Austin was that Governor Hubbard had received the petitions from Nacogdoches with some 2,000 signatures but he declined to commute the sentence of "the 'blood thirsty rascal' as the governor called Longley or words to that effect."[24]

On Wednesday, October 9, Longley admitted to Sheriff Brown that he had exaggerated the number of men that he killed. He claimed that he had killed but eight men, six white men and two black men, "though he had shot several others who did not die."[25] On this same date, under orders from the governor, Ranger Lewis S. Delony, according to his memoirs, said that he reported to Jim Brown to assist in carrying out the execution. He said that he was detailed to help guard the jail because of a rumor that Jim Longley and Wes Hardin would attempt to grab the prisoner. Of course, Hardin was not a free man at the time. Delony said that there was a large crowd of armed men camped near Giddings that was thought to be the "Hardin and Longley gang."[26]

On October 10, the day before the scheduled hanging and four days after his twenty-seventh birthday, Longley wrote his final letters to his brothers Jim and Cammie. They reflect the resignation of a man ready to die:

> Dear Brother
>
> I am in good spirits and old boy I think you will hear that I died the same way.
>
> Jim I haven't time to write much. I got your post card just now and now Jim Ill tell you for the last time that you must

always be gay and happy and love God with all your heart and soul. I don't dread this at all. Tomorrow this time I will be in a much better place. Oh it is a glorious thing to think of the beautiful change. Tell ma to rather rejoice than to grieve. I feel better than I ever fealt in my life.

I got Cammies letter and paps. Well Jim be a good boy and meet me in heaven. Good Bye.

Your most loving Brother forever.

W. P. Longley

My Dear Sweet little brother Cammie

I have not time to write much but allways be a good Boy and dont cry for me. I am all right. Give my love to all the family.

The priest is here tonight and will be with me tomorrow on the scaffold. Tell pap and ma and George and Lizzie and Matt and every body that I am all right. So no more. Goodbye Dearest little Buddie Cammie.

W. P. Longley[27]

A reporter for the *Galveston Daily News* visited Longley in jail, finding him "calm, collected and in good spirits." The reporter noted that, while the condemned man did not appear as "jocular" as in the past, Longley still spoke lightly of killing. He told the reporter that he had not prepared any statement to read on the gallows, but did not know if he would make a speech. "That depends upon how I feel at the time. I don't see what good it will do. Let others learn by experience as I have."[28]

The Galveston newspaper described the doomed man:

Longley appears heavier than ever known to be, and speaks most kindly of the treatment received in jail here, especially

Alexander Campbell "Cammie" Longley. *Courtesy of Juanita Longley, San Saba, Texas.*

> when comparing it with his incarceration in Galveston. The Catholic priest from Austin arrived this evening and spent some time with Longley. It is notable that Longley has left off using profane language entirely.[29]

The priest tending to Longley's spiritual needs in his last hours was the Reverend Daniel J. Spillard, an Irishman from Austin. The Reverend Spillard was the first Holy Cross priest at St. Mary's Church there.[30] On this Thursday evening, Spillard spent about three hours with Longley, who made his confession.[31]

Jim Brown rounded up about 100 armed men to make sure the hanging went off without any trouble. Half of them were to be mounted, while the other half would be on foot around the gallows.[32] The mounted men were under the direction of Zinna P. Eagleston (sometimes spelled Eggleston), who himself had once faced trial for murder. A forty-three-year-old native of North Carolina, Eagleston was indicted along with James Walker in April 1862 in Bastrop County for the murder of a Joseph McDavid, as well as indicted for assault with intent to kill a John McDavid. Probably because of the war, he was not tried until 1866 when a jury found him not guilty.[33] More recently Eagleston had been one of three partners in the Lee County Meat Market.[34] In charge of the "infantry" was William J. McClellan, who had been a deputy for Jim Brown in August 1877 prior to Longley's trial.[35]

Dawn of Friday, October 11, 1878, saw a murky morning and the threat of rain. It was estimated that by 7 a.m. there were about 2,000 people gathered in town, a large portion of them being black.[36] Wagons and carriages lined the roads leading to Giddings, along with horsemen, all compelled to witness the passing of the noted desperado. The newly erected gallows stood about six hundred yards northwest of the Giddings depot. One of Brown's guards spoke to Longley in his cell, and the condemned man told him that "if it were not for his faith in God he would break down at the last moment," and that he would now rather kill a man than take the name of the Lord in vain.[37]

The Reverend Daniel J. Spillard. *By permission of Catholic Archives of Texas, Austin.*

At 8 a.m., the Reverend Spillard and the Reverend Joseph Querat, a French-born priest who, because of failing health and eyesight, was assigned to a Galveston convent, met with Longley and administered the last rite of extreme unction.[38] Longley then asked the sheriff not to permit anyone to see him, much to the consternation of reporters outside the jail eager for a last interview.

The priests having left, Longley continued to prepare himself mentally. He asked some of the guards to join him in singing the hymn, "Amazing Grace," Longley singing in a bass voice. He prayed in his cell, then, "at leisure and with scrupulous taste," dressed himself for his death. He put on a "faultless" black suit, a white shirt with a turndown collar, and a black necktie. On his lapel he affixed a blue rosette. He combed his long hair and goatee, and readied a broad-brimmed, low-crowned hat to complete his ensemble.[39] Under his shirt and tied around his neck with a cord was a small Catholic medal.

Although it was being rumored that Jim Longley was in the crowd or in the area as part of a rescue attempt, none of Longley's immediate family came to see him. The only family member to visit him, after he had dressed, was his ten-year-old niece, Elizabeth Carnes, known as Lizzie. She was the daughter of Longley's sister, Martha Jane, who had married William Carnes.[40] One newspaper gave a melodramatic account of this brief meeting:

> She is a beautiful girl, and the last interview between uncle and niece was affecting in the extreme. She was admitted to the jail after the murderer had attired himself for the last time. Extremes again met, the innocent girl and the uncle steeped in crime, utterly abandoned and lost. When she gracefully arose to leave him forever the hardened and red-handed assassin implanted a last kiss on the pure brow of the child and turned away to hide the emotion that evidently welled up in his reprobate bosom. The scene touched the hearts of the stoutest minded of the rough guards of the prison.[41]

The Reverend Joseph Querat. *By permission of Catholic Archives of Texas, Austin.*

Outside the jail, one self-proclaimed witness, many years later, described the air as festive. According to him, popcorn and peanut vendors mingled with the crowd, and bunting hung across the main street of Giddings, connected to stores and saloons, of which there were two. Bartenders moved up and down the street serving whiskey from jugs for ten cents a drink. The witness, Everett Hagen, even asserted that "bands were playing and flags were flying," but all of this seems highly unlikely. During midmorning a rumor made the rounds that Longley had broken out of jail, and that story, along with other fantastic tales, "kept the crowd in a state of excitement."[42] None of the contemporary newspapers described such a circus-like atmosphere in Giddings.

At one twenty-five in the afternoon it was time to leave the jail. Jim Brown hustled Longley aboard a horse-drawn ambulance with four guards inside. Accompanied by Eagleston's mounted guards and McClellan's walking guards, the entourage slowly made its way up the street and headed for the waiting gallows. The crowd was kept back by guards and a rope placed around the wood frame gallows. Longley and his guard arrived at the gallows around 2:00 p.m. and he dismounted, a cigar clamped firmly in his mouth.

The two priests, Spillard and Querat, were at the scaffold to greet Longley, who was not restrained in any way. With a guard on either side of him, Longley walked to a chair beneath the gallows ladder and asked for some water. The water was brought to him, and as he drank it and smoked his cigar, he "alternately chatted and laughed with the guards." Longley had determined to affect a lighthearted approach in order to "die game." One newspaper reported that Longley asserted that his path to murder began with the killing of "helpless animals and birds,"[43] but such statement on the part of Longley does not seem likely.

At two fifteen it was time to ascend the gallows. The *Brenham Weekly Banner* said that as Longley climbed the steps leading to the platform, he put one foot down firmly and shook the stairs, telling his guards, "I wish to see if everything is firm. I don't care to be crippled."[44] The *Galveston Daily News* reported that the stairs came near giving way, and that Longley warned, "Look out, the steps are falling."[45] And another account many years later recalled that as Longley began to mount the steps, they wobbled, and he stepped back and asked that the steps be braced. "I don't want to get hurt climbing rickety stairs." The steps were braced as requested.[46] Deputy McClellan later remembered that the steps began to shake when Longley was about half way up, and the condemned man supposedly said, "Look out there, let's don't get crippled up before the show is over."[47]

On the scaffold, in addition to Longley, were Sheriff Brown, the two priests, and several guards, McClellan, Charlie Brown, Virgil Wooley, and Zinna Eagleston.[48] Jim Brown stepped up before the hushed crowd and announced that this was the first judicial execution to be carried out in Lee County, and that he hoped there never would be a necessity for another. The sheriff proclaimed that their object here was indeed solemn, that it was a disagreeable duty, but one that had to be performed.[49] He then read the death warrant to Longley, the command of Judge Turner that Brown hang Longley by the neck until he was "dead-dead-dead."[50] Longley was invited to address the crowd, and, discarding his cigar, he stepped forward. Although the exact words were not recorded, the following is the substance of what Longley said in a clear, calm voice:

> I have not much to say; but I have to die, I believe, surrounded by many enemies and but few friends. I hope you will all forgive me for anything I have done, as I have already forgiven all that ever did anything to me. God has forgiven me, and I owed him more than any of you. I know I have to die, and I hate it, for we all hate to die when the time comes; for I have killed men who hated to die as bad as I do. If I have any friends about here who think of revenge, I hope they will forego it, as it is wrong. I hear my brother is in the crowd. I hope not; but if he is, I hope he will let revenge alone and pray for me, as I ask all others to do. I have taken enough revenge myself, and am to be punished for it.[51]

Another account of his last words had him stating,

> in substance that, he had to die, but that he hated to die, no man was willing to die such a death, but that he recognized that the punishment was just and that he merited it; that he had taken the lives of other people which was as dear to them as his. He said, "I see present a large number of my enemies and a few of my friends; am told that my brother is present; if so, I want to admonish him not to attempt to avenge my death, nor do I wish any of my friends to attempt to do so; I have killed a good many persons and I believe that my punishment is just. I forgive everybody of every injury ever done me and I want everybody to forgive me. I have attempted to make my peace with my God and believe that I will be forgiven for the sins I have committed."[52]

Longley then knelt with the two priests and prayed. When he stood, he was pinioned by rope around the arms and legs after he shook hands with those on the scaffold. He kissed the priests, then kissed Jim Brown on the left cheek. To the hushed crowd he called out in a firm, clear voice: "Good bye, all; good bye." A number in the crowd responded with a similar farewell. A black cap was placed over his head after the noose was placed and adjusted around his neck, and he was positioned on the trapdoor of the scaffold. One newspaper reported that because the sheriff had received letters warning him that he would be shot on the scaffold by Longley's friends, Brown posted several of the guards around him so that the sheriff would be a difficult target.[53]

The trap was to fall when Jim Brown cut a rope with a hatchet, which had apparently been misplaced. Brown asked, "Where's the hatchet?" Longley's muffled voice came from under the black cap as he stood on the trap door, "What do you want with a hatchet? Are you going to split my head open?"[54] These were his last recorded words, for Jim Brown located the hatchet and chopped the rope in two.

Illustration from *The National Police Gazette* of October 26, 1878, dramatizing Longley on the gallows. *Courtesy Chuck Parsons, Luling, Texas.*

The trapdoor gave way and Longley plummeted down, falling eight feet, as had been intended to break his neck. One bystander recalled in 1926 that Longley's legs were hit forcefully by a heavy piece of iron rail tied to the end of a rope coming through the trap door.[55] But the rope slipped on the beam, and Longley continued to fall until his feet hit the ground beneath the scaffold. He stood, but it only took a second for the sheriff and a deputy to haul him up until his feet cleared the ground, refastening the rope to keep him suspended. Several moans could be heard from him, and he attempted to raise his feet and arms several times as he slowly strangled to death.

After seven minutes, his struggling ceased and Bill Longley was still. Four minutes later, three doctors—Gazley, Fields, and Johnson—checked the suspended body and confirmed that there was no heartbeat.[56] Longley's body was cut down, and it was determined that he had a broken neck, according to the *Galveston Daily News*.

Dr. Jacob A. Fields, Giddings, Texas. *From Mrs. James C. Killeen, ed.,* History of Lee County, Texas *(Quanah, Texas: Nortex Press, 1974.)*

Although none of the contemporary newspaper accounts mentioned it, Fuller alleged that one of the doctors took Longley's head in his hands and turned it completely around, and that a deputy from Washington County did the same to demonstrate that the neck was broken.[57] However, his neck was very likely not broken.

Texas Ranger Lewis Delony later wrote that Wilson Anderson's widow and two children were present and expressed satisfaction with the hanging, although he did not mention the bungling of the execution. He said that Longley's body was placed in a coffin, the coiled rope laid on his breast, and the coffin lid screwed shut.[58] Then the reports say that "the body was carried off and buried by the sheriff."[59] Fuller said that Brown placed Longley's body in a covered hack and took it to the cemetery on the western part of Giddings, on a hill, and "buried it outside the fence in the bushes."[60] This was the site of the present-day Giddings cemetery.

Jim Brown duly returned the death warrant to the court, and wrote on it:

> Came to hand on the 11th day of October 1878 and on the same day between the hour of 10 o'clock and sun down executed this writ by hanging W. P. Longley until he was dead as I am within directed.
>
> J. M. Brown
> Sheriff Lee Co
>
> The jail not being sufficient to erect a gallows Execution took place outside of the jail at the hour of 2:30 P.M. in the presence of the following five named freeholders of Lee County, viz, V. P. Woolley, W. M. Brown, R. E. Harris, S. F. Rainwater, W. A. Scoby. The body of the convict was buried by me.
>
> J.M. Brown
> Sheriff Lee Co.[61]

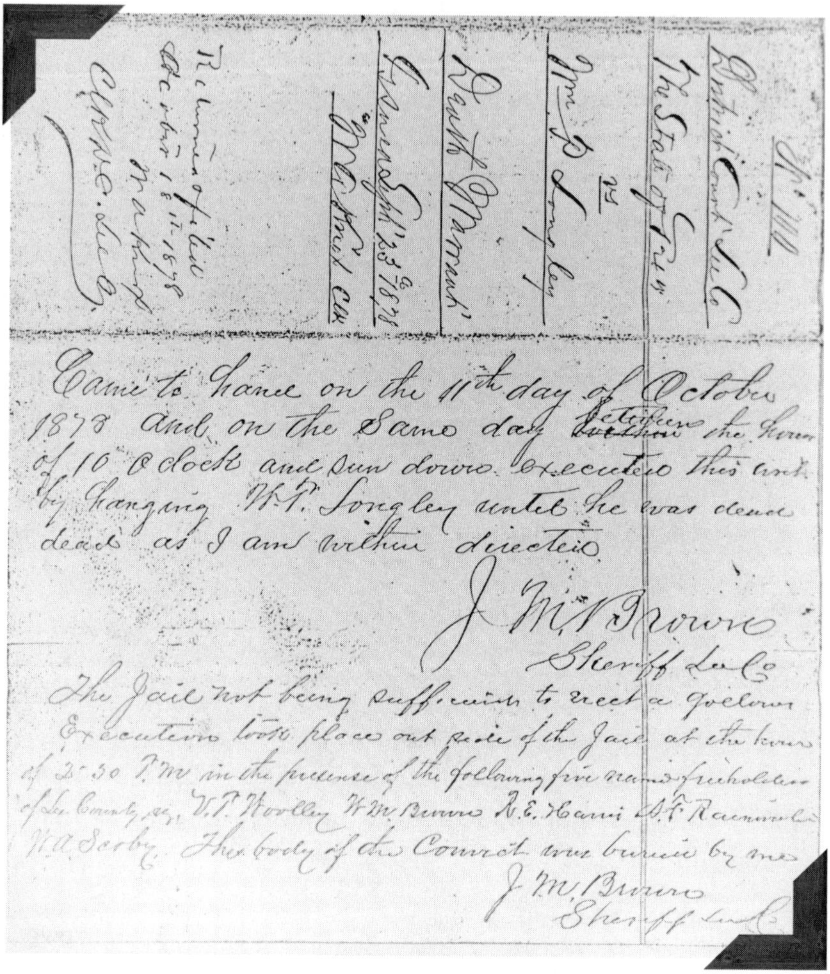
No. 111
District Court Lee Co
The State of Texas
vs
Wm. P. Longley
Death Warrant
Issued Sept 23rd 1878
[illegible] Clk

Came to hand on the 11th day of October 1878 and on the Same day between the hours of 10 o'clock and sun down executed this writ by hanging W. P. Longley until he was dead dead as I am within directed

J. M. V. Brown
Sheriff Lee Co

The Jail not being sufficient to erect a gallows Execution took place out side of the Jail at the hour of 3:30 P.M. in the presence of the following five named freeholders of Lee County viz. W. T. Woolley W. M. Burns R. E. Harris A. P. [illegible] W. A. [illegible]. The body of the convict was buried by me

J. M. Brown
Sheriff Lee Co

Bill Longley's death warrant. *Courtesy of Chuck Parsons, Luling, Texas.*

The execution of Bill Longley was duly reported by the press of Texas, giving him credit for dying as "game" as he had lived. The "majesty of the law" was declared vindicated. The *Galveston Daily News* celebrated Longley's violent passing:

> Thus one by one the desperadoes who formerly scandalized the state, parading murder and rapacity as a profession, and

> scorning all law except the law of the "drop" of the sixshooter, are made to answer for their crimes and pay their forfeit to society in the inexorable grip of the civil authority. A hundred tumultuous lynchings could not have one hundredth part of the remedial effect of these regular, orderly, quiet, but determined and relentless executions.[62]

In Missouri, the *St. Louis Globe-Democrat* detailed Longley's exploits, largely borrowed from stories in the *Galveston Daily News*, and the details of his execution were carried under a scarlet headline: "Bloody Bill, The Last of Longley, The Desperado."[63]

Bill Longley was dead, but he wasn't forgotten, at least not immediately. On the evening of his death, a reporter in Galveston went to a local medium, Mrs. Talbot, who announced that she would attempt to contact Longley's spirit. However, her séance produced no visit from the outlaw. Her explanation was that Longley preferred the quiet of his new surroundings, that conclusion being a better one than Longley's not being dead.[64] Also, the *Lone Star* in Giddings began advertising the sale of "*Life of William P. Longley, written by himself*" for fifty cents, and the *Galveston Weekly News* offered a full report of the execution with a woodcut and a sketch of his life.[65]

The Lee County commissioners authorized payment of $268.90 to Sheriff Jordan in Galveston County for keeping Longley in his jail. Sheriff Brown was authorized $339.45 for expenses that he had incurred in guarding and executing the prisoner.[66]

Bill Longley was dead and buried. His legacy as a deadly gunman, the product of a fierce imagination and boastful nature, would now be a firm part of Texas lore, the stories to be told and retold until they were accepted as fact.

Chapter 20

Not Upon His Doomed Neck

Bill Longley quickly passed from the pages of Texas newspapers, and his notoriety with him. Other gunmen, such as Hardin and Ben Thompson, stepped to the forefront of the public spotlight, their sort continuing to fascinate those who found glamour and excitement in the larger-than-life exploits of an outlaw, as opposed to the humdrum routine of school, farming, or other similar everyday callings. As with Longley, the notorious Jesse James also capitalized on the press to insure a place in history, although James took great pains to *deny* his nefarious deeds.

Only eight months after the hanging, however, stories were already being passed around in Dallas that the execution had been a hoax, thus commencing decades of confusion and speculation about the ultimate fate of Bill Longley. "Rich relatives supplied him with a steel corset and neck piece, which prevented the rope from choking him or pulling on his neck at all when the drop fell." Friends were supposed to have pretended to bury the body, smuggling Longley away and "setting him up in business in California, where he now lives a pious and model young man."[1] Although the story was briefly published in 1879, it did not garner a public response from those who knew better, apparently because it seemed so absurd on its face.

In January 1881, the gallows on which Longley was hung were sold to the sheriff of Milam County for the execution at Cameron of murderer Milam Hubby.[2] In that same year Bill's brother Jim married Elvira Anna "Vie" Draper near Florence in Williamson County on October 3.[3] Their first child, Mary, was born prematurely on July 31, 1882, near Salado in Bell County.[4] Jim and Vie Longley would ultimately have seven children.[5] A claim to the Texas Board of Veterans in Austin by Campbell Longley for a pension was rejected.[6]

Jim again ran afoul of the law, this time in Bell County. On April 19, 1884, the grand jury indicted him for robbery, stating that a C. D. Stephens had obtained a judgment on December 21, 1883, in justice court against Jim in the amount of $12, plus $14.55 in costs. Allegedly, on March 17, 1884, Longley devised a scheme to avoid paying the judgment by assaulting Stephens until he gave him a written receipt indicating that the debt had been fully paid.[7] The case was later dismissed.

In August 1887, the story of Longley's hanging being a hoax took on new life when informal comments made by Campbell Longley in Belton were carried statewide:

> Belton, Tx, Aug. 23—Campbell Longley, father of the once notorious and not yet forgotten Bill Longley, removed to this county from near Lexington, Lee County, several years ago, and has been during his residence here one of our most substantial farmers and respected citizens. At his former residence he bears the reputation as he does here of being a consistent Christian gentleman, a thrifty and well-to-do farmer, and a man whose word can be implicitly relied upon.
>
> In a conversation with some of our leading citizens a few days ago, he tells a story about his wayward son that but for the known character of the narrator would be put down as wildest fiction. He says in substance, that Bill Longley was publicly hanged some 12 years ago in Giddings by Sheriff Jim Brown, in

James Stockton Longley and family, around the turn of the twentieth century. *Courtesy of H. Jerry Longley, Farmington, New Mexico.*

the presence of the usual large assemblage which gathers out of morbid curiosity on such occasions, was not really and in fact hanged, but by a justifiable collusion (justifiable so far as the relations and friends of the condemned man were concerned) was allowed to escape unharmed.

Mr. Longley says that when Bill was sentenced to be executed to satisfy the plaint of outraged law, and when all hope

> had fled of the intervention of superior court and executive, that a rich uncle in California came to the rescue with $4,000 in filthy lucre, which, so worked upon the sympathy of the sheriff charged with the execution of the sentence, that the friends of Bill were permitted so to arrange things that when the drop fell, the weight of his body fell not upon his doomed neck, but upon an iron hook, supported by appropriate body harness, in such a manner that he escaped physically unharmed, and that, when he had drawn his legs up and down in the approved method two or three times, pronounced by the medical doctors in attendance dead, and was delivered over to his friends for decent interment, the coffin which was actually buried, contained not the remains of the alleged desperado, but only rocks, while Bill, in proper person, was himself again and even while the last sad rites were being pronounced, was well on his way out of the country.
>
> Mr. Longley says further, that his legally but not actually dead son is, and has been living since his supposed execution, in Central America, where he has reformed his ways and has become one of the largest land and cattle holders on that part of the globe.
>
> Those who know Campbell Longley will have no hesitation whatever in believing his story, which he says he now gives to the public for the first time, and now only, because the sheriff who officiated at the supposed execution is himself dead.[8]

Actually, Jim Brown was not dead. Leaving his position as sheriff of Lee County in 1884, he becomes a partner of the notorious gambler Luke Short in Fort Worth. It would not be until September 6, 1892, when Brown was shot to death by Chicago policemen while resisting arrest, at the age of fifty-four, after a controversy dealing with a Chicago racetrack.[9] But Brown also made no response to the report. Another Bell County newspaper suggested that the story of the hoax was the product of a "no doubt anxious and loving father, who would believe his son still lived and is doing well." The newspaper editor had been present for the hanging, had known Longley for years, and "can testify to the fact that he was hung dead, very dead, and was buried in the Giddings cemetery where his remains now are."[10] Doctor J. A. Fields, who attended the execution and examined Longley's body, swore in Giddings that the man was "hanged by the neck until he was dead, dead, dead, and that his body lies in the potter's field near" Giddings.[11]

The story flew in the face of other reports that Longley had been buried after the hanging. Hiram Craig and William McClellan, who assisted in the execution, recalled that Longley was buried "out at the edge of town . . . next to a blackjack tree."[12] Sheriff Brown wrote on Longley's death warrant that he had buried the body after the hanging. The *Brenham Weekly Banner* stated that the body was buried,[13] as did the *Galveston Daily News*.[14]

However, the story that the execution was a hoax and that Longley had survived took wing and became a longstanding legend. This led to a bizarre series of events over one hundred years later when extensive efforts were made to prove or disprove the story. One newspaper, making light of the story, asserted that Central America was a "regular summer resort in comparison to the country from which William should actually date his letters."[15]

Miley L. Wooley, the son of the Virgil Wooley who assisted at the execution,[16] recalled in 1931 that he witnessed the hanging as a thirteen-year-old boy. He saw Longley hauled back up after his feet touched the ground. "The body of Longley was lifted and placed in the coffin and, attended by the officers and hundreds of curious, was moved to the little community cemetery and deposited in a newly dug grave."[17] Wooley also alleged that Campbell had faked the story of Bill's survival to spare his frail wife, and that after her death he made a statement to the Texas press that the story was not true.[18] No mention of a recantation by Campbell Longley has been located in Texas newspapers of the period. Everett Hagen also recalled in 1938 that Longley's body was cut down, placed in a wooden coffin on a buckboard and, followed by a small army of deputies, taken across some railroad tracks to a cemetery in an area known as San Antonio Prairie and buried at the foot of a blackjack tree.[19]

Nevertheless, other versions expanded the mystery and added to the confusion of what happened to Longley's body. Without refuting that the execution had actually occurred, Texas Ranger Lewis Delony, in an account of the hanging written in the 1930s, put a little different twist on the story by writing that "a sorrowful father took charge of the remains of his former wayward son."[20] The *Brenham Weekly Banner* on October 25, 1878, quoted the *Georgetown Sun* that "The corpse of Bill Longley, who was hung at Giddings, was brought through here on Saturday, en route for his father's in Bell county."[21] Another news account asserted that "Bill Longley's corpse was carried to Bell County and there interred."[22] But none of these accounts asserted that the hanging was a hoax.

Sarah Longley, Campbell's wife of almost fifty-two years, died on April 14, 1890, at the age of sixty-eight years, and was buried in a cemetery in Bell County's Wilkinson Valley where the family farm was located. Her grave marker mourned: "Our Mother; In God's morn her orb will rise; once more a star of paradise."[23] Only three months later, on July 13, seventy-three-year-old Campbell married Mary Catherine Dockray Craighead, a twenty-eight-year-old widow with three children.[24]

According to the late A. C. Greene, a respected historian descended from Campbell's new bride, the Dockray family had initially approved the union because it was thought that old Campbell was quite wealthy, and the idea of four additional mouths to feed at the Dockray farm underscored the marriage as a more desirable solution. As an elderly woman, Mary Catherine expressed bitterness at being "pandered" off to Campbell by the family "subtly reminding him how sweet a warm, young woman could be in the bed. . . . He was a vigorous, decisive man and memory heated his veins and he got his new wife"[25] in spite of the protests of his own family.

Campbell allegedly tried to talk his new wife into placing her children in an orphanage, which she refused to do, and there is a family legend that he tried to poison them. Two of the children did die of a "vague fever." Mary Catherine was then supposed to have left the old man, telling the family that she did so without consummating the marriage (Greene wrote that he doubted that this was true, although another Dockray family rumor was that Campbell had been physically unable to meet his marital responsibilities). As the story went, Campbell urged her to return, which she did, but only on the condition that he build her a new house on the Lampasas River. The old house held memories of Sarah, and Campbell is supposed to have accommodated her.

As the Dockray family story went, word got out to the family that Mary Catherine was being shabbily treated, and a brother sent a stern warning that it would be dangerous for the Longleys to abuse her. Finally, some three years after the marriage, Mary Catherine left Campbell again, this time for good, but she never divorced him.[26]

Greene said that Mary Catherine, his great-grandmother, explained the reason behind Campbell Longley's 1887 assertion that Bill Longley's hanging was a hoax:

> Nobody talked about Bill Longley, . . . but to the people of Bell and Lee counties he was still alive. Because he had cheated death from the rope one time, it was popularly felt that his second hanging could not have been real. There were stories of how a special silver throat piece had been fashioned so that the rope would not choke him to death, or that a shoulder and chest harness had taken the terror out of the gallows' fall, or that the carcass of a hog had been substituted for Bill Longley and buried under his name while he fled south with the connivance of the sheriff. My grandmother saw letters supposedly from Bill in his South American hiding place, but she said the old man had had the letters written to help ease the sorrow of Bill's mother. These letters came even after Cam married Mary Catherine and he showed them to her. Cam had a girl who had married a Mormon, . . . and this daughter included Bill's purported letters in her own from Utah when she wrote home.[27]

Thus, one explanation for Campbell's statement in 1887, that his son's execution was a hoax, was simply to perpetuate for his heartbroken wife, Sarah, the calming story that Bill survived and was alive and doing well, finally living those Christian principles that she so dearly valued. Hiram Craig later claimed that when he was living in Bell County as a butcher, he had an occasion to go to Campbell Longley's farm to get two cows. When Campbell saw him looking at Bill's picture in the house, the old man supposedly told him that his wife was in bad health and that "I have written these letters to myself so I can read them to her and make her think he is still alive and with my brother in California. I am afraid she would lose her mind if she knew he was really dead."[28]

But, other than this statement by Campbell, and Craig's recollections many years later, what evidence was there to corroborate the claim that the hanging was or was not a hoax? According to T. U. Taylor, Longley's grave in Giddings remained unmarked except for a few "rude flint rocks" marking the outline of the grave, but that in the mid-1920s a petrified hollow log was placed at the grave as a headstone, projecting some eighteen inches in the air. "When recently visited, there was a small three-lobed cactus plant growing on the surface, and nearly over his heart was a single lone violet with no surrounding companions. The grave is in the center of a small circular opening in the postoak trees." However, this is not evidence that Longley's body was in that grave.

The story persisted that Longley survived his appointment with the hangman. Well into the twentieth century, an elderly Bob Wright of Dallas recalled that in the 1880s Bill Longley was living on the Longley farm with his parents in Bell County and that Bill tended bar at several saloons in Belton. He claimed to have ridden in a wagon with Bill many times to visit Wright's grandfather, Melville Wilkinson, where he would display his marksmanship. According to Wright, Lee County authorities learned of Bill's whereabouts and arrested him. On the way back to Lee County, Longley allegedly attempted to escape and was shot to death. Wright said that

Campbell brought the body by wagon back to the farm and buried it under a cedar tree.[29]

T. U. Taylor wrote in 1927 of stories that he had heard about Longley's escaping the noose. It was rumored that "powerful friends" of the condemned man had arranged for a "steel jacket to fit over his shoulders, around his arms, and up under his neck that would support his weight."[30] Taylor said that he encountered people who believed that Longley was killed "on the upstairs, east front porch of a building on East Avenue in the city of Austin" in 1893.[31] Another man assured Taylor that he had camped with Bill on the banks of the Colorado River in Austin in 1890, but the individual thought to be Longley turned out to be a boyhood friend of Taylor's. In 1895, according to Taylor, a fellow showed up in Mason, Texas, at the printing shop of the father of historian J. Marvin Hunter and had circulars printed up advertising the petrified body of Bill Longley. The "body" turned out to be a cleverly painted cement statue.[32]

Western writer Carl Breihan, without any documentation, passed on other rumors. One was that a Bell County neighbor of the Longleys, three days after the hanging, saw a covered wagon pull up at the rear of the farmhouse. The driver untied the covering and two men got out. The neighbor then witnessed an immediate and dramatic change in Sarah Longley from grief-stricken depression to cheerful happiness.[33] Breihan also claimed that a cousin of Longley was attending college in Russellville, Arkansas, in 1912, when a fellow student's father, a farmer, told him that he had once ridden with Longley, had been tried and acquitted for a murder in McLennan County, Texas, and that he had received correspondence from Longley in South America, which he burned at Longley's request.[34] Richard Rushing perhaps?

Breihan cited some unknown sexton of the Giddings cemetery who said that a tall, gray-haired man asked the location of Longley's grave, and when it was pointed out chuckled and said, "So that's where they say he's buried." Allegedly, the sexton believed that the stranger was Longley himself. Breihan also wrote, again without any documentation, that the name of "W. P. Longley, South American cattleman" was included on the passenger list of the *Lusitania*, which was torpedoed by Germany on May 7, 1915.[35] The National Archives could not locate such a name among American passengers aboard the ship.[36]

In 1976, an official Texas historical marker commemorating the presence of Longley's body in the Giddings cemetery was dedicated by the Lee County Historical Commission and the Texas State Historical Commission near a petrified log sticking out of the ground, over what was believed at the time to be Longley's grave. It did not make any difference that the petrified log had been moved several times since the 1920s whenever it was in the way, such as for expansion of the cemetery.

The legacy of a Bill Longley who had survived three hangings (one in Arkansas and two at Giddings) continued into the next century. In September 1987, almost one hundred ten years after the actual event, the late Woodrow Wilson of Giddings decided to prove that such a hoax could be carried off. A descendant of John Wilson, Longley's brother-in-law and close cohort, Wilson, sixty-seven, erected a gallows in front of his residence and flea market on U.S. Highway 290 outside of Giddings, and announced his intention to hang himself to show that it could be done with a harness that he had constructed. On September 20, with Wilson's hands secured by handcuffs and a hood over his head, Wilson's friend, Richard Schadke, chopped the rope holding the trap door, and Wilson dropped through, just as Longley had. The crowd gathered to watch this episode broke its silence with cheers when Wilson called out that he was okay, having suffered only minor injuries.[37]

However, the most serious claim that Longley survived was that of Ted Wax of Gonzales, Louisiana. In a book published in 1988, *Dead Man on the Bayou?*, Wax claimed that his grandfather, John Calhoun Brown, was really Bill Longley. According to Wax, Longley surfaced as John Calhoun Brown in Plaquemine, Iberia Parish, in Louisiana, first buying property in a remote part of the parish in 1886. Brown's obituary indicated that he had been a resident of the Parish since 1878, the same year that Longley was hanged. Labeled locally as a "mystery man," according to Wax, Brown was believed to be from Texas, but no one knew anything about his past.

Captain Brown, as he came to be known, married Emily Breaux in 1891, and their first child, a son, was named William and called Bill. The couple ultimately had ten children who survived. Brown became wealthy in the timber business, and his family became prominent in Plaquemine society. Captain Brown died on October 31, 1923, following an operation for a prostate condition.[38]

Wax said that he was entirely unsuccessful in trying to genealogically trace his grandfather prior to 1886. A chance conversation with a relative resulted in a comment that Captain Brown may have been Bill Longley. This led Wax to recall that in 1952, after his mother's death, he went through an old trunk belonging to her and found an unfinished manuscript in her handwriting that stated that her father, Captain Brown, was Bill Longley from Texas. The manuscript was later discarded while Wax was away on military service and no copies were retained. Wax also claimed that a photograph of Bill Longley was a "mirror image" of his grandfather.

As further evidence that the two men were the same, Wax had Brown's signature compared with the copy of one of Longley's letters by an attorney in New Orleans, who concluded they were written by the same person. In addition, Wax took photographs of both Longley and his grandfather to Dr. Douglas W. Owsley, an anthropology instructor at Louisiana State University at the time, who, after computer studies, concluded there were indeed similarities between the physical appearance of the two men.[39]

Wax and Owsley were intrigued by the possibility that Brown might actually be Longley and that the outlaw indeed escaped the hangman. Owsley subsequently became an associate curator of the Department of Anthropology of the National Museum of Natural History at the Smithsonian Institution. In conjunction with Drs. Brooks and Suzanne Ellwood of the Center for Geoarcheological Studies at the University of Texas at Arlington, who were interested in testing scientific approaches to locating unmarked graves, Owsley attempted over a three-year period to find Longley's grave at Giddings. Family hostility, according to Wax, prevented an exhumation of Brown's body for study and possible DNA testing.

Between 1992 and 1994, a major effort was made to find Longley's grave. Oral history by Giddings residents was relied on to try to isolate the area where he might be buried, although most accounts were vague. A photograph allegedly taken in the 1920s of Bill Longley's grave was consulted, but it too proved unreliable in locating the grave. The scientific methods relied on located over fifty unmarked graves in the portion of the Giddings cemetery where Longley was believed buried, but the thirty-one bodies ultimately exhumed as likely possibilities proved to be either the wrong sex, the wrong race, the wrong size, or the wrong age. In addition to not finding Longley's grave, neither did the scientists locate an empty grave shaft loaded with rocks or the carcass of a hog.

Ted Wax consults as to the possible location of Bill Longley's grave at Giddings, Texas. *Author's photo.*

Dr. Doug Owsley examines skull fragments in the Giddings Cemetery. *Author's photo.*

In a paper, the scientists acknowledged several problems with the validity of information available to them as a major reason for the failure specifically to find Longley's grave, but stated that they were pleased with the results of the technical methods they employed to identify the burial shafts.[40] A rock marked "Wild Bill Longley" was found at the base of a nearby tree, but it was determined to have been placed in the area many, many years after Longley was allegedly buried there. The term "Wild Bill" was never applied to Longley during his lifetime, but was first used by T. U. Taylor in the 1920s when writing about the outlaw.

However, the failure to find Longley gave some credence to Wax's contention that he wasn't there at all, and, instead, perhaps occupying the grave of John Calhoun Brown in Louisiana. Then again, maybe not.

First, the notion that the hanging was a hoax had a few problems by itself. Literally thousands of people, not to mention a coterie of lawmen, three doctors, and two priests were in attendance on the execution. The illusions achieved today by Hollywood special effects were not available in 1878, and it is difficult to imagine that such a hoax could be smoothly carried off in front of so many witnesses. Further, why would the three doctors share in such a conspiracy, much less the lawmen surrounding the gallows? It would not have taken very long for so-called witnesses to come forward to tell the story, but none of them did. Indeed, years later, those who were involved with the hanging, such as William McClellan and Dr. Fields, were convinced that Longley died that October day.[41]

As has been seen, Pres Longley in California was far from a rich man and, beyond sending a letter to the president of the United States, could not have sent a large amount of money sufficient to bribe everyone in attendance on the hanging.

Only rumor and the alleged quote by Campbell Longley sustained the story that Longley lived on. Ted Wax relied on a mysterious handwritten manuscript that has not survived, comparisons of photographs, and questionable handwriting analysis. Any competent,

The skeleton of Bill Longley is uncovered. *Author's photo.*

professional handwriting expert will confirm that a comparison of a *signature* with a letter written some forty years apart will prove highly unreliable. That is the evidence on which Wax based a belief that he was descended from Longley.

However, persistence finally paid off and most doubts laid to rest when, in July 1998, a skeleton was unearthed in the Giddings cemetery that gave every indication that it was Bill Longley. Although no clothing remained, there was a small Catholic medal around the neck of the skeleton, and a small piece of a plastic-like substance with a floral design, which could have been the backing for the blue rosette that Longley wore on his coat when he was hanged. The body was removed to the Smithsonian Institution in Washington, D.C., and in June 2001, after an unsuccessful effort to reconstruct the facial bones to match with photographs of Longley, comparison of mitochondrial DNA taken from the pulp of a tobacco-stained tooth with DNA from Helen Chapman, a great-granddaughter of one of Longley's sisters, established that the body had the same maternal lineage. Thus the body was more than likely that of Bill Longley.[42] On July 19, 2001, the body was returned to Texas and reinterred in the Giddings Cemetery, drawn to its final resting place by a horse-drawn hearse.

The old Longley homestead in the Wilkinson Valley of southern Bell County now lies under Stillhouse Hollow Lake. Sarah Longley's grave was removed from that cemetery and reinterred in another cemetery at the time the lake was engineered in the 1960s. Of those Bill Longley left behind, his brother Jim went on to serve as a constable in McCulloch County. Jim's wife, Vie, died in Temple, Texas, in 1928, and he died on April 15, 1938, and was buried near his father, Campbell, in Lometa, Lampasas County, Texas.[43] Campbell died on September 15, 1907, fifteen days shy of his ninety-first birthday.[44] Campbell's widow, the estranged Mary Catherine, who continued to use the Longley name, was ironically celebrated at the Texas Centennial in 1936 as one of three remaining widows of Texas Revolution veterans, and ultimately became the sole surviving widow with a $12 monthly pension for the rest of her life.[45]

Bill Longley did not attain that pantheon of illustrious Texas gunfighters which he so zealously sought. A brief television series in the 1950s that portrayed him as a noble character did little to give him the notoriety of a Wyatt Earp or John Wesley Hardin. Because little was done to corroborate the tales that he wove painting himself as a rip-roaring, hell-bent mankiller, aficionados of the Old West knew only what he claimed and tended to ascribe to him the legacy of a major gunfighter. But for the most part, he faded into anonymity.

The post-Civil War era produced a small number of men who had a singular bent for violence, and who subsequently received an inordinate amount of attention for their bloody deeds. Glorified through the years, many, if not most of them, took on a more noble veneer in the mold of the fabled Robin Hood, either unfairly led into criminal careers by forces beyond their control or, at the least, possessed of personal codes of honor which in some way justified their outlawry. These images, the product of legend rather than hard fact, have persistently clouded a true perspective of the roles of these gunfighters celebrated for their out-of-the-ordinary lives.

Bill Longley, on close inspection, was neither noble nor necessarily brave. The details of the five killings ascribed to him that can be corroborated, i.e., Green Evans, Wilson Anderson, George Thomas, Lou Shroyer, and William Lay, do not lead one to throw garlands in Longley's direction. In each case, Longley angled for a clear advantage over his victim. There was no dramatic facedown in the middle of the street. The Reverend Lay was shot while milking a cow. George Thomas was shot in the back. Wilson Anderson was plowing a field and likely unarmed. Green Evans was fleeing for his life. Only Lou Shroyer showed fight, but Longley initially tried to get "the drop" on him.

So Bill Longley, on closer examination, does not seem to merit any glorification as a significant gunfighter in the mold of John Wesley Hardin, Ben Thompson, Billy the Kid, or Jesse James. But then, perhaps on closer examination, neither will they.

THE END

Endnotes

Notes for Chapter 1

1. *Lometa (Texas) Reporter*, 4 October 1907.
2. Walter Prescott Webb, ed., *Handbook of Texas*, vol. 2 (Austin: Texas State Historical Association, 1952), 488.
3. *Lometa (Texas) Reporter*, 4 October 1907.
4. Mrs. Katherine Morgan to Texas Bureau of Pensions, 30 July 1931, Texas State Library, Austin.
5. Daughters of the Republic of Texas, *Muster Rolls of the Texas Revolution* (Lubbock, Texas: Craftsman Printers, 1986), 250. Longley is listed as "McCampbell Longley."
6. Audited Military Claims (Campbell Longley, 12 September 1836), Texas State Library, Austin; *Lometa (Texas) Reporter*, 4 October 1907.
7. Webb, *Handbook of Texas*, vol. 2, p. 336.
8. *Lometa (Texas) Reporter*, 4 October 1907.
9. Corrie Pattison Haskew, *Historical Records of Austin and Waller Counties* (Houston: Premier Printing and Letter Service, 1969), 19.
10. Gifford White, *1840 Citizens of Texas*, vol. 2 (Austin: Gifford White, 1984).
11. Longley Family Bible; 1850 U.S. Census (Austin County, Texas). See also Betty M. McCroskey and Mrs. W. F. Bradley, *Texas Marriage Records: Austin, Matagorda and Wharton Counties* (Wharton, Texas: Comfort Wood Chapter, D.A.R., 1955), 8, and Helen Swenson, *Texas Marriages* (Round Rock, Texas: Frances Terry Ingmire & Helen Smothers Swenson, 1981), vol. 1, p. 87.
12. Doris Johnson, "The Longley Family," unpublished manuscript.
13. Longley Family Bible.
14. A. J. Sowell, *Rangers and Pioneers of Texas* (Austin: State House Press, 1991), 204–210. See also Donaly E. Brice, *The Great Comanche Raid* (Austin: Eakin Press, 1987), which lists a "James P. Longley" as part of Colonel John H. Moore's contingent unit.
15. *Lometa (Texas) Reporter*, 4 October 1907.
16. *Ibid.*; Public Debt Claims (23 May 1853), Texas State Library, Austin; Joseph Milton Nance, *Attack and Counterattack* (Austin: University of Texas Press, 1964).
17. Longley Family Bible.
18. *Lometa (Texas) Reporter*, 4 October 1907.
19. Longley Family Bible.
20. Carolyn R. Ericson and Frances T. Ingmire, *First Settlers of the Republic of Texas*, vol. 2 (Nacogdoches, Texas: Ericson Books, 1982).

21. Christopher L. York to Mrs. P. B. Price, 29 May 1972, Center for American History, University of Texas, Austin.
22. Deed Records, Washington County, Texas, vol. M, 63, 66.
23. Longley Family Bible.
24. 1860 U.S. Census (Washington County, Texas, Evergreen Precinct), 194; Marriage Records, Washington County, Texas, vol. 1, p. 24.
25. Longley Family Bible.
26. *Ibid.*; Compiled Military Service Records (Alexander C. Longley), National Archives.
27. Longley Family Bible.
28. *Lometa (Texas) Reporter*, 4 October 1907.
29. Mrs. James C. Killen, ed., *History of Lee County, Texas* (Quanah, Texas: Nortex Press, 1974), 212–213; T. U. Taylor, "Bill Longley and His Wild Career," *Frontier Times* 3, no. 9 (June 1926): 17.
30. *Lometa (Texas) Reporter*, 4 October 1907.
31. Taylor, "Wild Career," 17–18.
32. Bill Longley to Bettie "Southrn," 19 September 1878, Center for American History, University of Texas, Austin.
33. *Galveston Daily News*, 12 October 1878.
34. T. R. Fehrenbach, *Lone Star* (New York: American Legacy Press, 1983), 407.
35. *Galveston Daily News*, 12 October 1878.
36. Taylor, "Wild Career," 18.
37. *Houston Daily Telegram*, 7 March 1876.
38. Charles William Ramsdell, *Reconstruction in Texas* (Austin: University of Texas Press, 1970), 67.
39. *Ibid.*, 188.
40. Edgar P. Sneed, "A Historiography of Reconstruction in Texas: Some Myths and Problems," *Southwestern Historical Quarterly* 72, no. 4 (April 1969): 445.
41. *Belton (Texas) Journal*, 20 September 1877.
42. Henry C. Fuller, *Adventures of Bill Longley* (Nacogdoches, Texas: Baker Printing Co., n.d.), [72–73]. Fuller's book was not paginated and the author has counted the pages.

Notes for Chapter 2

1. Ed Bartholomew, *Wild Bill Longley: A Texas Hard-Case* (Houston: Frontier Press, 1953), 5–13; Robert Elman, *Badmen of the West* (Secaucus, New Jersey: Ridge Press, 1974), 109; Carroll C. Holloway, *Texas Gun Lore* (San Antonio: Naylor Co., 1951), 103.
2. Bill Longley to Milton Mast, 29 October 1877, as quoted in Fuller, *Adventures of Bill Longley*, 72.

3. Taylor, "Wild Career," 18.
4. 1860 U.S. Census (Washington County, Texas, Evergreen Post Office), 689/689; 1870 U.S. Census (Washington County, Texas, Evergreen Post Office), 123/123.
5. *Galveston Daily News*, 12 October 1878.
6. Taylor, "Wild Career," 18.
7. Grant was born on June 27, 1860. Lee County Historical Commission, *Lee County, Texas, Cemeteries*, vol. 2 (Giddings, Texas: Lee County Historical Commission, 1991), 76.
8. Taylor, "Wild Career," 19.
9. *Galveston Daily News*, 16 September 1877.
10. *Ibid.*, 12 October 1878; Taylor, "Wild Career," 18.
11. Owen P. White, *Trigger Fingers* (New York: Knickerbocker Press, 1926), 271.
12. *Houston Sunday Times*, 15 November 1868.
13. *Daily Austin Republican*, 28 December 1868.
14. "Captain" Alfred Evans, a native of North Carolina, born in 1810, was a veteran of the Seminole Indian wars in Florida. Coming to Texas in 1838, he settled first in Brazoria County, then in Austin County where he farmed for twenty years. Evans served as an officer in the 1848 Mexican War before resuming civilian life on his farm, even serving as a state legislator from Austin County. In 1859 he moved to a new farm near Salado in Bell County in Central Texas. During the Civil War he commanded a group of Confederate volunteers in Bell County, at the same time maintaining his farm, which included eight slaves. His farm also consisted of a total of 1,055 acres, sixty horses, and eighty cattle in 1868. *A Memorial and Biographical History of McLennan, Falls, Bell and Coryell Counties, Texas* (Chicago: Lewis Publishing Co., 1893), 51–52; David Yeilding, ed., *Story of Bell County, Texas*, vol. 1 (Austin: Eakin Press, 1988), 759; 1860 Slave Schedule, Bell County, Texas, no. 11; 1868 Tax Assessment Rolls, Bell County, Texas.
15. "Squire" Maxwell could be John Maxwell, a thirty-four-year-old farmer who lived near Evergreen with his wife and two children. 1870 U.S. Census (Washington County, Texas, Evergreen Post Office), 57/57.
16. The 1870 census reveals only a twenty-two-year-old laborer from Texas named J. L. Gilmore living on the farm of C. S. Seals. A "James Gilmore" was briefly a suspect in an express robbery in Bryan, Brazos County, Texas, in April 1870. 1870 U.S. Census (Washington County, Texas, Evergreen Post Office), 28/28; *Galveston Daily News*, 8 April 1870.
17. Alfred Evans to Gov. E. M. Pease, 30 December 1868, Lucie Price Collection, Center for American History, University of Texas, Austin.

18. *Ibid.*
19. *Galveston Daily News*, 16 September 1877; *National Police Gazette*, 26 October 1878, p. 6.
20. William L. Richter, *The Army in Texas During Reconstruction* (College Station: Texas A&M University Press, 1987), 143.
21. An examination of census reports for Karnes County in 1860 and 1870 turns up only one possible person by the name of Reagan, William Reagan of Tennessee, spelled "Raygen" in the 1870 report. Reagan is shown as a farmer in 1860 with a wife and three children, but employing a John Reagan, twenty-two, likely a brother, as a stock keeper. In 1870 "Raygen" is described as a stock raiser, but John Reagan is no longer a part of the household nor in the county's census. Reagan's farm or ranch was near Helena, which is some five miles northeast of present-day Karnes City. There is no further information about Reagan or Longley's sojourn in the county. A John Reagan was a prominent Texas politician who served in the United States Congress both before and after the Civil War, including the period of time that Longley was confined in jail prior to his execution, when Longley related this story. Perhaps this was a joke by Longley, and perhaps he worked for William Reagan. *Galveston Daily News*, 12 October 1878; 1860 U.S. Census (Karnes County, Texas, Helena Post Office), 20, 1212/1155; 1870 U.S. Census (Karnes County, Texas, Helena Post Office), 9, 2/1.
22. *Galveston Daily News*, 16 September 1877, 12 October 1878; *Houston Daily Telegram*, 12 October 1878; Taylor, "Wild Career," 19–20.
23. Richter, *Army in Texas*, 145.
24. Lt. Col. W. H. Carter, *From Yorktown to Santiago with the Sixth U.S. Cavalry* (Austin: State House Press, 1989), 135.
25. *Daily Austin Republican*, 28 February 1870.
26. Carter, *From Yorktown to Santiago*, 135.
27. *Galveston Daily News*, 12 October 1878.
28. *Ibid.*, 16 September 1877; *Houston Daily Telegram*, 12 October 1878.

Notes for Chapter 3

1. *Galveston Daily News*, 16 September 1877.
2. Barry A. Crouch, *The Freedman's Bureau and Black Texans* (Austin: University of Texas Press, 1992), 94–96; Barry A. Crouch and Donaly E. Brice, *Cullen Montgomery Baker, Reconstruction Desperado* (Baton Rouge: Louisiana State University Press, 1997).
3. *Galveston Daily News*, 16 September 1877.
4. Ed Bartholomew, *Cullen Baker* (Houston: Frontier Press, 1954), 56.
5. *Galveston Daily News*, 16 September 1877.
6. *Ibid.*

7. Crouch, *Freedman's Bureau*, 97; Crouch and Brice, *Cullen Montgomery Baker*, 153.
8. Bartholomew, *Cullen Baker*, 58; Taylor, "Wild Career," 20; *Galveston Daily News*, 16 September 1877.
9. Fuller, *Adventures of Bill Longley*, 33.
10. Longley Family Bible; *Lometa (Texas) Reporter*, 4 October 1907.
11. Longley Family Bible; Mrs. Frances Terry Ingmire, *Washington County, Texas, Marriage Records, 1837–1870* (St. Louis: Mrs. Frances Terry Ingmire, 1980), 32.
12. Longley Family Bible.
13. 1860 U.S. Census (Burleson County, Texas, Evergreen Post Office), 496/488.
14. 1850 U.S. Census (Muscogee County, Georgia, Ninth District), 382; 1870 U.S. Census (Burleson County, Texas, Caldwell Post Office), 192, 518/551.
15. Fuller, *Adventures of Bill Longley*, 34.
16. *Galveston Daily News*, 16 September 1877, 12 October 1878; *Houston Daily Telegram*, 12 October 1878.
17. J. E. Brady to Gov. E. M. Pease, 7 February 1870, Book No. 5, no. 97, Civil Board, Fifth Military District of Texas, Gov. E. M. Pease Collection, Texas State Library, Austin.
18. *State of Texas v. James E. Brady*, Cause No. 696, vol. D, pp. 520, 550, District Court Minutes, Bastrop County, Texas.
19. *State Rights Democrat* (LaGrange, Texas), 21 January 1870.
20. *Houston Daily Times*, 29 January 1870.
21. *Daily Austin Republican*, 9 February 1870.
22. J. E. Brady to Gov. E. M. Pease, 11 February 1870, Book No. 5, no. 107, Civil Board, Fifth Military District of Texas, Gov. E. M. Pease Collection, Texas State Library, Austin.
23. Report by T. P. Woods, 12 July 1870, "Crimes Committed in Washington County," Texas State Library, Austin.
24. *Flake's Daily Bulletin* (Galveston), 1 March 1870.
25. *Galveston Daily News*, 10 March 1870.
26. Wagner was appointed sheriff of Llano County on September 11, 1869, by General Reynolds, Fifth Military District, and was removed from office in April 1870 when Reconstruction ended. Jung was appointed sheriff of Bastrop County in August 1869, reelected in December 1869, and served until his resignation in November 1871. Born in Bohemia, Jung's civilian trade was that of brick mason. He apparently wasn't the most politic of politicians, at least for Reconstruction Texas sensitivities, as he was criticized toward the end of his term for trying to dance with a "Negro damsel" at a barbecue hosted by the local black community of Bastrop and attended by white

elected officials. Joseph Jung to Gov. E. M. Pease, 30 March 1870, Book No. 5, no. 191, Civil Board, Fifth Military District of Texas, Gov. E. M. Pease Collection, Texas State Library, Austin; Sammy Tise, *Texas County Sheriffs* (Albuquerque: Oakwood Printing, 1989), 31, 344; 1880 U.S. Census (Bastrop County, Texas), 113/113; *Bastrop (Texas) Advertiser*, 5 August 1871.

27. Fuller, *Adventures of Bill Longley*, 34; James S. Longley, manuscript circa 1936.
28. *Brazos Eagle* (Bryan, Texas), 11 June 1870, as quoted in *Flake's Daily Bulletin* (Galveston), 16 June 1870.
29. *Galveston Daily News*, 21 March 1874.
30. John Wesley Hardin, *The Life of John Wesley Hardin* (Seguin, Texas: Smith & Moore, 1896), 25.
31. 1870 U.S. Census (Washington County, Texas, Brenham Post Office, Precinct 2), 3, 37/37.
32. 1870 U.S. Census (Washington County, Texas, Evergreen Post Office), 126/126.
33. *Brenham (Texas) Weekly Banner*, 18 May 1877.
34. Hardin, *Hardin*, 26–27.
35. As quoted in Richard C. Marohn, *The Last Gunfighter: John Wesley Hardin* (College Station, Texas: Creative Publishing Co., 1995), 141.
36. *Austin Texas Capitol*, 16 September 1877.
37. *Chicago Times*, as quoted in *Sedalia (Missouri) Daily Democrat*, 15 March 1878.
38. Deed Records, Washington County, Texas, vol. X, 170.
39. Deed Records, Bell County, Texas, vol. M, 129, 147, 163, and 196.
40. *Belton (Texas) Weekly Journal*, 7 and 14 May 1870.
41. Ramsdell, *Reconstruction in Texas*, 292.
42. W. C. Nunn, *Texas Under the Carpetbaggers* (Austin: University of Texas Press, 1962), 245.
43. *Flake's Daily Bulletin* (Galveston), 23 June 1870.
44. Fuller, *Adventures of Bill Longley*, 34–35.

Notes for Chapter 4

1. Fuller, *Adventures of Bill Longley*, 35–36.
2. *Ibid.*, 36.
3. *Ibid.*, 36–37.
4. *Galveston Daily News*, 16 September 1877.
5. *Ibid.*, 16 September 1877, 12 October 1878; Fuller, *Adventures of Bill Longley*, 37–38.
6. Fuller, *Adventures of Bill Longley*, 38.
7. *Dallas Daily Herald*, 25 May 1873.

8. Fuller, *Adventures of Bill Longley*, 37–39.
9. *Galveston Daily News*, 16 September 1877.
10. Fuller, *Adventures of Bill Longley*, 39–42.
11. *Ibid.*, 42.
12. *Ibid.*, 42–43; *Galveston Daily News*, 16 September 1877.
13. *Galveston Daily News*, 16 September 1877.
14. Fuller, *Adventures of Bill Longley*, 43.
15. Bartholomew, *Wild Bill Longley*; 51; Frank M. Canton, *Frontier Trails* (Norman: University of Oklahoma Press, 1972), 121–131; Robert K. DeArment, *Alias Frank Canton* (Norman: University of Oklahoma Press, 1996), 160–163.
16. Fuller, *Adventures of Bill Longley*, 44.
17. *Galveston Daily News*, 16 September 1877.
18. *The Daily Commercial* (Leavenworth, Kansas), 3 March 1870.
19. *Ibid.*, 11 March 1870.
20. Bill Longley to James S. Longley, 8 March 1871 or 1872.
21. Fuller, *Adventures of Bill Longley*, 44; *Galveston Daily News*, 16 September 1877.

Notes for Chapter 5

1. *Galveston Daily News*, 16 September 1877.
2. Fuller, *Adventures of Bill Longley*, 44–45.
3. Judge W. L. Kuykendall, *Frontier Days* ([Laramie, Wyoming]: J. M. & H. L. Kuykendall, 1917), 137–138.
4. 1870 U.S. Census (Cheyenne, Wyoming Territory), 421, 265/216.
5. Robert M. Utley, *The Indian Frontier of the American West, 1846–1890* (Albuquerque: University of New Mexico Press, 1984), 101.
6. Jerome A. Greene, *Battles and Skirmishes of the Great Sioux War, 1876–1877* (Norman: University of Oklahoma Press, 1993), xvi; Robert M. Utley and Wilcomb E. Washburn, eds., *The American Heritage History of the Indian Wars* (New York: American Heritage Publishing, 1977), 244.
7. Utley and Washburn, *Indian Wars*, 244.
8. *Ibid.*, 265.
9. Francis Paul Prucha, *A Guide to the Military Posts of the United States, 1789–1895* (Madison: State Historical Society of Wisconsin, 1964), 30; Robert G. Ferris, *Soldier and Brave*, National Survey of Historic Sites and Buildings, vol. 12 (Washington, D.C.: U.S. Department of the Interior, National Park Service, 1971), 386.
10. U.S. Census (Cheyenne, Wyoming Territory), 413, 11/10.
11. Kuykendall, *Frontier Days*, 137–138.
12. Fuller, *Adventures of Bill Longley*, 45.

13. Kuykendall, *Frontier Days*, 138; 1870 U.S. Census (Cheyenne, Wyoming Territory), 426, 412/357.
14. Fuller, *Adventures of Bill Longley*, 44–48.
15. Kuykendall, *Frontier Days*, 138.
16. James Chisholm (Lola M. Hunter, ed.), *South Pass 1868* (Lincoln: University of Nebraska Press, 1975), 216–217.
17. *South Pass (Wyoming) News*, 9 April 1870.
18. *Ibid.*
19. *Ibid.*
20. John D. McDermott, *Dangerous Duty: A History of Frontier Forts in Fremont County, Wyoming* ([Lander], Wyoming: Fremont County Historic Preservation Commission, 1993), 99.
21. *Ibid.*, 100.
22. David M. Delo, "Camp Stambaugh . . . The Miner's Delight," *Wind River Mountaineer* 3, no. 4 (Oct.–Dec. 1987): 5; Major Joseph I. Lambert, *One Hundred Years With the Second Cavalry* (Fort Riley, Kansas: Capper Printing Co., 1939), 110–111.
23. Delo, "Camp Stambaugh," 5; McDermott, *Dangerous Duty*, 100.
24. Kuykendall, *Frontier Days*, 138.
25. *Ibid.*; McDermott, *Dangerous Duty*, 102; Delo, "Camp Stambaugh," 6.
26. Kuykendall, *Frontier Days*, 140–141.
27. Joseph G. Rosa, *They Called Him Wild Bill* (Norman: University of Oklahoma Press, 1974), 313–317.
28. Fuller, *Adventures of Bill Longley*, 49–50.
29. *Ibid.*, 51–52.
30. Enlistment certificate (William P. Longley), National Archives, Washington, D.C.

Notes for Chapter 6

1. Fuller, *Adventures of Bill Longley*, 52–53.
2. *Ibid.*, 73–74.
3. *Galveston Daily News*, 25 October 1877.
4. Medical History, Camp Stambaugh, Wyoming Territory (December 1870), Records of the Office of the Adjutant General, American Heritage Center, University of Wyoming; Acting Assistant Surgeon A. S. Greenwell, Surgeon General's Office, U.S. War Department, *Report on the Hygiene of the United States Army with Descriptions of Military Posts* (Washington, D.C.: U.S. Government Printing Office, 1875), 378.
5. F. V. Hayden, *Eleventh Annual Report of the United States Geological and Geographical Survey of the Territories Embracing Idaho and Wyoming, 1877* (Washington, D.C.: U.S. Government Printing Office, 1879), 7.
6. Greenwell, *Hygiene*, 378.

7. Muster Roll, Company B, Second Cavalry Regiment, Camp Stambaugh, Wyoming Territory, 30 April–30 June 1870, RG 94, National Archives, Washington, D.C.
8. Reports of General Court-Martial, William P. Longley and John Miller, 15 August 1870, Camp Stambaugh, Wyoming Territory, National Archives, Washington, D.C.; Muster Roll, Company B, Second Cavalry Regiment, 30 June–31 August 1870, RG 94, National Archives, Washington, D.C.; *Galveston Daily News*, 25 October 1877.
9. Grugan, a Pennsylvania native, entered the Civil War as an artillery private, subsequently seeing considerable action as a lieutenant in the Union cavalry. He continued as a cavalry officer after the war, serving along with Wheelan in the Second Cavalry Regiment from 1866. The thirty-one-year-old Wheelan was also Pennsylvania-born, but served in the Union army during the Civil War with a New York cavalry unit. Reports of General Court-Martial, William P. Longley and John Miller; Theo. F. Rodenbough, *From Everglade to Canon with the Second Dragoons* (New York: D. Van Nostrand, Publisher, 1875), 378; 1870 U.S. Census (Wyoming Territory, Smith's Gulch), 508, 53/52.
10. Reports of General Court-Martial, William P. Longley and John Miller.
11. McDermott, *Dangerous Duty*, 100; Post Return, Camp Stambaugh, Wyoming Territory, September 1870, American Heritage Center, University of Wyoming.
12. Special Order No. 66, 25 September 1870, U.S. War Department Records, Camp Stambaugh, Wyoming Territory, American Heritage Center, University of Wyoming.
13. Post Return and Surgeon's Report, September 1870, Camp Stambaugh, Wyoming Territory, American Heritage Center, University of Wyoming.
14. Delo, "Camp Stambaugh," 9.
15. Chisholm, *South Pass, 1868*, 179–180.
16. Betty Carpenter Pfaff, *Atlantic City Nuggets*, 76.
17. Post Return, November 1870, Camp Stambaugh, Wyoming Territory, American Heritage Center, University of Wyoming.
18. Surgeon's Report, November 1870, Camp Stambaugh, Wyoming Territory, American Heritage Center, University of Wyoming.
19. Muster Roll, Company B, Second Cavalry Regiment, 31 October–31 December 1870, Camp Stambaugh, Wyoming Territory, RG 94, National Archives, Washington, D.C.
20. *Galveston Daily News*, 25 October 1877.
21. Surgeon's Report, December 1870, Camp Stambaugh, Wyoming Territory, American Heritage Center, University of Wyoming.
22. *Ibid.*; *South Pass (Wyoming Territory) News*, 14 December 1870; McDermott, *Dangerous Duty*, 101.

23. *Galveston Daily News*, 25 October 1877.
24. Lambert. *One Hundred Years*, 108–109.
25. Greenwell, *Hygiene*, 378–381.
26. Bill Longley to Jim Longley, March 8, 187[?].
27. Rodenbough, *Everglade to Canon*, 377–378.
28. Post Returns, April and May 1871, Camp Stambaugh, Wyoming Territory, American Heritage Center, University of Wyoming.
29. Muster Roll, Company B, Second Cavalry Regiment, 28 February–30 April 1871, Camp Stambaugh, Wyoming Territory, RG 94, National Archives, Washington, D.C.
30. McDermott, *Dangerous Duty*, 105.
31. Muster Roll, Company B, Second Cavalry Regiment, 30 April 1871–30 June 1871, Camp Stambaugh, Wyoming Territory, RG 94, National Archives, Washington, D.C.; Surgeon's Report, June 1871, Camp Stambaugh, Wyoming Territory, American Heritage Center, University of Wyoming.
32. Surgeon's Report, December 1871, Camp Stambaugh, Wyoming Territory, American Heritage Center, University of Wyoming.
33. General Order No. 34, 31 August 1871, Camp Stambaugh, Wyoming Territory, U.S. War Department Records, American Heritage Center, University of Wyoming.
34. Surgeon's Report, December 1871, Camp Stambaugh, Wyoming Territory.
35. Muster Roll, Company B, Second Cavalry Regiment, 31 October–31 December 1871, RG 94, National Archives, Washington, D.C.
36. Robert A. Murray, "Camp Stambaugh, Wyoming: Guarding the South Pass Gold Fields, 1870–1878," *Order of the Indian Wars Journal* 2, no. 2 (Spring 1981): 7.
37. Fuller, *Adventures of Bill Longley*, 53–55.
38. Surgeon's Report, January–March 1872, Camp Stambaugh, Wyoming Territory, American Heritage Center, University of Wyoming.
39. *Ibid.*, April 1872.
40. Muster Roll, Company B, Second Cavalry Regiment, 30 April–30 June 1872, Camp Stambaugh, Wyoming Territory, RG 94, National Archives, Washington, D.C.
41. *Galveston Daily News*, 25 October 1877.

Notes for Chapter 7

1. *Galveston Daily News*, 16 September 1877.
2. Fuller, *Adventures of Bill Longley*, 56–57.
3. *Ibid.*, 58.
4. *Ibid.*

5. *Ibid.*, 58–59; *Galveston Daily News*, 16 September 1877.
6. Fuller, *Adventures of Bill Longley*, 59.
7. *Galveston Daily News*, 25 October 1877.
8. Records, U.S. War Department, 1 July 1870, American Heritage Center, University of Wyoming.
9. Fuller, *Adventures of Bill Longley*, 59.
10. *Ibid.*, 60.
11. Writers Program, Works Project Administration, *Wyoming* (New York: Oxford University Press, 1941), 308–309.
12. Fuller, *Adventures of Bill Longley*, 60–61.
13. *Ibid.*, 61–62.
14. *Ibid.*, 62.
15. *Ibid.*, 63.
16. *Ibid.*, 64–66.

Notes for Chapter 8

1. *Galveston Daily News*, 16 September 1877, 12 October 1878.
2. Fuller, *Adventures of Bill Longley*, 66.
3. D. O. McCray, "Parkerville," Morris County Library, Council Grove, Kansas.
4. Fuller, *Adventures of Bill Longley*, 66–67.
5. *Galveston Daily News*, 16 September 1877, 12 October 1878.
6. Fuller, *Adventures of Bill Longley*, 67.
7. *Galveston Daily News*, 16 September 1877.
8. 1860 U.S. Census (Morris County, Kansas, Grove Township), 418, 32/32; 1870 U.S. Census (Morris County, Kansas, Clark Creek Township), 680, 37/38.
9. Fuller, *Adventures of Bill Longley*, 67.
10. *Ibid.*, 68; *Galveston Daily News*, 16 September 1877.
11. 1870 U.S. Census (Fayette County, Texas, LaGrange Post Office), 209/203; 1880 U.S. Census (Bastrop County, Texas, Smithville Post Office), 316/319.
12. *Galveston Daily News*, 16 September 1877.
13. Yeilding, *Story of Bell County, Texas*, vol. 1, p. 270.
14. *Galveston Daily News*, 16 September 1877.
15. *Ibid.*
16. Tevis Clyde Smith, *Frontier's Generation* (Brownwood, Texas: Moore Printing Co., 1980), 34–35.
17. Walter Prescott Webb, ed., *Handbook of Texas*, vol. 2 (Austin: Texas State Historical Association, 1952), 916–917; T. R. Havins, *Something About Brown* (Brownwood, Texas: Banner Printing Co., 1958), 12, 46; James C. White, *The Promised Land* (Brownwood, Texas: Brownwood Banner,

1941), 47–48; Historical Marker, Grave of John Williams (1804–1871), Williams Ranch Cemetery; Louise Gartman Smith, "The Williams Ranch," *The Cattleman* (December 1943), as quoted in Brown County Historical Society, *In the Life and Lives of Brown County People*, 36; 1870 U.S. Census (Brown County, Texas, San Saba Post Office), 1, 4/4.

18. Mrs. Jesse B. Bettis and Mrs. Mattie Baird, *Zephyr Yesterday and Today* (Brownwood, Texas: Banner Printing Co., 1980), 193; Smith, *Frontier's Generation*, 32; 1870 U.S. Census (Brown County, Texas, San Saba Post Office), 1, 4/4.
19. *Galveston Daily News*, 16 September 1877; *Houston Daily Telegram*, 12 October 1878.
20. *Galveston Daily News*, 26 July 1877, 3 August 1877.
21. Sgt. J. M. Redmon to F. L. Britton, 28 February 1873, State Police Correspondence, Texas State Library, Austin.
22. 1870 U.S. Census (Coleman County, Texas), 38/39; Donavon Duncan Tidwell, *Freemasonry in Brownwood* (Fort Worth: Masonic Home and School, 1966), 81–82; Leona Bruce, *They Came in Peace to Coleman County* (Fort Worth: Branch-Smith, 1970), 27–29; Chuck Parsons, *James Madison Brown: Texas Sheriff, Texas Turfman* (Wolfe City, Texas: Henington Publishing Co., 1993), 4; Deed Records, Coleman County, Texas, A/165, C/584, D/345, E/59, F/165, K/348; Robert W. Stephens, *Texas Rangers Indian War Pensions* (Quanah, Texas: Nortex Press, 1976), 34.
23. James B. Gillett, *Six Years with the Texas Rangers* (Lincoln: University of Nebraska Press, 1976), 9.
24. *Galveston Daily News*, 16 September 1877; Capt. John M. Elkins, *Indian Fighting on the Texas Frontier* (Amarillo, Texas: Russell & Cockrell, 1929), 56–57; 1870 U.S. Census (Coleman County, Texas), 39/39.
25. Stephens, *Indian War Pensions*, 34.
26. *Galveston Daily News*, 16 September 1877.
27. *Ibid.*
28. *State of Texas v. William Longley*, Cause No. 879, Bell County, Texas, District Court Records.
29. Yeilding, *Story of Bell County, Texas*, vol. 2, 578.
30. 1870 U.S. Census (Bell County, Texas), 113, 264/264; 1874 Tax Assessment Rolls, Bell County, Texas; Marriage Records, Bell County, Texas, vol. D, 130.
31. 1870 U.S. Census (Bell County, Texas), 37, 117/117.

Notes for Chapter 9

1. *Galveston Daily News*, 16 September 1877.
2. Deed Records, Mason County, Texas, vol. A/B, 51.
3. Tise, *Texas County Sheriffs*, 357.

4. *Galveston Daily News*, 16 September 1877.
5. *Ibid.*
6. Clara Watkins, *Kerr County, Texas, 1856–1976* (N.p.: Hill Country Preservation Society, 1976), 117.
7. *State of Texas v. Frank Eastwood*, Cause No. 4, vol. 25, p. 279, District Court Minutes, Kerr County, Texas.
8. *Ibid.*, vol. 25, p. 93.
9. *State of Texas v. Frank Eastwood*, Cause No. 6, vol. 25, p. 103, District Court Minutes, Kerr County, Texas.
10. *State of Texas v. Frank Eastwood and James Johnson*, Cause Nos. 49, 50, 51, 55, vol. 13, p. 99; vol. 27, pp. 62, 63, 65, District Court Minutes, Kerr County, Texas.
11. 1870 U.S. Census (Kerr County, Texas, Kerrville Precinct 4), 10/10.
12. *State of Texas v. James Johnson, Frank Eastwood, and Young Stockman*, vol. D, 38, 44, 47, 48, 51–54, 89–91, 123–126, District Court Minutes, Gillespie County, Texas.
13. *State of Texas v. Frank Eastwood*, Cause No. 219, vol. D, 153, 160–161, 308, District Court Minutes, Gillespie County, Texas.
14. *San Antonio Daily Herald*, 25 July 1873; *Austin Daily State Journal*, 15 August 1873.
15. *San Antonio Daily Herald*, 15 July 1873, 25 July 1873; *San Antonio Daily Express*, 15 July 1873.
16. *Austin Daily State Journal*, 15 August 1873.
17. *San Antonio Daily Herald*, 15 July 1873.
18. *Ibid.*
19. *Austin Daily State Journal*, 15 August 1873.
20. Tise, *Texas County Sheriffs*, 304; Watkins, *Kerr County, Texas*, 161.
21. *San Antonio Daily Herald*, 18 July 1873; *Austin Daily State Journal*, 15 August 1873.
22. *San Antonio Daily Herald*, 15 July 1873; *San Antonio Daily Express*, 15 July 1873.
23. *San Antonio Daily Herald*, 15 July 1873.
24. *Ibid.*, 25 July 1873; *San Antonio Daily Express*, 15 July 1873.
25. *San Antonio Daily Herald*, 18 July 1873.
26. *Ibid.*, 25 July 1873.
27. *San Antonio Daily Express*, 29 July 1873.
28. 1870 U.S. Census (Burleson County, Texas, Caldwell Post Office), 39/41.
29. 1870 U.S. Census (Fayette County, Texas, Lyonsville Post Office), 134/126.
30. Affidavit, 17 July 1873, Gov. E. J. Davis Papers, Texas State Library, Austin.

31. 1880 U.S. Census (Kerr County, Texas, Precinct Nos. 3 and 4), 117/123; Gloria Clifton Dozier, *Reconstructed 1890 Census of Kerr County, Texas* (Kerrville, Texas: Gloria Clifton Dozier, 1991), 26.
32. Gerald Witt, *The History of Eastern Kerr County* (Austin: Nortex Press, 1986), 33.
33. *San Antonio Daily Herald*, 25 July 1873.
34. *San Antonio Daily Express*, 29 July 1873.
35. *State of Texas v. William Ake*, vols. 3 and 4, District Court Minutes, Williamson County, Texas.
36. *Georgetown (Texas) Watchman*, 29 May 1869.
37. Requisition, 9 May 1877, Texas Governor's Office, Texas State Library, Austin (Courtesy Dave Johnson, Zionsville, Indiana).
38. Clara Stearns Scarbrough, *Land of Good Water* (Georgetown, Texas: Williamson County Sun Publishers, 1973), 151, 165–167.
39. Records, Governors Richard Coke and Richard Hubbard, Texas State Library, Austin (Courtesy Dave Johnson, Zionsville, Indiana).
40. *State of Texas v. Jeff Ake*, vols. 3 and 4, District Court Minutes, Williamson County, Texas; *Galveston Daily News*, 15 June 1877.
41. *Dallas Daily Herald*, 4 January 1882.
42. James B. O'Neil, *They Die But Once* (New York: Knight Publications, 1935), 100–101.
43. *San Antonio Daily Express*, 20 July 1873.
44. *Ibid.*, 23 July 1873.
45. *Galveston Daily News*, 16 September 1877.
46. *Austin Daily State Journal*, 21 July 1873.
47. *Galveston Daily News*, 16 September 1877.
48. 1870 U.S. Census (Travis County, Texas, Austin Post Office), 11/22; 1880 U.S. Census (Travis County, Texas, E.D. 129, First Ward, Austin), 173, 21/31.
49. *Galveston Daily News*, 16 September 1877.
50. *Ibid.*
51. *Ibid.*
52. Christine Dulaney, "McIver-Bostick," Madison County Historical Commission, *A History of Madison County, Texas* (Dallas: Taylor Publishing Co., 1984), 388.
53. *Bryan (Texas) Appeal*, 10 February 1870, as quoted in *Flake's Daily Bulletin* (Galveston), 26 March 1870.
54. *Calvert (Texas) Enterprise*, unknown date, as quoted in *Flake's Daily Bulletin* (Galveston), 26 March 1870.
55. Executive Record Book, Governor Richard Coke, Texas State Library, 219.
56. *State of Texas v. William McIver*, Cause No. 588, vol. 1, p. 281, District Court Minutes, Brazos County, Texas.

57. *State of Texas v. William McIver*, Cause No. 7, vol. A, 346, District Court Minutes, Madison County, Texas.
58. *Flake's Daily Bulletin* (Galveston), 17 September 1869.
59. *Brenham (Texas) Banner*, 10 November 1876.
60. *State of Texas v. Joseph McIver*, Cause No. 244, vol. A, 308; vol. B, 16, District Court Minutes, Madison County, Texas.
61. *State of Texas v. J. R. McIver*, Cause No. 268, vol. A, 314; vol. B, 9, District Court Minutes, Madison County, Texas.
62. *State of Texas v. John R. McIver*, Cause No. 116, vol. A, 108, 191–192, District Court Minutes, Madison County, Texas.
63. *State of Texas v. Joseph McIver*, Cause No. 373, vol. B, 14, 276, District Court Minutes, Madison County, Texas.
64. *State of Texas v. J. R. McIver*, Cause No. 374, vol. B, 14, 53, District Court Minutes, Madison County, Texas.
65. Leon County Genealogical Society, *Leon County Cemetery Records*, vol. 2 (Centerville, Texas: Leon County Genealogical Society, 1982), 210.
66. James S. Longley, circa 1936, Center for American History, University of Texas, Austin.

Notes for Chapter 10

1. Prucha, *Guide to the Military Posts*, 73.
2. J. Frank Dobie, *A Vaquero of the Brush Country* (Austin: University of Texas Press, 1985), 188.
3. *Galveston Daily News*, 16 September 1877.
4. *Ibid.*
5. *Ibid.*
6. *Ibid.*
7. *Ibid.*
8. James S. Longley, circa 1936.
9. *Belton (Texas) Journal*, 20 September 1877.
10. *Ibid.*
11. *Austin Daily Statesman*, 28 May 1874; *Colorado (Texas) Citizen*, 4 June 1874; George W. Tyler, *The History of Bell County* (San Antonio: Naylor Co., 1935), 301–303.
12. Mrs. Jean Shroyer and Mrs. Hazel Hood, *Williamson County, Texas: Its History and Its People* (Austin: Nortex Press, 1985), 323.
13. James S. Longley, circa 1936.
14. Shroyer and Hood, *Williamson County, Texas*, 216; 1860 U.S. Census (Williamson County, Texas), 339, No. 120; 1870 U.S. Census (Williamson County, Texas, Florence Post Office), 429, 767/767.

15. *State of Texas v. William Mullen*, Cause Nos. 198, 280, 316, 494, 500, 834, 836, and 928, vols. 3 and 4, District Court Minutes, Williamson County, Texas.
16. *State of Texas v. William Mullen*, Cause No. 555, vol. 3, 475; vol. 4, 397, District Court Minutes, Williamson County, Texas.
17. Shroyer and Hood, *Williamson County, Texas*, 12; 1870 U.S. Census (Williamson County, Texas, Pond Springs Post Office), 420, 658/658.
18. Scarbrough, *Land of Good Water*, 80, 110, 125.
19. James S. Longley, circa 1936; Shroyer and Hood, *Williamson County, Texas*, 343; Williamson County Genealogical Society, *Williamson County, Texas, Marriage Records* (Round Rock, Texas: Williamson County Genealogical Society, 1983), 8.
20. 1870 U.S. Census (Travis County, Texas, Precinct No. 5), 100/117.
21. James S. Longley, circa 1936.
22. *Ibid.*
23. *Ibid.*; 1880 U.S. Census (Bastrop County, Texas, Precinct No. 6), 410/410.
24. James S. Longley, circa 1936.
25. *Ibid.*
26. *Galveston Daily News*, 16 September 1877.
27. *Belton (Texas) Journal*, 20 September 1877.
28. *Ibid.*; James S. Longley, circa 1936.
29. Killen, *History of Lee County, Texas*, 64, 317, 376, 420; 1860 U.S. Census (Washington County, Texas, Doddville Post Office), 192, 669/669; 1870 U.S. Census (Washington County, Texas, Evergreen Post Office), 101/101; 1880 U.S. Census (Lee County, Texas, Precinct No. 1), 368/382.
30. James S. Longley, circa 1936.
31. 1860 U.S. Census (Washington County, Texas, Doddville Post Office), 192, 670/670; 1870 U.S. Census (Washington County, Texas, Evergreen Post Office), 178, 104/104; 1880 U.S. Census (Lee County, Texas, E.D. 91, Precinct No. 1), 22, 376/390; Yeilding, *Story of Bell County, Texas*, vol. 2, p. 1003; W. Broadus Smith, *Marriage Records, Washington County, Texas, 1837–1858* ([Brenham], Texas: W. Broadus Smith, 1968), 32.
32. Caroline E. Anderson to Archibald Willingham, 18 July 1853 (Courtesy Dr. Douglas Willingham, Salado, Texas).
33. Julia Jones, *Lee County* (Houston: Gulf Coast Baptist Print, 1945), 61; Killen, *History of Lee County, Texas*, 211.
34. *State of Texas v. Wilson Anderson*, Cause No. 9, vol. A, 3, 6, 13, District Court Minutes, Lee County, Texas.
35. *Belton (Texas) Journal*, 20 September 1877.

36. John W. Yeats, "Facts of Longley Hanging Explained," Magazine Section, *Houston Post Dispatch*, 25 October 1931.
37. 1870 U.S. Census (Washington County, Texas, Evergreen Post Office), 181, 158/158; Parsons, *James Madison Brown*, 3–4, 9–12, 14, 17–30.
38. Deed Records, Washington County, Texas, vol. X, 170.
39. James S. Longley, circa 1936.
40. *Belton (Texas) Journal*, 12 September 1877.
41. Taylor, "Wild Career," 25.
42. *New York Herald*, 13 October 1878.
43. *Ibid.*
44. James S. Longley, circa 1936.
45. *Galveston Daily News*, 12 October 1878.
46. Taylor, "Wild Career," 25.
47. *Galveston Daily News*, 3 April 1875.
48. *Galveston Weekly News*, 5 April 1875.
49. *Belton (Texas) Journal*, 20 September 1877.
50. *Galveston Daily News*, 26 October 1877.
51. Taylor, "Wild Career," 25; Fuller, *Adventures of Bill Longley*, 4.
52. *State of Texas v. William Longley and James Longley*, Cause No. 100, Indictment, 10 May 1875, District Court Records, Lee County, Texas, Texas State Library, Austin; District Court Minutes, Lee County, Texas, vol. A, 57.
53. Executive Record Book, Gov. Richard Coke, 1874–1876, 27 May 1875, 592, Texas State Library, Austin.

Notes for Chapter 11

1. Tise, *Texas County Sheriffs*, 330; Killen, *History of Lee County, Texas*, 321; 1860 U.S. Census (Washington County, Texas, Evergreen Post Office), 689/689; 1870 U.S. Census (Washington County, Texas, Evergreen Post Office), 123/123.
2. James S. Longley, circa 1936.
3. Marriage Records, Book 2, 185, Madison County, Texas.
4. James S. Longley, circa 1936.
5. Grayson County Genealogical Society, *Ancestors and Descendants, Grayson County, Texas* (Dallas: Taylor Publishing Co., 1980), 53.
6. Tise, *Texas County Sheriffs*, 213.
7. *Ibid.*, 360. Jim Longley may have been confused and was thinking of Ferdinand Niggles, who was sheriff of Medina County from 1876 to 1882.
8. James S. Longley, circa 1936.
9. Bentley & Pilgrim, *Texas Legal Directory, 1876–1877* (Austin: Democratic Statesman Office, 1877), 41.
10. *Galveston Daily News*, 13 October 1878.

11. *Biographical Souvenir of the State of Texas* (Chicago: F. A. Battey & Co., 1889), 669–670.
12. James S. Longley, circa 1936.
13. Ed Bartholomew, *Wyatt Earp: The Untold Story* (Toyahvale, Texas: Frontier Book Company, 1963), 148.
14. *Wichita (Kansas) Weekly Beacon*, 14 July 1875, 21 July 1875.
15. *Austin Daily Democratic Statesman*, 17 August 1875; Executive Record Book, Gov. Richard Coke, 1874–1876, 24 August 1875, Texas State Library, Austin.
16. Executive Record Book, Gov. Richard Coke, 42, Texas State Library, Austin.

Notes for Chapter 12

1. Bill Longley to James M. Brown, unknown date.
2. *Giddings (Texas) Tribune*, as quoted in *Brenham (Texas) Banner*, 24 September 1875.
3. *Nacogdoches (Texas) News*, 20 July 1877; Fuller, *Adventures of Bill Longley*, 7; Taylor, "Wild Career," 25.
4. W. R. (Bob) Poage, *McLennan County–Before 1980* (Waco, Texas: Texian Press, 1981), 260.
5. Patricia Ward Wallace, *Waco, Texas, Crossroads* (Woodland Hills, California: Windsor Publications, 1983), 29.
6. *State of Texas v. Robert Rushing and J. W. Longley alias J. W. Patterson*, Indictment, Cause No. 2606, 20 November 1875, District Court Records, McLennan County, Texas.
7. 1870 U.S. Census (McLennan County, Texas, East Waco Post Office), 71/56.
8. *State of Texas v. J. W. Longley alias J. W. Patterson*, Indictment, Cause No. 2590, 18 November 1875, District Court Records, McLennan County, Texas.
9. *Waco (Texas) Daily Examiner*, 13 November 1875.
10. *Nacogdoches (Texas) News*, 20 July 1877; Fuller, *Adventures of Bill Longley*, 7–8.
11. *Waco (Texas) Daily Examiner*. 16 November 1875.
12. *State of Texas v. J. W. Longley alias J. W. Patterson*, Cause No. 2591, Indictment, 18 November 1875, District Court Records, McLennan County, Texas.
13. 1870 U.S. Census (McLennan County, Texas, Waco Post Office), 71–72, 517/508.
14. *State of Texas v. J. W. Longley alias J. W. Patterson*, Cause No. 2602, Indictment, 20 November 1875, District Court Records, McLennan County, Texas.

15. *Waco (Texas) Daily Examiner*, 16 November 1875.
16. 1880 U.S. Census (McLennan County, Texas, E.D. 109), 20/20.
17. 1870 U.S. Census (McLennan County, Texas, Waco Post Office), 165/168.
18. *State of Texas v. Robert Rushing and J. W. Longley alias J. W. Patterson*, Cause No. 2606.
19. Executive Record Book, Governor O. M. Roberts, Letterpress Book No. 2, 737, 24 January 1880, Governor O.M. Roberts Correspondence, Texas State Library, Austin.
20. *Nacogdoches (Texas) News*, 20 July 1877; Fuller, *Adventures of Bill Longley*, 8.
21. Taylor, "Wild Career," 25.
22. *Nacogdoches (Texas) News*, 20 July 1877.
23. Compiled Service Records, Union Volunteers, Pennsylvania (Lewis Shroyer), National Archives, Washington, D.C.
24. J. Evetts Haley, *Charles Goodnight, Cowman & Plainsman* (Boston: Houghton Mifflin, 1936), 148.
25. 1870 U.S. Census (Lampasas County, Texas), 2/2.
26. *Ibid.*; Lampasas History Book Committee, *Lampasas County, Texas* (Marceline, Missouri: Walsworth Publishing Co., 1991), 337; Jonnie Elzner, *Relighting Lamplights of Lampasas County, Texas* (Lampasas, Texas: Jonnie Ross Elzner, 1974), 288.
27. 1880 U.S. Census (Lampasas County, Texas, Precinct No. 6), 339, 1/1; 1900 U.S. Census (Lampasas County, Texas), 203/230.
28. Lampasas History Book Committee, *Lampasas County, Texas*, 18.
29. *State of Texas v. W .L. Shroyier*, Cause No. 7, vol. A, 1, 20, District Court Records, Lampasas County, Texas. (Courtesy Jeff Jackson, Lampasas).
30. *State of Texas v. W.L. Shroyier*, Cause No. 61, vol. A, 69, 73, 111, 159, District Court Records, Lampasas County, Texas. (Courtesy Jeff Jackson, Lampasas).
31. *State of Texas v. W. L. Shroyier*, Cause No. 173, Indictment and Statement of Facts, 9 September 1873, District Court Records, Lampasas County, Texas.
32. *State of Texas v. W. L. Shroyier*, Cause No. 189, Indictment, 16 September 1873, District Court Records, Lampasas County, Texas.
33. Lampasas History Book Committee, *Lampasas County, Texas*, 24.
34. *State of Texas v. W. L. Shroyier*, Cause No. 189.
35. *State of Texas v. W. L. Shroyier*, Cause No. 63, vol. A, 270, District Court Records, Lampasas County, Texas. (Courtesy Jeff Jackson, Lampasas).
36. *State of Texas v. W. L. Shroyier*, Cause No. 173.
37. *Mrs. S. A. Horrell v. Lou Shroyer*, Cause No. 44, District Court Records, Lampasas County, Texas. (Courtesy Jeff Jackson, Lampasas).

38. 1880 U.S. Census (Lampasas County, Texas, Precinct No. 6), 339, 1/1; 1900 U.S. Census (Lampasas County, Texas), 203/228.
39. *Bastrop (Texas) Advertiser*, 21 August 1875.
40. *Ibid.*
41. Preemption Affidavit and Designation, No. 7, 19 February 1875, and Corrected Field Notes, File No. 905, 1 March 1875, Texas General Land Office, Austin.
42. Warranty Deed, File No. 905, 29 September 1875, Texas General Land Office, Austin.
43. Charles B. Jones, Affidavit of Loss of Deed, File No. 905, 28 April 1880, Texas General Land Office, Austin.
44. [T. U. Taylor], "More Light on Bill Longley," *Frontier Times* 4, no. 9 (June 1927): 18.
45. *Ibid.*
46. Florence Fenley, *Oldtimers of Southwest Texas* (Uvalde, Texas: Hornby Press, 1957), 165.
47. Tise, *Texas County Sheriffs*, 503.
48. Fenley, *Oldtimers of Southwest Texas*, 165.
49. *Ibid.*
50. *Estate of J. B. Gibson v. L. Shroyer*, Cause No. 155, vol. 2, p. 124, District Court Minutes, Uvalde County, Texas.
51. Taylor, "Wild Career," 24.
52. A.J . Sowell, *Early Settlers and Indian Fighters of Southwest Texas* (Austin: State House Press, 1986), 223; Bandera County History Book Committee, *History of Bandera County, Texas* (Dallas: Curtis Media Corporation, 1986), 444; Eldon Stephen Branda, ed., *Handbook of Texas*, vol. 3 (Austin: Texas State Historical Association, 1976), 1087; 1870 U.S. Census (Uvalde County, Texas, Sabinal Post Office), 76/79.
53. *Lampasas (Texas) Dispatch*, 28 June 1877; *Nacogdoches (Texas) News*, 20 July 1877.
54. *Ibid.*
55. 1860 U.S. Census (Leon County, Texas, Bear Grass Post Office), 283; *State of Texas v. Jack Bolt*, vol. 3, pp. 30, 50–51, District Court Minutes, Mason County, Texas; Dave Johnson, Zionsville, Indiana, to author, 11 September 1994.
56. William L. Shroyer, Personal Notebook (Courtesy Mrs. Opal Thomas, Belton, Texas).
57. *Lampasas (Texas) Dispatch*, 28 June 1877; *Nacogdoches (Texas) News*, 20 July 1877.
58. *Ibid.*; *State of Texas v. William Longley*, Cause No. 100, Attachment, 25 July 1877, District Court Records, Lee County, Texas, Center for American History, University of Texas, Austin.

59. *Ibid.*; Fenley, *Oldtimers of Southwest Texas*, 166; Interview with Mr. Sid Heard, Reagan Wells, Uvalde County, Texas, 30 November 1993.
60. *Lampasas (Texas) Dispatch*, 28 June 1877; *Nacogdoches (Texas) News*, 20 July 1877. The January 10, 1876, date is confirmed by Shroyer's widow in a petition that she filed in Lampasas County on April 25, 1876, seeking an injunction to stop the forced sale of land that Shroyer had not paid for. *Mary C. Shroyer et al. v. Louisa F. Grizzell et al.*, Cause No. 271, District Court Records, Lampasas County, Texas (Courtesy Jeff Jackson, Lampasas).
61. *Ibid.*
62. Taylor, "Wild Career," 24.
63. John Leakey, *The West That Was* (Dallas: Southern Methodist University Press, 1958), 38.
64. [Taylor], "More Light on Bill Longley," 19.
65. Fenley, *Oldtimers of Southwest Texas*, 166.
66. [Taylor], "More Light on Bill Longley," 19.
67. Interview with Mr. Sid Heard, 30 November 1993.
68. *Ibid.*; Fenley, *Oldtimers of Southwest Texas*, 216.
69. C. B. Jones, Affidavit of Loss of Deed, 28 April 1880, File No. 905.
70. Bill Longley to James S. Longley, 14 May 1878.
71. Sowell, *Early Settlers*, 612–619; J. Marvin Hunter, *100 Years in Bandera, 1853–1953* (Bandera, Texas: J. Marvin Hunter, 1953), 17; Allan A. Stovall, *Breaks of the Balcones* (Barksdale, Texas: Allan A. Stovall, 1967), 100; Fenley, *Oldtimers of Southwest Texas*, 190; 1870 U.S. Census (Uvalde County, Texas, Sabinal Post Office), 96/94; 1880 U.S. Census (Bandera County, Texas, Precinct No. 4), 17/17.
72. *Lampasas (Texas) Dispatch*, 28 June 1877; *Nacogdoches (Texas) News*, 20 July 1877.
73. 1880 U.S. Census (Lampasas County, Texas, Precinct No. 6), 339, 1/1; 1900 U.S. Census (Lampasas County, Texas), 203/228.
74. Probate Minute Book, 22 November 1876, vol. 1, p. 22, Lampasas County, Texas.
75. Marriage Record Book, 17 January 1878, vol. A, 198, Lampasas County, Texas; 1880 U.S. Census (Lampasas County, Texas, Precinct No. 6), 339, 1/1.
76. *Lampasas (Texas) Daily Times*, 17 July 1878.
77. Slaughter Cemetery, Lampasas County, Texas.

Notes for Chapter 13

1. *State v. James Longley*, vol. A, 121–122, 16 December 1875, District Court Minutes, Lee County, Texas; *Austin Daily Democratic Statesman*, 17 August 1875.

2. 1870 U.S. Census (Medina County, Texas, Castroville Post Office), 1/1; Tise, *Texas County Sheriffs*, 369; Castro Colonies Heritage Association, *The History of Medina County, Texas* (Dallas: National ShareGraphics, Inc., 1987), 14.
3. Fuller, *Adventures of Bill Longley*, 12.
4. Tise, *Texas County Sheriffs*, 369.
5. Fuller, *Adventures of Bill Longley*, 14.
6. 1880 U.S. Census (Lee County, Texas, Precinct No. 1), 301/312.
7. Killen, *History of Lee County*, 234; Lee County Historical Commission, *Lee County, Texas, Cemeteries*, vol. 1, p. 64.
8. Fuller, *Adventures of Bill Longley*, 14.
9. *Houston Daily Telegraph*, 1 March 1876; *Giddings (Texas) Tribune*, 3 March 1876, as quoted in *Fayette County (Texas) Record*, 9 March 1876. See also Parsons, *James Madison Brown*, 38–39.
10. *Fayette County (Texas) Record*, 18 May 1876.
11. *Ibid.*, 2 June 1876; *Austin Daily Democratic Statesman*, 10 February 1878.
12. 1870 U.S. Census (Travis County, Texas, Austin Post Office), 524/566.
13. Bentley & Pilgrim, *Texas Legal Directory, 1876–1877*, 28; Deed Records, vol. 24, p. 493, Bell County, Texas.
14. *Fayette County (Texas) New Era*, 2 June 1876.
15. James S. Longley, circa 1936.
16. In December 1875, Fay recorded in Bell County deed records that he was given power of attorney by a Joseph B. Haynes of St. Louis, Missouri, to sell property that Haynes owned in Bell and Falls counties for whatever price Fay thought "fit and convenient." In 1877 John and Emily Lewellen were approached by a man named Sharpe, supposedly a partner of Fay, who told the couple that he had purchased 200 acres from Haynes through Fay's power of attorney. A deal was struck for the Lewellens to swap their ninety acres of land for the 200 acres and three promissory notes from Sharpe for $200 each. The power of attorney turned out to be a forgery, and in March 1878 the Lewellens filed a civil suit against Fay. But the lawyer's whereabouts were unknown. The previous month, in February, he had been arrested in Belton for the forgery. When the officer taking Fay to Austin stopped at Round Rock to switch trains, Fay managed to escape. A reward of $250 was offered for his delivery to the Travis County jail, and in 1881, after being rearrested, he pleaded guilty and was sentenced to two years confinement in the state penitentiary. *Galveston Daily News*, 12–13 February 1878; *Belton (Texas) Journal*, 21 March 1878; Deed Records, vol. 27, p. 222, Bell County, Texas; *Austin Daily Democratic Statesman*, 8 February 1878; Governor R. M. Hubbard to Sheriff J. M.

Brown, 22 August 1878, Governor's Letterpress Book, vol. 2, p. 533, Texas State Library, Austin; *Dallas Daily Herald*, 23 February 1881.

17. 1870 U.S. Census (Lamar County, Ben Franklin Post Office), 463/463; Fuller, *Adventures of Bill Longley*, 14.
18. Fuller, *Adventures of Bill Longley*, 14–15.
19. 1870 U.S. Census (Lamar County, Texas, Ben Franklin Post Office), 463/463.
20. Katherine Dinsmore Beshears, Mesquite, Texas, to author, 2 November 1995.
21. Fuller, *Adventures of Bill Longley*, 15.
22. Grave marker, W. R. Lay, Simmons Cemetery, Ben Franklin, Delta County, Texas.
23. Grave marker, Mark L. Foster, Simmons Cemetery, Ben Franklin, Delta County, Texas.
24. *Biographical Souvenir of the State of Texas*, 305; 1870 U.S. Census (Red River County, Texas, Clarksville Post Office), 1705/1705; 1880 U.S. Census (Delta County, Texas, Precinct No. 3), 46.
25. Fuller, *Adventures of Bill Longley*, 15–16.
26. *Ibid.*, 16–17.
27. *Ibid.*, 17.
28. *Ibid.*, 18.
29. *Ibid.*, 19.
30. *State of Texas v. William Black et al.*, Cause No. 194, and *State of Texas v. Thomas Jack*, unknown cause nos., vol. B, 404, District Court Civil Minutes, Delta County, Texas.
31. Fuller, *Adventures of Bill Longley*, 19.
32. Tise, *Texas County Sheriffs*, 153; 1880 U.S. Census (Delta County, Texas, Precinct No. Three), 6/6.
33. 1860 U.S. Census (Lamar County, Texas, Paris Post Office, Precinct No. 10), 167–168, 122/122; 1870 U.S. Census (Hopkins County, Texas, Charleston Post Office), 129/131; 1880 U.S. Census (Delta County, Texas, Precinct No. 1), 151/154.
34. Fuller, *Adventures of Bill Longley*.
35. Ikie Gray, *Loose Leaves* (Dallas: Mathis Publishing Co., ca. 1935), 28; Delta County History Book Committee, *Delta County History* (Dallas: Taylor Publishing Co., 1991), 6.
36. Commissioners Court Minutes, 29 May 1876, vol. A, 245, Delta County, Texas.
37. Fuller, *Adventures of Bill Longley*, 19–20; *Galveston Daily News*, 12 July 1876.
38. *Galveston Daily News*, 12 July 1876.
39. Taylor, "Wild Career," 26.

40. Executive Record Book, Gov. Richard Coke, 1874–1876, 23 June 1876, 319, Texas State Library, Austin.
41. *State of Texas v. William Black*, *State of Texas v. William Kennedy*, and *State of Texas v. Ed Corbet*, Indictments, unknown cause numbers, 5 August 1876, vol. C, 404, District Court Civil Minutes, Delta County, Texas; *State of Texas v. William Black*, Cause No. 184, 8 August 1876, vol. C, 56, District Court Civil Minutes, Delta County, Texas.
42. Commissioners Court Minutes, 19 August 1876, Book A/B, 256, Delta County, Texas.

Notes for Chapter 14

1. Fuller, *Adventures of Bill Longley*, 20–22.
2. *Ibid.*, 22.
3. *Ibid.*, 22–24.
4. *Ibid.*, 24–25.
5. *Ibid.*, 25.
6. *Ibid.*, 25–26.
7. *Ibid.*, 26.
8. *Ibid.*, 26–27.
9. *Ibid.*, 27.
10. *Ibid.*, 28.
11. *Ibid.*, 29–30.
12. *Ibid.*, 30.
13. *Ibid.*, 30–31.
14. Prucha, *Guide to the Military Posts*, 76.
15. Fuller, *Adventures of Bill Longley*, 31.
16. *Ibid.*
17. *Houston Telegram*, as quoted in *Dallas Daily Herald*, 7 June 1878.
18. *Austin Texas Capitol*, 20 September 1877.
19. 1860 U.S. Census (Washington County, Texas, Union Hill Post Office), 167, 247/247.
20. *Brenham (Texas) Banner*, 7 April 1876; Parsons, *James Madison Brown*, n. 3, 71.
21. *List of Fugitives From Justice for 1878*, as cited in Parsons, *James Madison Brown*, 63.
22. Fuller, *Adventures of Bill Longley*, 31–32. Rachel Lavinia Jack married Mississippi-born James Monroe Wheeler in Lamar County, Texas, on 10 July 1880, and they ultimately settled with their eight children in the Choctaw Nation, Indian Territory. "Miss Louvenia" died in McCurtain County, Oklahoma, on 12 April 1942, having always denied any relationship with Bill Longley. Letter to author

from Katherine Dinsmore Beshears, Mesquite, Texas, 2 November 1995.

23. Fuller, *Adventures of Bill Longley*, 32–33; 1860 U.S. Census (Washington County, Texas, Union Hill Post Office), 167, 247/247; *List of Fugitives From Justice in 1878*, as cited in Parsons, *James Madison Brown*, 63.
24. Fuller, *Adventures of Bill Longley*, 33.
25. 1860 U.S. Census (Milam County, Texas, Cameron Post Office), No. 564; 1870 U.S. Census (Milam County, Texas, Cameron Post Office), No. 919; 1880 U.S. Census (Milam County, Texas, E.D. 104), 396/397; Perry C. Holder, *150 Years of Cemetery Records in Milam County* (Austin: D. Armstrong Co., 1991), 431.
26. Fuller, *Adventures of Bill Longley*, 33.
27. *Galveston Daily News*, 15 September 1877.
28. *Ibid.*, 25 November 1876.
29. Fuller, *Adventures of Bill Longley*, 33.
30. *Giddings (Texas) Tribune*, 24 November 1876, as quoted in *Houston Daily Telegram*, 26 November 1876.
31. Adjutant General William Steele to Sgt. J. Leverett, 10 March 1877, Adjutant General Records, 1867–1877, Texas State Library, Austin.
32. Captain John C. Sparks, 20 March 1877, *Statement of Arrests and Attempts to Arrest*, Company C, Frontier Battalion, Texas State Library, Austin.

Notes for Chapter 15

1. Statement of Arrests, March 1877, Company C, Special State Troops [Frontier Battalion], Texas State Library, Austin.
2. Fuller, *Adventures of Bill Longley*, 2.
3. *Ibid.*; Carolyn Reeves Ericson, *Nacogdoches: Gateway to Texas*, vol. 2 (Nacogdoches, Texas: Ericson Books, 1987), 82; Nacogdoches County Genealogical Society, *Nacogdoches County Families* (Dallas: Curtis Media Corp., 1985), 216; 1880 U.S. Census (Nacogdoches County, Texas, Precinct No. 2), 101/101.
4. Fuller, *Adventures of Bill Longley*, 2; Ericson, *Nacogdoches: Gateway to Texas*, vol. 2, p. 82; Nacogdoches County Genealogical Society, *Nacogdoches County Families*, 216.
5. Fuller, *Adventures of Bill Longley*, 2.
6. *Ibid.*
7. 1870 U.S. Census (Shelby County, Texas, Brooklin Post Office), 174, 20/20; 1880 U.S. Census (Shelby County, Texas), 38/39.
8. 1870 U.S. Census (Shelby County, Texas, Brooklin Post Office), 180, 112/112.
9. Fuller, *Adventures of Bill Longley*, 2.

10. J. E. Hewett to T. U. Taylor, quoted in [Taylor], "More Light on Bill Longley," 21.
11. *Biographical and Historical Memoirs of Northwest Louisiana* (Chicago: Southern Publishing Co., 1890), 246–247.
12. 1880 U.S. Census (DeSoto Parish, Louisiana, Keatchie Post Office).
13. [Taylor], "More Light on Bill Longley," 19–20; Fuller, *Adventures of Bill Longley*, 2.
14. J. A. H. Slawson, *DeSoto Parish History and Cemetery Records* (Nacogdoches, Texas: J. B. Sanders, 1967), 77; [Taylor], "More Light on Bill Longley," 20; Fuller, *Adventures of Bill Longley*, 2.
15. 1880 U.S. Census (DeSoto Parish, Louisiana, Keatchie Post Office), 26/26; Fuller, *Adventures of Bill Longley*, 2; [Taylor], "More Light on Bill Longley," 20.
16. Fuller, *Adventures of Bill Longley*, 2; [Taylor], "More Light on Bill Longley," 20.
17. *Ibid.*
18. *Biographical and Historical Memoirs of Northwest Louisiana*, 246, 276; Slawson, *DeSoto Parish History*, 95.
19. *Memorial and Genealogical Record of Texas (East)* (Chicago: Goodspeed Brothers, 1895), 205–207; Tise, *Texas County Sheriffs*, 387; Ericson, *Nacogdoches: Gateway to Texas*, vol. 2, p. 234; Gladys Hardeman, *The History of Melrose*, unpublished manuscript, 1954–1965, Special Collections Department, Steen Library, Stephen F. Austin University, 1–2; Carolyn Reeves Ericson, *The People of Nacogdoches County in 1860* (Nacogdoches, Texas: Carolyn Reeves Ericson, 1978), 48; 1870 U.S. Census (Nacogdoches County, Texas: Melrose Precinct), 343/343.
20. Ericson, *Nacogdoches: Gateway to Texas*, vol. 2, p. 193; Nacogdoches County Genealogical Society, *Nacogdoches County Families*, 193; Marriage Records, vol. B, 356, Nacogdoches County, Texas; *Record of Murders and Assaults, 1867–1868*, 171, Texas State Library, Austin.
21. *Panola (Texas) Watchman*, 27 June 1877; Taylor, "Wild Career," 29; Fuller, *Adventures of Bill Longley*, 3.
22. *State of Texas v. William Longley*, capias warrant, 28 May 1877, Cause No. 100, District Court Records, Lee County, Texas, Center for American History, University of Texas, Austin.
23. Slawson, *DeSoto Parish History*, 67.
24. [Taylor], "More Light on Bill Longley," 20; Fuller, *Adventures of Bill Longley*, 3–4.
25. Taylor, "Wild Career," 26–27.
26. [Taylor], "More Light on Bill Longley," 20–21.
27. *Shreveport Times*, as quoted in *San Antonio Daily Express*, 8 July 1877.

28. *Waco (Texas) Examiner*, as quoted in *Marshall (Texas) Tri-Weekly Herald*, 23 June 1877.
29. *Henderson (Texas) Times*, as quoted in *Panola (Texas) Watchman*, 27 June 1877.
30. *Ibid.*; Taylor, "Wild Career," 26; Fuller, *Adventures of Bill Longley*, 4; *Galveston Daily News*, 10 June 1877.
31. *State of Texas v. William Longley*, capias warrant, 28 May 1877, Cause No. 100, District Court Records, Lee County, Texas, Center for American History, University of Texas, Austin.
32. *Fort Worth Daily Democrat*, 18 July 1877.
33. *Brenham (Texas) Daily Banner*, 10 June 1877.
34. *Waco (Texas) Daily Examiner*, 19 June 1877.
35. *Waco (Texas) Daily Examiner*, as quoted in *Marshall (Texas) Tri-Weekly Herald*, 23 June 1877.
36. *Giddings (Texas) Tribune*, 11 June 1877, 22 June 1877, as cited in *Brenham (Texas) Daily Banner*, 16 June 1877, 24 June 1877.
37. Tise, *Texas County Sheriffs*, 330.
38. *Brenham (Texas) Banner*, 5 May 1876, 12 May 1876. See also Parsons, *James Madison Brown*, 38–40.
39. Parsons, *James Madison Brown*, 53.
40. 1860 U.S. Census (Washington County, Texas, Evergreen Post Office), 689/689.
41. *Galveston Daily News*, 7 July 1877; see also Parsons, *James Madison Brown*, 58, 61, who identifies him as Jeff Arendal, based on Lee County Records.
42. W. A. Knox to Milton Mast, 27 June 1877, as quoted in *Nacogdoches (Texas) News*, 20 July 1877; *Brenham (Texas) Daily Banner*, 30 June 1877, 22 July 1877.
43. W. A. Knox to Milton Mast, 27 June 1877.
44. *Galveston Daily News*, 7 July 1877.
45. *Ibid.*, 28 June 1877.
46. *Ibid.*, 10 July 1877.
47. *Brenham (Texas) Daily Banner*, 15 July 1877.
48. *Dallas Daily Herald*, 19 July 1877.
49. *State of Texas v. J. W. Longley alias J. W. Patterson*, Cause No. 2590, District Court Records, McLennan County, Texas.

Notes for Chapter 16

1. *Galveston Daily News*, 26 October 1877.
2. 1870 U.S. Census (Washington County, Texas, Evergreen Post Office), 171, 3/3.
3. *Brenham (Texas) Banner*, 2 March 1876.

4. *Ibid.*, 9 June 1876.
5. *State of Texas v. William Longley*, Attachment, 25 July 1877, Cause No. 100, District Court Records, Lee County, Texas, Center for American History, University of Texas, Austin.
6. *Ibid.*
7. *Dallas Daily Herald*, 4 August 1877.
8. *Brenham (Texas) Daily Banner*, 29 July 1877.
9. *Galveston Daily News*, 8 August 1877.
10. *Ibid.*, 1 August 1877.
11. *Dallas Daily Herald*, 26 July 1877.
12. *Bonham (Texas) News*, 10 August 1877.
13. *State of Texas v. William Longley*, 16 August 1877, vol. B, 480, District Court Civil Minutes, Delta County, Texas.
14. *Bonham (Texas) News*, 24 August 1877.
15. *Castroville (Texas) Era*, as quoted in *Dallas Daily Herald*, 23 August 1877.
16. Rick Miller, *Bounty Hunter* (College Station, Texas: Creative Publishing Co., 1988), 85–80; Chuck Parsons, *The Capture of John Wesley Hardin* (College Station, Texas: Creative Publishing Co., 1978), 46–55.
17. *Brenham (Texas) Daily Banner*, 25 August 1877.
18. *State of Texas v. William Longley*, 27 August 1877, vol. A, 183, Cause No. 100, District Court Minutes, Lee County, Texas.
19. Judge Turner was appointed by President Hayes to the federal bench in 1880. *Brenham (Texas) Banner*, 4 February 1876; 1870 U.S. Census (Travis County, Texas, Austin), 463/505; 1880 U.S. Census (Travis County, Texas, E.D. 121, Polling Place No. 5), 22, 153/158; James D. Lynch, *The Bench and Bar of Texas* (St. Louis: Nixon-Jones Printing Co., 1885), 365–366; William Neal Ramey, ed., *Texian (Annual)*, vol. 2, no. 1, Quarterly no. 4 (Austin: publisher unknown, 1886), 279; Hunter, *Handbook of Texas*, vol. 2, p. 809.
20. *State of Texas v. William Longley*, 27 August 1877, Cause No. 100, vol. A, 183, District Court Minutes, Lee County, Texas.
21. 1860 U.S. Census (Washington County, Texas, Evergreen Post Office), 685/685; 1870 U.S. Census (Burleson County, Texas, Evergreen Post Office), 17/17; 1880 U.S. Census (Lee County, Texas, Precinct No. 3); Killen, *History of Lee County*, 34.
22. Yeats, "Facts of Longley Hanging Explained," 3.
23. Bonnie Tom Robinson, "They Buried Bill Longley Next to a Blackjack Tree," *Frontier Times* 9, no. 12 (September 1932): 572–574.
24. 1870 U.S. Census (Washington County, Texas, Evergreen Post Office), 218/218; 1880 U.S. Census (Lee County, Texas, Giddings Post Office), 2, 35/38.
25. 1880 U.S. Census (Lee County, Texas, E.D. 91, Giddings), 1, 17/19.

26. 1880 U.S. Census (Lee County, Texas, Giddings Post Office), 87/94 and (Precinct No. 1), 129/135 [is listed twice]; Lee County Historical Commission, *Lee County, Texas, Cemeteries*, vol. 2, 124.
27. Tise, *Texas County Sheriffs*, 330.
28. *Galveston Daily News*, 29 August 1877; *Waco (Texas) Daily Examiner*, 4 September 1877; Bentley & Pilgrim, *Texas Legal Directory, 1876–1877*, 61.
29. Miss Mamie Yeary, *Reminiscences of the Boys in Gray, 1861–1865* (McGregor, Texas: Miss Mamie Yeary, 1912), 683; Frank W. Johnson, *A History of Texas and Texans*, (Chicago: American Historical Society, 1916), vol. 2, pp. 111–112; Webb, *Handbook of Texas*, vol. 2, p. 601; *Brenham (Texas) Banner*, 5 March 1874; Mrs. R. E. Pennington, *The History of Brenham and Washington County* (Houston: Standard Printing & Lithographing Co., 1915), 84–87; Lucian Lamar Knight, ed., *Library of Southern Literature* (Atlanta: Martin & Hoyt Co., 1910), vol. 15, p. 396.
30. Charles F. Greenwood, "Judge Seth Shepard," *Proceedings of the Thirty-Eighth Annual* [Texas Bar Association] *Session* (Houston: Gray, Dillaye & Young, Printers, 1917), 102–105.
31. Bentley & Pilgrim, *Texas Legal Directory, 1876–77*, 61; Judy and Nath Winfield, Jr., *Cemetery Records of Washington County, Texas, 1826–1960* ([Brenham], Texas: Judy & Nath Winfield, Jr., 1974), 93.
32. *Brenham (Texas) Banner*, 2 March 1876.
33. *State of Texas v. William Longley*, Cause No. 100, *Venire Facias*, 31 August 1877, District Court Records, Lee County, Texas, Center for American History, University of Texas, Austin.
34. Killen, *History of Lee County, Texas*, 48.
35. 1880 U.S. Census (Lee County, Texas, Giddings Post Office), 19/21.
36. *Giddings (Texas) Weekly Tribune*, 24 September 1874.
37. *State of Texas v. William Longley*, Cause No. 100, Motion for Continuance, 3 September 1877, District Court Records, Lee County, Texas, Center for American History, University of Texas, Austin.
38. *Galveston Daily News*, 4 September 1877.
39. *State of Texas v. William Longley*, Cause No. 100, 3 September 1877, vol. A, 190, District Court Minutes, Lee County, Texas.
40. *Galveston Daily News*, 4 September 1877.
41. *Ibid.*, 26 October 1877.
42. 1870 U.S. Census (Washington County, Texas, Evergreen Post Office), 91/91; 1880 U.S. Census (Washington County, Texas, Precinct No. 1, E.D. 91), 14, 250/259, 507/525; Lee County Historical Commission, *Lee County, Texas, Cemeteries*, vol. 1, p. 19.
43. 1870 U.S. Census (Burleson County, Texas, Lexington Post Office), 227/240; 1880 U.S. Census (Lee County, Texas, Precinct No. 3); Lee County Historical Survey Committee, *History of Lee County, Texas*,

271, 441; Lee County Historical Commission, *Lee County, Texas, Cemeteries*, vol. 1, p. 19.

44. Lee County Historical Commission, *Lee County, Texas, Cemeteries*, vol. 1, p. 101.
45. 1860 U.S. Census (Burleson County, Texas, Evergreen Post Office), 77, 521/573; 1880 U.S. Census (Lee County, Texas, Precinct No. 3).
46. 1870 U.S. Census (Burleson County, Texas, Lexington Post Office), 13/14; Lee County Historical Survey Committee, *History of Lee County, Texas*, 381; Lee County Historical Commission, *Lee County, Texas, Cemeteries*, vol. 2, p. 28.
47. 1860 U.S. Census (Burleson County, Texas, Lexington Post Office), 13, 84/84; 1880 U.S. Census (Lee County, Texas, E.D. 94), 327/328; *State of Texas v. Richard Puckett*, Cause Nos. 259, 570, 591, and 594, vol. D, 679, 692, and 758, December 1873, District Court Minutes, Burleson County, Texas.
48. 1870 U.S. Census (Burleson County, Texas, Blue Branch Post Office), 24/25; 1880 U.S. Census (Lee County, Texas, Precinct No. 3); Lee County Historical Survey Committee, *History of Lee County, Texas*, 168; Lee County Historical Commission, *Lee County, Texas, Cemeteries*, vol. 1, pp. 101–102; *Giddings (Texas) Tribune*, as quoted in *The Colorado Citizen* (Columbus, Texas), 6 January 1876.
49. 1870 U.S. Census (Burleson County, Texas, Lexington Post Office), 140, 161/173; 1880 U.S. Census (Lee County, Texas, Precinct No. 4), 244/245; Lee County Historical Commission, *Lee County, Texas, Cemeteries*, vol. 1, p. 217.
50. *Galveston Daily News*, 26 October 1877.
51. *State of Texas v. William Longley*, Cause No. 100, 3 September 1877, vol. A, 190, District Court Minutes, Lee County, Texas.
52. *Galveston Daily News*, 5 September 1877.
53. Thomas Ripley, *They Died With Their Boots On* (New York: Sun Dial Press, 1937), 61–62; Taylor, "Wild Career," 29.
54. *Galveston Daily News*, 5 September 1877; *Austin Daily Democratic Statesman*, 9 September 1877; *San Antonio Daily Express*, 13 September 1877; see also Parsons, *James Madison Brown*, 57.
55. Frances T. Ingmire, *Bastrop County, Texas, Marriage Records, 1851–1870* (St. Louis: Frances T. Ingmire, 1985), 10.
56. *State of Texas v. Jos. Hemphill*, Cause No. 2563, 13 December 1873, vol. F, 140, District Court Minutes, Bastrop County, Texas.
57. *Dallas Commercial*, as quoted in *Denison (Texas) Daily News*, 21 December 1878.
58. Fuller, *Adventures of Bill Longley*, 4.
59. *Belton (Texas) Journal*, 20 September 1877; *Lampasas (Texas) Dispatch*, 27 September 1877.

60. *Ibid.*
61. *Galveston Daily News*, 26 October 1877.
62. *Ibid.*
63. *Ibid.*
64. *Ibid.*, 21 October 1877.
65. *State of Texas v. William Longley*, Cause No. 100, Charge to the Jury, 4 September 1877, District Court Records, Lee County, Texas, Center for American History, University of Texas, Austin; Article 605, Chapter 15, Title 15, *Penal Code of the State of Texas* (Galveston: A.H. Belo & Co., 1879), 81.
66. Articles 607 and 609, Chapter 15, Title 15, *Penal Code of the State of Texas*, 81–82.
67. *State of Texas v. William Longley*, Cause No. 100, Charge to the Jury, 4 September 1877, District Court Records, Lee County, Texas, Center for American History, University of Texas, Austin.
68. Article 668, Chapter 15, Title 8, *Code of Criminal Procedure of the State of Texas* (Galveston: A.H. Belo & Co., 1879), 81.
69. Bill Longley to James M. Brown, unknown date.
70. *Galveston Daily News*, 21 October 1877.
71. *Ibid.*
72. *State of Texas v. William Longley*, Cause No. 100, Reverse of Indictment, 4 September 1877, District Court Records, Lee County, Texas, Texas State Library, Austin; District Court Minutes, Lee County, Texas, vol. A, 190.
73. *Galveston Daily News*, 5 September 1877.
74. *Houston Telegram*, as quoted in *New Orleans Daily Picayune*, 11 September 1877.
75. *New York Herald*, 13 October 1878.
76. *Belton (Texas) Journal*, 20 September 1877.
77. *State of Texas v. William Longley*, Cause No. 100, 11 September 1877, vol. A, 202, District Court Minutes, Lee County, Texas.
78. *Elyria (Ohio) Constitution*, 8 November 1877.
79. *Belton (Texas) Journal*, 20 September 1877; *Lampasas (Texas) Dispatch*, 27 September 1877.
80. *Ibid.*
81. *San Antonio Daily Express*, 13 September 1877.
82. *Frontier Echo* (Jacksboro, Texas), 2 November 1877.

Notes for Chapter 17

1. *State of Texas v. William Longley*, Cause No. 100, vol. A, 204, District Court Criminal Minutes, Lee County, Texas.
2. *Galveston Daily News*, 13 September 1877.

3. *Ibid.*
4. *Ibid.*
5. *Ibid.*, 14 September 1877.
6. *Ibid.*, 15 September 1877; *Brenham (Texas) Banner*, as quoted in *Dallas Daily Herald*, 22 September 1877.
7. Parsons, *James Madison Brown*, 58.
8. *Galveston Daily News*, 15 September 1877.
9. *Ibid.*
10. *Ibid.*, 16 September 1877.
11. *Ibid.*
12. *Dallas Daily Herald*, 18 September 1877.
13. Tise, *Texas County Sheriffs*, 202.
14. 1870 U.S. Census (Galveston County, Texas, Ward No. 1), 1043/1045; Galveston County Genealogical Society, *St. Joseph's Church, Galveston, Texas–Baptismal, Confirmation, Marriage and Death Records, 1860–1952* (Easley, South Carolina: Southern Historical Press, 1984), 31, 78, 102, 165; Galveston County Genealogical Society, *Early Texas Death and Legal Records From Joseph Franklin's Diary and John Griffin's Sexton Records* (Galveston: Galveston County Genealogical Society, 1990), 59, 69, 70.
15. *Galveston Daily News*, 10 July 1877, 18 September 1877.
16. *Ibid.*, 28 September 1877.
17. *Austin Texas Capitol*, 21 October 1877; *Weatherford (Texas) Exponent*, 23 March 1878.
18. *Nacogdoches (Texas) News*, as quoted in *Galveston Daily News*, 17 October 1877.
19. *Dallas Daily Herald*, 19 October 1877.
20. *Galveston Daily News*, 21 October 1877.
21. *Ibid.*
22. *Ibid.*
23. *Ibid.*, 26 October 1877.
24. *Ibid.*
25. *Ibid.*
26. *Ibid.*
27. Bill Longley to James S. Longley, 14 October 1877, Center for American History, University of Texas, Austin.
28. *Ibid.*
29. *Ibid.*
30. Bill Longley to Milton Mast, 29 October 1877, as quoted in Fuller, *Adventures of Bill Longley*, 70–72.
31. *Ibid.*; *Nacogdoches (Texas) News*, as quoted in *Galveston Daily News*, 13 November 1877.
32. *Galveston Daily News*, 26 December 1877.

33. *Ibid.*, 11 November 1877.
34. *Ibid.*, 22 November 1877.
35. James S. Longley to Campbell Longley, 24 November 1877, Center for American History, University of Texas, Austin; 1880 U.S. Census (Bastrop County, Texas, Precinct No. 14), 34/34; Bill Moore, *Bastrop County, 1691–1900* (Wichita Falls, Texas: Nortex Press, 1977), 85.
36. *Galveston Daily News*, 4 January 1878; Parsons, *James Madison Brown*, 64.
37. *Galveston Daily News*, 23 January 1878.
38. James S. Longley to Campbell Longley, 27 January 1878, Center for American History, University of Texas, Austin.
39. 1880 U.S. Census (Bastrop County, Texas, Precinct No. 6), 410/410.
40. *Galveston Daily News*, 5 February 1878, 12 February 1878.
41. Ramey, *Texian (Annual)*, vol. 2, no. 1, quarterly no. 4, 262–263; Webb, *Handbook of Texas*, vol. 2, p. 104; *Galveston Daily News*, 25 July 1878.
42. 1870 U.S. Census (Austin County, Texas, Bellville Post Office), 551/551.
43. *Galveston Daily News*, 7 March 1878.
44. *Ibid.*, 8 March 1878.
45. Webb, *Handbook of Texas*, vol. 2, p. 894; M'Arthur and Wickes, *The Twenty-Seventh Legislature and State Administration of Texas, 1901* (Austin: Ben C. Jones & Co., Printers, 1901), 13–14; Lynch, *The Bench and Bar of Texas*, 333–337.
46. *W. P. Longley v. State of Texas*, 3 Tex. Court of Appeals Reports 613, 13 March 1878.
47. *Ibid.*, 615.
48. *Ibid.*, 616.
49. *Ibid.*, 612.
50. *Ibid.*, 617.
51. *Galveston Daily News*, 15 March 1878.
52. Bill Longley to James S. Longley, 15 March 1878, Center for American History, University of Texas, Austin.
53. *State of Texas v. William Longley*, Cause No. 100, Mandate of Court of Appeals, 30 March 1878, District Court Records, Lee County, Texas, Center for American History, University of Texas, Austin.

Notes for Chapter 18

1. *Chicago Times*, as quoted in *Sedalia (Missouri) Daily Democrat*, 15 March 1878.
2. *Ibid.*
3. *Illustrated Police News*, 20 April 1878.

4. Bill Longley to Milton Mast, approximately April 1878, partially quoted in *Austin Daily Democratic Statesman*, 7 April 1878, 16 April 1878.
5. *Galveston Daily News*, 22 November 1877.
6. *Ibid.*, 1 December 1877.
7. *Ibid.*, 4 December 1877.
8. Bill Longley to Rudolph Hatcher, 12 April 1878, courtesy of Pauline Longley, San Saba, and partially quoted in *Austin Daily Democratic Statesman*, 24 April 1878.
9. *Galveston Daily News*, 10 July 1877, 16 April 1878, 5 May 1878.
10. *Brenham (Texas) Daily Banner*, 18 April 1878; *Victoria (Texas) Advocate*, 27 April 1878.
11. *Austin Daily Democratic Statesman*, 30 April 1878.
12. Bill Longley to James S. Longley, 14 May 1878, Center for American History, University of Texas, Austin.
13. 1880 U.S. Census (Bandera County, Texas, Precinct No. 4), 12/12.
14. Bill Longley to James S. Longley, 14 May 1878, Center for American History, University of Texas, Austin.
15. Bill Longley to Campbell and Sarah Longley, 16–17 May 1878, Center for American History, University of Texas, Austin; Lampasas County Historical Commission, *Lampasas County, Texas*, 76.
16. Bill Longley to Campbell and Sarah Longley, 16–17 May 1878, Center for American History, University of Texas, Austin.
17. Longley Family Bible; Mrs. Homer L. Roper and Mrs. Richard N. Grammar, *Cemeteries–Lampasas County* (Lampasas, Texas: Daughters of the American Colonists, 1978), 106.
18. Bill Longley to Campbell and Sarah Longley, 16–17 May 1878, Center for American History, University of Texas, Austin.
19. *William Taylor v. State of Texas*, 3 Tex. Court of Appeals Reports 387 (1878).
20. *Galveston Daily News*, 18 May 1878.
21. Bill Longley to Milton Mast, 22 May 1878, as quoted in *National Police Gazette*, 29 June 1878.
22. Fuller, *Adventures of Bill Longley*, 72–74.
23. Bill Longley to Campbell and Sarah Longley, 1 June 1878, Center for American History, University of Texas, Austin.
24. *Galveston Daily News*, 5 June 1878.
25. *Ibid.*, 9 June 1878.
26. Bill Longley to James S. Longley and Alexander C. Longley, 15 June 1878 (Courtesy of Dr. Brooks Ellwood, Arlington, Texas).
27. *Galveston Daily News*, 8 December 1880.
28. *Flake's Daily Bulletin* (Galveston), 13 February 1870; *Dallas Daily Herald*, 8 December 1880.

29. Baptismal Record, St. Mary's Cathedral, Galveston, Texas, 50, no. 391, Archives, Diocese of Galveston-Houston.
30. *Galveston Daily News*, 21 July 1878; *Lampasas (Texas) Daily Times*, 17 July 1878.
31. *Galveston Daily News*, 25 July 1878.
32. *Nacogdoches (Texas) News*, as quoted in *Lampasas (Texas) Daily Times*, 28 July 1878, and *Galveston Daily News*, 23 July 1878.
33. Bill Longley to Sarah Campbell and James S. Longley, 31 July 1878, Center for American History, University of Texas, Austin.
34. *Galveston Daily News*, 14 July 1878.
35. *Ibid.*, 6 August 1878.
36. *Ibid.*, 13 August 1878.
37. *Ibid.*, 16 August 1878.

Notes for Chapter 19

1. Republic of Texas Pension Application, 14 August 1878, Texas State Library, Austin.
2. *Ibid.*, 22 May 1874.
3. Registry of Letters, Rutherford B. Hayes Presidential Center, Fremont, Ohio, 25–26 August 1878; *New York Herald*, 13 October 1878.
4. *New York Herald*, 13 October 1878.
5. Mildred Forester, Paradise, California, to author, 25 April 1994; Lee Albright, Paradise, California, to author, 17 August 1994.
6. *New York Herald*, 13 October 1878.
7. *Galveston Daily News*, 27 August 1878; *Brenham (Texas) Daily Banner*, 27 August 1878.
8. *Austin Statesman*, as quoted in *San Antonio Daily Express*, 28 August 1878.
9. *Galveston Daily News*, 31 August 1878.
10. *Ibid.*, 10 September 1878.
11. *New York Herald*, 13 October 1878.
12. *Galveston Daily News*, 7 September 1878; Parsons, *James Madison Brown*, 68. Parsons cited a September 4 trial date, based on a Lee County criminal minute book.
13. *Panola (Texas) Watchman*, 23 October 1878.
14. *Ibid.*; *Galveston Daily News*, 7 September 1878; see also *State of Texas v. William Longley*, Cause No. 100, vol. A, 239, District Court Minutes, Lee County, Texas.
15. Bill Longley to Mrs. Bettie "Southrn," 19 September 1878, Center for American History, University of Texas, Austin.
16. *Ibid.*

17. Bill Longley to Campbell and Sarah Longley, 26 September 1878, Center for American History, University of Texas, Austin.
18. Bill Longley to James S. Longley, 27 September 1878, Center for American History, University of Texas, Austin.
19. Taylor, "Wild Career," 27.
20. Stephens, *Indian War Pensions*, 65. See also Dora Neill Raymond, *Captain Lee Hall of Texas* (Norman: University of Oklahoma Press, 1982), 75 *et seq*.
21. Taylor, "Wild Career," 27; Everett Hagen, "I Saw Wild Bill Longley Hang," *Real West* 2, no. 7 (May 1959): 21.
22. Letterpress Book, Governor Richard Hubbard, 7 October 1878, 322, Texas State Library, Austin.
23. G. K. Martin, "Land of the Noose–Yegua Knobbs," *Old West* 5, no. 3 (Spring 1969): 8–9.
24. *Houston Daily Telegram*, 12 October 1878.
25. *Galveston Daily News*, 11 October 1878.
26. Lewis S. Delony, "40 Years a Peace Officer," *Old West* 7, no. 2 (Winter 1970): 82.
27. Bill Longley to James S. Longley and Alexander C. Longley, 10 October 1878 (Courtesy of Dr. Brooks Ellwood, Arlington, Texas).
28. *Galveston Daily News*, 11 October 1878.
29. *Ibid*.
30. Catholic Directory Record, Catholic Archives of Texas, Austin; 1880 U.S. Census (Travis County, Texas, E.D. 136, Austin), 265, 293/328.
31. *Brenham (Texas) Weekly Banner*, 18 October 1878.
32. *Houston Daily Telegram*, 12 October 1878.
33. *Galveston Daily News*, 12 October 1878; 1880 U.S. Census (Lee County, Texas, Precinct No. 1), 185/193; *State of Texas v. Z .P. Eggleston*, Cause Nos. 418, 419, 465, 466, vol. D, 183, 184, 187, 272, 281, 335, District Court Minutes, Bastrop County, Texas; Fuller, *Adventures of Bill Longley*, 5–6.
34. *Giddings (Texas) Weekly Tribune*, 24 September 1874.
35. *Galveston Daily News*, 12 October 1878; Fuller, *Adventures of Bill Longley*, 5; Robinson, "They Buried Bill Longley," 572–574.
36. *Brenham (Texas) Weekly Banner*, 18 October 1878.
37. *St. Louis Globe-Democrat*, 12 October 1878; *Houston Daily Telegram*, 12 October 1878.
38. *Houston Daily Telegram*, 12 October 1878; 1880 U.S. Census (Galveston County, Texas, St. Mary's Orphan Asylum), 140/141; *Sunday Times* (Houston), 27 September 1868; Rev. James Vanderholt, "Rev. Joseph Querat," Archives, Diocese of Galveston-Houston.
39. *St. Louis Globe-Democrat*, 12 October 1878.

40. 1870 U.S. Census (Burleson County, Texas, Blue Branch Post Office), 128, 52/55.
41. *Houston Daily Telegram*, 12 October 1878.
42. Hagen, "I Saw Wild Bill Longley Hang," 20–21.
43. *Austin Daily Democratic Statesman*, 1 December 1878.
44. *Brenham (Texas) Weekly Banner*, 18 October 1878.
45. *Galveston Daily News*, 12 October 1878.
46. Yeats, "Facts of Longley Hanging Explained," 3.
47. Robinson, "They Buried Bill Longley," 573.
48. *Ibid.*; Hiram G. Craig to *Frontier Times*, unknown date.
49. *Galveston Daily News*, 12 October 1878.
50. *State of Texas v. William Longley*, Cause No. 100, District Court Records, Lee County, Texas, Center for American History, University of Texas, Austin.
51. *Galveston Daily News*, 12 October 1878.
52. *Brenham (Texas) Weekly Banner*, 18 October 1878.
53. *St. Louis Globe-Democrat*, 12 October 1878.
54. *Ibid.*
55. L. C. Rummel to *Frontier Times* 3, no. 10 (July 1926): 11.
56. *Galveston Daily News*, 12 October 1878; *Brenham (Texas) Weekly Banner*, 12 October 1878; *St. Louis Globe-Democrat*, 12 October 1878; *Houston Daily Telegram*, 12 October 1878. Dr. Edward T. Gazley was a forty-five-year-old physician whose father had represented a community in Bastrop County at the Texas Constitutional Convention in 1836. Secretary of the Lee County Medical Examining Board, Gazley advertised that he gave "special attention to diseases peculiar to females" and that his Giddings office at Gazley and Clark's Drug Store was at the "sign of the golden mortar." Dr. Jacob A. Fields, born in Virginia in 1852, originally studied for the Methodist ministry, but graduated as a doctor from Tulane University in 1874 and came to Giddings in 1875. In addition to his medical practice, he had also established a drugstore. He helped found the First National Bank there, and would also serve in the Texas legislature and later as mayor of Giddings in 1920. The third doctor, William Lafayette Johnson, came to Evergreen from Mississippi after the Civil War, then later moved his practice to Giddings. Doctor Johnson was also president of the Lee County Medical Examining Board. Lee County Historical Survey Committee, *History of Lee County, Texas*, 48; 1880 U.S. Census (Lee County, Texas, Giddings Post Office), 6/6 and 43/49; 1880 U.S. Census (Travis County, Texas, E.D. 123, Town of Manor), 55, 84/84; Lee County Historical Commission, *Lee County, Texas, Cemeteries*, vol. 2, pp. 85, 92; *Giddings (Texas) Weekly Tribune*, 24 September 1874.
57. Fuller, *Adventures of Bill Longley*, 6.

58. Delony, “40 Years a Peace Officer,” 82.
59. *Galveston Daily News*, 12 October 1878; *St. Louis Globe-Democrat*, 12 October 1878.
60. Fuller, *Adventures of Bill Longley*, 6.
61. *State of Texas v. William Longley*, Cause No. 100, Death Warrant, District Court Records, Lee County, Texas, Center for American History, University of Texas, Austin.
62. *Galveston Daily News*, 12 October 1878.
63. *St. Louis Globe-Democrat*, 12 October 1878.
64. *Galveston Daily News*, 12 October 1878.
65. *Ibid.*, 13 October 1878.
66. Minutes, 21 October 1878, vol. A, 182, Commissioners Court, Lee County, Texas.

Notes for Chapter 20

1. *San Antonio Daily Express*, 22 June 1879.
2. *Brenham (Texas) Daily Banner*, 14 January 1881, 16 January 1881.
3. Wayne Spiller, “His Brother’s Long Shadow,” *True West* 19, no. 3 (January–February 1972): 7; Williamson County Genealogical Society, *Williamson County, Texas, Marriage Records, 1848–1888*, 46.
4. Spiller, “His Brother’s Long Shadow,” 7.
5. *Lometa (Texas) Reporter*, 4 October 1907.
6. *Austin Daily Statesman*, 29 July 1881.
7. *State of Texas v. James S. Longley*, Cause No. 2399, Indictment, District Court Records, Bell County, Texas.
8. *San Antonio Daily Express*, 27 August 1887.
9. Parsons, *James Madison Brown*, 119, 133–138.
10. *Temple (Texas) Weekly Times*, 27 August 1887.
11. *Belton (Texas) Weekly News*, 6 September 1887.
12. Robinson, “They Buried Bill Longley Next to a Blackjack Tree,” 574.
13. *Brenham (Texas) Weekly Banner*, 18 October 1878.
14. *Galveston Daily News*, 12 October 1878.
15. *Victoria (Texas) Advocate*, 10 September 1887.
16. Woolley was born in Lee County on January 12, 1866, marrying Rebecca Wilson in 1886. The two had five children. When she died in 1896, Woolley married Jennie Lou Bryan, and they had six children. He served as deputy sheriff in Fort Bend County for six years, beginning in 1905, then served four years as a justice of the peace, subsequently being elected sheriff. Frank W. Johnson (Eugene C. Barker, ed.), *A History of Texas and Texans* (New York: American Historical Society, 1914), vol. 3, pp. 1545–46.

17. Yeats, "Facts of Longley Hanging Explained," 3.
18. *Ibid.*
19. Hagen, "I Saw Wild Bill Longley Hang," 76.
20. Delony, "40 Years a Peace Officer," 82.
21. *Brenham (Texas) Weekly Banner*, 25 October 1878.
22. *San Antonio Daily Express*, 30 October 1878.
23. Grave marker, Sarah A. Longley, Cedar Knob Cemetery, Bell County, Texas.
24. Marriage Records, vol. J, 187, Bell County, Texas; A. C. Greene, *A Personal Country* (College Station: Texas A&M University Press, 1979), 288–289.
25. Greene, *A Personal Country*, 288–290.
26. *Ibid.*, 290–291.
27. *Ibid.*
28. Robinson, "They Buried Bill Longley Next to a Blackjack Tree," 574.
29. Bob Wright, "More About Bill Longley," *Texas Parade* 20, no. 5 (October 1959): 4.
30. [Taylor], "More Light on Bill Longley," 21.
31. *Ibid.*
32. *Ibid.*, 21–22.
33. Carl W. Breihan, *Great Gunfighters of the West* (San Antonio: Naylor Co., 1971), 62.
34. *Ibid.*, 63.
35. *Ibid.*, 63–64.
36. Ruth Priest Dixon, Researcher, to author, 28 January 1994.
37. Grace Lim, "Man Doesn't Want Legend Left Hanging," *Austin American-Statesman*, 21 September 1987.
38. Ted Wax, *Dead Man on the Bayou?* (Gonzales, Louisiana: Ted Wax, 1988), 80–91.
39. *Ibid.*, 93–99.
40. Brooks B. Ellwood, Douglas W. Owsley, Suzanne H. Ellwood, and Pat Marcado-Allinger, "Search for the Grave of the Notorious Texas Gunfighter William 'Wild Bill' Longley," unpublished manuscript, 1994.
41. See also Chuck Parsons, "Bill Longley's Ghost Escapes," *True West* 39, no. 12 (December 1992): 24–25.
42. "Mystery of Texas Outlaw Solved by Smithsonian-led Team of Scientists," news release, Smithsonian Institution National Museum of Natural History, 13 June 2001; *University of Texas at Arlington Magazine Online* 24, no. 1 (Fall 2001).
43. Spiller, "His Brother's Long Shadow," 44, 48.
44. *Lometa (Texas) Reporter*, 4 October 1907.
45. Greene, *A Personal Country*, 291.

Bibliography

Books

Bandera County History Book Committee. *History of Bandera County, Texas*. Dallas: Curtis Media, 1986.

Bartholomew, Ed. *Cullen Baker*. Houston: Frontier Press, 1954.

———. *Wild Bill Longley: A Texas Hard-Case*. Houston: Frontier Press, 1953.

———. *Wyatt Earp: The Untold Story*. Toyahvale, Texas: Frontier Book Company, 1963.

Bentley and Pilgrim. *Texas Legal Directory, 1876–1877*. Austin: Democratic Statesman Office, 1877.

Bettis, Mrs. Jesse B., and Mrs. Mattie Baird. *Zephyr Yesterday and Today*. Brownwood, Texas: Banner Printing Co., 1980.

Biographical and Historical Memoirs of Northwest Louisiana. Chicago: Southern Publishing Co., 1890.

Biographical Souvenir of the State of Texas. Chicago: F. A. Battey & Co., 1889.

Branda, Eldon Stephen, ed. *The Handbook of Texas*, vol. 3. Austin: Texas State Historical Association, 1976.

Breihan, Carl W. *Great Gunfighters of the West*. San Antonio: Naylor Co., 1971.

Brice, Donaly E. *The Great Comanche Raid*. Austin: Eakin Press, 1987.

Brown County Historical Society. *In the Life and Lives of Brown County People*. Brownwood, Texas: Brown County Historical Society.

Bruce, Leona. *They Came in Peace to Coleman County*. Fort Worth: Branch-Smith, 1970.

Canton, Frank M. *Frontier Trails*. Norman: University of Oklahoma Press, 1972.

Carter, Lt. Col. W. H. *From Yorktown to Santiago with the Sixth U.S. Cavalry*. Austin: State House Press, 1989.

Castro Colonies Heritage Association. *The History of Medina County, Texas*. Dallas: National ShareGraphics, 1987.

Chisholm, James. *South Pass, 1868*. Edited by Lola M. Homsher. Lincoln: University of Nebraska Press, 1975.

Crouch, Barry A. *The Freedman's Bureau and Black Texans*. Austin: University of Texas Press, 1992.

Crouch, Barry A., and Donaly E. Brice. *Cullen Montgomery Baker: Reconstruction Desperado*. Baton Rouge: Louisiana State University Press, 1997.

Daughters of the Republic of Texas. *Muster Rolls of the Texas Revolution*. Lubbock, Texas: Craftsman Printers, 1986.

DeArment, Robert K. *Alias Frank Canton*. Norman: University of Oklahoma Press, 1996.

Delta County History Book Committee. *Delta County History*. Dallas: Taylor Publishing Co., 1991.

Dobie, J. Frank. *A Vaquero of the Brush Company*. Austin: University of Texas Press, 1985.

Donavon, Duncan Tidwell. *Freemasonry in Brownwood*. Fort Worth: Masonic Home and School, 1966.

Dozier, Gloria Clifton. *Reconstructed 1890 Census of Kerr County, Texas*. Kerrville, Texas: Gloria Clifton Dozier, 1991.

Elkins, Capt. John M. *Indian Fighting on the Texas Frontier*. Amarillo, Texas: Russell & Cockrell, 1929.

Elman, Robert. *Badmen of the West*. Secaucus, New Jersey: Ridge Press, 1974.

Elzner, Jonnie. *Relighting Lamplights of Lampasas County, Texas*. Lampasas, Texas: Jonnie Ross Elzner, 1974.

Ericson, Carolyn Reeves. *Nacogdoches: Gateway to Texas*, vols. 1 and 2. Nacogdoches, Texas: Ericson Books, 1987.

———. *The People of Nacogdoches County in 1860*. Nacogdoches, Texas: Carolyn Reeves Ericson, 1978.

Ericson, Carolyn Reeves, and Frances T. Ingmire. *First Settlers of the Republic of Texas*, vol. 2. Nacogdoches, Texas: Ericson Books, 1982.

Fehrenbach, T. R. *Lone Star*. New York: American Legacy Press, 1983.

Fenley, Florence. *Oldtimers of Southwest Texas*. Uvalde, Texas: Hornby Press, 1957.

Ferris, Robert G. *Soldier and Brave*. National Survey of Historic Sites and Buildings, vol. 12. Washington, D.C.: U.S. Department of the Interior, National Park Service, 1971.

Fuller, Henry C. *Adventures of Bill Longley*. Nacogdoches, Texas: Baker Printing Co., n.d.

Galveston County Genealogical Society. *St. Joseph's Church, Galveston, Texas–Baptismal, Confirmation, Marriage and Death Records, 1860–1952*. Easley, South Carolina: Southern Historical Press, 1984.

———. *Early Texas Death and Legal Records from Joseph Franklin's Diary and John Griffin's Sexton Records*. Galveston: Galveston County Genealogical Society, 1990.

Gillett, James B. *Six Years with the Texas Rangers*. Lincoln: University of Nebraska Press, 1976.

Gray, Ikie. *Loose Leaves*. Dallas: Mathis Publishing Co., circa 1935.

Grayson County Genealogical Society. *Ancestors and Descendants, Grayson County, Texas*. Dallas: Taylor Publishing Co., 1980.

Greene, A. C. *A Personal Country*. College Station: Texas A&M University, 1979.

Greene, Jerome A. *Battles and Skirmishes of the Great Sioux War, 1876–1877*. Norman: University of Oklahoma Press, 1993.

Greenwell, A. S. *Report on the Hygiene of the United States Army with Descriptions of Military Posts*. Washington, D.C.: U.S. Government Printing Office, 1875.

Haley, J. Evetts. *Charles Goodnight: Cowman and Plainsman*. Boston: Houghton Mifflin, 1936.

Hardeman, Gladys. *The History of Melrose*. Unpublished manuscript, 1964–1965. Special Collections Department, Steen Library, Stephen F. Austin State University, Nacogdoches, Texas.

Hardin, John Wesley. *The Life of John Wesley Hardin*. Seguin, Texas: Smith & Moore, 1896.

Haskew, Corrie Patterson. *Historical Records of Austin and Waller Counties*. Houston: Premier Printing and Letter Service, 1969.

Havins, T. R. *Something About Brown*. Brownwood, Texas: Banner Printing Co., 1958.

Hayden, F. V. *Eleventh Annual Report of the United States Geological Survey of the Territories Embracing Idaho and Wyoming, 1877*. Washington, D.C.: U.S. Government Printing Office, 1879.

Holder, Perry C. *150 Years of Cemetery Records in Milam County*. Austin: D. Armstrong Co., 1991.

Holloway, Carroll C. *Texas Gun Lore*. San Antonio: Naylor Co., 1951.

Hunter, J. Marvin. *100 Years in Bandera, 1853–1953*. Bandera, Texas: J. Marvin Hunter, 1953.

Ingmire, [Mrs.] Frances T[erry]. *Bastrop County, Texas, Marriage Records, 1851–1870*. St. Louis: Frances T. Ingmire, 1985.

———. *Washington County, Texas, Marriage Records, 1837–1870*. St. Louis: Mrs. Frances Terry Ingmire, 1980.

Johnson, Frank W. *A History of Texas and Texans*, vol. 2. Chicago: American Historical Society, 1916.

Jones, Julia. *Lee County*. Houston: Gulf Coast Baptist Print, 1945.

Killen, Mrs. James C., ed. *History of Lee County, Texas*. Quanah, Texas: Nortex Press, 1974.

Knight, Lucian Lamar, ed. *Library of Southern Literature*, vol. 15. Atlanta: Martin & Hoyt Co., 1910.

Kuykendall, Judge W. L. *Frontier Days*. [Cheyenne, Wyoming]: J. M. & H. L. Kuykendall, 1917.

Lambert, Major Joseph I. *One Hundred Years with the Second Cavalry*. Fort Riley, Kansas: Capper Printing Co., 1939.

Lampasas History Book Committee. *Lampasas County, Texas*. Marceline, Missouri: Walsworth Publishing Co., 1991.

Leakey, John. *The West That Was*. Dallas: Southern Methodist University Press, 1958.

Lee County Historical Commission. *Lee County, Texas, Cemeteries*, vols. 1 and 2. Giddings, Texas: Lee County Historical Commission, 1991.

Leon County Genealogical Society. *Leon County Cemetery Records*, vol. 2. Centerville, Texas: Leon County Genealogical Society, 1982.

Lynch, James D. *The Bench and Bar of Texas*. St. Louis: Nixon-Jones Printing Co., 1885.

Madison County Historical Commission. *A History of Madison County, Texas*. Dallas: Taylor Publishing Co., 1984.

Marohn, Richard C. *The Last Gunfighter: John Wesley Hardin*. College Station, Texas: Creative Publishing Co., 1995.

M'Arthur & Wickes. *The Twenty-Seventh Legislature and State Administration of Texas, 1901*. Austin: Ben C. Jones & Co., Printers, 1901.

McCroskey, Mrs. Betty M., and Mrs. W. F. Bradley. *Texas Marriage Records: Austin, Matagorda and Wharton Counties*. Wharton, Texas: Comfort Wood Chapter D.A.R., 1955.

McDermott, John D. *Dangerous Duty: A History of Frontier Forts in Fremont County, Wyoming*. [Lander], Wyoming: Fremont County Historic Preservation Commission, 1993.

A Memorial and Biographical History of McLennan, Falls, Bell and Coryell Counties. Chicago: Lewis Publishing Co., 1893.

Memorial and Genealogical Record of Texas (East). Chicago: Goodspeed Brothers, Publishers, 1895.

Miller, Rick. *Bounty Hunter*. College Station, Texas: Creative Publishing Co., 1988.

Moore, Bill. *Bastrop County, 1691–1900*. Wichita Falls, Texas: Nortex Press, 1977.

Nacogdoches County [Texas] Genealogical Society. *Nacogdoches County Families*. Dallas: Curtis Media Corp., 1985.

Nance, Joseph Milton. *Attack and Counterattack*. Austin: University of Texas Press, 1964.

Nunn, W. C. *Texas Under the Carpetbaggers*. Austin: University of Texas Press, 1962.

O'Neil, James B. *They Die But Once*. New York: Knight Publications, 1935.

Parsons, Chuck. *The Capture of John Wesley Hardin*. College Station, Texas: Creative Publishing Co., 1978.

Parsons, Chuck. *James Madison Brown: Texas Sheriff, Texas Turfman*. Wolfe City, Texas: Henington Publishing Co., 1993.

Penal Code of the State of Texas. Galveston: A. H. Belo & Co., 1879.

Pennington, Mrs. R. E. *The History of Brenham and Washington County*. Houston: Standard Printing & Lithographing Co., 1915.

Poage, W. R. (Bob). *McLennan County–Before 1980*. Waco, Texas: Texian Press, 1981.

Prucha, Francis Paul. *A Guide to the Military Posts of the United States, 1789–1895*. Madison: State Historical Society of Wisconsin, 1964.

Ramey, William Neal, ed. *The Texian Annual*, vol. 2, no. 1, quarterly no. 4. Austin, 1886.

Ramsdell, Charles William. *Reconstruction in Texas*. Austin: University of Texas Press, 1970.

Raymond, Dora Neill. *Captain Lee Hall of Texas*. Norman: University of Oklahoma Press, 1982.

Richter, William L. *The Army in Texas During Reconstruction*. College Station: Texas A&M University Press, 1987.

Ripley, Thomas. *They Died With Their Boots On*. New York: Sun Dial Press, 1937.

Rodenbough, Theo. F. *From Everglade to Canon with the Second Dragoons*. New York: D. Van Nostrand, Publisher, 1875.

Roper, Mrs. Homer L., and Mrs. Richard N. Grammer. *Cemeteries–Lampasas County*. Lampasas, Texas: Daughters of the American Colonists, 1978.

Rosa, Joseph G. *They Called Him Wild Bill*. Norman: University of Oklahoma Press, 1974.

Scarbrough, Clara Stearns. *Land of Good Water*. Georgetown, Texas: Williamson County Sun Publishers, 1973.

Shroyer, Mrs. Jean, and Mrs. Hazel Hood. *Williamson County, Texas: Its History and Its People*. Austin: Nortex Press, 1985.

Slawson, J. A. H. *DeSoto Parish History and Cemetery Records*. Nacogdoches, Texas: J. B. Sanders, 1967.

Smith, Tevis Clyde. *Frontier's Generation*. Brownwood, Texas: Moore Printing Co., 1980.

Smith, W. Broadus. *Marriage Records, Washington County, Texas, 1837–1858*. [Brenham], Texas: W. Broadus Smith, 1968.

Sowell, A. J. *Rangers and Pioneers*. Austin: State House Press, 1991.

———. *Early Settlers and Indian Fighters of Southwest Texas*. Austin: State House Press, 1986.

Stephens, Robert W., ed. *Texas Ranger Indian War Pensions*. Quanah, Texas: Nortex Press, 1975.

Stovall, Allan A. *Breaks of the Balcones*. Barksdale, Texas: Allan A. Stovall, 1967.

Swenson, Helen. *Texas Marriages*, vol. 1. Round Rock, Texas: Frances Terry Ingmire & Helen Smothers Swenson, 1981.

Tise, Sammy. *Texas County Sheriffs*. Albuquerque: Oakwood Printing, 1989.

Tyler, George W. *The History of Bell County*. San Antonio: Naylor Co., 1936.

Utley, Robert M. *The Indian Frontier of the American West, 1846–1890*. Albuquerque: University of New Mexico, 1984.

Utley, Robert M., and Wilcomb E. Washburn. *The American Heritage History of the Indian Wars*. New York: American Heritage Publishing Co., 1977.

Wallace, Patricia Ward. *Waco: Texas Crossroads*. Woodland Hills, California: Windsor Publications, 1983.

Watkins, Clara. *Kerr County, Texas, 1856–1976*. N.p.: Hill Country Preservation Society, 1976.

Wax, Ted. *Dead Man on the Bayou?* Gonzales, Louisiana: Ted Wax, 1988.

Webb, Walter Prescott, ed. *The Handbook of Texas*, vols. 1 and 2. Austin: Texas State Historical Association, 1952.

White, Gifford. *1840 Citizens of Texas*, vol. 2. Austin: Gifford White, 1984.

White, James C. *The Promised Land*. Brownwood, Texas: Brownwood Banner, 1941.

White, Owen P. *Trigger Fingers*. New York: Knickerbocker Press, 1926.

Williamson County Genealogical Society. *Williamson County, Texas, Marriage Records*. Round Rock, Texas: Williamson County Genealogical Society, 1983.

Winfield, Judy, and Nath Winfield, Jr. *Cemetery Records of Washington County, Texas, 1826–1960*. [Brenham], Texas: Judy and Nath Winfield, Jr., 1974.

Witt, Gerald. *The History of Eastern Kerr County*. Austin: Nortex Press, 1986.

Works Project Administration. *Wyoming*. New York: Oxford University Press, 1941.

Yeary, Miss Mamie. *Reminiscences of the Boys in Gray, 1861–1865*. McGregor, Texas: Miss Mamie Yeary, 1912.

Yeilding, David, ed. *Story of Bell County, Texas*, vols. 1 and 2. Austin: Eakin Press, 1988.

Articles

Delo, David M. "Camp Stambaugh . . . The Miner's Delight," *Wind River Mountaineer* 3, no. 4 (Oct.–Dec. 1987).

Delony, Lewis S. "40 Years a Peace Officer," *Old West* 7, no. 2 (Winter 1970).

Dulaney, Christine. "McIver-Bostick." In *A History of Madison County, Texas*. Dallas: Taylor Publishing Co., 1984.

Ellwood, Brooks B., Douglas W. Owsley, Suzanne H. Ellwood, and Pat Mercado-Allinger. "Search for the Grave of the Notorious Texas Gunfighter William 'Wild Bill' Longley." Unpublished manuscript, 1994.

Greenwood, Charles F. "Judge Seth Shepard," *Proceedings of the Thirty-Eighth Annual* [Texas Bar Association] *Session*. Houston: Gray, Dillaye & Young, Printers, 1917.

Hagen, Everett. "I Saw Wild Bill Longley Hang," *Real West* 2, no. 7 (May 1959).

Lim, Grace. "Man Doesn't Want Legend Left Hanging," *Austin American-Statesman*, 21 September 1987.

Martin, G. K. "Land of the Noose–Yegua Knobbs," *Old West* 5, no. 3 (Spring 1969).

McCray, D. O. "Parkerville." Manuscript in Morris County Library, Council Grove, Kansas.

Murray, Robert A. "Camp Stambaugh, Wyoming: Guarding the South Pass Gold Fields, 1870–1878," *Order of the Indian Wars Journal* 2, no. 2 (Spring 1981).

Parsons, Chuck. "Bill Longley's Ghost Escapes," *True West* 39, no. 12 (December 1992).

Richardson, Vivian. "Scribbling Bill, the Fiddler Outlaw," *Dallas Morning News*, 4 January 1931, Feature Section, p. 3.

Robinson, Bonnie Tom. "They Buried Bill Longley Next to a Blackjack Tree," *Frontier Times* 9, no. 12 (September 1932).

Rummel, L. C. Letter to *Frontier Times* 3, no. 10 (July 1926): 11.

Sneed, Edgar P. "A Historiography of Reconstruction in Texas: Some Myths and Problems," *Southwestern Historical Quarterly* 72, no. 4 (April 1969).

Smith, Louise Gartman. "The Williams Ranch," *Cattleman* (December 1943).

Spiller, Wayne. "His Brother's Long Shadow," *True West* 19, no. 3 (Jan.–Feb. 1972).

Taylor, T. U. "Bill Longley and His Wild Career," *Frontier Times* 3, no. 3 (June 1926).

[———]. "More Light on Bill Longley," *Frontier Times* 4, no. 9 (June 1927).

Wright, Bob. "More About Bill Longley," *Texas Parade* 20, no. 5 (October 1959).

Yeats, John W. "Facts of Longley Hanging Explained," *Houston Post Dispatch*, Magazine Section, 25 October 1931.

Newspapers

Austin American-Statesman
Austin Daily Democratic Statesman
Austin Daily State Journal
Austin Daily Statesman

Austin Texas Capitol
Bastrop (Texas) Advertiser
Belton (Texas) Journal
Belton (Texas) Weekly Journal
Bonham (Texas) News
Brenham (Texas) Daily Banner
Brenham (Texas) Weekly Banner
Colorado (Texas) Citizen
Daily Austin Republican
Dallas Daily Herald
Denison Daily News
Elyria (Ohio) Constitution
Fayette County New Era (La Grange, Texas)
Fayette County Record (La Grange, Texas)
Flake's Daily Bulletin (Galveston)
Fort Worth Daily Democrat
Galveston Daily News
Galveston Weekly News
Georgetown (Texas) Watchman
Giddings (Texas) Weekly Tribune
Houston Daily Telegram
Houston Daily Times
Houston Sunday Times
Illustrated Police News
Jacksboro (Texas) Frontier Echo
La Grange (Texas) State Rights Democrat
Lampasas (Texas) Daily Times
Lampasas (Texas) Dispatch
Leavenworth (Kansas) Daily Commercial
Lometa (Texas) Reporter
Marshall (Texas) Tri-Weekly Herald
Nacogdoches (Texas) News
National Police Gazette
New Orleans Daily Picayune
New York Herald
Panola Watchman (Carthage, Texas)
San Antonio Daily Express
San Antonio Daily Herald
Sedalia (Missouri) Democrat
South Pass (Wyoming Territory) News
St. Louis Globe-Democrat
Victoria (Texas) Advocate
Waco (Texas) Daily Examiner

Weatherford (Texas) Exponent
Wichita (Kansas) Weekly Beacon

Public Records

Texas County Records

Bastrop County, Texas:
District Court Records:
State of Texas v. James E. Brady, Cause No. 696
State of Texas v. Jos. Hemphill, Cause No. 2563
State of Texas v. Z. P. Eggleston, Cause Nos. 418, 419, 465, and 466
Bell County, Texas:
Deed Records, vols. M, 24, 27
District Court Records:
State of Texas v. James S. Longley, Cause No. 2399
State of Texas v. William Longley, Cause No. 879
State of Texas v. William Longley, Cause No. 1148
Grave marker, Sarah A. Longley, Cedar Knob Cemetery
Marriage Records, vols. D, J
Slave Schedule, 1860
Tax Assessment Rolls, 1868, 1874
Brazos County, Texas:
District Court Records:
State of Texas v. William McIver, Cause No. 588
Burleson County, Texas:
District Court Records:
State of Texas v. Richard Puckett, Cause Nos. 259, 570, 591, and 594
Coleman County, Texas:
Deed Records, vols. A, C, D, E, F, and K
Delta County, Texas:
Commissioners Court Minutes, vols. A, A/B, 1876
District Court Records:
State of Texas v. Thomas Jack
State of Texas v. William Black et al., Cause No. 194
State of Texas v. William Kennedy
State of Texas v. Ed Corbet
Grave marker, William Roland Lay, Simmons Cemetery
Grave marker, Mark L. Foster, Simmons Cemetery
Gillespie County, Texas:
District Court Records:
State of Texas v. James Johnson, Frank Eastwood, and Young Stockman

State of Texas v. Frank Eastwood, Cause No. 219

Kerr County, Texas:

District Court Records:

State of Texas v. Frank Eastwood, Cause No. 4

State of Texas v. Frank Eastwood, Cause No. 6

State of Texas v. Frank Eastwood and James Johnson, Cause Nos. 49–51, 55

Lampasas County, Texas:

District Court Records:

State of Texas v. W. L. Shroyier, Cause No. 7

State of Texas v. W. L. Shroyier, Cause No. 63

State of Texas v. W. L. Shroyier, Cause No. 173

State of Texas v. W. L. Shroyier, Cause No. 189

Mrs. S. A. Horrell v. Lou Shroyer, Cause No. 44

Marriage Records, vol. A

Probate Records, Book No. 1

Slaughter Cemetery

Lee County, Texas:

Commissioners Court Minutes, vol. A

District Court Records:

State of Texas v. Wilson Anderson, Cause No. 9

State of Texas v. William Longley and James Longley, Cause No. 100

Madison County, Texas:

District Court Records:

State of Texas v. J. R. McIver, Cause No. 268

State of Texas v. J. R. McIver, Cause No. 374

State of Texas v. John R. McIver, Cause No. 116

State of Texas v. Joseph McIver, Cause No. 244

State of Texas v. Joseph McIver, Cause No. 373

State of Texas v. William McIver, Cause No. 7

Marriage Records, Book 2

Mason County, Texas:

Deed Records, vol. A/B

District Court Records:

State of Texas v. Jack Bolt

McLennan County, Texas:

District Court Records:

State of Texas v. Robert Rushing and J. W. Longley alias J. W. Patterson, Cause No. 2606

State of Texas v. J. W. Longley alias J. W. Patterson, Cause No. 2590

State of Texas v. J. W. Longley alias J. W. Patterson, Cause No. 2591

State of Texas v. J. W. Longley alias J. W. Patterson, Cause No. 2602

Mills County, Texas:
Grave marker, Williams Rancho Cemetery (John Williams)
Nacogdoches County, Texas:
Marriage Records, vol. B
Uvalde County, Texas:
District Court Records:
Estate of J. B. Gibson v. L. Shroyer, Cause No. 155
Washington County, Texas:
Deed Records, vols. M, X
Marriage Records, vol. I
Williamson County, Texas:
District Court Records:
State of Texas v. Frank Eastwood, Cause No. 458
State of Texas v. William Ake
State of Texas v. Jeff Ake
State of Texas v. William Mullen, Cause Nos. 198, 280, 316, 494, 500, 555, 834, 836, and 928

Texas State Records

Texas Court of Appeals (Galveston):
W. P. Longley v. State of Texas, 3 Tex. Ct. of Appeals Reports 613 (1878)
William Taylor v. State of Texas, 3 Tex. Ct. of Appeals Reports 387 (1878)
Texas General Land Office:
File No. 195 (Uvalde County, Texas)
Texas State Library and Archives:
Adjutant General Records, 1867–1877
Audited Military Claims (Campbell Longley), 12 September 1836
Gov. E. J. Davis Collection, 1873
Gov. E. M. Pease Collection, 1870
Gov. Richard Coke Collection, 1874–1876
Gov. Richard Hubbard Collection, 1876–1878
Gov. O. M. Roberts Collection, 1880
Public Debt Claims, 23 May 1853
Record of Murders and Assaults, 1867–1868
Republic of Texas Pension Applications
State Police Correspondence, 1873
Texas Bureau of Pensions, 1931
Texas Ranger Correspondence
T. P. Woods, "Crimes Committed in Washington County," 12 July 1870

United States Records

United States Census Records:

1850 Austin County, Texas
1860 Burleson County, Texas
Karnes County, Texas
Lamar County, Texas
Leon County, Texas
Milam County, Texas
Morris County, Kansas
Washington County, Texas
Williamson County, Texas
1870 Austin County, Texas
Bell County, Texas
Brown County, Texas
Burleson County, Texas
Coleman County, Texas
Fayette County, Texas
Galveston County, Texas
Hopkins County, Texas
Karnes County, Texas
Kerr County, Texas
Lamar County, Texas
Lampasas County, Texas
McLennan County, Texas
Medina County, Texas
Milam County, Texas
Morris County, Kansas
Red River County, Texas
Shelby County, Texas
Travis County, Texas
Uvalde County, Texas
Washington County, Texas
Williamson County, Texas
Wyoming Territory
1880 Bandera County, Texas
Bastrop County, Texas
Delta County, Texas
DeSoto Parish, Louisiana
Galveston County, Texas
Kerr County, Texas
Lampasas County, Texas
Lee County, Texas

McLennan County, Texas
Milam County, Texas
Nacogdoches County, Texas
Shelby County, Texas
Travis County, Texas
1900 Lampasas County, Texas

United States National Archives and Records Service:

Compiled Military Service Records (Alexander C. Longley)
Compiled Military Service Records (William P. Longley)
Compiled Military Service Records (Lewis Shroyer)
Court-Martial Records (William P. Longley, John Miller)
Muster Rolls, Co. B, Second Cavalry Regiment, U.S. Army (1870–1872)

Archives and Private Collections

Archives, Catholic Diocese of Galveston-Houston.
Camp Stambaugh Records. American Heritage Center, University of Wyoming, Laramie.
Catholic Archives of Texas, Austin.
Ellwood, Brooks. Private collection. Arlington, Texas.
Johnson, Doris. "The Longley Family." Unpublished manuscript.
Longley Family Bible. Collection of Kenneth Longley, Abilene, Texas.
Longley, Pauline. Private collection. San Saba, Texas.
"Longley, William P. (Bill)." Center for American History, University of Texas, Austin.
Lucie Price Collection. Center for American History, University of Texas, Austin.
Rutherford B. Hayes Presidential Center, Fremont, Ohio.
Steen Library, Special Collections Department, Stephen F. Austin State University, Nacogdoches, Texas.
Thomas, Mrs. Opal. Private collection. Belton, Texas.
Willingham, Dr. Douglas. Private collection. Salado, Texas.

Correspondence And Interviews

Albright, Lee, Paradise, California, to author, 17 August 1994.
Beshears, Katherine Dinsmore, Mesquite, Texas, to author, 2 November 1995.
Forester, Mildred, Paradise, California, to author, 25 April 1994.
Heard, Sid, Reagan Wells, Texas, interview with author, 30 November 1993.
Johnson, Dave, Zionsville, Indiana, to author, 11 September 1994.
Rudderow, John, Chico, California, to author, 28 December 2009.
Thomas, Opal, Belton, Texas, interviews with author, March–April 1994.

INDEX

A

B

C

D

E

F

G

H

I

J

K

L

M

N

O

P

Q

R

S

W

Y

Z

Y

Z